THEORIZING THE AMERICANIST TRADITION

Edited by Lisa Philips Valentine and Regna Darnell

This collection challenges the prevailing notion that the Americanist Tradition in anthropology, typified by Franz Boas and his colleagues, is atheroretcal. Contributions from twenty-five distinguished scholars are brought together here to provide a comprehensive, accessible, state-of-the-art appraisal of interdisciplinary research in the areas of anthropology, linguistics, and Native Studies.

Participants in this dialogue accepted the challenge of making their underlying theoretical assumptions explicit. Topics range from historical debates in anthropology and linguistics to recent innovations within the Americanist Tradition. The search for authenticity is brought to bear on discussion of changing traditions in texts and literacy, in linguistics and education, and in contemporary discourse spanning the Americas.

Debate on the future of the Americanist Tradition forms a critical part of this collection. The volume juxtaposes Canadian and American theoretical work on language and revitalizes a shared tradition centred on the study of meaning. Readers are invited to enter this vibrant and open-ended Americanist discourse.

LISA PHILIPS VALENTINE is Associate Professor and REGNA DARNELL is Professor in the Department of Anthropology at the University of Western Ontario.

Edited by
LISA PHILIPS VALENTINE and REGNA DARNELL

Theorizing the Americanist Tradition

UNIVERSITY OF TORONTO PRESS
Toronto Buffalo London

Toronto Buffalo London
Printed in Canada
Reprinted in 2018

ISBN 0-8020-4229-5 (cloth)
ISBN 978-0-8020-8077-6 (paper)

Printed on acid-free paper

Canadian Cataloguing in Publication Data

Main entry under title:

Theorizing the Americanist tradition

(Anthropological horizons)
Includes bibliographical references.
ISBN 0-8020-4229-5 (bound) ISBN 978-0-8020-8077-6 (paper)

1. Anthropological linguistics – Canada. 2. Anthropological linguistics – United States. 3. Indians – Languages.
I. Valentine, Lisa Philips, 1954– . II. Darnell, Regna, 1943– .

PM108.T43 1999 306.44′08997 C98-932490-7

University of Toronto Press acknowledges the financial assistance to its publishing program of the Canada Council for the Arts and the Ontario Arts Council.

Contents

CHANGING TRADITIONS

In Text and Literacy

In Linguistics and Education

And Changing Discourses

THEORIZING ACROSS BOUNDARIES: THE AMERICANIST TRADITION AND OTHERS

THEORIZING THE AMERICANIST TRADITION

1 Introduction: Timely Conversations

LISA PHILIPS VALENTINE and REGNA DARNELL

This volume represents pieces of conversations about and from within the Americanist Tradition. Distinctive features of these conversations include multiple perspectives: the participants' talk is co-created, emergent, messy, takes unexpected directions, is open for input, and builds from prior conversations. The conference from which this volume arises had its own roots in conversations between the editors, who, in the serendipity of academia, encountered each other in 1990 in the Anthropology Department at the University of Western Ontario. We promptly began joint research on comparative Native American[1] identities as performed through English discourse in southwestern Ontario, with its complex and fascinating juxtaposition of Algonquian and Iroquois traditions. Our collaboration often led to conversations about contemporary anthropological theory as our research led us across the boundaries of disciplines and deeper into the philosophical foundations of our own Americanist practice at the intersection of linguistics and anthropology.

Our conversations moved from the historical place of the Americanist Tradition in anthropology to the range of contemporary theoretical concerns that are appropriately addressed within an Americanist framework, to the theoretical discourses originated by those trained in the Americanist Tradition which have been appropriated without acknowledgment in the general profession. We felt it was time to extend our dialogue to make explicit the unique contributions of Americanists and to create an overt discourse about future directions in anthropology from such a perspective.

Periodically in the course of academic work, otherwise reasonable persons are inspired to organize a conference. After each bout of such activity, the academic resolves never to do it again. But then a burning issue arises that calls out for conversation, both formal and informal, with like-minded colleagues whose experiences both overlap with and differ from one's own. In such a state of mild insanity, instigated by our conversations, we resolved to assemble some key thinkers on these matters, most of them known to both of us for a long time (and many known to each other as well), and think together about what it is we do, with whom we do it, and why. We invited scholars who worked in different regions of the world to cross multiple borders and boundaries. Authors from Canada and the United States are equally represented in this volume in large part because the Aboriginal collaborators laid claim to what is now North America long before the United States and Canada emerged as geo-political entities.

In our initial conceptualization of the conference, we proposed five topics: History and Emergent Traditions, Text and Translation, Native Writing / Native Experience, Contemporary Discourse, and Performance and Dialogue in Ethnography. While both the overall project and subcategories within it appeared to us relatively straightforward, the response was surprisingly consistent: in the three and a half days of presenting papers at the conference, participant after participant began with a ritual disclaimer of the form: 'I don't know why I was invited or what "Theorizing the Americanist Tradition" is, but ...' indicating that we Americanists are not accustomed to theorizing our practice. The disclaimer was invariably followed by an absolutely wonderful (re)thinking of some aspect of the tradition and reflection on why we have not thought explicitly of ourselves this way all along.

The topical clusters were the immediate catalyst of the conversation, but what emerged following the conference was something quite different. When, about a year and a half later, we seriously badgered our colleagues to finalize their (revised) papers for this volume, we found that the papers had been transformed. The authors had entered into new and overlapping conversations with others at the conference, interacting with others' ideas in a way that we had only imagined before the gathering – we were delighted that the conversations had taken on lives of their own over the intervening year. The structure of the volume had to be invented anew. Using Americanist tools of inductive text analysis, we are again rethinking and retheorizing the Americanist Tradition. The conversation between the participants continues. In another reflexive move, we look at the narrative ordering of the articles for this book (Contents) where, in our overt attempt to 'order social life' by creating linear and other contingent relations between articles, we are theorizing indeed. The irony of such practices, as implied in most papers in this volume, is that a monologic theory is anathema to contemporary Americanist positioning.

In *Theorizing the Americanist Tradition* (or, in the practice of theorizing the Americanist Tradition), the authors enter into dialogue with these Native American traditions as well – the theorizing remains conversational/dialogic.

Perhaps this is part of the reason why the Americanist Tradition has been declared by the monologically committed to be a-theoretical or anti-theoretical. We begin this volume by framing **THEORIZING ...** through the interaction between Robin Ridington, Thomas King, Coyote, and the audience in Ridington's 'Coyote's Cannon: Sharing Stories with Thomas King.' Ridington beautifully theorizes theory in this playful reading of Coyote and Thomas King. As he writes, 'Native American [as opposed to non-Native Americanist] theorizing ... is fundamentally dialogic. Theorizing comes about through stories and conversation' (pp. 22–3). The alternative to such theorizing is presented when the 'Dog Dream says, "I am god" ... Playing God can lead to a monologue that attempts to manage without the other' (p. 26). Ridington/Coyote/King hits at the heart of our enterprise: in the Americanist Tradition, we attempt to theorize in such a way that we remain (dialogic) dogs and not 'get everything backwards' to become (monologic) gods. Dennis Tedlock repeats virtually the same message as he illustrates the transformation of the Judaeo-Christian version of creation as a single deity 'speaking the monologue of absolute power' to a K'iche' version of the same story as a 'dialogue among gods whose power is not absolute' (pp. 164, 165).

For the most part, Americanists don't like to play God. We have heard too much about the tricksters – Coyote, Wiihsahkecaahk, Raven, and Carcajou – to follow them unawares into their self-deceiving follies. (Most of *their* problems arise from trying to subvert a dialogic world into a monologue that they control, as Ridington so eloquently argues.) Many of the other papers in this volume reveal similar self-examination – even at times, self-reproach – for our propensity, as academics and anthropologists, for getting too close to becoming gods, for producing monologues. Another observation by Ridington helps to frame our introduction, '"Each story," I says, "like each piece of a hologram, contains information about the entire structure of which it is a part"' (p. 35). The stories in this volume are also holographic, giving insight into a large and complex Americanist Tradition. Our 'Timely Conversations' is also a holographic piece of this volume.

... THE AMERICANIST TRADITION

From History. The dialectic among the papers by Regna Darnell, Stephen O. Murray, and Raymond Fogelson sets foundations critical for contextualizing the multiple readings of the Americanist Tradition found elsewhere in this volume. These three authors present different renditions of history internal to our own discipline(s). Their differing perspectives create a productive triangulation of thought and practice; they combine to present a richly textured discussion of what scholars approaching the twenty-first century understand as the Americanist Tradition. Part of their analyses and practices emerge as products of Americanist methodology, where access to the history of anthropology comes most often through the study of objects (that is, text or discourse) that in turn are based on interviews (especially life stories) or other material documents including the cylinders, tapes, books, letters, and calendric fragments discussed in various ethnographic contexts throughout this volume. The disciplinary matrix within anthropology entails attention to the linguistic forms within textual objects, but it also engages other disciplines, including linguistics, history, sociology, politics, and archaeology.

Regna Darnell's 'Theorizing Americanist Anthropology: Continuities from the B.A.E. to the Boasians' formed the 'first turn' in many of the conversations evident in this volume. In this paper, Darnell proposes seven 'distinctive features' of the Americanist Tradition. These include the inseparability of language, thought, and reality, culture as a system of symbols, discourse as the basis for both ethnographic and linguistic study, a commitment to preserving oral knowledge, the mutability and historicity of culture, and an emphasis on long-term fieldwork that is reflected in the Americanist focus on dialogic research between the researched and those researching. She reads history onto itself in her search for continuities between pre-Boasian Americanists centred in the Bureau of American Ethnology and contemporary theoretical issues in anthropology. Moving beyond a simple equation of Americanist anthropology with the work of Franz Boas and his students, the paper sets a baseline from which to trace the distinctive features of the tradition through the concrete practices of contemporary practitioners. Her suggestion that anthropologists 'come by their theories from ... the symbolic capital of the discipline itself, and ... through a dialogic reflexivity with the peoples they study' began a dialogue engaged by many of the later papers. Theory is *not* something that belongs to anthropologists but not to Native American / First Nations persons. Rather, Americanist theory is constructed in a dialogic space shared by Native American intellectuals and the anthropologists they seek to educate into their ways of civilization.

Steve Murray,[2] in partial contrast to Darnell, approaches the Americanist Tradition with the double vision of an Americanist practitioner who is also an observer of other practitioners. He relies more heavily on the archival record of anthropological practice than on the self-image of anthropologists socialized in disciplinary oral history. The stories we all tell one another often lack the critical edge brought by the partial outsider. In his paper 'The Non-Eclipse of Americanist Anthropology during the 1930s and 1940s,' Murray, unlike many contributors, defines the tradition primarily in geographical terms, contrasting overseas work with its ties to colonialism and ethnic genocide to work done 'at home.' Nonetheless, he acknowledges that certain topics are peculiarly Americanist, regardless of their illustrative data; for instance, ethnopoetics, ethnography of speaking, and linguistic anthropology more generally. Murray's characteristically impeccable footnotes provide both verisimilitude (he claims nothing without extensive evidence) and internal multivocality (this is the claim, but on the other hand ...). The sense of marginality to anthropology in general, even in North America, is perceptually real to many of the contributors, but does not hold up under documentary examination.[3]

Ray Fogelson plays the themes of 'Nationalism and the Americanist Tradition' against each other to suggest ways in which the specific histories of American nationalism and the Americanist Tradition informed each other in their earliest manifestations. He begins his discussion of the Americanist Tradition with Thomas Jefferson's interest in Indian ethnology, linguistics, and archaeology. Fogelson traces academic and (American) governmental concerns with aboriginal groups through the nineteenth century, illustrating ways in which the questions addressed by both groups diverged and converged as they dealt with both historical and contemporary issues. He writes that the 1893 World Colombian Exposition (World's Fair) in Chicago marked a 'transition point in Americanist anthropology' from studying the 'traditional Indian' to addressing more contemporary groups. Fogelson's reading of Americanist history presents a basis for his admonitions to contemporary researchers that they will 'have to become wards to the people they purport to study ... [and] will have to pledge allegiances to new nationalisms,' as the term is used by many contemporary Native American / First Nations groups.

To the Present. The papers by Dell Hymes and John Cove develop further the alternative readings of the history of the Americanist Tradition, rereading early theoretical issues onto and/or against contemporary theory.

Dell Hymes builds an intriguing conversation between history and theory in 'Boas on the Threshold of Ethnopoetics.' His 'side-shadowing' of Boas's interest in repetition and rhythm builds a dialogue between Boas's texts and analyses on the one hand and contemporary work in ethnopoetics on the other. Hymes discusses culturally appropriate conventions of genre, and the irony of Boas's postponement of at least certain kinds of generalizations until the historically particular traditions of various Native American groups were understood ethnographically and linguistically, thereby setting the baseline for contemporary investigations that Boas and his students and protégés began to explore. As an integral part of his substantive project, Hymes theorizes both historical and contemporary practices of text collection and analysis.

In 'Cultural Relativism in the Americanist Tradition: From Anthropological Method to Indigenous Emancipation,' John Cove traces the standpoint perspective to Max Weber rather than to Boasian anthropology, making it, at least in the first instance, an import, a grafting on North American experience. But he comes around to arguing that the Americanist Tradition fuses 'the Native point of view,' Weber's standpoint, with an indigenous pragmatism grounded in science and natural history, aspiring to valid and replicable cross-cultural comparison. Cove's engagement with Fourth World (aboriginal) peoples outside North America, particularly with the Maori, triangulates issues of ethics, epistemology, and advocacy. The crucial concept is cultural relativism, arguably twentieth-century anthropology's most significant contribution to North American public culture. Cove argues that, far from invalidating ethical and political activism, anthropological relativism potentially empowers cultural others. But he also warns that this key intellectual index of our identity as a discipline is highly endangered. Recent court decisions disempower both anthropologists and the aboriginal peoples with whom they collaborate by the imposition of an outdated positivism upon minority cultures and academic disciplines – which have long known better, yet have failed to make this case effectively in public discourse.

Addressing Authenticity. The papers by Chris Wolfart, Dick Preston, and Dennis Tedlock each address aspects of authenticity, a hotly contested issue in contemporary anthropology, which Preston and Tedlock, in particular, play against history. This history is both disciplinary history and the history of European-Aboriginal contact throughout the Americas. Each of the three considers aspects of cross-cultural translations of language, text, traditions, and culture.

Chris Wolfart, in 'Authenticity and *Aggiornamento* in Spoken Texts and Their Critical Edition,' argues for the legitimacy and feasibility of collaboration with Native speakers who come from communities in which languages of interest to Americanist linguists are actually spoken. His own work, based on a two-decade collaboration with Plains Cree linguist Freda Ahenakew, aspires to critical editions of texts that meet the standards of careful philology in the languages of Western tradition (cf. Hymes 1983). Wolfart is careful to note the humanistic value of texts as 'distinct expressions of the human mind,' sufficiently complex and language-specific that translations must be considered new texts. The fieldworker must beware of his/her own limitations and of the courtesy of teachers who will simplify texts not only grammatically but also in terms of the spiritual values that give them their intelligibility and cultural significance. Although the naive linguist may (and demonstrably does) improve over a career, the later stages of this 'progression' still fall far short of what the native speaker knows through socialization and life-long learning. Wolfart also provides an invaluable historicist commentary on the need to evaluate the exemplary Algonquian work of Leonard Bloomfield in its own context, neither ignoring its limitations by contemporary standards nor failing to appreciate its importance in linking Algonquian to general linguistics.

Many of the participants are elders or at least elders-in-training, consistent with our premise that it takes a long time to come to understand *anything* in the Americanist Tradition. Dick Preston most reflexively adopts the stance of an elder passing on his own reflections about disciplinary practice over a career. In 'Reflections on Culture, History, and Authenticity,' he engages in a dialogue with some very un-Americanist contemporary theory about invented tradition and the oddities of attributing authenticity to much of anything. Preston takes his conversation with John Blackned seriously, to the point of replicating Blackned's pedagogical strategies whereby he was taught. These strategies take seriously the form as well as the content of the teachings. Conventional social-scientific prose is narrativized and contextualized, as Preston uses the rhetorical strategy of repetitions, each with increasing depth and familiarity. The aesthetic of stark minimalism leaves the reader/listener to infer relevance and interconnection; again each story is a hologram. Authenticity resides in the authoritative words of the elder; we learn through Preston's acquired model that authenticity is not a thing but a process of knowing, of maintaining continuity from a non-static past to an emergent future that is the very essence of the tradition. In contrast to the use of this term in other anthropological discourse, authenticity in the Americanist Tradition resides in personal agency. Tradition itself is constituted in the flux of ongoing social relations.

Dennis Tedlock applies Americanist methods of dialogic and textual analysis to the origin myths of Spanish-Indian contact in Mexico in 'Dialogues between Worlds: Mesoamerica after and before the European Invasion.' What we can reconstruct of the Aztec view of the contact with Corteź in 1519 involves dialogue, albeit constructed in indirect discourse mediated through two slave interpreters. Moreover, Tedlock suggests that dialogic models are implicit in the epistemologies of most if not all aboriginal Americans. As noted earlier, his citation of Keresan origin stories complements Ridington's dialogic engagement of Thomas King's Coyote figure/actor. Tedlock provides a new lens on the dialogic strategies of the classic Mesoamerican ethnographies that differs from those of Landa and Sahagún. In this reading, Landa's omniscient third-person narration becomes less a matter of scientific objectivity than of stylized suppression of dialogue. Sahagún errs in the reverse: he presents texts in which the Natives speak but he distances himself from any dialogue or engagement – in what now seems to be an evasion of ethical responsibility to enter into dialogue and to report it as two-sided and agentive. Tedlock's own preference is for the third term, the multivocal text of Duran, which acknowledges an indigenous pre-contact theory of history and entails the possibility of meaningful dialogue with the newcomers. The 'kind of world theorized' by the indigenous texts is hermeneutic, dialogic, and fundamentally alien to our own decontextualized monologic literacy. It is, therefore, only by reversing the anthropological lens and using indigenous perceptions of invaders that we may see our own tradition clearly, in contrast.

CHANGING TRADITIONS

In Text and Literacy. Another theme that permeates many of the papers is the explicit recognition of the place of creating *new* discourses about *old* discourses within the Americanist Tradition. But, as Americanists, we also learn that *our* stories about old texts are, in turn, discourses to be analysed and critically addressed. The process is ongoing. The reflexivity of the inscription process informed by contemporary research is, in essence, an uncovering of the multiple histories of a given utterance. Those histories inform, enrich, transform, and provide movable frameworks for understanding and interpretation.

In 'The Meaning of Writing and Text in a Changing Americanist Tradition,' Jane Hill turns to the missing link in many conversations among anthropologists about their shared culture: the Native view of the anthropologist. She is particularly concerned about the links between writing and text *and* text and discourse, emphasizing that the traditions most of us study are oral traditions. She implies that many anthropologists have not noticed the change in our discipline from the need for urgent salvage linguistics and ethnography to a need for language maintenance and development in communities whose practices of textuality and literacy may contrast dramatically with those we take for granted (a call directly addressed by Danielle Cyr, this volume). Hill worries that each layer of text and text production moves further from the 'dialogic moment' of interaction between linguist/anthropologist and (speaking) consultant. We have, she suggests, our priorities backwards: only naive students ask if we speak the languages we analyse, while our academic peers care mostly about what we say and publish, rather than what is told to us. Our own deeply ingrained literary bias, moreover, operates against the likelihood of understanding variation in dialect and performance, especially of genres that are highly contextualized, for instance, the rapid-fire teasing of the Tohono O'odham. Genuine dialogue is more often piously invoked than illustrated.

Barbara Tedlock, in order to document the continuity of a Mayanist literary tradition in the highlands, turns to the few classic Mayan texts that have been preserved. The discussion of a precontact literary tradition in 'Continuities and Renewals in Mayan Literacy and Calendrics' elegantly subverts the neocolonial stereotype of 'oral' versus 'literate' cultures. Tedlock's analysis of a newly discovered text highlights cultural continuities in meaning, and shows how a contemporary Mayan intelligentsia adapts literary entextualization to emerging agendas in which the traditional oral and written traditions interweave and inform one another. The Americanist and Mayan textual traditions are finely interwoven to create a new, genuinely dialogic, discourse.

Blair Rudes uses a single case, the study of Tuscarora, to illustrate the complex interaction of multiple traditions of text collection and use in 'Why Collect Texts? The Native, Evangelical, and Americanist Traditions among the Tuscaroras.' Rudes outlines how the Americanist Tradition has treated Tuscarora texts primarily as input to linguistic analysis, rarely transmitting them in full form to any audience. In contrast, the Tuscarora tradition has been carried forward by listeners who 'collect' texts by hearing, memorizing, and practising to transmit them, also orally, as a community service. He also notes a Christian evangelical tradition designed for (one-way) dissemination only. Rudes suggests that the Americanist Tradition in the narrowest sense (cf. the one lamented by Hill) enlarges to a 'convergent tradition' in which Americanists and Natives work reciprocally on joint publications, using past Americanist work to replace currently irretrievable knowledge for the benefit of contemporary communities.

The papers by Doug Parks, Ray DeMallie, and Bea Medicine are connected in revisiting earlier Americanist research conducted by experts who were themselves Native Americans. In each case, the author presents the richness of the work done and insights into these remarkable individuals who, in all cases, worked in less than optimal circumstances and yet left phenomenal legacies for contemporary community interpretation and use.

Both Parks and DeMallie have used archival documents to reconstruct the ritual knowledge of late-nineteenth- and early twentieth-century elders and priests in collaboration with contemporary speakers for the use of both anthropologists and the Native American communities whose cultural property was recorded. In 'George A. Dorsey, James R. Murie and the Textual Documentation of Skiri Pawnee,' Douglas Parks details James R. Murie's (Skiri Pawnee) association with the anthropologist George A. Dorsey. Murie's wax-cylinder recordings of Roaming Scout, collected in collaboration with Dorsey, passed through the hands of Franz Boas and Gene Weltfish before reaching Parks, who is reworking them with Nora Pratt, the last fluent speaker of old-style formal Skiri. Mrs Pratt, although she does not know the ritual practices described by Roaming Scout, belongs to a conservative Skiri family and is an inheritor of Roaming Scout's narrative authority.

Addressing another collaboration, Ray DeMallie's '"George Sword Wrote These": Lakota Culture as Lakota Text' outlines Sword's Oglala Sioux texts, written by him in Oglala and preserved through the intervention of anthropologist Clark Wissler and agency physician James R. Walker.[4] Franz Boas encouraged Ella Deloria (see Medicine, this volume) to rework the Sword materials. DeMallie has reworked the products of the genealogy yet again, in collaboration with the late Vine Deloria, Sr, and restored the wax cylinders produced by Sword. The editorial labours reflected in these projects demonstrate the ongoing continuity of textual collaborations over generations, a recurrent feature of the Americanist Tradition.

Bea Medicine, herself a Lakota anthropologist and Elder, provides a commentary on another Lakota woman anthropologist, her aunt Ella Cara Deloria. In 'Ella C. Deloria: Early Lakota Ethnologist (Newly Discovered Novelist),' Medicine, writing in a style characteristic of Elders, emphasizes the constraints of standing between a traditional culture and language and an academic discipline that too often fails to accord professional and personal respect to those who mediate between cultures. Such collaborations of anthropologists and linguists with aboriginal peoples are valued highly in Americanist rhetoric, but are harder to locate in practice. Medicine's commentary is corrective in that it goes beyond the substantial academic and professional achievements of Ella Deloria to situate her in a community at a given time and place, in interaction with the author and other persons known to her, foregrounding the human dimension of cross-cultural conversation.

In Linguistics and Education. The papers by Danielle Cyr, Margaret Seguin Anderson and Deanna Nyce, and Barbara Burnaby all focus on aspects of Canadian education. Cyr addresses community literacy efforts, Anderson and Nyce write collaboratively about building a joint program between the newly founded University of Northern British Columbia and the Nisg̱a'a Nation, and Burnaby looks at Canadian Native language policies from before Canadian Confederation (1867) through the 1990s. In each case, the authors tease out different types of dialogues among those who traditionally control First Nations' language issues: the linguist/anthropologist, the university, and the government.

In 'Past and New Directions for Fieldwork in Ethnolinguistics,' Danielle Cyr suggests the importance of taking time to build the rapport, trust, and long-range involvement to serve as catalyst for what Rudes calls a 'convergent tradition' operating between Native and Americanist researchers. Her discussion of the slow emergence of community collaboration toward Micmac language revitalization is an object lesson in the ethics called for by Hill, Rudes, Anderson and Nyce, and others in this volume. Work in these areas is often dismissed as 'merely descriptive' within the broader anthropological and linguistic academic communities, but Cyr makes clear that the luxury of description is not allowed to those of us who extend our linguistic work back into the communities with which we work. These communities are not deluded that what we do is mere description! They recognize the philosophical entailments in alternative systems of literacy, grammatical presentation, and standardization at all levels, including the choice and use of orthographic systems and grammatical treatises, and the preparation of pamphlets and books for use in the classroom and elsewhere.

Margaret Seguin Anderson and Deanna Nyce ('Nisga'a Studies and the Americanist Tradition: Bringing First Nations Research and Teaching into the Academy') emphasize the need for adequate institutional frameworks of reciprocal or collaborative research, in the particular context of the innovative Nisga'a language and culture program at the University of Northern British Columbia. Their collaborative paper – which is itself a performative act, accomplishing what it proposes – chronicles a continuing journey to bring the University of Northern British Columbia and the Nisga'a Nation together. This is not a seamless construction, as the paper melds together two separate discourses that attack asymmetrical power relations from differently situated positions. The writing maintains the integrity of these discrete positions. The discomfort this poses for conventional academic writing is precisely the challenge of Americanist collaboration. The paper presents precedents for 'Native Control of Native Education' (National Indian Brotherhood of Canada Declaration, 1972) in Nisga'a territory, building on the early work of William Beynon with various linguists and anthropologists, and within School District 92 and its program built on aboriginal traditions of life-long learning. But Anderson and Nyce emphasize that, however promising the current initiatives, true partnership cannot emerge in client-patron relationships reflecting and perpetuating the power inequities of mainstream institutions. Funding for Nisga'a academic programs remains dependent on university control and is not yet grounded within the communities requesting the development and implementation of educational services.

In 'Policy on Aboriginal Languages in Canada: Notes on Status Planning,' Barbara Burnaby outlines how aboriginal language development and revitalization have been plagued by Canada's policy of two official languages, English and French, and of 'multiculturalism' for immigrant groups. Because these categories are taken as given, First Nations languages have been excluded from the policy concerns. Burnaby reviews the historical development of assimilationist policies, expressions of sympathy for cultural retention without attention to language, and contemporary political concerns around land and constitution. From the point of view of aboriginal language retention, Burnaby argues that the unintended consequences of policy have been and remain those of assimilation, that is, linguistic genocide. The Canadian political context outlined by Burnaby sets the foundation for some of the contemporary problems discussed in Cyr and Anderson and Nyce.

And Changing Discourses. The lesson of these Americanist stories is one of ethics, applicable not only to those working within the Americanist Tradition but also to those working in other anthropological traditions. Our focus on the study of discourse within the Americanist Tradition opens many doors to understanding. But having worked in and through discourse, we are acutely aware of the upside and the downside of our methodology, the length of time it takes to understand that discourse. The fieldwork of most of the contributors in this volume spans decades. It takes time and commitment to say anything interesting to community members in the language of their community or, conversely, to our colleagues about those discourses. But by attending to discourse, by learning the communicative norms of a community and by learning how to (begin to) understand in terms of the categories of someone else's system, we are able to extend knowledge into new domains far beyond those currently in vogue in anthropology. The three papers in this section by Ellen Basso, Charles Briggs, and Lisa Valentine work to address different aspects of individual agency, role, and structural power as performed through public and private discourses.

Ellen Basso's contribution, '"Interpersonal Relations" in a Kalapalo Shaman's Narrative,' might be read as another example of 'sideshadowing' of areas of concern in an earlier era of the Americanist Tradition. Basso untangles an intellectual genealogy of interpersonal relations as understood by psychologist Harry Stack Sullivan and his co-conspirator in interdisciplinary social science of the interwar years, Edward Sapir. Sapir, she argues, positioned himself far from the culture and personality work that developed after his death with his emphasis on the inseparability of culture and the individual; they were sides of the same coin. For Sapir, the study of personality was a way to link history and psychology, the twin concepts of Boasian culture theory. What Sullivan added was the focus on interpersonal relations. Basso's argument, grounded in this history of the Americanist Tradition, makes sense of her presentation of a story and ways of listening to it from the point of view of an ordinary male person among the Kalapalo. Her distinction between the talents and social consequences of the shaman/trickster role and the interpersonal awareness required in the role of the bowmaster emerges from an 'imaginative intimacy with the storytellers,' who use quoted speech to draw listeners into community life. These polar traditional roles reside not solely in the individuals but in the conventional forms whereby personality is channelled in accordance with interpersonal norms that transcend the talents or idiosyncrasies of any given individual who may hold one of these roles. Sullivan's clinical practice and Kalapalo traditional knowledge arrive at parallel analyses. The Kalapalo storytellers use story action to develop implicit historical consciousness based on individual action in an interactional context. The manner of writing evokes that of Dennis Tedlock and Robin Ridington in this volume. The use of narratives to explore personal understandings and constructions of the external world also echoes themes in Briggs's paper.

One theme that emerges in recurrent ways throughout the entire volume is temporality: real and imagined, linear and non-linear. Charles Briggs's paper, 'Sequentiality and Temporalization in the Narrative Construction of a South American Cholera Epidemic,' examines this theme directly. In outlining the chronological structuring of a Warao healer's narrative, Briggs illustrates an emergent relationship between linear temporality and cultural authority. As we read Briggs, we are made aware that 'individuals and communities use temporalization in objectifying and ordering social life' (p. oo). Briggs's analysis of the structuring of stories about a cholera epidemic illustrates ways in which several of a healer's discourses, narrated at different times during the epidemic, were used to discover and name causality for the devastating event, creating a performance of increasing power and authority over those events. Over time, the healer's constructions of the events within the cholera epidemic became increasingly structured in chronology and location; with each subsequent telling he became more specific, locating the events along a clear time line and within the local landscape. This temporal and linear structuring indexed the healer's emerging understanding of the epidemic and also his emerging ability to address cause and cure for those events. This analysis of the healer's discourse is equally appropriate to an analysis of location and temporalization (see the organization of the table of contents of this volume for examples, particularly 'THEORIZING THE AMERICANIST TRADITION – From History') by researchers who display their authority and power in presenting research. Our academic narratives are heavily imbued with power through assumptions or assertions of disciplinary chronology, genealogy, and place.

As illustrated in Lisa Valentine's article, 'Personal Agency in Systemic Discourse,' the flexibility of Americanist methodology or perspective allows it to be used at all levels of system, in any context, including those within our own Western, industrialized, recognizably complex society. Valentine analyses a single political speech by former Canadian Prime Minister Pierre Trudeau to suggest ways in which an Americanist perspective might be used to integrate micro-and macro-level analysis. In a case of apparent linguistic accommodation, Trudeau speaks to a predominantly Native American audience, using rhetorical devices and lexical choices that are presumably constructed to sound sympathetic to First Nations peoples. However, when one examines the alternative 'norms of interpretation' of his audience, the seeds of cross-cultural misunderstanding become apparent.

THEORIZING ACROSS BOUNDARIES: THE AMERICANIST TRADITION AND OTHERS. The final papers in the volume create a dialogue across theoretical and disciplinary traditions. This crossing of boundaries is a key feature of the Americanist Tradition. As we find from the sample of authors in this volume, research in the Americanist Tradition is not limited by geographical or political boundaries: we find virtually equal representation of Americanist research from North, Central, and South America, and increasingly from other parts of the world. The Americanist Tradition crosses disciplinary boundaries equally fluidly. We find evidence of Americanist influence in linguistics, anthropology, folklore, psychology, and women's and gender studies, Native studies, literary theory and criticism, history, and ethnomusicology. Karen Adams from linguistics, Peter Denny from psychology, and Bill Leap from gender studies examine such disciplinary interactions directly.

Karen Adams situates the aims of a European tradition of critical linguistics alongside those of the Americanist Tradition in '"Critical Linguistics": Alternative Approaches to Text in the American Tradition.' In linguistics, at least in recent decades, American (as opposed to Americanist) linguistic models have been narrower and less eclectic than European ones. Despite the centrality placed on political activism by key linguists in the USA, political commitment has proceeded separately from linguistic analysis. Adams identifies gender studies and the ethnography of communication as exceptions to this pattern within linguistics; not surprisingly, both fields have moved from Americanist anthropology into the domain of linguistics. The Americanist message, long available but marginalized (e.g., Bolinger), has yet to filter through to much of American linguistics. Insofar as cross-fertilization has occurred, Adams shows that its locus is to be found in the intersection of Americanist anthropology and linguistics.

Peter Denny both calls for and illustrates a cross-cultural cognitive psychology that combines the sophisticated experimental methods of psychology with data from equally sophisticated anthropological fieldwork in 'Current Extensions of Sapir and Whorf in Cross-Cultural Cognitive Science: Cognitive Styles and Ontological Categories.' He argues that cognitive style should be understood as social, a matter of what Basso (this volume) calls interpersonal relations. At one end of an implicit continuum of cross-cultural variability is the decontextualized style of Western industrial culture, in which background assumptions of language and culture cannot be assumed to be shared. He then turns, in good Americanist procedure, to the culture history of particular groups, comparing the ontological categories of hunters and gatherers with those of agriculturalists, arguing that cognitive differences are not random.

In 'Anticipating Queer Theory,' Bill Leap offers insights into ways in which the Americanist Tradition forms a platform for moving into new fields. Indeed, his explanation of 'Queer moments' during the discussion period of the conference moved performance of identity into new ethical and theoretical positioning. Leap, who is well known for his work on Native American English(es), demonstrates that the Americanist Tradition is defined by theory, methodology, and a network of interacting scholars, that it is not restricted to the study of 'the American/Canadian Indian.' Leap is particularly articulate in applying the Americanist theoretical emphasis on authenticity (cf. Preston) that is 'engaged, situated, insider-centred,' in which text is 'a performative by-product of textual reading.' Marginality applies as well to multiple identities in/of that amorphous entity loosely identified as 'our society.' Gender diversity, indeed, is an issue frequently raised by the Boasian in-group, particularly Ruth Benedict and Margaret Mead. Leap's analysis focuses around a dialogic symbolic interactional strategy of 'deniability' that leads the emic perspective of the Americanist Tradition into complex societies and multiple standpoints from which to read the 'same' interaction (cf. Valentine).

And once again the Americanist enterprise circles back on itself. By focusing on discourse, rooted in people's own experience, moving toward more direct representation, the Americanist Tradition maintains the integrity of the individual while allowing for alternative 'world-views' that are consistent within a given community, although they may appear incommensurate to an outsider. We Americanists have often called our own work descriptive, which it is in no small part – because readers must be trained through the use of extensive examples to see the nuances of the discourse. We have been branded as a-theoretical because we often have presented discourse as artefact, rather than as means of discovery. Part of the mandate of the conference and of this book is to make explicit the theoretical underpinnings of our endeavours, in their multiple dimensions.

A number of individuals gave papers at the conference that they did not submit for inclusion in this volume: Robert Brightman, Virginia Hymes, Bruce Mannheim, John Nichols, Jay Powell, and Brian Swann. In addition, we were honoured to have Eric Hamp as a wonderful discussant for several of the papers. These participants added much to the conversations negotiated herein and their input is evident in many of the papers. Graduate students were integral to the conference discussions and to the pervasive sense of transmitting a tradition across academic generations. We acknowledge the efforts of Tim Bisha, Bruce Lawrence, Susanne Miskimmin, Molly Turnbull, and Rob Wishart. Particular thanks go to Julian Sonik, whose organizational talent over a period of months culminated in outstanding culinary feats much appreciated by the participants. György Ozoray put up with conference potlucks, all-night conversations, and our obsession with the constitution of a self-conscious Americanist community. Allan McDougall was invaluable backstage, beginning with the initial grant writing, continuing with his help in the physical arrangements at the conference, through his thoughtful questioning (over a period of almost four years) of what the Americanist Tradition was, is, and will be, and finally during the preparation of the book manuscript itself.

We gratefully acknowledge conference grants from the Social Sciences and Humanities Research Council of Canada and the Wenner-Gren Foundation for Anthropological Research. At the University of Western Ontario, we received support for the conference from the Faculties of Social Science, Arts, Graduate Studies, and Part-Time and Continuing Education, and from the Department of Anthropology and the Centre for Research and Teaching of Canadian Native Languages. The Dean of Social Sciences, Peter Neary, particularly facilitated the publication of this volume. We also wish to recognize Virgil Duff of the University of Toronto Press, who has been consistently enthusiastic in support of the project.

And, finally, we invite readers to join our ongoing Americanist conversations ...

NOTES

1 The term 'Native American' is common in the United States. In Canada, the equivalent term is 'First Nation,' when referring to a single Native American group or community, or 'First Nations,' referring to multiple communities. This usage follows an early Canadian model of three founding nations: Aboriginal, English, and French.

2 'Steve Murray' is Stephen O. Murray (see Contributors list). Our use of naming practices in the introduction shall proceed in the conversational style used at the conference and as the volume was constructed.

3 Similarly Darnell ('Changing Patterns of Ethnography in Canadian Anthropology,' *Canadian Review of Sociology and Anthropology* 34 [1997]:269–96) explodes the inaccurate perception of practising anthropologists that First Nations anthropology in Canada is no longer salient in academic contexts or in scientific programs.

4 See also *Blessings for a Long Time* (1997) in which Robin Ridington reads Francis La Flesche and Alice Fletcher against his own work with Dennis Hastings, the Omaha tribal historian.

2 Theorizing Coyote's Cannon: Sharing Stories with Thomas King

ROBIN RIDINGTON

So. In the beginning ...

When Regna Darnell and Lisa Valentine invited me to the conference on 'Theorizing the Americanist Tradition,' I followed standard academic practice and sent them the abstract of a paper I had not yet written. It read as follows:

The oral traditions of many First Nations code information in a way that is analogous to the distribution of visual information in a holographic image. Each story, like each piece of a hologram, contains information about the entire structure of which it is a part. Stories function as metonyms, parts that stand for wholes. Stories in the First Nations traditions I am familiar with are part of a highly contextualized discourse which assumes familiarity with biography and shared experience.

First Nations novelist Thomas King replicates genre conventions of oral tradition in *Green Grass, Running Water*. This paper describes my experience of teaching his book in conjunction with telling stories from my own experience of First Nations oral traditions. It concludes that by using the genre conventions of Native storytelling, King successfully communicates the quality of Native experience in his writing.

As the conference drew closer, I decided that rather than presenting a conventional paper, I would demonstrate how Native American theorizing might be different from theorizing by non-Native Americanist scholars. I would do this by reading a piece written in the style of Coyote discourse Thomas King used in his novel. Academics, I theorized, conventionally theorize in writing. First Nations thinkers, I thought, conventionally theorize in a medium of narrated discourse. If academic theorizing is usually the product of argument and monologue, First Nations theorizing would have to be the product of conversation and dialogue. My reading would be, I theorized, a narrated example of discourse shared with a Native author. My purpose was to show that First

Nations epistemology is an inherent property of discourse rather than separate from it.

Thomas King is both an academic and a First Nations storyteller. His theorizing lopes across the borderlands between written and oral communication. His novel is, among other things, a Coyote creation story. As Margery Fee and Jane Flick observe in a paper about King's prodigious crossings of textual, political, and ethnographic borders, 'borders are constructed by what you know and don't know. Coyote epistemology requires training in illegal border crossing' (Fee and Flick 1955: 1). Fee and Flick write about King's use of parts in relation to the whole of his novel. 'King's strategy for writing for an audience primarily composed of the uninformed,' they say, 'is not to pander to its preconceptions or to produce explanations.' Rather, they say, King plays Coyote to 'trick this audience into finding out for themselves' (ibid., 2–3).

'Stories function as metonyms,' I said in my abstract. They are 'parts that stand for wholes.' I went on to say that First Nations stories 'are part of a highly contextualized discourse which assumes familiarity with biography and shared experience.' As Fee and Flick observe, 'borders are constructed by what you know and what you don't know.' I wanted to cross some borders by venturing into the realm of 'Coyote epistomology' in my reading of Tom King. What happens to stories when Indians and non-Indians try to share a cultural landscape? What happens when Coyote epistemology encounters the Western canon?

Green Grass, Running Water is King's reading of North American literature, literary theory, Native American history, and popular culture through the images and genre conventions of American Indian oral tradition. No single reader will understand all the references, since the communities with which King shares experience include Indians and academics, Americans and Canadians, mythic characters and friends. He contextualizes his story within a multitude of biographies and experiences. By crossing borders, King also expands them. Just as Herman Melville read the Bible, Shakespeare, and classical mythology into an American whaling saga, King reads all of the above as well as Melville, Northrop Frye, James Fenimore Cooper, John Wayne, and a host of other literary and cultural icons into a quartet of American Indian creation cycles as seen through the juggled eyes of Coyote.

The Case for Sharing Theoretical Authority

Sharing ethnographic authority is now an accepted, if not universal, strategy in ethnographic writing. The reasons for sharing authority are more than political and aesthetic. An ethnography that places the ethnographer's monologue above the voices of people being represented risks sacrificing effective engagement with its subject. Monologic ethnography is likely to be bad (and ethnocentric) ethnography because its claim to objectivity may actually disguise the subjectivity of its singularly isolated author. Mikhail Bakhtin wrote the following general caution about monologic writing as an authorial strategy: 'Monologue is finalized and deaf to the other's response, does not expect it and does not acknowledge in it any *decisive* force. Monologue manages without the other, and therefore to some degree materializes all reality ... Life by its very nature is dialogic. To live means to participate in dialogue' (Bakhtin 1984: 292–3).

An anthropology that 'manages without the other' is a contradiction in terms. But although it may now be common to share ethnographic authority, it is less common for academics to share theoretical authority. Most Americanist anthropologists and literary critics view theorizing as their business, not that of the Native Americans whose lives generate the theorizing. While theorists need 'the other' as a source of data, they generally practise theoretical writing as a genre that is uniquely their own. Even when theorizing reflects 'the other' rather than attempting to manage without it, the language of theory continues to be culturally monologic. It almost invariably replicates the genre conventions of Western academic expression rather than those of Native Americans. It sounds something like what I have been writing so far. It is more like one side of an argument than it is like a story.

Elsewhere (Ridington 1988), I suggested that many of the anthropologists who studied people of the Subarctic also made contributions to anthropological theory that were significantly influenced by the theoretical constructs of the people they studied. A. Irving Hallowell, for instance, wrote that 'a higher order of objectivity' may be obtained 'by adopting a perspective which includes an analysis of the outlook of the people themselves as a complementary procedure' (Hallowell 1960: 21). But despite his recognition that 'the outlook of the people' is complementary to academic theorizing, he continued to frame his theoretical writing within the vocabulary and genre conventions of conventional academic discourse. His theoretical writing was complementary to 'the outlook of the people themselves,' rather than a dialogue with it in its own terms.

With a few exceptions, such as Dennis Tedlock's polyvocal essay 'The Speaker of Tales Has More than One String to Play On' (Tedlock 1991), most Americanist theoretical writing situates itself relentlessly within the canons of formal academic discourse. Perhaps this is because most academic theorizing is done by Americanists who are not, themselves, Native Americans. The academy guards its language closely, as Greg Sarris observes in a book he subtitled 'A Holistic Approach to American Indian Texts' (1993). Native American writers are doing more than challenging what may be included in the canon of

English literature. They challenge the very language in which the canon may be described. Native authors who write theory by telling stories include Gerald Vizenor, Greg Sarris, Jeannette Armstrong, and Thomas King.

Diaglogical Theory and Native American Creation Stories

In his paper for this volume, Dennis Tedlock notes that Native American theorizing about social and natural relations begins with their creation stories. These stories differ from those of the Judaeo-Christian tradition, he suggests, because they bring the world into being through dialogue rather than monologue. A truly dialogical anthropology, he says, is difficult but possible (Tedlock, this volume). Dialogical ethnography is certainly easier to accomplish than dialogical theory. While it is easy to publish theory about dialogics, it is considerably less easy to publish theory written in a dialogic form. Theoretical writing in the Americanist Tradition uses different genre conventions than narrated dialogue, although theory in the Western tradition generally is deeply rooted in the dialogues of Socrates as narrated by his student Plato.

Native American dialogue includes both human and non-human persons. Conversation between the myriad human, animal, natural, or mythical persons of a storied world is at the heart of Native American poetics. By poetics, I mean more than just the formal properties of oral narrative, as important and interesting as these may be as seen in the work of people like Dell Hymes. Here, I use poetics in a more inclusive sense to mean the ways in which people create meaning through language. Native American storytelling is, I believe, the key to their way of theorizing. Stories function as metonyms; parts that stand for wholes. Each story is connected to every other and to a highly contextualized discourse that assumes familiarity with biography and shared experience. Storied characters converse with one another to create the world.

'Life by its very nature is dialogic,' says Bakhtin. 'To live,' he says, 'means to participate in dialogue.' Tagish Athapaskan elder Angela Sidney made a similar point when she told Julie Cruikshank that she tried to live her life right, 'just like a story' (Cruikshank 1990: 1). As Rodney Frye points out in his introduction to a collection of stories from the Inland Northwest, 'Knowledge is embedded within stories and their telling' (Frye 1995: 145). With good reason he called the collection 'Stories That Make the World.' Native American stories are more than about the world. They actually talk it into being. They are parts and they are wholes in conversation with one another.

Native American theorizing sounds different from that of non-Native Americanists. Its vocabulary and genre conventions are those of oral narrative, ceremony, and visual representation. It is fundamentally dialogic. Theorizing comes about through stories and conversation. It is the product of shared authority. Human and non-human persons talk to one another. Coyote is one of these people. He is one of the great Native American theorists. Thomas King knows this well, and so did the late Okanagan storyteller Harry Robinson. In one of Harry's stories, the world as we know it begins with a conversation about names between Coyote and the Creator:

> So, Coyote,
>   well, he's not Coyote yet at that time.
> He must have different name.
> His name, Shim-ee-OW.
> That's his name, Shim-ee-OW.
> That's Indian word, Shim-ee-OW.
> And the way I always say,
>   I don't know what that means.
> I don't know which language to call that to be Shim-ee-OW.
>   But that's his name.
> At that time he's not Coyote yet.
> He's not Shin-KLEEP
> He's Shim-ee-OW.
> (Robinson 1989: 55)

In Harry Robinson's story, Coyote embodies paradox. His name is not a name that means something. How can he have a name that is not a name and still be Coyote before he has been given it as a name? 'I don't know which language to call that,' Robinson tells us philosophically. Robinson's Coyote challenges the listener to think about signs and signification. His conversation is about semiotics. Coyote thinks about all the names. He thinks about being Wolf, about being Cougar, about being Fox. 'I want to tell you,' he says to the Creator. 'There are three names. I want one of them.' But the Chief tells Coyote he is too late. There are only two names left. The Chief says:

> The one name can be KWEELSH-tin.
> That's Sweathouse.
> And the other name, it can be Shin-KLEEP.
> That's Coyote.
> (ibid., 60)

Coyote and the Creator continue their conversation. The Chief tells Coyote what he will have to do if he takes the name Sweathouse. The job description is a succinct account of an important sacred ceremony. Coyote is not interested. He does not want to stay in one place and grant the wishes of shtil-SHKAYL (human people, 'come alive person'). Then the Chief says:

> But if you take the name, Shin-KLEEP,
> (well, that's Coyote),
> If you take the name Shin-KLEEP
> you going to be named Shin-KLEEP
> and I can give you power
> and you'll have the power from me.
> Then you can go all over the place.
> You can walk anywhere.
> You can go all over this island here.
> And wherever you was in this island,
> that's your right wherever you are.
> And there's a lot of danger,
> a lot of bad animal and monster in the country
> and I want you to get rid of that.
> You try to kill 'em
> You kill the monster.
> The monster,
> that's the animals they can kill and eat people.
> (ibid., 62)

Coyote takes the name and the rest is history. He takes on the task of killing the monsters that prey on people. He takes on the job of culture hero, but he does so within the character of Coyote, the trickster, not that of KWEELSH-tin, the Sweathouse. No matter what his name and job description, Coyote retains his essential nature. Through his storied life, he helps bring the world into being. Each story, like each piece of a hologram, contains information about the entire structure of which it is a part. Shin-KLEEP 'can go all over the place.' Shin-KLEEP 'can walk everywhere.' Shin-KLEEP is a character in the highly contextualized discourse that assumes familiarity with biography and shared experience. He already knows about Wolf, about Cougar and about Fox.

Shin-KLEEP enters into a life that is by its very nature dialogic. Wherever he goes, he enters the stories of that place. He is equally familiar to the human and non-human people with whom he shares stories. He talks his way in and out of dicey situations. He shares stories with just about everyone. That Coyote gets around. The stories he shares are a Native American canon. Enter Thomas

King. That Coyote even shares his stories with a Cherokee who hangs out with Blackfoot basketball players in Alberta. 'So. In the beginning, there was nothing. Just the water' (King 1993: 1).

Green Grass, Running Water

Both Harry Robinson and Coyote share stories with Thomas King in *Green Grass, Running Water*. But Coyote and Harry Robinson are not the only authors who share stories with that Native American writer. Herman Melville shares stories with him. Northrop Frye shares stories with him. James Fenimore Cooper shares stories with him. John Wayne shares stories with him. So do the authors of the Bible. I am trying to share stories with him in this paper. That Native American author is very generous with his credits. It is rumoured he looked at the text of my reading with a smile on his face (Hoy, personal communication).

What would happen, King asks, if Coyote rather than Jehovah created the world? What would happen if Jehovah turned out to be Joseph Hovaugh, the head doctor in a mental institution for old Indians? What would happen if an Indian author read the canon of white history through the narrative conventions of Indian history? The first thing that would happen, in King's version of the story, is that Coyote would be asleep and fall into conversation with his own dream. Creation, as Tedlock points out, has to begin with dialogue. Somewhere, too, there has to be the voice of an author. For Melville, that voice calls himself Ishmael. For King, the first person singular will suffice.

In Harry Robinson's stories, the voice of an omniscient third person narrator carries the story line. Robinson leads with that authorial voice and cites the voices of characters in the story as directly quoted dialogue. The result is vivid and compelling. 'I can go for twenty-one hours or more when I get started,' Harry told editor Wendy Wickwire, 'because this is my job. I'm a storyteller' (Robinson 1992: 7). In an interview with Peter Gzowski on CBC Radio, King talked about Robinson's influence on his work. 'I couldn't believe the power and the skill with which Robinson could work up a story in English (they weren't translated, they were just simply transcribed) and how well he understood the power of the oral voice in a written piece' (Gzowski 1993).

Harry Robinson's eponymous Coyote understands the power of the oral voice as he begins to tell the story of creation. The story is, of course, a dialogue about names and identities. King's Coyote enters a similar creative dialogue with himself:

> Who are you? says that Dream. Are you someone important?
> 'I'm Coyote,' says Coyote. 'And I am very smart.'

> I am very smart too, says that Dream. I must be Coyote.
> 'No,' says Coyote. 'You can't be Coyote. But you can be a dog.'
> Are dogs smart? says that Dream.
> 'You bet,' says Coyote. 'Dogs are good. They are almost as good as Coyote.'
> Okay, says that Dream. I can do that.
> But when that Coyote Dream thinks about being a dog, it gets everything mixed up. It gets everything backward.
> (King 1993: 1–2)

At this point in the dialogue, an author's voice breaks in to say, 'That looks like trouble to me.' That author is right, too. Pretty soon that Dog Dream says, 'I am god.' Playing God can lead to big trouble. Playing God can lead to a monologue that attempts to manage without the other. Playing God can lead to parts who think they are wholes.

King plays sagaciously with an intercultural vocabulary of biography and experience that can be shared only partially by any given reader. Some of it, like the Sundance and the Dead Dog Cafe, is Indian business. Some of it belongs to literary critics. Some belongs to anthropologists and historians. Some comes from the border towns of cultural trivia. 'There is no reader of this novel,' Fee and Flick observe, 'except perhaps Tom King, who is not outside some of its networks of cultural knowledge' (1995: 1). King's story is so multivocal that no single reader can expect to know every reference, from Melville's Benito Cereno and Moby Dick (who becomes Moby Jane), to the Navaho stories of Changing Woman. Most North Americans will get the reference to a faded Italian movie actor named Crystal Bell Cologne, but only Canadians and historians will recognize Louis, Ray, and Al in the Dead Dog Cafe as Louis Riel. Most will groan with a flood of outrage when they get the shaggy-dog story about the Nissan, the Pinto, and the Karmann-Ghia that sail over the edge of the world in the novel's fulfilling denouement.

Canadians may not know that a bit player named Henry Dawes was responsible for the 'Dawes Act' that privatized Indian lands in the United States, nor will they be aware that Richard Pratt founded the Carlisle Indian School with prisoners from Fort Marion, Florida, and pledged to 'kill the Indian, save the man.' Americans probably won't know that an Englishman named Archie Belaney made his name as the 'Indian' writer Grey Owl, nor that Elijah Harper said 'No' to the proposed Meech Lake Canadian constitutional accord. They may not get Polly Johnson and Susanna Moodie, who is 'roughing it,' but they will recognize those Native American heroines Sally-Jo Weyaha and Polly Hantos. Literary critics will recognize Northrop Frye's 'literal, allegorical, tropological, anagogic' categories when Dr Hovaugh charts a course, Balthazar-like, towards a certain star (King 1993: 324). They will remember that Frye saw Canadian literature as being dominated by a 'garrison mentality' and described the Bible as 'The Great Code.' But King and Coyote manage to scramble Frye's canonical borders with images from John Wayne and Richard Widmark movies.

Yes, but 'borders are constructed both by what you know and what you don't know.' Borders are also broken down (or deconstructed) by transforming what you don't know into what you know and, conversely, by transforming what you know into something strange. Indians and colonizers have been doing both to one another for five hundred years. King and Coyote are adept at both transformations. And as Fee and Flick point out, King's Dead Dog Cafe evokes Nietzsche's famous aphorism, 'God is Dead' (Fee and Flick 1995: 12).[1] The Dead Dog Cafe is clearly a 'site of contestation,' as lit-crit voices might have it. In King's narrative, it is a site of contestation between Canadian and American versions of Indian history. On a larger scale, the entire book is a site of contestation between conflicting Indian and white versions of a shared history. Sharing stories with Thomas King is not always unproblematic, but it is guaranteed to increase one's knowledge by connecting what you do know to something you ought to know. If you are lucky, you may even deconstruct something you thought you knew.

Following Coyote's opening dialogue with his dog dream, the rest of the book carries on a series of conversations that attempt to make the world right again. These conversations appear as the stories of First Woman, Changing Woman, Thought Woman, and Old Woman, four mythic persons from Native American tradition. In the novel, these goddess figures first appear disguised as four old Indians who have escaped from a mental institution run by Dr Joseph Hovaugh and his black assistant, Babo, a gender-shifted refugee from Melville's *Benito Cereno.* In Melville's novella, Babo is a slave who leads a rebellion against the Spanish slave-ship captain Benito Cereno. When an American whaling captain, Amasa Delano, boards Cereno's ship, the *San Dominick*, Babo pretends to be Cereno's slave when, in fact, he has reversed roles and become his master. King's Babo recalls the role played by Melville's Babo, but with a Coyote twist. Melville's Babo was a black slave who overthrew his master; King's Babo is a black woman who knows more than her master, the God-like Dr J. Hovaugh.

'Babo's right,' King told Peter Gzowski in the CBC interview. 'Babo's always right. The Sergeant [of course, named Cereno] is always wrong.' Dr Hovaugh plays the role of God, but with no more success than Coyote's dog dream. Babo is right that the four old Indians are actually women. She is right that J. Hovaugh is a fraud. The real deities, in King's story, are four female creators who have masked themselves with the names of whitemen from Western literary tradition. Each one of these whitemen is famous for having been paired with an aboriginal person. First Woman of Navaho tradition becomes The Lone Ranger (Kemo sabe, 'the one who knows,' paired with Tonto, 'the stupid one'); Changing Woman of Navaho tradition becomes Ishmael (son of Abraham and the slave girl Hagar; also the narrator of Melville's Moby Dick, who is paired with the 'cannibal,' Queequeg); Thought Woman of Pueblo tradition becomes Robinson Crusoe, paired with Friday; and Old Woman becomes the deerslayer, Hawkeye, paired with Cooper's Chingachgook.

Like Coyote in Harry Robinson's story, these creators play with names and the stories they invoke. Also like Coyote, Thomas King plays with a multitude of mutually intersecting stories. Some of the stories he cites are classic Native American myths. Some of them are from the canon of Western literary tradition. Some are from the lives of fictional characters who live only within the world of King's writing. Within the novel, Blackfoot history professor Alberta Frank wishes to become pregnant without having to bother with the stupid satin sheets of her boyfriend, Charlie Looking Bear. Within Navaho oral tradition, Changing Woman was lonely and wished to communicate with the sun. Her sister wished to communicate with the rain clouds. The story relates: 'So it was that they made up their minds. At dawn the next morning each would do what *Azdzqq nadleehe* the Changing Woman suggested. Accordingly, she found a flat, bare rock near the summit of *Ch'ool'i'i* on whose sides the giant spruces grow to this very day. She lay upon it, face up, with her feet to the east and her legs spread comfortably apart. That way she could relax as she observed the sun make its path across the sky. That way it could shine its warmth fully upon her' (Zolbrod 1984: 181).

From this encounter, Changing Woman became pregnant. Her sister became pregnant from a rain cloud. In *Green Glass, Running Water*, the same thing happened to Alberta on her way to the Sundance. In a moment of wetness and with the help of Coyote, playing at least the Annunciator and maybe even God the Father, she went the way of her sister, Changing Woman. As the Sundance commences, Alberta, like Changing Woman, blossoms. The novel, of course, is set in a place called Blossom, Alberta. As any English professor knows, the placement of a comma can change the meaning of words. Blossom Alberta really is the book's simple, life-affirming message. Sun and life-giving water centre the Sundance in a forked cottonwood pole. The People blossom there. So. In the beginning there was a reading. These are the words I spoke:

The Reading (3 June 1995)

So. Theorizing the Americanist Tradition. Native Writing – Native Experience. Mmmm. I'm an Anthro; and I'm not an Indian. So what voice do I use?

> So.
> In the beginning, there was nothing. Just water.
> Coyote was there, but Coyote was asleep. That Coyote was asleep and that Coyote was dreaming. When that Coyote dreams, anything can happen.
> 'I can tell you that,' says Tom.
> (King: 1)

Wait a second, says Anthro. This is my story. I'm sharing stories with Tom, not the other way around. It says so right here on the program; 10:00–10:30 Saturday, June 3, 1995. Theorizing the Americanist Tradition: Native Writing – Native Experience. 'Sharing Stories with Thomas King.' Theorizing is my business. Tom's is Native writing, Native experience. Tom is an Indian, an Indian storyteller. Telling stories is his business. I wrote an abstract. Anthros are good at abstract thought. Indians are good at oral thought. Walter Ong says so. He's a Jesuit and he should know. Anthros are good at theorizing. They are good at theorizing the Americanist Tradition. Indians are good at being informants. Indians are the first Americans. Anthros are the first Americanists.

In my abstract I wrote:

> The oral traditions of many First Nations code information in a way that is analogous to the distribution of visual information in a holographic image.

In *Green Grass, Running Water* (327–8) Tom wrote (sort of):[2]

> Anthros are patient.
> Indians can run fast.

I wrote:

> Each story, like each piece of a hologram, contains information about the entire structure of which it is a part.

Tom wrote:

> Anthros are spiritual.
> Indians can endure pain.

I wrote:

> Stories function as metonyms; parts that stand for wholes.

Tom wrote:

> Anthros are cognitive.
> Indians have quick reflexes.

I wrote:

> Stories in the First Nations traditions I am familiar with are part of a highly contextualized discourse which assumes familiarity with biography and shared experience.

Tom wrote:

> Anthros are philosophical.

Indians don't talk much.

I wrote:

First Nations novelist Thomas King replicates genre conventions of oral tradition in *Green Grass, Running Water.*

Tom wrote:

Anthros are sophisticated.

Indians have good eyesight.

I wrote:

This paper describes my experience of teaching his book in conjunction with telling stories from my own experience of First Nations oral traditions.

Tom wrote:

Anthros are sensitive.

Indians have agile bodies.

I wrote:

It concludes that by using the genre conventions of Native storytelling, King successfully communicates the quality of Native experience in his writing.

'Phew,' I says.

'Each story,' I wrote, 'like each piece of a hologram, contains information about the entire structure of which it is a part.'

'That's a lot of information,' says Coyote.

'You bet,' I says.

'Indian stories are cosmic,' says Coyote. 'They are about goddess figures like First Woman, Changing Woman, Thought Woman, and Old woman. Whiteman's stories are fictional. They are about made-up characters like the Lone Ranger, Ishmael, Robinson Crusoe, and Hawkeye.'

'But what happens if an Indian knows about these other guys too?' I says. 'What happens if Indians use microwave ovens?' 'You mean microwave pizza?' says Coyote. 'You mean the pizza test?'[3]

'No,' I says. 'I mean what if an Indian has read James Fenimore Cooper and Herman Melville and Northrop Frye? What if this Indian knows that Margaret Atwood wrote a book of poems called *The Journals of Susanna Moodie*?'

'I am a word in a foreign language,' says Margaret (Atwood 1970: 11).

'What if this Indian knows that Grey Owl was actually an Englishman named Archie Belaney? What if this Indian has a degree in English literature?'

'Sounds like Eli Stands Alone in *Green Grass, Running Water*,' says Coyote.

'Sounds like Thomas King,' I says.

'Maybe that Indian author would be a contrary,' says Coyote. 'Maybe she would write about a great black lesbian whale called Moby Jane. Maybe she would turn Babo, the slave who took over Benito Cereno's ship, into Dr J. Hovaugh's omniscient cleaning lady.'

'Now we gotta figure out which of the characters is real,' says Peter Gzowski in an interview with Tom on CBC Radio, 'which one you made up, and where the resonance is in some of the names. Let's start with the four old Indians.'

'The four old Indians, yeah,' says Tom. 'Lone Ranger, Ishmael, Robinson Crusoe, Hawkeye. Well, I wanted to create archetypal Indian characters. I wanted to create the universe again.'

'Tom!' says Peter. 'The Lone Ranger's not an archetypal Indian character.'

'Well, actually, he sort of is in some kind of a strange way in North American popular culture,' says Tom. 'You know, you've got the Lone Ranger and Tonto, and you've got Ishmael and Queequeg, and you have Hawkeye and Chingachgook, and you have Robinson Crusoe and Friday, and these are all kind of ... they're not archetypal characters in literature, but they're Indian and white buddies, I suppose. Not buddy movies but buddy books, I suppose. But those are just the names that the old Indians have at the time we meet them. In actual fact, these are four archetypal Indian women who come right out of oral creation stories and who have been more or less ...'

'Ah!' says Peter.

'So each one of the women who open up the various sections that come out of the oral stories are really those old Indians as they come along,' says Tom, 'but they've just been forced to assume these guises by history, by literature, by just the general run of the world, and so that's what they call themselves now.'

'So when Babo tells the sergeant who's looking for them that they're women ...' says Peter.

'Yeah, Babo's right,' says Tom. 'I mean, Babo's always right. The sergeant's always wrong' (Gzowski 1993).

'Well,' I says. 'Each piece of a hologram contains information about the entire structure of which it is a part. I mean, Benito Cereno is about when the relations between slaves and masters aren't what they seem to be. The structure is there but the roles are reversed.'

'When Coyote dreams, anything can happen,' says Tom. 'Coyote's there from the get-go, from the very beginning and you have to look over your shoulder when you're dealing with Coyote,' says Tom to Peter.

'Or Tom King, I think,' says Peter.

'Moby Dick is part of the canon of American literature,' I says. 'So is Natty Bumppo who became Hawkeye, the deerslayer. So is Ishmael.'

'And he will be a wild man; his hand will be against every man, and every man's hand against him; and he shall dwell in the presence of all his brethren,' says the author of Genesis (16:12).

'Maybe Ishmael is a wild card, not a wild man,' says Coyote. 'Maybe Ishmael is actually Changing Woman,' says that one. 'That Indian contrary might find Changing Woman in her Bible. She might write about Thought Woman making lists like Robinson Crusoe. She might turn Old Woman into a leather-stocking. She might think First Woman was The Lone Ranger. When Coyote dreams, anything can happen,' says Coyote.

'That's right,' I says. 'Stories function as metonyms; parts that stand for wholes.'

'Oh boy!' says Coyote. 'My part is good at standing for holes. I hope that contrary Indian author writes me into her story.'

'Get lost, Coyote,' I says. 'I'm talking about stories. Stories in First Nations traditions are part of a highly contextualized discourse which assumes familiarity with biography and shared experience.'

'Would that First Nations author write a biographical novel about Coyote?' says Coyote. 'Would that one write about a Coyote dream?'

'I can't speak for Tom,' I says. 'You'd have to ask him if he intended to tell Coyote's story. He's the Indian author.'

'Hey,' says Coyote. 'Telling my story would be appropriation of voice. Only Coyotes can write about Coyotes.'

'I rest my case,' I says.

'So how can that one write about fictional characters from nineteenth-century American novels?' says Coyote.

'I guess he experienced them,' I says. 'Maybe he read a book on reader response theory.'

'Maybe he spent a lot of time hanging out with Blackfoot storytellers,' says Coyote.

'Really,' says Tom to Peter. 'It began with just being around other Native people when I was in my teen-age years, and then I began to sort of make that my field of study.'

'First Nations novelist Thomas King,' I says, 'replicates genre conventions of oral tradition in *Green Grass, Running Water*.'

'The people I know best,' says Tom, 'I suppose, are the people around Lethbridge and many of the people off the reserve and just my own family. That's the way conversations go a lot of the time. You have two people who are talking about the same thing but you'd never know it to listen to them. But in the end it all comes out all right.'

'Sure,' says Coyote. 'So he floats his whole Indian novel on *Benito Cereno* by Herman Melville and *The Deerslayer* by James Fenimore Cooper, not to mention trashy John Wayne and Richard Widmark movies and the *Anatomy of Criticism*.'

'The novel does deal with some of the primary attitudes that Canadians and in fact North Americans have towards Indians,' says Tom to Peter.

'Sounds like a garrison mentality,' I says.

'It also deals with the fact that that line that we think is so firm between reality and fantasy,' says Tom, 'is not that firm at all; that there's a great deal of play in it, that the line itself is an imaginary line.'

'I think Peter liked the book,' says Coyote.

'That's one of the reasons why you have these historical and literary characters who sort of float across time and in and out of this novel to affect the present or at least be a part of the present,' says Tom to Peter.

'Maybe that contrary Indian author would write a biographical novel about Coyote floating across time and in and out of the novel,' says Coyote. 'Maybe she would write about that Coyote Dream thinking about being a dog. Maybe that one would get everything mixed up. Maybe she would get everything backward.'

'You mean that dog dream might want to be a god,' I says.

'I am god,' says that Dog Dream.

'Isn't that cute,' says Coyote. 'That Dog Dream is a contrary. That Dog Dream has everything backward.'

'But why am I a little god,' shouts that god.

'Not so loud,' says Coyote. 'You're hurting my ears.'

'I don't want to be a little god,' says that god. 'I want to be a big god! *Big one*!'

Okay, okay,' says Coyote. 'Just stop shouting.'

'There,' says that GOD. 'That's better' (King: 2).

'Let's get back on topic,' says Coyote. 'Would Elijah Harper be in that contrary's story? Would Henry Dawes be there, and Louis Riel and Pauline Johnson and Duncan Campbell Scott?'

'You bet,' I says. 'They're all part of the shared Indian experience ... sort of.'

'How about Christopher Columbus,' says Coyote. 'We all share stories with that guy whether we want to or not.'

'Sure,' I says. 'That contrary Indian author would probably call him something like Crystal Bell Cologne and turn him into a red-headed Italian actor who recruits Indians for grade "B" westerns.'

'Right,' says Coyote, 'and he'd make up an elaborate shaggy-dog story to name his ships the Nissan, the Pinto, and the Karmann-Ghia and have them sail over the edge of the world because of a dam on Indian land in Alberta.'

'I like shaggy-dog stories,' says Coyote.

'Alberta,' I says. 'That's who the novel is about. It's about a Blackfoot university professor named Alberta Frank. She wants a kid but doesn't want to be responsible for some silly guy like one of her two boyfriends, Charlie Looking Bear and Lionel Red Dog.'

'And Coyote helped that woman who wanted a baby just like he did for that other one before,' says Coyote.

'Sshh,' I says. 'Someone might be offended.'

'Lionel thought he could see a yellow dog dancing in the rain the night Alberta got pregnant,' says Tom.

'The sky in Alberta,' says one of Charlie's teachers, 'is like a deep clear ocean into which you can look and see the soul of the universe.'

'*Green Grass, Running Water* is about a place called Blossom, Alberta,' says Coyote.

'You bet,' I says, 'and Blossom Alberta is also the book's simple life-affirming message.'

'What I wanted to do when I started writing the novel,' says Tom to Peter ... 'I started off not knowing this, of course, but working on the assumption that Christian myth was the one that informed the world that I was working with.'

'Sounds like appropriation to me,' says Coyote.

'And the more I got into the novel,' says Tom, 'I discovered that I couldn't work with that. It didn't give me enough freedom to work with my fictions, so all of a sudden one day I thought, My God, why don't I just recreate the world along more Native lines and use Native oral stories, oral creation stories, rather than the story you find in *Genesis*?'

'Uh-oh,' says Coyote. 'Sound's like another dog's dream.'

'So I went back and I began to, uh, use *that* as my basis for the fiction,' says Tom to Peter, 'and then all I had to do, no, not all I had to do but one of the things I wanted to do was to sort of drag that myth through Christianity, through Western literature and Western history and see what I came up with.'

'Sound like theorizing the Americanist Tradition,' I says.

'Sort of, you know,' says Tom to Peter, 'push it through that grinder if you will, as Native culture has been pushed through that sort of North American grinder.'

'Anthros are good at theorizing,' says Coyote. 'Is Tom an Anthro?'

'And so that's partly what happens,' says Tom. 'You get this movement in each one of the sections, you get this movement from an oral creation story through a Biblical story, through a literary story, through a historical story, and that repeats itself each of the times in the four sections.'

'That's why there are four old Indians in Dr J. Hovaugh's hospital,' says Coyote. 'Four is an Indian number.'

So.

In the beginning, there was nothing. Just the water.

'And so in each of those sections you have this archetypal woman who does come out of the sky,' says Tom, 'winds up, you know, somehow in a body of water, and the whole process begins from there.'

'Stories function as metonyms; parts that stand for wholes,' I says.

'There's what they call the earth diver story,' says Tom to Peter, 'where the main characters in the drama of creation come out of the sky and land in the ocean and start things from there.'

'Each story,' I says, 'like each piece of a hologram, contains information about the entire structure of which it is a part.'

'It was kind of nice too,' Tom says, 'because it gave me a chance to talk about a more Native sense of the creation of the world within the novel.'

'I thought the book was a Coyote creation story,' says Coyote.

'That's unlikely,' says Tom.

'No, no,' says Coyote. 'It's the truth.'

'There are no truths, Coyote,' Tom says. 'Only stories.'

'Okay,' says Coyote. 'Tell me a story' (King: 326).

'Sit down,' Tom says to Coyote.

'But there is water everywhere,' says Coyote.

'That's true,' Tom says. 'And here's how it happened' (King: 360).

Conclusion

Tom King's knowledge of Indian and Western tradition is both ethnographic and literary. He hung out with Blackfoot and Cree people. He read Harry Robinson. He took in most of what popular culture has to say about Indians. He is a good listener with a good voice. He likes Melville's literary tricks.

Episodic interrelated vignettes performed by a knowledgeable narrator are typical of traditional Indian oral literatures. Tom King's work is neo-premodern,[4] not postmodern. Reading the book as a romp through North American literature and history is a game for academics. That is why this paper is called 'Coyote's Cannon.' The book is being taught by professors of English literature as we speak.

The book's simple and life-affirming message really is Blossom Alberta. Once again, Coyote recreates the world through annunciation and the Sundance.

Postscript (a relaxation after writing)

There's lots more left for tropological sleuthing. Tom knows a lot. Maybe I little bit know something. For further references, consult your local Coyote.

NOTES

1 Thanks to Margery Fee and Jane Flick for reading the Dead Dog Cafe as 'God is Dead.'
2 By 'sort of,' I mean that in King's parody of Cooper, he contrasted Indians with whites. I have taken the liberty, in my quotation of this passage, to substitute anthropologists for whites, thus turning them into parts that stand for wholes.
3 The 'Pizza Test' is part of recent Canadian folklore shared by Indians and anthropologists. It refers to a court case in which a lawyer for the Crown supposedly attempted to discredit an Indian claim by implying that Indians who eat pizza couldn't be truly aboriginal and thus retained no aboriginal rights.
4 As far as I know, I am the first (and perhaps the only) person to use the term neo-premodern. The term could make sense only to a person already exposed to the pasticherie of postmodernism. People who lived before the 'modern' era obviously did not think of themselves as pre-modern. While they cannot have known about us, we can know about them. We can recognize a resonance between ourselves and people who never experienced the modernist agenda. Tom King plays upon this possibility. His Old Indians are pre-moderns held captive by American modernism, but they are also the thoroughly anachronistic Thought Woman, Old Woman, First Woman, and Changing Woman. Their time transcends our own and circles back to touch it. By masking them in the icons of modernism, King reveals himself to be a neo-premodernist.

REFERENCES

Atwood, Margaret. 1970. *The Journals of Susanna Moodie*. Toronto: Oxford University Press.

Bakhtin, Mikhail. 1984. *Problems of Dostoevsky's Poetics*. Edited and translated by Caryl Emerson. Minneapolis: University of Minnesota Press.

Cruikshank Julie. 1990. *Life Lived Like a Story*. Lincoln: University of Nebraska Press.

Fee, Margery, and Jane Flick. 1995. 'Knowing Where the Borders Are in Thomas King's *Green Grass, Running Water*.' Paper presented at a meeting of the Association for Canadian Studies in the United States.

Frye, Rodney. 1995. *Stories That Make the World*. Norman: University of Oklahoma Press.

Gzowski, Peter. 1993. CBC Morningside interview with Thomas King, 5 April 1993.

Hallowell, A. Irving. 1960. 'Ojibwa Ontology, Behavior, and World View.' In Stanley Diamond, ed., *Culture and History: Essays in Honor of Paul Radin*, 19–52. New York: Columbia University Press.

Hoy, Helen. 1995. Personal communication (e-mail message reporting her husband's response to 'Coyote's Cannon').

King, Thomas. 1993. *Green Grass, Running Water*. Toronto: HarperCollins. (The pagination cited refers to the hardcover edition, which comes full circle with 360 pages.)

Melville, Herman. 1856. *Benito Cereno*. Chicago: University of Chicago Press.

Ridington, Robin. 1988. 'Knowledge, Power and the Individual in Subarctic Hunting Societies.' *American Anthropologist* 90(1): 98–110 (reprinted in Ridington 1990: 100–18).

– 1990. *Little Bit Know Something: Stories in a Language of Anthropology*. Iowa City: University of Iowa Press.

– In press. 'Coyote's Cannon: Sharing Stories with Thomas King.' *American Indian Quarterly* (a somewhat different version of the present paper adapted for *AIQ* readers).

Robinson, Harry. 1989. *Write It on Your Heart: The Epic World of an Okanagan Storyteller*. Compiled and edited by Wendy Wickwire. Vancouver: Talon Books.

– 1992. *Nature Power: In the Spirit of an Okanagan Storyteller.* Compiled and edited by Wendy Wickwire. Vancouver: Douglas and McIntyre.

Sarris, Greg. 1993. *Keeping Slug Woman Alive: A Holistic Approach to American Indian Texts.* Berkeley: University of California Press.

Tedlock, Dennis. 1991. 'The Speaker of Tales Has More than One String to Play On.' In Ivan Brady, ed., *Anthropological Poetics.* Savage, MD: Rowman and Littlefield.

– 1995. 'Dialoguing with the Invader.' Paper presented at conference on Theorizing the Americanist Tradition, University of Western Ontario.

Zolbrod, Paul. 1984. *Dine bahane: The Navaho Creation Story.* Albuquerque: University of New Mexico Press.

3 Theorizing Americanist Anthropology: Continuities from the B.A.E. to the Boasians

REGNA DARNELL

Isaiah Berlin once claimed that thinkers – among whom I include philosophers, literary critics, perhaps even anthropologists and linguists – come in two varieties: there are hedgehogs, who have one great idea, worried through myriad potential instantiations, and there are foxes, who flit from one idea to another and seek connections among them. I have always prided myself on being a fox, perhaps even a butterfly. But I have discovered a deeply suppressed hedgehog in my long-ongoing thinking about the history and legacy in praxis of Americanist anthropology and linguistics.

Recently, in relation to my current commitment to delineating the parameters of an Americanist anthropological tradition that is firmly based in, yet reaches beyond, the study of the American Indian, I reread my 1969 dissertation, entitled 'The Development of American Anthropology, 1879–1920: From the Bureau of American Ethnology to Franz Boas.' My present reading documents a continuity in how we Americanists do anthropology, as well is in what we study. I am now prepared to argue that this tradition constitutes a theoretical substratum for virtually all sociocultural anthropologists trained in North America.

This reading of the Americanist Tradition, needless to say, creates some strange bedfellows. For example, one of the pieces of Claude Lévi-Strauss's structuralism (Darnell 1995b) is Americanist; there can be no question of the French anthropologist's enthusiasm for Bureau of American Ethnology monographs about the aborigines of North America or for the austere commitment to ethnographic representation of disappearing cultures by which he characterized the Boasians. He seems to have seen more ties *between* the B.A.E. and the Boasians than reasons to distinguish them; there was something about theory and method in relation to the cultures of this place that produced an identifiable amalgam that has persisted through anthropological history in North America.

A second piece of superficially unlikely Americanism is the text-based interpretive anthropology of Clifford Geertz (Darnell 1995a). Although Geertz did not work with aboriginal peoples of the Americas, he was trained in an anthropology that attended to symbolic thought as constructed across cultures. In Bali, throughout Indonesia, and in Morocco, Geertz often proceeded in ways familiar to colleagues with training similar to his own who continued to work in traditional Americanist communities like those usually studied by the founders of anthropology in North America.

Finally, there are the self-styled postmodernists (Darnell 1995a), whose ardour for a contemporary 'experimental moment' sometimes seems to preclude the very possibility of intellectual ancestry, Americanist or otherwise. George Marcus, James Clifford, and Paul Rabinow are certainly not students of Native North Americans; but in the larger sense toward which I aim here, they come by their Americanist roots honestly, in great part by way of Clifford Geertz.

Such bedfellows may be real without being present to the conscious awareness of latter-day inheritors of underlying Americanist assumptions. Several years ago, I read a paper to the Canadian Anthropology Society (Darnell 1992) about the Boasian tradition in the study of Native peoples in what is now Canada. A distinguished francophone colleague from Quebec accosted me afterwards, saying: 'You almost make me want to be a Boasian!' I responded somewhat flippantly: 'Ah, but you already are.' This colleague was trained in a distinguished North American department, one that also went into the making of Clifford Geertz; he played a significant role in rendering Lévi-Strauss's structuralism accessible to North American anthropologists. That he does not work with Native Americans is, I would argue, beside the point in terms of intellectual affinities and continuities. The superficial equation of the Americanist Tradition with the study of the American Indian obscures more general styles of scholarly production.

In general, I would argue that continuity with this broadly defined Americanist Tradition resides out of awareness for most practitioners most of the time. It thus behooves us to explore the underlying regularities, the essential tenets that have been absorbed into the mainstream, rising to consciousness largely when called into contrast with the underlying assumptions and intellectual styles of other national traditions, particularly British social anthropology. From an Americanist standpoint, there is something fundamentally alien about the behaviourism and God's-eye-view positivism of the latter. The early Boasians encountering Bronislaw Malinowski and A.R. Radcliffe-Brown as immigrants to the New World were less than impressed by what they perceived as the arrogance of the self-styled functionalists. For example, Ruth Benedict, in correspondence with Edward Sapir, retaliated for Radcliffe-Brown's high-handedness by refusing to use his hyphenated surname; he was 'Mr Brown.' Sapir, in turn, dismissed Radcliffe-Brown as 'a supercilious gentleman' (to Fay-Cooper Cole, 22 May 1932: University of Chicago Archives). Similarly, I find myself alternately bemused by the narrow and often ahistorical assumptions of the self-styled functionalists and defensive of what the Americanists had/have been doing all along.

The fundamental conflict between the Americanist and the British models for anthropology emerged most clearly in the debates between Sapir and Radcliffe-Brown (cf. Darnell 1990), his successor at the University of Chicago, about publication of the Navajo texts of Father Berard Haile, Sapir's long-time protégé and collaborator. For Radcliffe-Brown (Department of Anthropology memorandum, University of Chicago, May 1932: UC), 'authoritative' texts were useless to scholars: 'If they are to be treasured merely because they are disappearing, and because they are accurately transcribed ... their publication would then be supported by mere antiquarian sentiment.' Radcliffe-Brown was not a sentimental man. Sapir fulminated at Radcliffe-Brown's apparent belief that 'we in America had better get busy and learn something from functionalism as to how a truly readable volume should be prepared' (to Cole, 2 June 1932: UC). Less than a year before his death, still in defence of the Haile texts, Sapir made perhaps the most lyrical and self-conscious statement we have of the premises of the Americanist text-based method as a way of doing ethnography (to Cole, 25 April 1938): 'I'm not particularly interested in "smoothed-over" versions of native culture. I like the stuff in the raw, as felt and dictated by the natives ... the genuine, difficult, confusing, primary sources. These must be presented, whatever else is done ... There are too many glib monographs, most of which time will show to be highly subjective performances.' In contrast, Sapir praised 'that anxious respect for documentary evidence' that bridged the native's knowledge and the anthropologist's synthesis. The natives would be permitted to speak for themselves.

My own training is unabashedly Americanist, at least in retrospect; indeed, it was some time before I came to distinguish the Americanist Tradition from the whole of anthropology. My first teacher of anthropology, Frederica de Laguna, was Franz Boas's last Ph.D. student. As an undergraduate, I also studied with the late A. Irving 'Pete' Hallowell, dean of northern Algonquian (Ojibwe) studies. In a spurious and short-lived attempt to break away from the consistent tenor of my emerging professional socialization, I proposed, as a beginning graduate student at the University of Pennsylvania, to study culture and personality in East Africa. But intellectually the interesting game in town was linguistic anthropology and history of anthropology with Dell Hymes. Anthony F.C.

Wallace, the late John Witthoft, and Elizabeth Tooker cemented the inevitable long before I moved from the ivory tower to the First Nations (Native American) community.

In Canada, since 1969, the Americanist Tradition has continued to frame what I do. There are, to be sure, potentially enabling differences of scale: a Canadian anthropologist can easily obtain access to policy makers. First Nations issues, as evidenced by the ongoing assimilation of the report and recommendations of the Royal Commission on Aboriginal Peoples, are (at least occasionally) more salient in the minds of non-Native Canadians than are Native American issues in most parts of the United States. But the essential concerns of the Americanist Tradition have spanned the border (which, in any case, was deemed irrelevant for the aboriginal peoples of the continent by the Jay Treaty of 1823). My hedgehog's determination to link the history of anthropology and linguistics in the Americanist Tradition to my own ethnographic practice does not seem to me unique in Canadian anthropology. There is substantial continuity from the work of Edward Sapir as director of the Anthropological Division of the Geological Survey of Canada from 1910 to 1925 to the salvage-ethnography commitment of the Mercury Series of the National Museum of Man, now the Canadian Museum of Civilization.

In any case, my own situated position is part of what I can say about the Americanist Tradition. It is not, and is not intended to be, 'objective.' My own intellectual genealogy is set forth precisely to contextualize my interpretation of this tradition of which I am a part. To the extent that my own position is nuanced and self-conscious, it may fit together with other views from within, overlapping to produce a richer and more complex portrait of Americanist work. To facilitate that multilogue is one way to 'Theorize the Americanist Tradition.' There are many commonalities with the movement loosely called postmodernism, but the Americanist Tradition has its own distinctive take thereupon.

In foregrounding the Americanist Tradition, I am not suggesting, of course, that national traditions are incommensurable or that they have been isolated fully from one another in their historical emergence. However reflexively examined, national traditions remain somewhat amorphous and overlapping; like cultures, they are normative constructs, held uniquely by each member (Sapir, passim) and continuously emergent.

The cross-connections among national traditions, however, have proceeded as though what were at issue were *the same* anthropology, without acknowledgment of a mutual solitude, of a need for translation and calibration of language and intentionality. All too often the Americans, the British, the French, and the Germans have seemed to talk about the same things. But they have used different professional terminologies and have laid claim to different intellectual genealogies. Our wheels have been invented many times (although they have also been borrowed, thereby obscuring their histories). That is, diffusion and genetic relationship serve as theoretical models for disciplinary history as well as for linguistic change. Words like culture, society, function, structure, history, personality, rationality, relativism, translation, commensurability, etc., have divided artificially what might more productively be seen as mutually informative approaches to common interests in the variability and commonality of humankind across time and space.

Individual anthropologists adhere to, and modify, existing traditions, always in relation to the situated history of the discipline. Whether the rhetoric of professional socialization is continuous or revolutionary (Murray 1983, 1995), individual choices are non-random, in relation to and development from previously existing traditions. Self-awareness about starting points, about traditions and alternatives to them, deeply informs praxis – at least, I would argue, in relation to the Americanist Tradition.

The ongoing significance of Americanist anthropology has been eclipsed to a remarkable degree in the recent history of our discipline. To articulate the strawperson in its baldest form: the Boasian historical particularists were *mere descriptivists* who set back anthropology by decades in failing to allow nomothetic generalization, whether it be of the variety proposed by Leslie White's levels of sociocultural integration (1966) or Marvin Harris's techno-environmental determinism (1968), although the latter is far more subtle in acknowledging the depth of Boas's influence on anthropology, not just in America. Whatever was to be admired in the work of Franz Boas and his early students was portrayed as insufficient to carry anthropological theory forward without an infusion from elsewhere.

In anthropology, the obvious candidates for theoretical progress were evolutionism (purportedly stripped of its nineteenth-century ethnocentrisms in the multilinear evolutionism of Julian Steward, Marshal Sahlins, and Elman Service) and British social anthropology (wherein structure and function would frame generalizations for a 'natural science of society' as suggested by A.R. Radcliffe-Brown). In linguistics, Sapir's so-called mentalism receded before Bloomfieldian structuralism (Hymes and Fought 1975).

Americanists, whether in anthropology or linguistics, allowed this redefinition of the theoretical centre of gravity to happen without much in the way of protest. History of anthropology emerged as a reputable specialization within the North American discipline in the early 1960s around the work of George W. Stocking, Jr, with his distinction between 'presentism,' based on contemporary theoretical hobby horses, and 'historicism,' aiming for primary understanding of ideas in the situated context of their own time. Nonetheless, after publishing his collected papers on Boasian anthropology in 1968, Stocking largely defected to the history of the British tradition, presumably in search of a more enthusiastic audience for the history of anthropology among those widely assumed to be the victors in the unstated turf wars to supersede and/or marginalize the Americanist Tradition.

Whatever the theoretical triumphs of British social anthropology on North American soil since the 1970s, the British tradition (in spite of some honourable exceptions) has remained profoundly uninterested in the historical emergence of currently functioning social systems. One might almost believe that anthropologists, like members of cultures, can function in a vacuum, outside history. If this is so, then there is no distinction between history and theory, and no need for the history of anthropology. The resulting audience for disciplinary history, featuring post-Geertzian Chicago-trained postmodernists, retains little if any commitment to the historicism of Stocking in 1968. Exemplars of the movement away from historical context toward contemporary theoretical concerns include *Romantic Motives* (1989), volume six of Stocking's monograph series and Stocking's own paper (1991) speculating on why four British social anthropologists failed to complete major promised work, reaching permanent impasse.

Against the grain or otherwise, my own work has attempted in various directions to rehabilitate the Americanist Tradition. I have taken as a starting point the assumption that contemporary practice operates in a dialectic with disciplinary history. I believe that to be an Americanist involves, therefore, a choice rather than a necessity for cultural interpretation. Following Hallowell (1965), I further assume that anthropologists who are interested in disciplinary history will (and should) approach it using the same methods they learned in order to do ethnographic fieldwork in supposedly alien societies. It is a fundamental, and shared, Americanist attitude toward cause and effect, towards the nature of social explanation, rather than merely a passion for burrowing in archival and other obscure sources, that puts me at ease when I talk to ethnohistorians about the *theoretical* overlap between their work and my own. It really shouldn't come as a surprise that the American Society for Ethnohistory involves a great deal of Americanist research in the narrower, ethnographic, as well as in the philosophical, sense.

The continuities in Americanist anthropology unquestionably result in part from its focus on the study of the American Indian. Perhaps this focus was inevitable given the overwhelming presence (and resistance) of aboriginal peoples as the nation-states of the United States and Canada were forged by newcomer settlers. At the very least, there was a need to forge a common history for aboriginal peoples and foreign invaders determined to become 'natives' themselves. Hallowell (1960) suggested that the close relationship of Native Americans and settlers forced integrated attention to their cultures, languages, prehistories, and physical remains. In any case, North America's form of colonialism was an intimate, interactive, symbolically loaded one. Moreover, at least through the end of the Second World War, most anthropologists in North America worked at home, in aboriginal communities. Anthropologists and anthropological linguists trained more recently, regardless of where their research is done, remain heirs to this tradition.

The Americanist Tradition has been person-focused. Life history was the privileged methodology of the interwar effort to untangle the role of the individual in creating culture from the impact of culture on the individual, best articulated in the work of Edward Sapir. The term culture-and-personality, popularized by Margaret Mead and Ruth Benedict, bridges less clearly between ethnographic and historicist projects. My own book-length biographies of Sapir and of Daniel Garrison Brinton (whose edited monograph series, *Library of Aboriginal American Literature*, falls firmly within the Americanist Tradition that preceded as well as incorporated Boas) have approached the professional career of a subject by way of the discipline as seen through the eyes of a single subject (based on whatever records remain, whether in archives or in oral history). In a surprisingly discordant 'rhetoric of discontinuity' (Murray 1983, 1995), life history has been rehabilitated in recent postmodernist reflections on ethnography as writing; yet there is no acknowledgment of the roots of this methodology in Americanist studies of personality and culture.

It remains problematic that those trained within the Americanist Tradition – by Boas and his students and his students' students – have protested rarely against the eclipse of their own centrality to anthropology over the last half-century. Dedicated Americanists have been content, for the most part, to work within their own parameters, talking to each other. They employ a 'rhetoric of continuity' (Murray 1983, 1995) and a social organization based on consensus and collaboration.

This rhetoric of continuity derives, at least in part, from a political style widely found among the hunting and gathering societies of Native North America, in which one withdraws from confrontation and moves somewhere else to maintain personal autonomy. I would argue that anthropologists come by their theories from two major sources: first, from the symbolic capital of the discipline itself and, second, through a dialogic reflexivity with the peoples they study. If Americanists have tended to study the aboriginal peoples of the Americas, it should not surprise us that their resulting strategies of professional discourse parallel those of ethnographic discourse.

Such a non-confrontational strategy has the advantage of avoiding dissipation of energy for resolving strife. For anthropologists as well as for Native North Americans, it requires self-confidence, personal and in our cases also professional, that our ways of doing things are unassailable and more significant in the doing than in the disputing with outsiders who do not understand or care to understand. The disadvantage of such a strategy is that it abandons the larger field to others who are allowed by default to define themselves as victors in an undeclared disciplinary war. The alternative model is intensely competitive, assuming a zero-sum game in academic production, without much input from the subjects of study, and contrasting sharply with the multivocality foregrounded by the Americanist Tradition.

The failure to contest theoretical dominance of anthropology and linguistics in North America may be dated in part to the aftermath of the death of Sapir in 1939. Sapir's linguistic students failed to challenge Leonard Bloomfield's behaviourist dominance of linguistics; indeed, Bloomfield became a mentor to many of the Sapirian survivors. Likewise, Sapir's students of personality in a variety of North American Native cultures failed to engage in debate with contemporaries who turned overseas in search of genuine primitiveness, the exotic. For Sapir, 'genuine' culture was a question of integration, of satisfaction provided for the individual. Increasingly, after the memorandum on acculturation by Robert Redfield, Ralph Linton, and Melville Herskovits in the *American Anthropologist* in 1936, genuine culture in Sapir's sense could be found in the adaptation of traditional values and patterns of action to contemporary circumstances. The Americanist exotic was subordinated to the making of common sense in everyday lives.

In the process, the rest of anthropology apparently forgot that the Americanists existed. This conference asserts that it is time to see what has been preserved in and what has emerged from the backwater.

Far from being atheoretical – mere description of moribund memory cultures of former buffalo hunters on the Great Plains – the Americanist Tradition challenges the static structural-functionalist 'ethnographic present,' implicitly claiming to represent a pristine pre–European contact traditionalism. The distinctive features of the Americanist Tradition have moved into the broader framework of global anthropology, albeit often without explicit acknowledgment of their provenance. Perhaps it is time to document the appropriations.

Although each practitioner within the Americanist Tradition could doubtless propose other distinctive features, or explicate them differently, I propose the following as a baseline:

1. Language, thought, and reality are inseparable. The particular triad comes from John Carroll's title for the collected works of Benjamin Whorf, but the concern with the construction of cultural worlds from linguistic categories dates

from the introduction to the *Handbook of American Indian Languages* by Boas in 1911 (which in turn draws on the Germanic tradition of linguistic relativity emanating from Hermann Steinthal, Wilhelm von Humboldt, and Johann Herder). The work of Sapir, Morris Swadesh, more recently John Lucy, Stephen Levinson, and others on grammatical categories elaborates this tradition.

2. The Americanist Tradition defines culture as a system of symbols. It is contained in people's heads. Their behaviour certainly provides evidence of it; but behaviour without insider explication of its meaning remains opaque, exotic, to an outsider. It is merely 'man-from-Mars ethnography.'

3. Texts, with varying degrees of relationship to spontaneous discourses but in any case produced by native speakers in native languages, constitute the database for both Americanist ethnography and linguistics (Darnell 1992). I have argued elsewhere (Darnell 1990) that the link between Sapir's work in linguistics and in culture and personality resides in the necessity for a linguist to work closely with a small number of 'informants' and thereby to be drawn into the way they organize their knowledge into a coherent world-view. Study beginning from the point of view of the member of culture or speaker of language leads to life history, eye-witness accounts of historical events, and integration of personality as evidenced in characteristic narrative structures (both cultural and individual).

4. There is an Americanist commitment to preserving the knowledge encoded in oral traditions so that it shall not be lost from the permanent record of human achievement. The texts are 'precious and to be preserved, as all testimony of the working of the human spirit in the shaping of distinctive symbolic form' (Hymes 1983). Sapir is said by oral tradition in Americanist anthropology to have left Indo-European philology after he met Franz Boas because of the irrevocable urgency of the work. The contemporary concern over 'endangered languages' among linguists and anthropologists is rooted in this Americanist experience.

5. 'Traditional cultures' are not static, to be preserved in amber for some future archaeologist. The contemporary skills, as well as past products, of anthropological and linguistic work are increasingly valuable to aboriginal communities seeking their own balances of tradition and innovation. For contemporary Ojibwe peoples of southwestern Ontario, at least, 'traditional' is not abstract and idealized, frozen somewhere in the distant past; rather, it is a moving target, located in harmony with both past and future, the latter measured in terms of seven generations of children to come. Like 'us,' the mainstream inheritors of Euro-American 'civilization,' the Americanist Tradition asserts, the aboriginal peoples of our continent also have history. Whether that history

is recorded in oral form or written, traditionally or in contemporary praxis, really does not matter. Present-day cultures are historical products. To be unaware of historical process (or disciplinary history) is to be cut off from the sources of one's own tradition.

6. Native peoples are not objects to be studied. Many of them are anthropologists and linguists. Many are commentators on our disciplines. The commentaries are not always flattering. Many feel that early Americanists objectified their so-called informants. Certainly, the multivocality of the present tradition came into being gradually over several generations of professional anthropology in America. It would, however, be a mistake to assume that Americanists are less responsive to issues of appropriation and representation than other anthropologists or scholars from other disciplines. We are the first targets of such attack, I submit, precisely because we are the ones who engage in dialogue. While our erstwhile colleagues in other traditions or disciplines speak about 'the native,' we attempt to engage him/her in conversation. As Dennis Tedlock is wont to remind us, we have the option of putting the response in quotation marks and respecting its narrative integrity and personal agency. Neither anthropologists/linguists nor Native persons and communities are locked in an unbreakable solitude. Our communication creates a new community, partially shared.

7. The anthropologists and linguists of the Americanist Tradition take a long time to do their work. Many of us have been working with the same communities for twenty, thirty, or more years now. We have grown through large portions of our own life cycles alongside trusted consultants, whose understanding has also grown over the time we have spoken together. Our conversations have been part of the changing understanding of each. Moreover, these conversations are often held in shared space; we live and work in the same places and are known where we live, thus being held continuously and immediately accountable for what we say and who we are. It is a spiral, a circle whose closure is only possible when it has returned to its beginning. You can't just 'get the culture' and go on to the next one.

These distinctive features are so obvious that most of us would not think to state them explicitly. I believe they are closely linked, as a set, to the inextricable connection between cultural anthropology and linguistics in the Americanist Tradition. Such links are virtually absent in other national traditions. This brings us back to the question of how the contemporary but historically constituted Americanist Tradition grew out of Boasian anthropology, with its own roots in the work of the Bureau of American Ethnology under John Wesley Powell.

In 1969, I argued that Boasian anthropology, as it emerged by about 1920, constituted a scientific revolution in the terms proposed by Thomas Kuhn

(1962). Nonetheless, there was considerable continuity to the work of the B.A.E.; I emphasized institutional continuity. The B.A.E. was the institutional base from which Boas grounded his initial attempt to wrest control of North American anthropology away from the museum-based, archaeologically oriented Washington and Boston establishments (see also Hinsley 1981). In Ottawa from 1910 to 1925, Sapir, as a museum curator of linguistics, faced similar dichotomies. (The question of how one curates a linguistic fact is itself a fascinating example of the reification of cultural artefacts as though they, rather than the knowledge underlying them, were the point. Thus, Boas's Northwest Coast diaries report his glee in obtaining not only a mask, but the story to go with it.) In any case, both Boas and Powell faced considerable pressures to define culture in observable, preferably materially preservable, form.

Kuhn's model did not disallow transitional continuities in cases of paradigm shift. Murray (1983, 1995) suggests that the missing piece, analytically, is the virulent rhetoric of revolution employed by Boas in cementing his own position as the dominant figure in North American anthropology, both theoretically and organizationally. Oral tradition in anthropology has it that Boas conquered his hidebound evolutionary predecessors in a single fell swoop with his appointment to Columbia University in 1899.

Reality is somewhat more complex. It was not obvious at the time that the forces of Boasian good would defeat the incumbent evils of evolution. It was not even obvious that universities would be the wave of the future and museum/government work become increasingly marginal; indeed Boas depended heavily in the years between 1880 and 1920 on the interdependence of university instruction and museum funding of field research (Darnell 1969, 1998).

Boas eschewed historicism in favour of presentist rhetoric. His 1904 paper in *Science* on 'the history of anthropology' attacked his predecessors, especially Daniel Brinton, without even naming them. He implied that the critique of evolution was already complete and that the 'new' anthropology (that is, Boasian anthropology) was firmly in control in North America. In fact, the battle lines were only then being drawn. Moreover, many of Boas's associates, particularly Alfred Kroeber and Robert Lowie, urged their former teacher to take more conciliatory positions toward his competitors over the first two decades of the century.

In 1969, I emphasized that Boas's ability to overwhelm the discipline within less than a full scientific generation was due in part to the unilinear process of professionalization. B.A.E. anthropologists were progressively marginalized by their lack of access to universities where they could train their own successors. Indeed, the U.S. Congress piously expected them to put themselves out of business as the Indians were settled on reservations and banished from public visibility until such time as they should die out or become acculturated. If there were any new jobs, university-trained anthropologists were increasingly available to fill them.

Boas chose his institutional base wisely, as time has demonstrated. He built on his own German university training and unwavering commitment to professionalization through graduate education. The German model was in the air in all North American academic disciplines in the late nineteenth and early twentieth centuries. It was the ideal time for anthropology to come of age. The result was the establishment of several major urban centres under Boasian control combining academic instruction and museum support for research and fieldwork. New York, Boston, Chicago, Philadelphia, Berkeley, and Ottawa all developed such institutional alternatives. Although these collaborations of museum and academy were often uneasy, the wave of the future moved relentlessly.

So, institutionally, there was a scientific revolution and a paradigm shift. After a brief transitional period, social networks in anthropology also shifted toward the Boasians (as Kuhn would have predicted had he ever seriously addressed cases from the social sciences). Unquestionably, historical particularism succeeded evolution as the theory of choice in North American anthropology.

Nevertheless, there was substantially greater continuity in ethnographic practice than in theoretical stance. The priority placed by the B.A.E. on mapping the diversity of languages and cultures of the continent maintained its saliency under the early Boasians. In spite of Powell's commitment to the evolutionary theory of Lewis Henry Morgan, B.A.E. researchers stayed fairly close to the data for collaborative projects like the linguistic classification or the synonymy. Although Boas personally chafed under the restrictions of survey fieldwork on the Northwest Coast for the American Association for the Advancement of Science and B.A.E., he also insisted that there must be an ethnographic baseline before grand generalization could proceed. Although he defined the ultimate questions of anthropology as historical and psychological (1911), the historical had to come first. Powell and Boas were not so far apart in practice.

What did not emerge in my 1969 reading of this history was the continuity in a symbolic or mentalist reading of culture from Powell and his associates to Boas and his students. Although the B.A.E. did some archaeological and museum work, Powell himself tended to ignore it. He was interested in other things, most of which were also of interest to Boas.

First, Powell focused on non-material culture. He had little choice, being a specialist in the Ute and Shoshone cultures, which were stereotyped by many of his contemporaries as the so-called root-digging savages of the southwestern desert.

Second, Powell was interested in language. Language was his chosen index for classifying tribal relationships in Native North America; believing that grammar reflected evolutionary stage and was therefore common to all American Indian tribes, Powell pioneered in assembling the lexical data necessary for an Americanist philology.

Third, Powell encouraged the B.A.E. staff to amass text collections as evidence of the native point of view (at least to a degree). He hired Boas as Honorary Philologist of the B.A.E. and facilitated a series of grammars (with illustrative texts) that ultimately appeared in four volumes (beginning in 1911, long after his own death and Boas's separation from the institutional auspices of the B.A.E.).

Finally, Boas and Powell shared a four-square definition of the scope of anthropology. In the quadratic format, archaeology and physical anthropology could go their own ways, while linguistics and cultural anthropology, for both, remained inextricably linked. (Boas, of course, worked intensively in physical anthropology; most of his students in cultural anthropology and linguistics, however, did not.)

All of this sounds very Boasian. Indeed, it is. To be sure, Boas arrived from Germany with a familiarity with the *Volkerkunde*, *Lebenswelt*, *Weltanschauung* tradition of Herder, Steinthal, von Humboldt, and the Brothers Grimm. This led him to give more prominence to texts than did Powell and his contemporaries. But Boas's emphasis was not all that alien to the established Powell tradition (though it must have seemed so to the rest of the Washington establishment, centred in the United States National Museum under the leadership of Boas's sometime nemesis, evolutionist archaeologist Otis T. Mason). The Washington anthropology that fit well with Boas's version of the discipline rested solidly on the personality and political visibility of Powell, as illustrated by the rapid disintegration of the Powell-McGee enterprise after Powell's death in 1902.

Boas could graft a version of German folklore onto Powell's version of the Americanist Tradition with reasonable facility. This shared position contrasted sharply with the museum anthropology based on evolution and diffusion of items of material culture espoused equally by the disciples of Frederick Ratzel in Germany and those of Mason in Washington. With his usual cavalier disregard of acknowledgments, however, Boas ignored both the institutional and the theoretical continuities in the Americanist Tradition, thereby eclipsing them in professional memory.

The above analysis resolves two major worries of my earlier treatment. First, I paid little heed to the archaeological and museum side of the B.A.E. and Washington enterprises. I felt guilty because I thought it was due to my personal disinterest with these topics and did not fully acknowledge the corresponding bias of Powell and his closest associates. Second, some of my favourite exemplars of the Boasian tradition, as I then wanted to call it, were

B.A.E. folks. What was then an embarrassment now seems to me to lie at the heart of a more complex view of the emergence of the Americanist Tradition (see Darnell, 1998).

Although detailed exposition awaits another occasion, this interpretation sets us up to trace continuities from Americanist anthropology (in its classical period between the two world wars) to contemporary postmodernist, post-structuralist, interpretive, symbolic anthropology as we now know (or do not know) it (see Darnell, forthcoming).

REFERENCES

Darnell, Regna. 1969. 'The Development of American Anthropology 1879–1920: From the Bureau of American Ethnology to Franz Boas.' Unpublished Ph.D. thesis, University of Pennsylvania.

– 1990. 'Franz Boas, Edward Sapir and the Americanist Text Tradition.' *Historiographia Linguistica* 17: 129–44.

– 1992. 'The Boasian Text Tradition and the History of Canadian Anthropology.' *Culture* 17: 39–48.

– 1995a. 'Deux ou trois choses que je sais du postmodernisme.' *Gradhiva* 17: 3–15.

– 1995b. 'The Sources of Lévi-Strauss's Structuralism.' *Historiographia Linguistica* 22(1–2): 217–35.

– 1998. *And Along Came Boas: Continuity and Revolution in Americanist Anthropology*. Amsterdam and Philadelphia: John Benjamins.

– Forthcoming. *Invisible Genealogies: Americanist Persistences in Contemporary Anthropology*. Lincoln: University of Nebraska Press.

Hallowell, A. Irving. 1960. 'The Beginnings of Anthropology in America.' In F. de Laguna, ed., *Selected Papers from the American Anthropologist 1888–1920*: 1–90.

– 1965. 'The History of Anthropology as an Anthropological Problem.' *Journal of the History of the Behavioral Sciences* 1.

Harris, Marvin. 1968. *The Rise of Anthropological Theory*. New York: Crowell.

Hinsley, Curtis. 1981. *Savages and Scientists*. Washington: Smithsonian Institution.

Hymes, Dell. 1983. 'The Americanist Tradition.' In *Essays in the Historiography of Linguistics*. Amsterdam and Philadelphia: John Benjamins.

Hymes, Dell, and John Fought. 1975. 'American Structuralism.' *Current Trends in Linguistics* 13: 903–1156.

Kuhn, Thomas. 1962. *The Structure of Scientific Revolutions*. Chicago: University of Chicago Press.

Murray, Stephen O. 1983. *Group Formation in Social Science*. Edmonton-Champaign: Linguistic Research.

– 1995. *Theory Groups and the Study of Language in North America*. Philadelphia and Amsterdam: John Benjamins.

Stocking, George W., Jr. 1991. *Books Unwritten, Turning Points Unmarked: Notes for an Anti-History of Anthropology*. Bloomington: Indiana University Press.

Stocking, G.W., Jr, ed. 1989. *Romantic Motives*. Madison: University of Wisconsin Press.

White, Leslie. 1966. *The Social Organization of Ethnological Theory*. Houston: Rice University Press.

4 The Non-Eclipse of Americanist Anthropology during the 1930s and 1940s*

STEPHEN O. MURRAY

Before undertaking the research for this chapter, I accepted too easily the conventional view ('folklore' in the pejorative sense) that American anthropologists' turn away from studying Native North American peoples began with Margaret Mead in Samoa and Robert Redfield in Mexico during the late 1920s, became more general with the importation (partly by Mead and Redfield, and directly by the American sojourns of A.R. Radcliffe-Brown and Bronislaw Malinowski) of British functionalisms during the 1930s, and final with the mobilization into the U.S. war effort during the 1940s. When I looked more closely, I saw that the eclipse of Americanist work was lesser, later, and more endogenously American than many Americanists suppose.

Clearly, Mead and Redfield and the visiting functionalists articulated an already widespread impatience with listing and mapping traits salvaged from the memories of those no longer living in aboriginal societies.[1] They and many students of the 1930s sought to study the functional integration of intact, distinct 'primitive' cultures and scorned examination of how Native Americans lived on the reservations to which they had been confined. These anthropologists' own fieldwork was mostly far from intensive, and often did not even involve prolonged residence with the people studied.[2] About the Omaha, with whom she reluctantly – and, I might add, clandestinely[3] – worked in the summer of 1930, Mead (1972: 190–1) wrote that 'there was very little out of the

* I use 'Americanist' here as a site of research (mostly, in the restricted sense of Native North America; 'First Nations' in Canadianese) not as a theory, method, or approach (cf. Hymes 1983: 116). My primary focus in this paper is on cultural anthropology. My 1994 book, especially pp. 174–6, discusses the relative decline of Americanist research in American linguistics and linguistic anthropology. Comments by Ellen Basso, Regna Darnell, Raymond DeMallie, Raymond Fogelson, Paul Kutsche, William Leap, Lisa Valentine, and Murray Wax strengthened my confidence in some interpretations, and deterred me from making some others.

past that was recognizable and still less in the present that was aesthetically satisfying ... I had the unrewarding task of discussing a long history of mistakes in American policy toward the Indians and prophesying a still more disastrous fate for them in the future.'[4] As Hymes (1972: 231) noted, 'Some anthropologists stopped studying Indians in the 1930s, because they had become like any other minority group.' For instance, Elizabeth Colson, whose first fieldwork was in California, recalled, 'Many of us thought by the 1930s that what could be recorded here at home about the Native Americans' pre-conquest past had been recorded, and we wanted a chance to write about living people. Today we no longer share a regional focus and probably have not done so since about 1950' (1985: 121). In addition to stressing that last date – coincidentally the year of my birth and the high tide of British functionalist social anthropology of Africa – I would note that interbellum Americanists had practically no systematic knowledge of reservation life to apply. Kelly (1985: 129) discusses the critique that Scudder Mekeel and Julian Steward made in 1936 and Steward (1977 [1969]): 336) reiterated that 'in 1934 anthropologists were ill-equipped with basic understanding of culture change in the modern world,' because 'ethnologists were not interested in the factors, processes, and dynamics of change that had occurred during the many years following European contact' (also see Villa Rojas 1979: 50).

The acculturation studies of the 1930s continued to focus on (shared/normative) cultural traits, not on communities, let alone communities in the context of states. Indian reservations could have been, but were not, the site of community studies. I don't think that anyone thought to treat the Native Americans living in the 1930s as outside of history or as examples of endogenously maintained social equilibrium, as social anthropologists treated groupings in colonized Africa.

Radcliffe-Brown did not undertake fieldwork during his Chicago tenure (1931–7) and greatly antagonized many Americanists, including Edward Sapir, who had been partly responsible for bringing him to Chicago.[5] Although she put in some time on a reservation, Mead was very emphatic that she did not want to make a career as an Americanist, and, famously, insisted on going to Polynesia for her first fieldwork in defiance of Boas's wish for her to work with some American tribe (Mead 1972: 128–30). In that Derek Freeman (1983) has cast her as the Boasian archetype,[6] there is a special irony in her refusal to study Native Americans. The irony is increased by the markedly nationalistic American defence of Mead in that she was heavily influenced by British functionalists before almost any other American was, and that no one since Radcliffe-Brown has occasioned so uniform and nationalistic a rejection as an uppity alien disrespectful of what American anthropologists do as has Derek Freeman,[7] even though what Mead did was much closer to the detested Radcliffe-Brown than to the work of her Boasian elder brothers. She was even 'under the direction of Radcliffe-Brown' in her first Admiralty Islands fieldwork (Mead 1959: 553n34). In contrast, her Boasian 'elder brothers' were uncomfortable with her methods and epistemology. Robert Lowie (1929, 1940) was particularly troubled (specifically, by Mead 1928, 1939); also see the dismay in Kroeber (1931). However, neither in published reviews nor in unpublished correspondence do I see any of the locus of their discomfort (bordering on anxiety even) being her abandonment of Native America as a research site.

Mead and Redfield were certainly harbingers of functionalism, of disregarding material culture, and of globalizing the scope of American anthropology,[8] but when I was looking more closely at who was doing what, when, the marginalization of Americanist work within American anthropology appears both more gradual and less complete than many Americanists suppose. Anthropology Ph.D.'s from the 1930s, especially from Berkeley and Yale, and to a lesser extent from Harvard, mostly worked on Americanist dissertation topics (Ebihara 1985: table 1).

It is indisputable that professionalizing Canadian and United States anthropology began with attempts to identify general/normative traits of what the oldest then-living members of pacified North American aboriginal tribes remembered (Darnell 1969, 1971; Cole 1973; cf. Preston 1983). However, it is useful to recall that especially Roland Dixon, Edward Gifford, Alfred Kroeber, Berthold Laufer, and Robert Lowie had broader interests than aboriginal North America and considerable erudition. Boas-trained anthropologists such as Fay Cooper Cole, Laura Watson Benedict, and William Jones studied indigenous groups in the colony of the Philippines that the United States seized in 1898. Zora Neale Hurston and her enemy Melville Herskovits, both of whom were Boas students, did fieldwork in U.S.-occupied Haiti. Herskovits and Ruth Landes worked among Afro-Brazilians during the 1930s, while Lowie and Benedict fostered fieldwork in the South American jungles. Lowie also conveyed and amplified Baron Nordenskiold's pressure on the National Research Council's Division of Anthropology and Psychology to survey South American Indians in 1932, which led to the B.A.E. *Handbook of South American Indians* edited by Julian Steward (1946–50) during the 1940s (Frantz 1985: 89–90).[9]

It is apposite to remember that, depending on whether one counts Anglo America, Benedict's (1934) ever-popular restatement of cultural description as personality was either two-thirds or three-fourths Americanist and that before the Second World War her fieldwork was Americanist. So was most American anthropologists' work on acculturation and much of the work on culture and personality.[10] Practically all of Devereux's ethnographic publications are on

Native Americans, as is most of La Barre's ethnographic and historical work. Even much of the culture and personality work done in the decade and a half after the Second World War – notably that of Irving Hallowell, Anthony F.C. Wallace, John Honigmann, Victor Barnouw, and George and Louise Spindler – was Americanist. Ralph Linton, probably the most influential non-Boasian, non-Chicago anthropologist of the 1930s and 1940s and the author of the most widely used textbook of the late thirties, obviously got around. Before going to Madagascar, he was Field Museum curator of North American ethnology and worked up Pawnee material from notes of George Dorsey's work with James Murie (Linton and Wagley 1971: 25; Parks, this volume). During his Wisconsin tenure Linton worked on Comanche, and once he got to Columbia, he pulled together Columbia Americanist students' fieldwork in *Acculturation in Seven American Indian Tribes* (1940). His own chapters in that book, along with what he wrote in *The Study of Man* (1936) seem to me relatively continuous with Boasian[11] study of the movement of culture 'items' and 'traits' and their adaptation into 'complexes.' Although not exclusively an Americanist, Linton clearly did Americanist work.[12]

With the exception of John Embree, Radcliffe-Brown's Chicago students also worked on Native American topics.[13] Indeed, it seems fairly obvious that Radcliffe-Brown came to America believing that he would sort out Native America as he had aboriginal Australia (Stocking 1979: 21; DeMallie 1994: 6–7), and that some Chicago students thought that they accomplished this under his tutelage. Radcliffe-Brown's Chicago students became and remained Americanists. Indeed, there is a sense in which Radcliffe-Brown's Chicago tenure and the reaction of Boasians stimulated a renewal of theoretical interest in Native America. At the very least, his stay produced some Americanists who might otherwise have worked elsewhere.[14]

Although they produced a florescence of kinship 'system' studies, neither Radcliffe-Brown nor his Chicago students produced holistic ethnographies of Native American 'social systems.' And they did not 'progress' towards modelling how local groups are affected by nation-states and world economies. As late as 1950, even ethnography done as part of early 'area studies' continued to fail to relate parts to any whole, moving Julian Steward (1950: 22) to note: 'Most studies have treated the community ... as if it were a self-contained structural and functional whole which could be understood in terms of itself alone ... Individual communities are often studied as if the larger whole were simply a mosaic of such parts' or 'as if the larger society did not exist.'[15]

Redfield's introduction and Sol Tax's opening chapter in *Social Anthropology of North American Tribes* (Eggan 1937) pressed Radcliffe-Brown's claims to be developing a science of society with rigorous 'scientific laws' against

Boasian theoretical nihilism and Kroeberian historical inference. While struggling diplomatically to give Boas his due – for doing what was needed at an *earlier* time[16] – Redfield proclaimed that 'no one in America has offered a strictly nonhistorical scientific method, equipped with a self-consistent body of concepts and procedures for getting specific jobs done in relation to ultimate scientific objectives. Radcliffe-Brown has done just that ... [He] has offered an explicit and systematic method for the scientific study of societies' (1955 [1937]: xii). Redfield also attempted to anticipate the objections to the sterility and unimportance of the results that Julian Steward was going to make (in his 1938 review of the book in the *American Anthropologist*).[17] More than half a century later, I do not think many anthropologists are impressed with the vapid so-called 'social laws' promulgated by Radcliffe-Brown (e.g., 1952b: 44–5),[18] or are expecting any to emerge from his approach. Many of us would agree with Steward's 1938 criticism that Radcliffe-Brownian dogma 'precluded serious attention to available history and that concern with standard behavior largely prevented inclusion of material on individual differences,' not just in that volume, but in the oeuvre of Robert Redfield, among others.[19] Still, for all the arrogant dismissal of American Americanist work that Radcliffe-Brown and his Chicago students made, despite the bad manners of their 'revolutionary rhetoric,'[20] and, despite his own lack of acquaintance with 'every day facts of life in particular [Native American] societies,'[21] Radcliffe-Brown did not divert Chicago students from working on Americanist topics. He did not even entirely stifle historical research by them.[22] *Social Anthropology*'s editor, Fred Eggan, who had been a student of Cole, Sapir, and Leslie Spier, before Radcliffe-Brown arrived, was more cautious in making claims than was Radcliffe-Brown, and continued to focus on circumscribed, historical comparisons and to avoid the rhetoric of a functionalist revolution against Boasian historicism. Although he did fieldwork in the U.S. colony of the Philippines before Japan conquered it, his major theoretical and ethnographic work remained Americanist (DeMallie 1994: 12).

It bears stressing that the early-twentieth-century shift of anthropology's primary institutional basis from museum to university (Eggan 1955: 488; Darnell 1969) did *not* lead to a de-emphasis on (Native North) America. Not that the shift in institutional base and fieldwork practice was without theoretical consequences. George Foster (1982) contrasted a period in which fieldwork involved a summer visit to a reservation or 'white-room ethnography,' with key informants interrogated off a reservation, to a community study period.[23] The *length* of study rather than the choice of a particular people to study yielded more data, which made it possible for some anthropologists to write synchronic, noncomparativist monographs. The earlier focus on 'ethnological specimens' – that is, culture-wide 'traits' – undoubtedly related to the museum base of research. Because they had to be generalists, Boasians at least implicitly considered cultures holistically (Foster 1982: 146–7) – more so, I would argue, than British social anthropologists did, despite the rhetoric about integrated 'systems' the latter mouthed. Excluding language and psychology and 'material culture,' Radcliffe-Brown and his students chose to ignore what Boasians saw as evidencing cultural configurations. In particular, functionalists' de-emphasis on 'material culture' collection is inseparable from the lack of interest in technology and physical environment that is a hallmark of social anthropology of the Radcliffe-Brown school, in maximal contrast to Americanists such as Julian Steward, Leslie White, and (to a lesser extent) Ralph Linton. Boas and most of his students wanted to know how people did things, including weaving (Gladys Reichard), making pots (Ruth Bunzel), hunting (Frank Speck), and even making blueberry pies (Boas).[24] Creative British work on the social implications of technology came not from social anthropologists but from the chemist turned historian Joseph Needham and archaeologist Gordon Childe, influenced, like Steward, by Marxist (albeit un-dialectical) materialism.

New Deal agencies funded ethnographic and historic research on American communities and made some attempts to apply scientific knowledge to rural America, including Indian reservations. If the Rockefeller Foundation had continued to expand support for anthropological work, as many expected, rather than curtailing it in 1933, globalization might have begun in earnest during the 1930s, but this did not happen.[25] Moreover, before the United States began to win the war and think about administering territories from which the Japanese would be driven – and Japan itself – the U.S. government employed anthropologists in administering the concentration camps of West Coast Japanese-Americans (Suzuki 1981; Starn 1986; see Gregg and Williams 1948: 607).

In common with other anthropologists, Americanists have at least indirectly maintained colonial and neo-colonial domination.[26] Some anthropologists have been eager to serve power – few more explicitly than Malinowski and Radcliffe-Brown – but customers have been few and strikingly successful 'application' of 'knowledge' non-existent. Admittedly, some anthropologists have sometimes challenged particular policies, but few have exerted real influence in long-term policy.[27] To the best of my knowledge none has produced an ethnography of, say, the Department of the Interior, although anthropologists have given (mostly informal) advice to Indian organizations on how to manage such bureaucracies, and written decades later of mistaken attempts to employ anthropologists and to apply anthropology (e.g., Steward 1977: 33–6; Nash 1979; Hall 1994).

Although foreshadowed by earlier research in the Philippines, service by

American anthropologists to colonial domination seems to me to have begun in earnest only with the Roosevelt administration, which reorganized the Indian reservations[28] and later established the Japanese-American concentration camps. John Collier, Roosevelt's Commissioner of Indian Affairs, sold anthropologists to Milton Eisenhower, warden of the Japanese-American concentration camps, as a means 'to perfect the science of human management' that would be useful in 'our post-war job in the Far East' (quoted in Kelly 1985: 135). At the very least, anthropologists were complicit with attempts at ethnocide.[29] How many copies of Alexander Leighton's (1945) *The Governing of Men* reached the Allied Armies of Occupation and whether this new knowledge on 'human management' or the 'culture at a distance' discourse, including Ruth Benedict's (1946) *The Chrysanthemum and the Sword*, was applied are historical topics that have yet to be researched.[30]

Americanist work remained predominant not just through the 1930s, but into the 1950s, despite the mobilization and dispersion to many places of American anthropologists during the Second World War. In a major and quasi-official historical retrospect, Robert Murphy (1976: 6) wrote that, until the Second World War, '[t]he bulk of our research had previously been in the study of the American Indian, which served more than any other influence to produce the rather flat, descriptive tone of our writings. It was the reservation situation, the culling of memory culture unvitalized by extant patterns of activity, that led to American nominalism, and not the anti-evolutionism of Boas[31] ... Financed by an influx of new funds that were clearly responsive to the country's expanded overseas interests, [American anthropologists] broke out of their traditional insularity and embarked on research on global scale' (also see Geertz 1995: 103).[32]

Looking at the immediately postwar volumes of the official journal of the American Anthropological Association does not substantiate this, as figure 4.1 shows. More than half the articles dealing with specific locales published in the *American Anthropologist* between 1946 and 1951 were Americanist, and almost all of these were North Americanist. Immediately before the tenure of its current Americanist editors, a plurality of articles with specific locales still were North American, as figure 4.2 shows. Similarly, as contrast of figures 4.3 and 4.4 shows, in recent years the *American Ethnologist* has published substantially more Americanist work than has *Man*.[33] In Canada around 1980, Burridge (1983: 309) classified the regional expertise of 57.8 per cent of 270 Canadian ethnologists as New World, along with 79 per cent of the dissertation field sites for 142 ethnology Ph.D. degrees from Canadian universities.

In 1925, when the Linguistic Society of America was founded, there were more than nine philologists and more than ten teachers of written languages for every two anthropological linguists (Murray 1994: 162; nearly all of the latter were Americanists). In the first fifteen volumes (1925–39) of its official journal, *Language*, 9.5 per cent of the articles about a language group dealt with Native American ones. In the next decade, this dropped to 6.6 per cent (while the percentage of articles on languages that were not Indo-European, not Semitic, and not Native American rose from 5.0 to 13.5).[34]

If not within American linguistics, at least within linguistic anthropology, Native American languages remained central. The major focus in linguistic anthropology during the 1950s, the so-called Whorf hypothesis, was rooted in assertions about Hopi language and culture, while Dorothy Lee's writings on values and world-view were rooted in research on Wintu and Lakota; the Navajo and their neighbours were the central site for Harvard Social Relations' contrast of diverse value patterns within a particular habitat (Vogt and Albert 1966), as well as for trying to test what was interpreted as Whorf's claim.[35] The neo-Bloomfieldians who attempted to extend linguistic methods to cultural classifications and social interaction during the 1950s and 1960s, notably C.F. Hockett, Kenneth Pike, and George Trager (with Edward Hall) were all Americanists first and foremost. Although some of the important exemplars (by Harold Conklin and Charles Frake) of ethnoscience derived from the Philippines, those of Floyd Lounsbury, Brent Berlin, Duane Metzger, and Gerald Williams were based on Native American data, and other major exemplars were Americanist in the broader sense, that is, Anglo-American (see Murray 1994: 403, 410). Certainly the analysis of ethnopoetics in recent years has been mostly Americanist (e.g., Hymes 1981; Tedlock 1993), along with outstanding analyses of creolization (Scollon and Scollon 1979), linguistic play, and intercultural stereotyping (Basso 1979).

As for reflexive accounts of fieldwork, I would recall Diamond Jenness, whose participant observation was as early as Malinowski's, while being more intensive, more extensive, and more sympathetic. Gladys Reichard's (1934) *Spider Woman* provides another early example of reporting on participation. And in the more recent self-conscious literature, Jean Briggs's (1970) *Never in Anger* continues the genre of writing about living with Inuit inaugurated by Jenness. It also continues to strike me as being the best exemplar of reflexive writing that conveys something about another culture, not just about the anthropologist's sensibilities.[36]

Lévi-Strauss's structuralist mill ground up North and South American native materials. George Peter Murdock's fieldwork was Northwest Coast and Leslie White's Pueblo, although I am among those who do not see how the theorizing of either relates to his ethnographic work. Julian Steward's development of ecological analysis more clearly derived from his Americanist work,[37] as did the

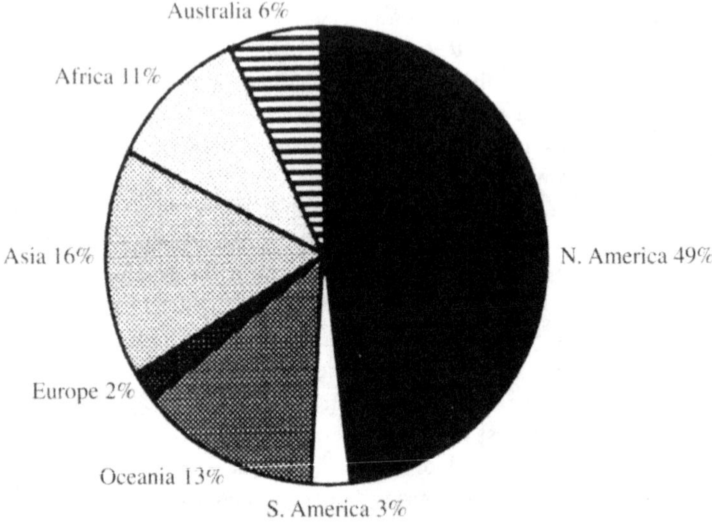

FIGURE 4.1 Areal distribution of articles in *American Anthropologist*, 1946–1951

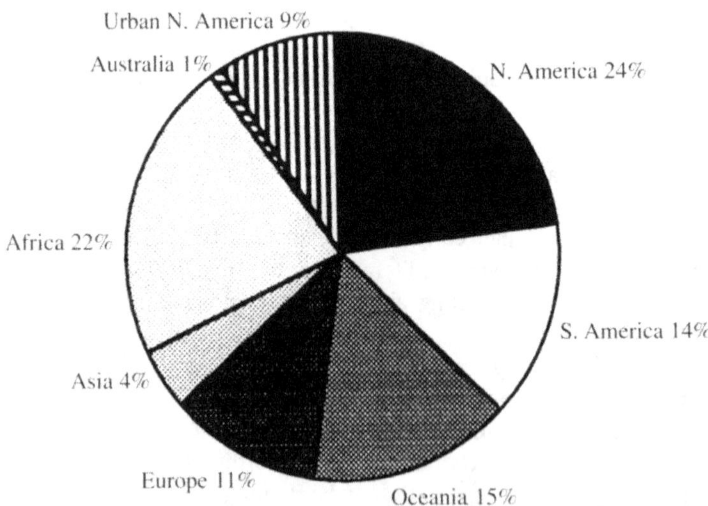

FIGURE 4.2 Areal distribution of articles in *American Anthropologist*, 1989–1993

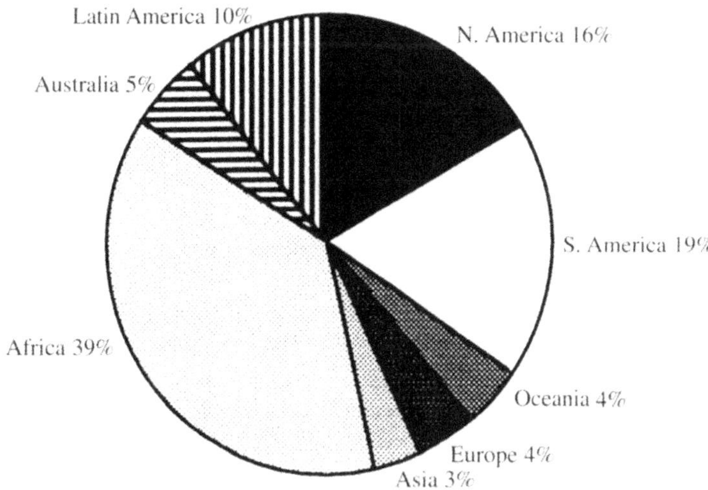

FIGURE 4.3 Areal distribution of articles in *American Anthropologist*, 1949–1958

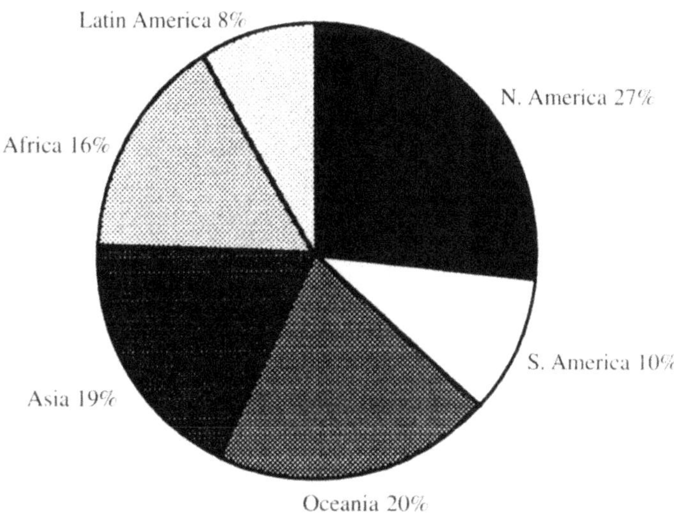

FIGURE 4.4 Areal distribution of articles in *American Anthropologist*, 1959–1968

influential theorizing about nativist revitalization movements by Linton, Wallace, and others; Wallace's explorations of intracultural variability; and Wallace's and Steward's exemplary use of documented history. Lowie remained a force through much of the 1950s and Kroeber through the entire decade.

Certainly Mesoamericanists (e.g., Ralph Beals, George Foster, John Gillin, Edward Spicer, Eric Wolf) and some South Americanists (Jules Henry, Charles Wagley) were prominent by the 1950s, while Lloyd Warner and his students (including sociologist Erving Goffman) mostly studied American groups other than First Nations / Native Americans.

I have already noted that Radcliffe-Brown's Chicago students did not turn away from Native America. Insofar as the dominance of functionalism was accompanied by such a turn, it was postwar Harvard Social Relations students such as Clifford Geertz, David Schneider, and Robert Bellah, and Yale students such as Ward Goodenough, Harold Conklin, and Charles Frake, who looked west of the American West Coast, not the Chicago students of Radcliffe-Brown. Looking at 1946 to 1960 in the *American Anthropologist* greatest-hits collection (Murphy 1976), one notes that the authors not trained as Americanists were mostly not from North America (Fredrik Barth, Meyer Fortes, Siegfried Nadel, along with Goodenough and Geertz, and linguist Zellig Harris, who was trained as a Semiticist philologist, but at the time was working on Cherokee. Those I classify as 'Americanists' from this collection are John Adair, John Atkins, Fred Eggan, Goffman, Steward, C.F. Voegelin, Evon Vogt, Leslie White, and Eric Wolf).

Although there are more Americanists in academia now than there were in the decade after the Second World War, the number of specialists on other areas increased more rapidly during the 1950s and 1960s. Still, I think that it would be difficult to construct a plausible claim that Africanists or Oceanists or Europeanists or Asianists have succeeded Americanists in dominating American anthropology at any time.[38] There are 'theorists' who have worked outside the Americas, but it seems to me that they are not concentrated in the study of any one other place. I certainly have heard anthropologists whose work is outside the Americas complaining of being marginal, marginal to 'theory'[39] in particular. I do not mean to underestimate the extent to which area studies were underwritten by Cold War interests, or the extent to which the illusion of cultures outside history continued, or the extent to which functionalists' derision of detailed Americanist data collection as theoryless has outlasted the dominance of functionalist theory and the recognition that cultures are neither as discrete, unchanging, or integrated as functionalists supposed.[40]

In addition, I would suggest at least one more general component in the postwar diversification of American anthropology: the GI Bill–spurred expansion of university enrolment in general, and the rapid growth of the number of anthropologists in particular, on the magnitude of 71 per cent between 1947 and 1951 (Goldschmidt 1985: 179). Demographic pressure pushed U.S. anthropologists' fieldwork beyond Native American reservations.[41] Areal studies were well funded, but, simultaneous with the pull of money was the push of diversifying to avoid competition. As Durkheim (1893) recognized in *The Division of Labor*, an expanding labour force usually leads to specialization.[42] In the case of anthropology, this has meant that an anthropologist has his or her own village or own cultural domain within a culture with several fieldworkers, instead of having a monopoly over a culture or (still earlier) over a culture area. Replication, though nominally regarded as desirable, has not been common.[43] Flight from American research sites seems to me, historically, in part, to have been a means to avoid competition, while competition-avoiding growth has sometimes led to amassing data that are not only non-comparable but frequently are invalid.

I think, as Regna Darnell's chapter in this volume also contends, that Americanists in recent years have been more cautious than other kinds of anthropologists about rejecting native interpretations and trampling native sensibilities.[44] In that more and more tribal governments restricted who could study and publish what, and set priorities for those employed or allowed to do fieldwork, Americanists in recent decades have had to take native concerns seriously or not have access to new data. While I think that increased sensitivity to native concerns is a positive value, I think that it was forced on anthropologists more than spontaneously developed by them. Whatever its sources, I would suggest that important examples of native analysis, of genuine dialogue between natives and alien analysts, of encouragement of native texts (particularly individual narratives),[45] along with careful, comparative use of historical materials,[46] have the potential to overcome such stigmatization of Americanist anthropology as lingers on after totalizing functionalist and structuralist paradigms have themselves been discredited, and as stories people tell about their experience have become not merely respectable but the preferred object of anthropological attention.[47]

NOTES

1 Franz Boas (1940 [1936]: 311) retrospectively claimed that 'when I thought these historical methods were firmly established, I began to stress, about 1910, the problems of cultural dynamics, of integration of culture and of the interaction between individual and society.' This contention is ill supported by his polemics into the 1920s with alien diffusionists (see 1940 [1920]: 286–8) and by the trait-distributional dissertation topics of Spier, Herskovits, Benedict, and Mead. (Herskovits [1953: 23] asserted that 'dissertation topics were brought to Boas for

approval, not suggested by him.' Cf. Mead [1959: 309; 1972: 126–9]. Mead [1972: 128] and Hoebel [1982: 9] suggested that there was greater freedom for students to pursue their own interests later in Boas's tenure than earlier.) A positive theory (age and area) may have hastened Boas's departure from the topic of diffusion, but surely not before 1920! See Darnell (1977) on the Boasian segue from trait distribution to psychological configurations after Lowie (1920) gave the coup de grâce to unilinear cultural evolution theorizing, and other Boasians crystallized the paradigm of the first generation of Boas students. On the insularity of Columbia anthropology, see Hoebel (1982: 8), Goldfrank (1978).

2 Brown's 'fieldwork' of Andamanese and Australians was primarily 'white room ethnography' rather than observation of functioning aboriginal cultures (Langham 1981). Much of Mead's Samoan research consisted of questioning Samoans on the verandah of a colonial government house where she lived. Redfield lived in Tepoztlán 76 days (minus two stays in Mexico City) and commuted in for interviews during some of the three remaining months before his earlier-than-scheduled return to Chicago (Godoy 1978). The length of Malinowski's Trobriand stay was partly a result of his being stranded as an enemy alien during the First World War.

3 Mead (1966: xxi) claimed that 'unawareness was essential to the successful prosecution of a study involving intimate details of contemporary life.' 'Prosecution' is a particularly apt choice of words. As Thorne (1980: 287) noted, many fieldworkers prefer misrepresenting what they are doing to trying to see how much informed consent to be studied and written about is possible. Also see M. Wax (1991: 451).

4 Also see Mead (1959: 313–17, 1966: xv). She recalled that, after her Omaha fieldwork, she and Reo Fortune 'explained that we would like to work among the Navaho, as an American Indian group whose culture was still alive and intact,' but 'Boas told us that the Navaho "belonged" to Gladys Reichard' (Mead 1972: 193).

5 'I was responsible for having brought him to Chicago,' Sapir wrote Louis Wirth in a 25 November 1931 letter (in the Regenstein Library at the University of Chicago). Sapir had been acting chair of the anthropology department the previous year, while Cole was in Washington, DC, and I do not think he would have made this assertion if his role had been only titular (reiterating what I put on record in Murray 1983: 339n35). It was primarily Radcliffe-Brown's ill-disguised contempt for previous Americanist work (in particular, publishing native texts – see the Sapir-Cole letters of 2 May and 2 June 1932 quoted in Darnell 1990: 250–1; reproduced in Stocking 1979: 20) that antagonized Boasians. The Benedict to Mead letter of 28 Dec. 1932 included in Mead (1959: 326–7) is typical of the irritation at the combination of arrogance, pretentiousness, ignorance, and cultism that non-Chicago anthropologists saw. Before Radcliffe-Brown's arrival on the American scene, Lowie (1923) sympathized with Radcliffe-Brown's 'attempt to explain the parts of Andamanese culture not as isolated fragments but as parts of an organic unity,' even while demurring from making the discovery of general laws the sole purpose of anthropology. There was plenty of American scepticism towards followers of W.H.R. Rivers, both the 'Children of the Sun' diffusionist branch and the functionalists. Kroeber had crossed swords with Rivers in 1909, and many American anthropologists in the interwar years remained sceptical of British anthropologists' psychological, historical, and sociological views. Lowie (1915) expressed criticism even of earlier, more restrained Rivers methods of inference, and he unequivocally objected to the wilder later inferences (Lowie 1937: 156–66). Brown could have made common cause with them, since it was the conjectures (and 'method') of William Perry, Grafton Elliott-Smith, and Rivers himself (after the time he trained Brown), not the more cautious reconstructions of Boasians, that Brown originally rejected (publicly, only after Rivers's 1922 death), and there was at least an implicit sense that there was a whole under the details of Boas's particularistic data. In response to Murdock's (1951) blistering attack on the narrowness

of British social anthropology (as the kind of antiquated sociology from which Murdock with great effort had freed himself), Radcliffe-Brown (1952a: 276) provided a mythical history, tracing the ethnology / social anthropology division of labour to the contrast of A.C. Haddon and James G. Frazer, with no mention of Rivers, the dead Laius of the story, or of the evolutionist focus of Frazer, Herbert Spencer, and E.B. Tylor that underlay Brown's interrogations of Andamanese prisoners.

6 Freeman's assumption that Margaret Mead was the most orthodox Boasian (having to bear, all but alone, the burden of demonstrating cultural determinism!) perhaps stems partly from his choosing to accept what she wrote uncritically in the case of her claims of legitimate descent from 'Papa Franz,' while treating what she wrote about Samoa very sceptically. Boas undeniably wrote a foreword to *Coming of Age in Samoa*, an act not unreasonably interpreted as a ritual laying on of hands. Still, her methods, topics, and theories bear little resemblance to those of Boas or of prominent Boasians such as Dixon, Kroeber, Lowie, Paul Radin, Sapir, Leslie Spier, and John Swanton, and it is obvious that she did what she wanted to do (going to Samoa, the research she actually did there and elsewhere), not what others commanded her to do (or even what she was funded to do). See Freeman (1991), Murray (1990, 1991a).

7 The irritation of the first generation of Boasians with Radcliffe-Brown mostly did not make it to print, or was expressed with exceptional restraint (Lowie 1937: 222–6). Slashing public attacks were made by some American anthropologists not notable for Boasian orthodoxy. Although the criticisms of British social anthropology in Steward (1938), Gregg and Elgin (1948), and Murdock (1951) are general, it is not at all difficult to distinguish whom the authors blame for what appalled them.

8 Mead (but not Redfield) moved a bit away from eliciting norms to observing behaviour and even in *Coming of Age in Samoa* (Mead 1928) discussed intracultural variability more than functionalist reportage did even decades later. She and Gregory Bateson gathered many artefacts on Bali (though they were 'art' rather than 'technology').

9 I fail to see American anthropological 'isolationism' in the interbellum years as a 'revolution against the destructive and immoral First World War' or as 'an unavoidable consequence of the Great Depression,' as Goldschmidt (1985: 165) does. I recall Murray Emeneau telling me that it was cheaper for his sponsors to support him in India than in America during the late 1930s. Boas and Sapir elicited information from Africans resident in the U.S., and Leonard Bloomfield's descriptions of Tagalog and Ilocano were based on work in the U.S. with native speakers. Both linguistic and psychological anthropological work done during the Second World War relied on natives of other societies resident in the U.S.

10 Besides Mead, another exception was Cora Du Bois, who had earlier done Wintu fieldwork, collaborated with Dorothy Lee, and wrote a standard work on the 1870 ghost dance before Abraham Kardiner financed her psychological anthropology of Alor. John and Beatrice Whiting did Paiute fieldwork before going to New Guinea or Africa. The flow was not entirely out from North America to Pacific islands; e.g., Felix Keesing's (1939) monograph on Menomini-white contact, and Laura Thompson's work on the Indian Personality, Education, and Administration Research Project during the 1940s (see Thompson and Joseph 1944; Joseph, Spicer, and Chesky 1949; Thompson 1951).

11 Roland Dixon's, in particular (as Linton and Wagley 1971: 14).

12 I consider Melville Herskovits's African research as seeking antecedents for African-American culture, i.e., the New World Negro, as in a serious sense 'Americanist,' as is that of the third member of the SSRC acculturation subcommittee, Robert Redfield in the Yucatán and Guatemala (and, arguably, also in Morelos). Redfield notably continued the substitution of space for time in analysing processes ('acculturation' in the Yucatán). Linton sponsored Charles Wag-

ley's fieldwork in Brazil and Carl Withers's in 'Plainsville' (Linton and Wagley 1971: 52–3), also 'Americanist' in the wider-than-First-Nations sense.

13 Lloyd Warner, Radcliffe-Brown's first American protégé, had studied at Berkeley with Kroeber and Lowie before going to Australia, and then studied European-Americans. (Warner supervised some New Deal studies of Native American personality and education – see Thompson 1951). Redfield was already fledged (Ph.D. 1928), without having worked on a Native American dissertation topic, and was already extolling Radcliffe-Brown's 'social anthropology' in invidious contrast to Americanist 'ethnology' (Redfield 1930: 11, 218) before Radcliffe-Brown was 'called' to Chicago in the fall of 1931. In a quite laudatory review of Redfield's (1930) *Tepoztlan* Kroeber (1931: 237) noted Redfield's 'leaning toward sociology,' that Redfield had not seriously used archive documentation, and that he touched history and geography 'as lightly as possible' in trying to analyse 'processual generalizations' and 'natural laws of social change' in social anthropology à la Radcliffe-Brown. On Linton's non-conversion see Linton and Wagley (1971: 38–40).

14 Raymond DeMallie (2 July 1995 letter) suggested the points in the preceding two sentences. Paul Kutsche (6 July 1995 letter) suggested that 'the heyday of [anthropologists'] interest in Native Americans was pretty much isomorphic with the height of interest in comparative kinship studies' and declined with them in a combination of paradigm exhaustion and exogenous political processes, not least of which was availability of funding for anthropological research outside the U.S.

15 Steward (1956) set out to remedy this in the project on Puerto Rico he directed.

16 See M. Wax (1956), heavily influenced by Redfield's impatience with Boasian particularism.

17 Kroeber (1936: 341) had already published his view that what Radcliffe-Brown's method had produced was (to date) sterile, after noting that 'determinants are multiple and variable' (p. 340), and that the fit between kinship terms and social usage is partial, not exact (p. 339; retreating from his 1909 total rejection of any fit).

18 Lowie (1937: 225) invidiously noted that 'Newton did not tell us that bodies either rise or fall,' but managed to be more specific in promulgating laws of gravitation.

19 The first criticism clearly does not apply to Fred Eggan, who sought whatever historical documentation existed. A chapter about 'change' was tacked on to many functionalist books on the supposed equilibrium of what was treated as a closed system (or, occasionally, as one disrupted by European agency).

20 See Murray (1994) on the social bases of rhetorics of continuity or revolution in human sciences.

21 Steward (1938: 720) quoted this desideratum from Tax (1937: 14), noting Tax's lack of intimate knowledge of California peoples (in implicit contrast to Steward's and Kroeber's considerable knowledge, and of Radcliffe-Brown's lack of Americanist fieldwork). Truman Michelson (1938) attacked Tax's understanding of Fox terms and practices.

22 One of the chapters in *Social Anthropology of North American Tribes* even dealt with a social process (nativist religious revivalism) in an intercultural community, using archival records, rather than with the kinship system of an aboriginal 'tribe.' Nash (1937: 378–9) noted Lloyd Warner's concern about using the psychological notion of 'deprivation' for society (a seemingly more Malinowskian than Radcliffe-Brownian tack). Concerned with the rejection of historical data by Radcliffe-Brown et al., Steward (1938: 722) extolled Nash's 'well-documented' chapter as illustrating 'the value of history in giving the fullest meaning to the function of an institution.' Within the Radcliffe-Brown school in England, Daryll Forde's insistence on historical and ecological considerations perhaps owed something to his Berkeley sojourn in the late 1920s (as well as to his initial archaeological training).

23 Foster identified an earlier period in which theorizing was done by armchair ethnologists reading secondary sources and/or querying missionaries and colonial officials. After the community study period, he saw a 'longitudinal, repeat-visit' period, pioneered by Clyde Kluckhohn among the Navajo. The periodization fits Foster's ontogeny from graduate student to supervisor of ongoing observation of Tzintzutzan Michoacán very well, but also seems more plausible to me for the phylogeny of American anthropology than other periodizations not based on fieldwork practices.

24 Hall (1992: 74–5) on 'frozen motor habits' (specifically in making pots), and the Whitings' (1978: 42) recollection that the most important lesson they learned from Leslie Spier was that, if you describe something, you must know how it works (specifically a Paiute rabbit trap).

25 The oft-repeated folklore of anthropologists is that American anthropologists outside the University of Chicago preferred no funding to funding directed by Radcliffe-Brown. Not having examined the internal Rockefeller Foundation documents, I suspect that the worldwide economic depression was a more important factor, and that lack of agreement among anthropologists was at most a minor factor in the Foundation's decision to refocus on health-related issues.

26 Leaving aside the propriety of trampling the sensitivities of subordinated peoples to gather materials (of all sorts, including religious secrets and plundering burial sites) for Science, I find it hard to imagine the payoff for governments of elicitation by Harrington et al. of memories and lexicons from the last survivors of a California people, etc. I do not think that utility for dominating regimes was either the goal or the result of Boasian work. Kroeber was especially sceptical of government employment of anthropology/anthropologists, and Boasians did not advertise useful application of their knowledge as Malinowski and Radcliffe-Brown tried to do (Asad 1973; Kuper 1983: 100–20).

27 One Chicago-trained anthropologist, Philleo Nash, was Indian Commissioner from 1961–6 (see Nash 1979). Gordon Macgregor was for a short time Agency Superintendent of the Oglala Pine Ridge Reservation, before moving on to the Indian Health Service.

28 Imposing a romantic sense of primitive communism along with liberal assumption about leadership and the engineering of people and of land (see Hall 1994). As Murray Wax stressed to me, legal recognition of Indian land was important and there were severe (Congressional/popular) limits on what the executive branch could do about empowering native people. Collier and anthropologists who became bureaucrats thought they were defending the interests of native people while trying to guide them.

29 See Suzuki (1981), Starn (1986), and R. Wax (1971: 69–174). Stocking (1979: 31) noted that Captain Fred Eggan proposed that the University of Chicago's training of those who were to administer captured territories include stints at the concentration camps. In contrast to eager attempts to involve anthropologists, the major sociological project dealing with the camps refused to supply any information to the government and trained 'native' analysts (Murray 1988).

30 The Society for Applied Anthropology emerged from wartime projects. Afterwards there were major projects in Peru, but also the Cornell Many Farms project in the U.S. Southwest (as Murray Wax reminded me).

31 Murphy (1976: 12) also considered Native American 'deculturation' as an explanation for the resistance to the shiny new toys of functionalism: 'However handy [a model of society in which norms guide actions which then feed back to reinforce the system of norms] may be as a starting point for the analysis of functioning social systems, it was less than useful when studying the shattered remnants of American Indian societ[ies].'

32 He further asserted that 'the change in scale of the research subject wrenched anthropology out of its age of innocence and ended forever ethnographies written from the head of one old infor-

mant sitting in the anthropologist's hotel room' (Murphy 1976: 7, adding 'until ethnoscience' resurrected the omniscient prime informant).

33 There were fluctuations, but no trends in percentage of articles that were Americanist within these time spans.

34 Murray (1994: 162) contains a more detailed breakdown of Bloch's (1950: 16) official report. I have excluded the 10.5 per cent (in both periods) of articles he coded as being about 'general topics' rather than dealing with a particular language or family.

35 No final report of the Southwest Project appeared (see Murray 1994: 195–6). In some sense all the linguistic eggs for the anthropological market were put in the Whorfian basket. (This image is from Hymes 1983 [1969]: 175.) The basket was then fumbled, although other linguistic eggs were hatched and carried by Lévi-Strauss and by cognitive scientists.

36 Two of the three sites discussed in the more instrumental pioneering discussion of fieldwork in R. Wax (1971) were Native North American ones.

37 This is especially clear in Steward (1937).

38 There is certainly some sense to saying that British social anthropology was dominated by Africanists.

39 'Theory' is not as distinct a field (separate specialty) in anthropology as it is in sociology, though some distinction between those who gather empirical data and those who theorize goes far back – before the Bureau of American Ethnology and Daniel Garrison Brinton, at least to Albert Gallatin, or, arguably, to Thomas Jefferson (see Murray 1994: 27–35).

40 Murphy (1976: 13) considered structural functionalism to have climaxed and been exhausted (in Kroeber's sense of both climax and pattern exhaustion) in 1963, though it continued, zombie-like, to stalk the earth after its demise. Elsewhere, he wrote that functionalism had reached an intellectual dead end in 1955 (Murphy introduction to Steward 1977: 35). I do not know why he chose that date, and would myself date the climax to Radcliffe-Brown and Forde (1950), followed quickly by the onslaught of Murdock (1951) and the apostasies of Evans-Pritchard (1951), with Firth (1954) and Leach (1954) constituting major (if incomplete) turns against the assumption of synchronic equilibrium of (what were treated as) closed systems.

41 Expansion seems to have been more gradual (or later) in Canada. See Burridge (1983) and Preston (1983), the latter markedly uneasy about overspecialization.

42 Hagstrom (1965) applied this generalization to scientific specializations.

43 If we extended this concern for replicability further and began to examine how well anthropologists understand what they see or hear, or the slender and shaky bases of many anthropological claims, such credibility as anthropology has might disappear, and as literate natives challenge the authority of short-term visitors' understanding of them, anthropologists might be regulated or banned in more and more places.

Of course anthropology is not the only profession substituting specialization for competition or the only one reluctant to examine the incompetence and misconduct of delinquent professionals, or the only one eager to keep anyone else from questioning what professionals choose to do (see Murray 1980 and Deloria 1991: 459–62), but contemporary anthropology gatekeepers have what I can only describe as a special horror of confronting the possibility that what a properly certified anthropologist produces might be wrong, not just the result of a difference of interpretation or a function of slight geographical or temporal difference between observations. Perhaps the protectiveness extended to white Americans' purportedly fieldwork-based pronouncements is especially strong because anthropologists got away for so long with making claims with little understanding of what was going on in front of them. As John Szwed (1972: 153) wrote, 'Working in distant places, largely with nonliterate peoples, anthropologists have seldom had to face their informants as critics of their published work; and having luxuriated in a sparsely populated discipline, they have often been able to avoid even the critical assessments of colleagues who have worked with the same people.' Understandably, those with shaky or no knowledge of the languages spoken do not like attention being called to the deficiencies of their material, or to the inadequacies of their comprehension (or the validity) of what they were told or of what they imagined was happening around them, and anthropology gatekeepers strive to perpetuate the pattern Szwed described. However, 'natives' from many places are writing back, often rejecting anthropologists' interpretations, questioning their competence – linguistic and other – as well as their recurrent complicity with domination: neo-colonialist and internal colonialist, as well as historically colonialist (see Hong and Murray 1989). Statements such as 'Two Crows denies this' are important data that should be recorded and taken seriously: somewhat, but not completely, 'privileged.' See Murray (1994: 500–1); Jackson (1989, 1995).

44 Those whose practices I have focused on recently, Sinologist anthropologists who worked on Taiwan (Hong 1994a, b; Hong and Murray 1989, 1993, 1997; Murray and Hong 1994) are, I hope (and we have argued), extreme in ideological service to contemporary domination by a neo-colonial regime. I have endeavoured not to overgeneralize from them and from Nancy Scheper-Hughes's various apologias for Cuban HIV+ concentration camps, but am aware that their work and anthropologists' refusal to address criticism of them may have coloured (jaundiced) my view of contemporary American anthropological praxis overseas.

45 As Ellen Basso shows in this volume, such narratives differ from 'life histories,' but portray individual characters, not schematic types.

46 I consider Eggan (1950, 1966) and Steward (1955, 1977) as having supplied exemplars of controlled comparison of aboriginal patterns; Spicer (1962), Dozier (1970), and M. Wax (1971), of more recent and/or long-term 'acculturations.' I also think that what Leach (1961: 1) wrote continues to apply, i.e., that anthropologists 'are giving up the attempt to make comparative generalizations; instead they have begun to write impeccably detailed historical ethnographies of particular peoples.'

47 In my view, the stories that anthropologists tell about themselves in various locales threaten to drown out the stories that other people tell them. Geertz (1995: 120) suggests that they misrepresent what is very public activity as introspection and provide little insight into how 'knowledge' is constructed in fieldwork.

REFERENCES

Asad, Talal. 1973. *Anthropology and the Colonial Encounter*. London: Ithaca Press.

Basso, Keith H. 1979. *Portraits of the Whiteman*. New York: Cambridge University Press.

Benedict, Ruth. 1934. *Patterns of Culture*. Boston: Houghton-Mifflin.

– 1946. *The Chrysanthemum and the Sword*. Boston: Houghton-Mifflin.

Bloch, Bernard. 1950. Publication Committee Report. *Linguistic Society of America Bulletin* 23: 12–17.

Boas, Franz. 1940. *Race, Language and Culture*. New York: Free Press.

Briggs, Jean L. 1970. *Never in Anger: Portrait of an Eskimo Family*. Cambridge, MA: Harvard University Press.

Bunzel, Ruth. 1929. *The Pueblo Potter: A Study of Creative Imagination in Primitive Art*. New York: Columbia University Press.

Burridge, Kenelm. 1983. 'An Ethnology of Canadian Ethnology.' In Frank Manning, ed., *Consciousness and Inquiry: Ethnology and Canadian Realities*, 306–20. Ottawa: National Museums of Canada (Mercury Series 89E).

Cole, Douglas. 1973. 'The Origins of Canadian Anthropology.' *Journal of Canadian Studies* 8: 33–45.

Colson, Elizabeth. 1985. 'Defining American Ethnology.' In Helm 1985: 177–84.

Darnell, Regna D. 1969. 'The Development of American Anthropology, 1880–1920.' Ph.D. dissertation, University of Pennsylvania.

– 1971. 'The Professionalization of American Anthropology.' *Social Science Information* 10: 83–103.

– 1977. 'Hallowell's *Bear Ceremonialism* and the Emergence of Boasian Anthropology.' *Ethos* 5: 13–30.

– 1990. *Edward Sapir*. Berkeley: University of California Press.

– 1995. 'Continuities in Americanist Anthropology.' Presidential address presented to the North American Association for the History of the Linguistic Sciences annual meeting, New Orleans.

Deloria, Vine, Jr. 1991. 'Research, Redskins, and Reality.' *American Indian Quarterly* 15: 457–68.

DeMallie, Raymond. 1994. 'Fred Eggan and American Indian Anthropology.' In R. DeMallie and A. Ortiz, eds, *North American Indian Anthropology*, 3–22. Norman: University of Oklahoma Press.

Dozier, Edward P. 1970. *The Pueblo Indians of North America*. New York: Holt, Rinehart & Winston.

Du Bois, Cora. 1939. *The 1870 Ghost Dance*. Berkeley: University of California Anthropology Record 3.

– 1944. *The People of Alor*. Minneapolis: University of Minnesota Press.

Durkheim, Émile. 1893. *De la division du travail social*. Paris: Alcan.

Ebihara, May. 1985. 'American Ethnology in the 1930s.' In Helm 1985: 101–21.

Eggan, Fred. 1955 [1937]. *Social Organization of North American Tribes*. Chicago: University of Chicago Press.

– 1950 [1933]. *Social Organization of the Western Pueblos*. Chicago: University of Chicago Press.

– 1966. *The American Indian: Perspectives for the Study of Social Change*. Chicago: Aldine.

Evans-Pritchard, E.E. 1951. *Social Anthropology*. New York: Free Press.

Firth, Raymond. 1954. 'Social Organization and Social Change.' *Journal of the Royal Anthropological Institute* 84: 1–20.

Foster, George M. 1982. 'Relationships between Anthropological Field Research and Theory.' In E.A. Hoebel, R. Currier, and S. Kaiser, eds, *Crisis in Anthropology: Views from Spring Hill, 1980*, 141–53. New York: Garland.

Frantz, Charles. 1985. 'Relevance: American Ethnology and Wider Society, 1900–1940.' In Helm 1985: 83–100.

Freeman, Derek. 1983. *Margaret Mead and Samoa*. Cambridge, MA: Harvard University Press.

– 1991. '"There's Tick i' th' World": An Historical Analysis of the Samoan Researches of Margaret Mead.' Unpublished manuscript.

Geertz, Clifford. 1995. *After the Fact: Two Countries, Four Decades, One Anthropologist*. Cambridge, MA: Harvard University Press.

Godoy, Ricardo. 1978. 'The Background and Context of Redfield's *Tepoztlan*.' *Journal of the Steward Anthropological Society* 10(1): 47–79.

Goldfrank, Esther Schiff. 1978. *Notes on an Undirected Life*. Flushing, NY: Queens College Press.

Goldschmidt, Walter. 1985. 'The Cultural Paradigm in the Post-War World.' In Helm 1985: 164–76.

Gregg, Dorothy, and Elgin Williams. 1948. 'The Dismal Science of Functionalism.' *American Anthropologist* 50: 594–611.

Hagstrom, Warren O. 1965. *The Scientific Community*. New York: Basic Books.

Hall, Edward T. 1992. *An Anthropology of Everyday Life: An Autobiography*. New York: Doubleday.

– 1994. *West of the Thirties: Discoveries Among the Navajo and Hopi*. New York: Doubleday.

Helm, June. 1985. *Social Contexts of American Ethnology, 1840–1984*. Washington: American Ethnological Society.

Herskovits, Melville J. 1953. *Franz Boas*. New York: Scribners.

Hoebel, E. Adamson. 1982. 'Ancient Times.' In E.A. Hoebel, R. Currier, and S. Kaiser, eds, *Crisis in Anthropology: Views from Spring Hill, 1980*, 3–13. New York: Garland.

Hong, Keelung. 1994a. 'Experiences of Being a "Native" while Observing Anthropology.' *Anthropology Today* 10(3): 6–9.

– 1994b. 'Anthropology in Taiwan.' *Anthropology Today* 10(5): 26–7.

Hong, Keelung, and Stephen O. Murray. 1989. 'Complicity with Domination.' *American Anthropologist* 91: 1028–30.

– 1993. 'Ethnographic Irresponsibility.' *Typhoon* 3(4): 4–6.

– 1997. 'A Taiwanese Woman Who Became a Spirit Medium: Native and Alien Models of How Taiwanese Identify Spirit Possession.' Paper presented at the third North American Taiwan Studies Conference, Berkeley.

Hymes, Dell H. 1972. *Reinventing Anthropology*. New York: Random House.

– 1981. *In Vain I Tried to Tell You : Essays in Native American Ethnopoetics*. Philadelphia: University of Pennsylvania Press.

– 1983. *Essays in the History of Linguistic Anthropology*. Amsterdam: John Benjamins.

Jackson, Jean 1989. 'Is There a Way to Talk about Making Culture without Making Enemies?' *Dialectical Anthropology* 14: 127–43.

– 1995. 'Culture, Genuine and Spurious: The Politics of Indianness in the Vaupés, Colombia.' *American Ethnologist* 22: 3–27.

Joseph, Alice, Rosamond B. Spicer, and Jane Chesky. 1949. *The Desert People: A Study of the Papago Indians*. Chicago: University of Chicago Press.

Keesing, Felix M. 1939. *The Menomini Indians of Wisconsin: A Study of Three Centuries of Cultural Contact and Change*. Philadelphia: American Philosophical Society (Memoir 10).

Kelly, Lawrence C. 1985. 'Why Applied Anthropology Developed When It Did.' In Helm 1985: 122–38.

Kroeber, Alfred L. 1909. 'Classificatory Systems of Relationship.' *Journal of the Royal Anthropological Institute* 39: 77–84.

– 1931. Review of *Growing Up in New Guinea* by Margaret Mead. *American Anthropologist* 33: 248–50.

– 1936. 'Kinship and History.' *American Anthropologist* 38: 338–341.

Kuper, Adam. 1983. *Anthropology and Anthropologists: The Modern British School*. London: Routledge & Kegan Paul.

Langham, Ian. 1981. *The Building of British Social Anthropology*. Dordrecht: Reidel.

Leach, Edmund. 1954. *Political Systems of Highland Burma*. Boston: Beacon Press.

– 1961. *Rethinking Anthropology*. London: Athlone Press.

Leighton, Alexander H. 1945. *The Governing of Men*. Princeton, NJ: Princeton University Press.

Linton, Adelin, and Charles Wagley. 1971. *Ralph Linton*. New York: Columbia University Press.

Linton, Ralph. 1936. *The Study of Man*. New York: D. Appleton-Century.

– 1940. *Acculturation in Seven American Indian Tribes*. New York: D. Appleton-Century.

Lowie, Robert H. 1915. Review of *The History of Melanesian Society* by W.H.R. Rivers. *American Anthropologist* 17: 588–91.

– 1920. *Primitive Society*. New York: Boni & Liveright.
– 1923. Review of *The Adaman Islanders* by A.R. Brown. *American Anthropologist* 25: 572–5.
– 1929. Review of Mead 1928. *American Anthropologist* 31: 532–4.
– 1937. *The History of Ethnological Theory*. New York: Holt, Rinehart & Winston.
– 1940. 'Native Languages as Ethnographic Tools.' *American Anthropologist* 42: 81–9.
Mead, Margaret. 1928. *Coming of Age in Samoa*. New York: Morrow.
– 1939. 'Native Languages as Field Work Tools.' *American Anthropologist* 41: 189–205.
– 1959. *An Anthropologist at Work*. Boston: Houghton-Mifflin.
– 1966 [1932]. *The Changing Culture of an Indian Tribe*. New York: Capricorn.
– 1972. *Blackberry Winter*. New York: Morrow.
Michelson, Truman. 1938. 'Sol Tax on the Social Organization of the Fox Indians.' *American Anthropologist* 40: 177–79.
Murdock, George Peter. 1951. 'British Social Anthropology.' *American Anthropologist* 53: 465–73.
Murphy, Robert F. 1976. *Selected Papers from the American Anthropologist 1946–1970*. Washington: American Anthropological Association.
Murray, Stephen O. 1980. 'The Invisibility of Scientific Scorn.' In R. de Mille, ed., *The Don Juan Papers*, 197–202. Santa Barbara: Ross-Erikson.
– 1983. 'Historical Inferences from Ethnohistorical Data: Boasian Views.' *Journal of the History of the Behavioral Sciences* 19: 335–40.
– 1988. 'The Reception of Anthropological Work in American Sociology, 1921–1951.' *Journal of the History of the Behavioral Sciences* 24: 135–51.
– 1990. 'The Poverty of a Historicism in Freeman's Account of Boasian Culture.' *Current Anthropology* 31: 401–7.
– 1991a. 'Boasians and Margaret Mead.' *Current Anthropology* 32: 448–52.
– 1991b. 'The Rights of Research Assistants and the Rhetoric of Political Suppression: Morton Grodzins and the University of California Japanese-American Evacuation and Resettlement Study.' *Journal of the History of the Behavioral Sciences* 27: 130–56.
– 1994. *Theory Groups and the Study of Language in North America: A Social History*. Amsterdam: John Benjamins.
Murray, Stephen O., and Keelung Hong. 1994. *Taiwanese Culture, Taiwanese Society*. Lanham, MD: University Press of America.
Nash, Philleo. 1937. 'The Place of Religious Revivalism in the Formation of the Intercultural Community on Klamath Reservation.' In Eggan 1937: 377–442.
– 1979. 'Anthropologist in the White House.' *Practicing Anthropology* 1(3): 3, 23–4.
Preston, Richard J. 1983. 'The Social Structure of an Unorganized Society: Beyond Intentions and Peripheral Boasians.' In Frank Manning, ed., *Consciousness and Inquiry: Ethnology and Canadian Realities*, 286–305. Ottawa: National Museums of Canada. (Mercury Series 89E.)
Radcliffe-Brown, A.R. 1922. *The Andaman Islanders*. Cambridge: Cambridge University Press.
– 1923. 'The Methods of Ethnology and Social Anthropology.' *South African Journal of Science* 20: 124–47.
– 1935. 'Kinship Terminologies in California.' *American Anthropologist* 37: 530–5.
– 1952a. 'Historical Note on British Social Anthropology.' *American Anthropologist* 54: 275–7.
– 1952b. *Structure and Function in Primitive Society*. Glencoe, IL: Free Press.
Radcliffe-Brown, A.R., and Daryll Forde. 1950. *African Systems of Kinship and Marriage*. New York: Oxford University Press.
Redfield, Robert. 1930. *Tepoztlan*. Chicago: University of Chicago Press.
– 1937. Introduction to Eggan 1937: vii–xii; 1955: ix–xiv.

Reichard, Gladys. 1934. *Spider Woman: A Story of Navajo Weavers and Chants*. New York: Macmillan.
Scollon, Ronald, and Suzanne Scollon. 1979. *Linguistic Convergence: An Ethnography of Speaking at Fort Chipewyan, Alberta*. San Francisco: Academic Press.
Spicer, Edward H. 1962. *Cycles of Conquest: The Impact of Spain, Mexico, and the United States on the Indians of the Southwest, 1533–1960*. Tucson: University of Arizona Press.
Starn, Orin. 1986. 'Engineering Internment: Anthropologists and the War Relocation Authority.' *American Ethnologist* 13: 700–20.
Steward, Julian. 1937. 'Ecological Aspects of Southwestern Society.' *Anthropos* 32: 87–104.
– 1938. Review of Eggan 1937. *American Anthropologist* 40: 720–2.
– 1946–50. *Handbook of South American Indians*. Washington: Smithsonian Institution (Bulletin 143, in 7 volumes).
– 1950. *Area Research: Theory and Practice*. New York: Social Science Research Council (Bulletin 63).
– 1955. *Theory of Culture Change: The Methodology of Multilinear Evolution*. Urbana: University of Illinois Press.
– 1956. *The People of Puerto Rico*. Urbana: University of Illinois Press.
– 1977. *Evolution and Ecology*. Urbana: University of Illinois Press.
Stocking, George W., Jr. 1976. *Selected Papers from the American Anthropologist 1921–1945*. Washington: American Anthropological Association.
– 1979. *Anthropology at Chicago*. Chicago: Regenstein Library.
– 1984. 'Radcliffe-Brown and British Social Anthropology.' *History of Anthropology* 2: 131–91.
Suzuki, Peter T. 1981. 'Anthropologists in the Wartime Camps for Japanese Americans.' *Dialectical Anthropology* 6: 23–60.
Szwed, John F. 1972. An American Anthropological Dilemma: The Politics of Afro-American Culture. In Hymes 1972: 153–81.
Tax, Sol. 1937. 'Some Problems of Social Organization.' In Eggan 1937: 3–32.
Tedlock, Dennis. 1993. *Breath on the Mirror: Mythic Voices and Visions of the Living Maya*. San Francisco: HarperCollins.
Thompson, Laura. 1951. *Personality and Government: Findings and Recommendations of the Indian Administration Research*. Mexico, D.F.: Ediciones del Instituto Indigenista Interamericano.
Thompson, Laura, and Alice Joseph. 1944. *The Hopi Way*. Chicago: University of Chicago Press.
Thorne, Barrie. 1980. '"You Still Takin' Notes?": Fieldwork and Problems of Informed Consent.' *Social Problems* 27: 284–97.
Villa Rojas, Alfonso. 1979. 'Fieldwork in the Mayan Region of Mexico. In G. Foster, T. Scudder, E. Colson, eds, *Long-Term Fieldwork in Social Anthropology*, 45–64. New York: Academic Press.
Vogt, Evon Z., and Ethel M. Albert. 1966. *People of Rimrock: A Study of Values in Five Cultures*. Cambridge, MA: Harvard University Press.
Wallace, Anthony F.C. 1961. *Culture and Personality*. New York: Random House.
Wax, Murray L. 1956. 'The Limitations of Boas' Anthropology.' *American Anthropologist* 58: 63–74.
– 1971. *Indian Americans*. Toronto: Prentice-Hall.
– 1991. 'The Ethics of Research in American Indian Communities.' *American Indian Quarterly* 15: 431–56.

Wax, Murray L., and Rosalie H. Wax. 1968. 'The Enemies of the People.' In H. Bahr, B. Chadwick, and R. Day, eds, *Native Americans Today*, 177–92. New York: Harper & Row.
Wax, Rosalie Hankey. 1971. *Doing Fieldwork: Warnings and Advice*. Chicago: University of Chicago Press.
Whiting., John, and Beatrice Whiting. 1978. 'A Strategy for Psychocultural Research.' In George Spindler, ed., *The Making of Psychological Anthropology*, 41–61. Berkeley: University of California Press.

5 Nationalism and the Americanist Tradition

RAYMOND D. FOGELSON

Anthropology, especially in its British mode following Evans-Pritchard, has often been referred to as 'the step-child of colonialism.' American anthropology and the development of the Americanist Tradition, I will argue, can best be considered as the *ward* of nationalism. The ideology of Americanism was certainly conditioned by previous colonial experiences. New nations in the Western hemisphere were created out of the wreckage of overseas European empires large and small. Such world powers and power-failures as Sweden, Portugal, Holland, Spain, France, and England all had their variable moments in the New World sun before retreating to the post-colonial shade.

The treatment of the indigenous and mestizo populations by the modern successors to the initial invaders can be regarded as a form of colonialism. Indeed, the late Robert K. Thomas coined the term 'internal colonialism' to describe the dependent condition of reservation and otherwise spatially segregated Indian populations (1966–7). Thomas's notion of 'internal colonialism' has recently been rediscovered and endorsed by Marxist theorist and outspoken American Indian Movement spokesman Ward Churchill (1993).

Despite the analytic robustness and rhetorical appeal of the colonial model, I find efforts at nation-building, international competition, and competing forms of nationalism to be more compelling stimuli in accounting for the emergence of the Americanist Tradition and ethnic nationalism within the United States and Canada. Not only did new nations usually strive mightily to separate themselves from their parental motherlands or fatherlands, but they actively attempted to create a distinctive identity of their own. This identity work included such things as the framing of constitutional law, the creation of national symbols, the establishment of traditions, the setting of annual ceremonial calendars, the maintenance of boundaries, and efforts to merge and blend into the newly enclosed landscape. I use the notion of identity here not only in terms of self-image as contrasted with the alter-images of others, but also in its literal sense: identity emphasizes a sense of *sameness* and *continuity* over time. Nationhood thus involves both newness in the process of separation and the forging of a distinctive polity and national character, but it also seeks legitimacy through perpetuation of enduring values and connections with an essentialized or primordial state of being.

Nations and nationalism are difficult to define. Their meanings change radically over time and space. Ideas of nationalism can be traced back to antiquity, but modern nationalist movements are thought to have begun in pre-pre-modern Western Europe, first with England, and later spreading into North America and Central and Eastern Europe, where bitter issues of nationalism and ethnicity continue to be contested. Eventually nationalism diffuses globally to the so-called Third and Fourth Worlds, where some of them become First Nations or one of the Five Hundred Nations.

Just as nationalism spreads globally, with various changes in meaning, over time, so does nationalism change internally. European or American nationalism is not the same in 1840 as it is in 1890. In 1840 nationalism could be regarded as a democratic revolutionary movement of the people; by 1890 it had become predominantly a conservative and reactionary movement pitting the upper classes against the people, and manifesting strong opposition to internationalism. Exclusivity and self-centred closed societies became the norm (Kohn 1973: 328).

Defining nation and nationalism is a bit like trying to nail jello to the wall. However, most definitions require as a *sine qua non* the notion of a community of people, real or theoretical, occupying a common territory, or at least once occupying a common homeland or promising to do so in the future. Often the community speaks a common language, possesses distinctive customs, and, at least formerly, believes itself to be connected by common descent through a mystical chain of blood. The last feature seems anachronistic today when race and racism are taboos, politically wrong topics. Nevertheless, etymologically, we must recognize that the term nation derives from the Latin 'to give birth,' or 'to breed.' Nationality is still considered by us to be a birthright, and the process by which an alien attains membership in the nation is called 'naturalization'; in crossing national borders one must have customs checked.

Nations are also sometimes defined in terms of scale, being larger than a tribe or a localized ethnic group and more stable and historically developed than a federation. Issues of scale confront us directly in the manner in which Europeans classified Native American polities. My impression is that, while the term tribe is used fairly commonly, and confederacy or empire occurs exceptionally, a large number of groups in the colonial records are referred to as nations.

The designation is only roughly correlated with size or scale, since we read of the Huron Nation, the Catawba Nation, the Cherokee Nation, the Sioux Nation, and the Pequot Nation, and so on. What seems to be occurring here is the recognition of sovereignty, independence, and power. When a nation is defeated it either ceases to exist, its remnants are scattered, or it is reduced to the status of a tribe. Pauline Strong and Barrik Van Winkle (1993: 12) date the shift from Indian 'nations' to Indian 'tribes' to the Commerce Clause of the United States Constitution in 1787.

Pequot history is recorded in all these registers. In the early seventeenth century, the Pequots were considered a powerful nation controlling the wampum trade up and down the rivers of southern New England. After they were massacred by the Puritans in 1636 at Fort Mystic, buckle-headed Captain John Mason declared that the Pequots ceased to be a people. Indeed, they achieved some measure of literary immortality in Melville's *Moby Dick* by being referred to as 'extinct as the Medes.' Yet, as we know, individual Pequots survived, banded together, and became a federally recognized tribe. They now proudly refer to themselves as a nation, with an open line to Washington and with transnational connections, by virtue of their present control of another kind of wampum trade in southern New England, big-time casino gambling.

The attribution of nationhood to Indians was never a simple evolutionary correlate of civilization. The major Indian groups in the southeastern United States attained the trappings of civilization before their removal to the West in the 1830s. However, they were collectively referred to as the Five Civilized *Tribes*, not the Five Civilized *Nations*, even though individually the groups were still referred to as Indian Nations – the Seminole Nation, the Creek Nation, the Cherokee Nation, the Choctaw Nation, and the Chickasaw Nation.

I want to turn now to consider the Americanist Tradition in relation to nationalism. As far as I can determine, the term Americanist first appears in 1881 in connection with the first meeting of the Congress of Americanists in Madrid in September of 1881. It is interesting to note that the Congress was international in scope and dominated by European scholars, as is the Society of Americanists today. However, the roots of the Americanist Tradition go far back into the colonial period, when interests in recording information on native customs and manners, languages, physical types, and antiquities were all pursued in hopes of ascertaining *who* the New World Natives were and how they related to known Old World populations. These quests for knowledge were also inspired by religious and political concerns.

After the American Revolution, the Americanist Tradition began in earnest. Perhaps no figure is more quintessentially Americanist than Thomas Jefferson. He disputed with European scholars over the thesis that America was an inferior habitat for plants, animals, and human beings. His keen interest in Indian ethnology can be seen in his instructions to the explorers Lewis and Clark; he was a serious student of American Indian linguistics and was directly or indirectly responsible for many of the early word lists that found their way to the American Philosophical Society. He also is remembered for conducting the first stratigraphically controlled excavation of a burial mound located near his home of Monticello. This did not immediately inaugurate scientific archaeological excavation techniques, but it did demonstrate continuity of the past with the present; Jefferson even reports periodic visits of living Indians to the grave site. On the practical side, Jefferson's Indian policy, while superficially liberal, aimed to transform what were thought to be wild, warlike, nomadic hunting groups into tame, peaceful, settled agriculturalists. The implicit choice was acculturation and assimilation or cultural death and disappearance.

The theme of disappearance continues to haunt the nineteenth century. The issue of Indian sovereignty in the United States is addressed in the 1831 Supreme Court case of the Cherokee Nation vs. Georgia, in which Chief Justice John Marshall articulates the doctrine of 'domestic dependent nation' status in which the Federal Government's relationship to the Cherokee Nation is compared to that of a 'guardian to his ward.' The full implications of this ruling have remained open to variable legal interpretation down to the present day.

On the one hand, wardship suggests immaturity and vulnerability. On the other hand, the relationship suggests definite obligations on the part of the more powerful protector to assist and defend the interests of the ward. Domestic dependent nation status entails loyalty, such that Indian Nations coming under this ruling were no longer permitted to make independent alliances with foreign powers or take up arms against the federal government. It was implicitly expected that Indian wards would perish long before reaching full maturity or that they would grow up in such a fashion as to be unrecognizable to their ancestors.

The main thrust of emerging nineteenth-century scholarly studies of the American Indian was oriented to the past. Several learned societies and multifaceted institutions and projects provided a support structure for research. I have already mentioned the American Philosophical Society, which took the lead in philological studies and ethnology. The American Antiquarian Society became a nerve centre for archaeological work during the second quarter of the nineteenth century. The American Ethnological Society was founded in 1842 and stimulated important research during the middle part of the century. Henry Rowe Schoolcraft's elephantine six-volume encyclopedia, *Information Regarding the History, Condition, and Prospects of the Indian Tribes of the United States*, brought together much valuable material. However, Schoolcraft's compilation was long on history and past traditions, but short on prospects and current conditions.

The Smithsonian Institution made an auspicious debut in 1848 with the publication of Squier and Davis's *Ancient Monuments in the Mississippi Valley*, but it had to wait until the latter part of the century for more sustained research under the aegis of the Geological Survey, the Bureau of Ethnology, and the U.S. National Museum. The Anthropological Society of Washington and the Woman's Anthropological Society, the parents of the American Anthropological Association, were already formed in the late 1880s, and the American Association for the Advancement of Science was an active arena for presenting the results of Americanist research. A comparable institutional survey could be done for nineteenth-century Canada.

Archaeology occupied centre stage in the nineteenth-century focus on the past. The mystery of the mound builders preoccupied many notable and unnotable minds. The question of the antiquity of human occupation of the New World and the search for early skeletal material formed important arenas of inquiry and speculation. The discovery of ancient monuments and evidence of early man were legitimizing efforts to provide the New World with parity to sites and finds in the Old World. Indeed, American archaeology develops almost as a reflex to European prehistory. Neanderthal skeletons are countered with claims for specimens like the Natchez pelvis; the contemporaneity of European Palaeolithic populations with elephants and mammoths is matched in America by the fraudulent elephant pipes in Davenport, or the false depiction of mammoths on the Lenape Stone unearthed in Eastern Pennsylvania. It should be noted that Henry Chapman Mercer, who published the major report on the Lenape Stone, had already participated in extensive excavations in France and Spain. To continue: an analogue to European Palaeolithic stone industries was thought to be present in the Trenton gravels and in the Upper Delaware Valley. Soon after the mesolithic remains of the Swiss Lake dwellers were revealed to an interested public, Frank Hamilton Cushing brought to destructive light complex wooden artefacts from the muck of Key Marco. This kind of transatlantic ping-pong began to slow down as the twentieth century approached.

The fusion of nationalism with the Americanist Tradition is clearly revealed in the nineteenth-century history of archaeological site preservation and antiquities laws. Frederick Ward Putnam purchased the Great Serpent Mound in Southern Ohio for Harvard's Peabody Museum, which later turned the site over to the Ohio Archaeological and Historical Society for safe keeping. The discovery of spectacular Anasazi sites in the Southwest drew visitors, pot hunters, and scholars. However, it was only when Nordenskjold started to crate up artefacts for shipment to European museums that legislative action was taken to protect what was now considered a national heritage.

Later, when Yellowstone was declared a national park, part of the motivation for doing so was to keep out Shoshone and Crow visitors (Peter Nabokov, personal communication). Antiquity laws were enacted to preserve sites for archaeological science. Only in recent years have Indians been consulted about site conservation and the possible religious significance to current Native historical consciousness. Thus, the process of assimilation and appropriation of Indian culture concerns not only the living, but the dead as well.

If any figure most fully embodied the culmination of the nineteenth-century Americanist position, it was Daniel Garrison Brinton. Regna Darnell has written definitively about this gentlemanly Philadelphia polymath (1988). He was, at once, a trained physician, a talented linguist, a critical interpreter of ethnological and archaeological data and theory, a significant student of folklore and myth, and an early specialist in comparative religion and primitive psychology. In many ways, he resembles an American E.B. Tylor, not only in his range of interests, in his Quaker tolerance, and in his abiding evolutionism, but also in his preference for the armchair over the field and his tenure as an early but inactive professor of anthropology of his time.

As Darnell notes, Brinton declares his divergent stance from most anthropologists in the preface of his *Essays of an Americanist* (1890). He believed in a considerable antiquity for humans on this continent, in a distinct American race, in genetic similarities in all American languages, in the importance of the abstract and symbolic features of myth, in the phonetic character of graphic methods, in the existence of poetic feelings in American tribes, and in an autochthony of American cultures that denied late immigration by way of the Bering Straits. Brinton also felt that the psychology of savage life was greatly underrated by most anthropologists owing to superficial observation, judging the past conditions of a tribe from modern and degenerate representatives, an inability to speak the languages, and the imposition of preconceived theories about Native thought and feeling. The anthropologists from whom Brinton distanced himself included younger scholars like Franz Boas, who emphasized fieldwork, whose outlook was more international, and who didn't subscribe to all of Brinton's parochial Americanist tenets.

The 1893 World Columbian Exposition marked a transition point in Americanist anthropology. Several Americanist crises of representation were played out at the Chicago fair. The scientists of the Smithsonian, particularly Otis Mason and William Henry Holmes, took a taxidermist turn, creating life figures of dead Indians and encasing them in simplified dioramas. Buffalo Bill and his Congress of Rough Riders employed show-business Indians, mostly Oglala

Sioux, to portray dramatic episodes in the losing of the West. Frederick Ward Putnam and Franz Boas favoured replicas of traditional Indian habitations populated by living Indians recreating the traditional cultures of their forebears. Finally, government boarding-school children sat properly at their desks in model Indian schools displaying their penmanship and lace-making ability. Meanwhile, the Carlisle brigades of Colonel Richard Henry Pratt marched under the banner of 'civilization and citizenship.'

Archaeology figured prominently at the Chicago fair: there were state, national, and international archaeological exhibits, including a massive replica of a Cliff Dweller site, and reconstructed stelae and public buildings from Yucatan.

However, one sensed that the progress celebrated at the fair sounded the death knell of the traditional Indian. As is well known, Frederick Jackson Turner announced the closing of the frontier at a history convention held in conjunction with the Chicago World's Fair. As is probably less well known, Daniel Brinton delivered a presidential address at the International Congress of Anthropology, also convened at the fair. Significantly, Brinton's talk was entitled 'The Nation as an Element in Anthropology' (1894). The address is a curious mixture of outworn evolutionary dogma combined with some forward-looking insights into the effects of nationality on various anthropological domains. Brinton's lecture reflects the old and the new, the nineteenth century and the twentieth century.

Another set of World's Fair documents that has recently surfaced is a series of predictions by various commentators about the state of the world a century into the future, that is, 1993 (Walter 1992). One of the prognosticators was Thomas Jefferson Morgan, then Commissioner of Indian Affairs. He predicted that Indian tribes as political entities would disappear, even though the Indian population would increase four-fold. He foresaw 'wandering bands of blanket beggars ... aboriginal tramps [who] will perpetuate the absurdities and enormities of Indian life either as a profession or as a providential object lesson for students of history.' Moreover, '[t]he great body of Indians will become merged in the indistinguishable mass of our population' (Morgan, in Walter 1992: 44).

This feeling of imminent loss of Indian culture pervades the activities of the first generation of trained, professional anthropologists after the turn of the century. Americanist anthropology was assumed from the start to be a salvage operation. The dominant Boasian modus operandi favoured short-term fieldwork, collaboration with key elder informants, and the co-production of texts, preferably in the native language. Sometimes these one-on-one interactions became so intense as to resemble a *folie à deux*. The ultimate ethnological aim, however, remained the reconstruction of cultural history.

By the late 1920s and 1930s, new theoretical currents began to affect the Americanist Tradition from both within and without. Functionalism in its various guises placed greater emphasis on the wholeness and integration of cultures and social structures. The dynamics of social and cultural change were sought in more complex processes than simple evolution and diffusionism. Finally, and most important, attention shifted away from an unknowable, idealized past and more toward a more accessible, realistic present. It is difficult to single out specific works that signal this transformation, but if pushed to the wall, I'd nominate Margaret Mead's study of the Omaha, *The Changing Culture of an Indian Tribe* (1932), despite its many flaws. I'd also dust off Clark Wissler's seldom cited work, *Indian Cavalcade* (1938), which looked at reservation communities as apt subjects of study in and of themselves. It should be noted that Wissler sponsored Mead and Reo Fortune's Omaha work, and that he was also influential in the Lynds' study of Muncie, Indiana, better known as *Middletown*, which was a pace-setting American community study.

During this period, American anthropologists began to take a more active interest in the welfare and survival of the societies they observed and analysed. Applied anthropology came to the fore as anthropologists worked closely with government agencies to enact legislation and to administer programs intended to benefit and empower Indians. The anthropological role began to shift from passive undertakers of Indian culture to active take-over policy makers in Indian affairs.

Subsequent debates have witnessed a steady decline in anthropological studies in Native North America. Although heirs to a rich and important research tradition, Americanist scholars are increasingly marginalized and made to feel irrelevant within the wider anthropological profession. This marginalization seems to have less to do with quality of work or the neglect of significant theoretical issues and more to do with conditions of work.

As Indian sovereignty has been reaffirmed, as movements for self-determination have gained momentum, and as formerly mute Indian voices become more strident, Native confrontations with anthropology and anthropologists become inevitable. For many, these developments herald the death of the Americanist Tradition. It takes almost the zeal of a missionary to convince funding agencies, sceptical colleagues, and reluctant tribal government officials about the significance of Americanist research. It is hard to persuade intelligent graduate students to forego the attractions of postcolonial studies in Africa, the Pacific, and elsewhere, or the allure of postmodern, transnational research in Eastern Europe, or the narcissism of self-reflective analyses of American society. They are dissuaded by the ordeal of negotiating research permissions with tribal councils; they are not enchanted with the pleasures of reservation life; they want to avoid the great, white American guilt trip; and they are uncomfortable with being the butt of 'anthro' jokes and being subjected to chronic 'anthro-bashing.'

If there is to be a resurrection of Americanist studies, and I think there will be, anthropologists will have to become wards to the people they purport to study. They will have to pledge allegiances to new nationalisms. They will have to face the challenges of transmitting and translating the past and continuing results of Americanist research to new audiences in new contexts.

REFERENCES

Brinton, Daniel G. 1890. *Essays of an Americanist*. Philadelphia: David McKay.

– 1894. 'The "Nation" as an Element in Anthropology.' In D. Staniland Wake, ed., *Memoirs of the International Congress of Anthropology*, 19–34. Chicago: Schulte Publishing.

Churchill, Ward. 1993. *Struggle for the Land: Indigenous Resistance to Genocide, Ecocide and Expropriation in Contemporary North America*. Monroe, ME: Common Courage Press.

Darnell, Regna. 1988. *Daniel Garrison Brinton: The 'Fearless Critic' of Philadelphia*. Philadelphia: University of Pennsylvania Publications in Anthropology.

Mead, Margaret. 1932. *The Changing Culture of an Indian Tribe*. New York: Columbia University Press.

Strong, Pauline Turner, and Barrik Van Winkle. 1993. 'Tribe and Nation: American Indian and American Nationalism.' *Social Analysis* 33: 9–20.

Thomas, Robert K. 1966–7. 'Colonialism: Classic and Internal.' *New University Thought* 4(4).

Walter, Dave (compiler). 1992. *Today Then: America's Best Minds Look 100 Years into the Future on the Occasion of the 1893 World's Columbian Exposition*. Helena, MT: American and World Geographic Publishing.

Wissler, Clark. 1938. *Indian Cavalcade or Life on the Old-Time Indian Reservations*. New York: Sheridan House.

6 Boas on the Threshold of Ethnopoetics

DELL HYMES

History is part of what there is to be 'theorized.' Let me suggest that it has two aspects: what did happen, what did not happen.

As to what did happen, there is need to overcome stereotypes and misconceptions, not least on the part of linguists, for whom part of the past has become unintelligible. Today the contexts and climates of opinion in which linguistic work developed in American anthropology often are lost from sight. (Cf. Hymes and Fought 1981 [1975]: 67–77; Hymes 1983 [1976]: 118–19, 131n70). Saussure, for example, is likely to be generalized as an influence, when in fact he was hardly noticed in the United States until after the Second World War. Present-day comments on the formative period of the first half of the twentieth century often overlook major factors in the development of descriptive linguistics in the United States (it was not then 'structuralism') such as sheer pleasure in the discovery of pattern for its own sake, desire to show that unwritten languages had pattern analogous to that of written languages, concern to void reductionist explanations in terms of psychology and biology, and concern for regularities that gave linguistics status in a horizon dominated by images of science.

To be sure, the need to recover contexts and actualities from documents and manuscripts is not recent. The initial stimulus to my own reading in the American Tradition came as a graduate student forty-five years ago, when history was mostly what a teacher could remember. Meaning then was under a cloud in American linguistics, a distant cloud, and my professor, a leader in linguistics in anthropology, asked in class, in a genuinely puzzled tone, 'Why was Boas interested in grammatical categories?' I discovered that one had only to open the *Handbook of American Indian Languages* (Boas 1911) and read its introduction to find out.

Valuable work has been accomplished and continues, to be sure. For me, the start of serious sustained history of the Americanist Tradition, with its roots in both linguistics and anthropology, is associated with its being taken up by George Stocking, and with papers he contributed to three conferences, one in 1962, two in 1968 (see Stocking 1968, 1974b, 1974c). It was in preparing to take part in a conference in his honour in the spring of 1995 that I returned to his paper on the Boas plan for American Indian languages, thinking about the relation between Boas's work with grammar and his work with texts. Stocking represented Boas's work with texts in his Boasian anthology by a Kathlamet narrative, 'Swan's Myth,' reproducing its initial page from the field notebook, its initial published page, and the full English translation. I found myself analysing the narrative, and rereading Boas on mythology, particularly on what he called style.

Reading Boas, one finds a number of statements about form. They seem to be calls for a new kind of analysis. If one recalls his 'analytic' approach to grammar, describing languages in their own terms, their own processes and categories (cf. Stocking 1974c), an 'analytic' approach to narrative form would seem a natural extension. Thoroughgoing analysis of a grammar in terms of its own processes and categories seems an analogue and starting point for thoroughgoing analysis of texts in terms of their own processes and categories.

This did not happen, of course. It was at least in some way a possibility, perhaps, a horizon now forgotten. Two recent experiences have made me especially appreciate such a horizon.

A few years ago I was asked to read an impressive manuscript on intellectual foundations for linguistic anthropology. I found myself slotted into a narrow genealogical niche. The manuscript was wide-ranging, for the most part, but for the period into which I was slotted for consideration omitted most of what I remembered as having mattered. I felt compelled to reconstruct for several pages what to me had been circumambient horizons of what to the writer was only a notch on a line from past to present.

A few months later I came upon a book on just this theme (composed in intellectual collaboration with a friend, Gary Morson). In *Foregone Conclusions*, Michael André Bernstein argues against histories and literature that assign people responsibility for outcomes they could not know, while denying their sense of futures for them still open. He is first of all concerned with writing about the Holocaust, but addresses as well Christian appropriation of the Hebrew Bible as merely preparation for a New Testament, and explores Robert Musil's novel, *A Man Without Qualities*, for its account of Austrians on the eve of the First World War (see now the English translation [Musil 1995]), full of plans and expectations. Writing in terms of foregone conclusions, of course, is 'foreshadowing.' Writing in terms of actual horizons is 'sideshadowing.' It is concerned with the quotidian, what Bernstein and Morson call 'prosaics,' what an anthropologist would call ethnography.

What follows is not a full scale 'sideshadowing' of Boas on narrative style. I do take up statements by Boas about literary form and 'rhythmic repetition' that seem to imply a new kind of work. I analyse a text taken down in Kathlamet Chinook by Boas in 1894, the one chosen by Stocking to represent Boas's work of this kind, to show what results if one seeks regularities of kinds of repetition and rhythm throughout such a narrative. I also present a few examples from other Chinookan texts that in their ritual-like action, and lyric suspension of time, seem akin to Boas's own recognition of 'repetitions ... rhythmic in form, varied in contents' (RLC [1940] 314). If Boas had followed up his own statements with more extended work, he might have come first to such passages.

In Boas's statements there was a seed, then, even if it did not take root. I shall consider why it did not, and comment on an irony in that, an irony that in the long run dissolves.

Boas on Form in 'Primitive Literature'

Boas was moved by verbal art in his earliest fieldwork (cf. Boas 1887a, b). In the 1917 'Introduction' to the *International Journal of American Linguistics* he did not limit himself to questions of language in a narrow sense, but declared, 'The problems treated in a linguistic journal must include also the literary forms of native production' (1917: 7), and observed, 'The most promising material for the study of certain aspects of artistic expression are the formal elements that appear with great frequency in the tales of all tribes' (ibid.). He goes on to say: 'Most of these are stereotyped to such an extent, that little individual variation is found. Even in poorly recorded tales, written down in translation only, and obtained with the help of inadequate interpreters, the sameness of stereotype formulas may sometimes be recognized. Conversation in animal tales and in other types of narrative, prayers and incantations, are probably the most important material of this character.' Early in 'Mythology and Folk-Tales of the North American Indians' (1914) Boas remarks again on literary form (emphasis mine): 'Even the best translation cannot give us material for the study of *literary form* – a subject that has received hardly any attention and the importance of which, as I hope to show in the course of these remarks, cannot be overestimated' (RLC 452). Later he elaborates:

> While much remains to be done in the study of the local characteristics of folk-tales in regard to the points referred to, a still wider field of work is open in all that concerns *their purely formal character*, and I can do no more than point out the necessity of study

of this subject. On the basis of the material hitherto collected, we are hardly in a position to speak of *the literary form of the tales*. I am inclined to count among their formal traits the typical repetition of the same incident that is found among many tribes; or the misfortunes that befall a number of brothers, until the last one is successful in his undertaking. These have the purpose of exciting the interest and leading the hearer to anticipate with increased eagerness the climax. (478, emphasis added)

To be sure, Boas sets 'poetry' apart: 'The literary style is most readily recognized in the poetic parts of tales; but, since these fall mostly outside of the purely narrative part of the stories, I do not enter into this subject' (479). But having contrasted the style of poems (song texts) in the Northwest and the Southwest, he goes on to remark: 'Equally distinct are the *rhythmic structures* that are used by the Indians of various areas' (479, citing Fletcher 1901 [emphasis added], presumably for patterns of repetition in the songs and chants of the Pawnee Hako ceremony).

In my own work, the indication of thoroughgoing patterning in Chinookan narratives came through pursuing the hypothesis that a cultural pattern number ('sacred number'), five, and its correlate, three, played a part. It is striking to find Boas associating such numbers with literary composition, with rhythmic repetition as a source in his 1914 study, 'Mythology and Folk-Tales of the North American Indians': 'I am not inclined to look at these [so-called sacred numbers] primarily as something of transcendental mystical value; it seems to me more plausible that the concept developed from the aesthetic values of rhythmic repetition. Its emotional effect is obviously inherent in the human mind; and the artistic use of repetition may be observed wherever the sacred number exists, and where it is not only used in reference to distinct objects, but also in rhythmic repetitions of tunes, words, elements of literary composition and of actions' (RLC 489). In the later paper 'Stylistic Aspects of Primitive Literature' (1925), Boas continues to make statements that are strikingly suggestive. The goal of the article is 'to discuss in how far general mental traits account for the development of poetry and of the art of narrative, and in how far special historical conditions have exerted an important influence' (RLC 491). Again, the notion of poetry is equated with song: 'Song and tale are found among all the people of the world and must be considered the primary forms of literary activity. It does not require special mention that primitive poetry does not occur without music, and that it is frequently accompanied by expressive motions or by dance. It is, therefore, more correct to speak of song rather than of poetry' (RLC 491). At the same time Boas stresses that primitive prose is based on the art of oral delivery, and therefore is more closely related to modern oratory than to printed literary style. The stylistic difference is considerable

(RLC 491). And he speaks of 'this pleasure given by the rhythmic repetition of the same or similar elements, in prose as well as poetry' (RLC 494). He concludes: 'We have found the literatures of all the peoples about which we have information share one feature, namely rhythmic form' (RLC 502).

Near the beginning is a statement that could be taken to anticipate ethnopoetics: 'The investigation of primitive narrative as well as of poetry proves that repetition, particularly rhythmic repetition, is a fundamental trait' (RLC 491). But the continuation of the paragraph does seem to identify form with what is fixed or with what is musical: 'All prose narrative consists in part of free elements the form of which is dependent upon the taste and the ability of the narrator. Inserted among those passages we do find others of fixed form which give the narrative to a great extent its formal attractiveness. Quite often these passages consist of conversation between the actors in which deviation from the fixed formula is not permitted. In other cases they are of rhythmic form and must be considered poetry or chants rather than prose.' In short, form must be recognizable either by fixity, or by rhythm in the sense that song or chant has rhythm.

Boas does recognize variation of contents within a pattern. Citing Kwakiutl speeches, for instance, a passage such as 'I have come Northerners; I have come Great Kwakiutl, I have come Rich Side' (1927: 314), he remarks: 'The repetitions discussed so far are rhythmic in form, varied in contents. They may be compared to an orderly succession of decorative motives that agree in the plan of the unit, but vary in details'; but continues, 'In poetry rhythmic repetitions of identical formal units are frequent.' In sum, the discussion never gets very far from identity.

Decorative Art

Boas's work on material art shows the generality of his conception of the role of aesthetic form in human life. It may also contribute to a conception of verbal form that, as it were, hugs the material ground. In this regard attention should be paid to the work of his student, Gladys Reichard.[1] Boas himself cites her early article, 'The Complexity of Rhythm in Decorative Art,' in his own discussion of rhythmic repetition in decorative form as the rhythm of time translated into space (Boas 1927: 40; Reichard 1922 in Boas 1927: 41–2). Reichard states the question as, 'Do primitive people have a definite plan in carrying out their ideas in beadwork, embroidery and other handicrafts?' (183). She analyses beadwork and embroidery from the Thompson River Indians of British Columbia, bands of skin used in decorating fur coats from Siberia, and Roman stripes on modern ribbons, girdles, and silks. Letters are assigned elements to chart their occurrence. Boas is not mentioned, but probably his conception of rhythmic repetition was assumed as known.

Years later Reichard (1944) dedicated her book, *Prayer: The Compulsive Word*, to Boas's memory. She remarks that her 1924 paper, and one by Cora Stafford on Peruvian embroideries, 'were inspired and aided by Professor Boas, who had a perennial interest in the subject. He felt that similar elaborations could be found in the literary sphere of art, even as it had been demonstrated in the music of primitive peoples. The possibilities of adding new forms of rhythmic repetition in music forms suggested by Navajo chant setup of music, song and song sequence are limitless and they await a detailed and time-consuming analysis which is at present impossible.' She goes on to quote Boas on the possibility of complex rhythms being found in narrative literary forms (1927: 310–11)[2] and to say that there is little doubt Navajo has a great deal to offer on this question, much of it in prayers. When she discussed this matter with Boas a short time before his death, he told her that he had 'something of the kind' in Kwakiutl prayers, which however were not as complicated as those of the Navajo. 'The obvious questions came up in our discussion: Does the person who uses the prayer realize its significance as a whole pattern? If he does, is that realization felt in the ways in which we might feel it? How would one proceed to answer such a question? In what way or ways does the Navajo memory function, for surely its demands are burdensome beyond any which our own culture furnishes? ... Can we devise a method for answering these questions? The following analysis aims to present the material which arouses them and in part to answer them, but it could profit greatly by suggestions regarding procedure' (1966 [1944]: 35–6). Reichard treats the prayers as rhythmic prose, since they are intoned, but adds that if it later should be decided that the form is nearer to poetry (when the prosody has been worked out), there is nothing in her discussion to prevent it (37). The grouping of lines on the page and problems of translation are taken up, together with the division of most prayers into three parts – invocation, petition, and benediction – and the patterning of individual prayers. She notes that four and its multiples are not as common as often assumed (46). A prayer from the Male Shooting Chant Evil-chasing is presented in full with explanation (chap. 6).

Repetition and number were important to Reichard also in her book on *Navajo Religion* (1950), as shown in chapter 14 on 'Number' and 16 on 'Word, Formula, and Myth,' and the many entries in the index under the heading 'repetition' (p. 792).

Gill's book on Navajo prayer (1981) takes its departure from Reichard (cf. pp. xx and 3–5). 'She is the first and only person to have attempted such an analysis' (4). He notes the origin of her interest in patterns of repetition in the

Thompson River work (not mentioning the other bodies of data in Reichard's article, or Boas). Examining prayer texts not included in Reichard's book, but for which she prepared diagrams, Gill finds many errors, and notes that the criteria for analysis of form and content are usually indeterminate. (See appendix A, 'Critique of Reichard's Analysis of Prayer.') Still, he says, the vision she undoubtedly saw and followed is clear.

Gill himself analyses Navajo prayers in terms of constituents, a set of twenty-two in all (p. 14). He discusses 'Navajo Prayer as Oral Poetry' (180–3), with some observations on overlapping repetition within the performance, and notes that rhythm and repetition are essential elements. He presents diagrams of prayer texts (32–4, 211–35), in terms of their constituents (and catalogues). The constituents are kinds of act and topic. The status of the prayers as poetry seems to be assumed, rather than needing demonstration.

Some Navajo and Apache narratives have in fact been found to have the kind of poetic relations discussed below (unpublished work by myself, Keith Basso, Mary Beth Culley, and Anthony Webster), but that is independent of the line of influence just described.

Poetry without Music

In contrast to statements that indicate universality for rhythmic repetition in verbal art, Boas at one point goes so far as to say (1927: 301): 'Poetry without music, that is to say forms of literary expressions of fixed rhythmic form, are found only in civilized communities, except perhaps in chanted formulas. In simpler cultural forms the music of language alone does not seem to be felt as an artistic expression, while fixed rhythms that are sung occur everywhere.' Again, recurrence is associated with fixity.

I like to think that, if Boas had had time and opportunity to explore verbal form more fully, he would have discovered further dimensions of it in unsung language. Or if he were alive when such dimensions came to be recognized, especially in languages that he himself wrote down and knew intimately, such as Kathlamet Chinook (Hymes 1994b) and Kwak'wala (Kwakiutl) (Berman 1991), he would have accepted them.

Over the past thirty years it has become apparent that in many, perhaps all, communities there are oral narratives that are organized in terms of regularities of recurrence. Sometimes these regularities are obviously marked, as when the Wishram Chinook texts, dictated by Louis Simpson, commonly mark units that can be called 'verses' by an initial pair of particles (usually, *aGa kwapt* 'now then,' sometimes *aGa wit'aX* 'now again,' or contrastively *kwapt aGa*).[3] Generally, where one can hear a narrative, such verse units are marked by potentially final intonation contours. Even without intonation contours, a variety of features enter into patterning – expressions of time, turns at talk, and, most of all, pattern numbers. Broadly speaking, there are two types: use of relations of three and five, as in Chinookan and American English, and use of relations of two and four, as in Kwakiutl, Takelma, and Zuni.

The recurrent regularities of such narrative for the most part are not within lines, that is, they are not metrical. Rather, they hold between lines, or groups of lines, and can be called *measured.* There can be variation in the way in which relations are deployed. A sequence of three may be a sequence of three pairs. A sequence of five may be a sequence of five pairs. Within sequences that answer to an expected cultural pattern, there may be more than one kind of internal rhythm. Five verses may constitute a rapid run, or may consist of two pairs and an outcome (cf. Hymes 1992 and Swan's myths below).

The kind of repetition focused upon by Boas does of course occur. In 'Swan's Myth,' a 'conjugal duet' between Swan and his wife about a roasting smelt ('my' vs. 'our,' a pattern that occurs in Kathlamet Texts between a man and woman in 'Panther and Owl' as well) is formal in the first sense: similar pairs of repeated lines with, to be sure, a significant contrast. Repetition involves repetition of content. The relations among verses marked initially by *aqa* 'now' (see below) are formal in another sense. The relations give rise to recurrent patterns that shape and express content, but the content need not be repeated.

Instead of 'repetition' and 'fixed,' terms such as 'recurrent' and 'abstract' are appropriate. To stick to the recurrence of overt forms is to miss underlying relations. In terms of grammar, it is as if one could not recognize that the category of person-marker has occurred in three positions in a row in a Kathlamet verb, because the same person marker has not occurred three times in a row. That last in fact cannot happen, so far as first and second person markers are concerned, and overlooks the positions in which person-markers occur and the relations among them.[4]

In sum, Boas pioneered in discovering recurrent relations among grammatical elements, and the patterns of words constituted by them. A similar step is to discover recurrent relations among narrative elements, and the patterns of texts constituted by them. The concept of rhythmic repetition is a step in that direction, but a limited step so long as it does not go beyond elements to relations.

Rhythms Change

If one extends Boas's phrase 'rhythmic repetition,' a text can be said to have a consistent rhythm in the sense of making use of an underlying principle. In Chinookan narratives the informing principle is not just of one pattern but of two: three- or five-step relations. Moreover, there is not just one level of organization, but several: the number of verses within a stanza, the number of stanzas within a scene, the number of scenes within an act, possibly the number of acts within a myth or major part. Choice is possible at each point. And even with similar choices, the pace may differ.

The Deserted Boy. The three scenes of the second act of 'The Deserted Boy,' told by Louis Simpson to Edward Sapir in 1905, are a striking example (see Hymes 1994a). The first act has ended with the boy deserted. The second act begins with him facing winter, alone.

[II] [i] [He survives]

Now then the boy wept. (A)
Now then he heard,
'TL' TL' TL''
Now then he turned his eyes,
he looked,
he dried his tears.

Now then he saw a *very* little bit of flame in a shell. (B)
Now then he took that very same flame.
Now then he built up a fire.

Now again he saw fibre, (C)
again a little bit of it,
straightway he took it.
Now again he went to the cache,
he saw five wild potatoes.
Now then he thought: 'My poor father's mother saved me potatoes,
and fire was saved for me by my father's mother,
and my mother's mother saved me fibre.'

Now then the boy made a small fish-line, (D)
and he made snares with string;
he set a trap for magpies.
Now then he caught them.
Then he made a small cloak with magpie's skin.
He just put it nicely around himself.
Again he lay down to sleep.
Again he just wrapped himself nicely in it.

Now then he fishes with hook and line; E(ab)
he caught one sucker,
half he ate,
half he saves.
Again, morning, he ate half.

Now again he fishes, (cd)
he caught two,
one he ate,
one he saved.
Again, morning, he ate one.

Now again in the morning he fishes, (ef)
he caught three suckers,
he ate one and a half.
Again, morning, he ate one and a half.

Now again he went to fish,
he caught four suckers,
two he ate,
two he saved.
Morning, now he ate all two.

Now again did he go to fish for the fifth time.
Now five times the boy had fished.
Now he had become a grown man.

[ii] [He sings]

Now then he examined his fish-line. (A)
Indeed, ats'ə´pts'əp fills to the brim a cooking-trough.
He stood it up on the ground.
Now then the boy sang.
Now then all the people watched him.
Now then they said:
'What has he become?'

Indeed! he became glad, (B)
he had caught ats'ə´pts'əp.
Thus he sang:
'Atséee, atséee,
'Ah, it waves freely over me,

'Ah, my feathered cloak.'
'Atséee, atséee,
'Ah, it waves freely over me,
'Ah, my feathered cloak.'
'Atséee, atséee,
'Ah, it waves freely over me,
'Ah, my feathered cloak.'
Indeed! Iœə́xian's daughter had given him food.

Now then the boy had camped over four times; (C)
he camped over a fifth time.
Now then he awoke,
a woman was sleeping with him,
a very beautiful woman:
her hair was long,
and bracelets right up to her on her arms,
and her fingers were full of rings,
and he saw a house all painted inside with designs,
and he saw a mountain-sheep blanket covering him,
both he and his wife.
Indeed! Iœə́xian's very daughter had given him food,
and plenty of Chinook salmon,
and sturgeon,
and blueback salmon,
and eels,
plenty of everything she had brought.

[iii] [The two are together]

Now he married her.
Now the woman made food.
Now, morning, it became daylight.
Now the two stayed together quietly that day.
Now the two stayed together a long time.

The opening act has moved precisely in threes and fives to the desertion of the boy. Now in a scene of five stanzas, each of different formal complexion, the boy's status changes. In (A) he weeps, hears, and finds. The three verses are formally coordinate, each beginning with 'Now then,' describing an arc of onset, ongoing outcome, but the third verse has that same arc again within its smaller compass (turn, look, dry his tears).

The second stanza has that arc (see, take, build a fire) in three lines, each a verse. The third stanza is an outcome for seeing and finding. In one verse of three steps, the boy finds fibre. In a second of two lines, he finds potatoes. In a concluding third he gives three lines of thanks.

In Chinookan narratives a sequence of five groups often has its third group as an intermediate outcome. Having summed up what he is thankful for at the end of the third stanza, the boy deploys his resources. In five verses in the fourth stanza he mainly provides himself with a cloak against the winter. In the fifth stanza he fishes, step by step, to a surprising result. Now the framework of the scene expands, so that the fifth stanza itself has five parts, each of them having itself a pair of verses. The first of each pair begins 'Now then / Now again.' The second of each pair ends with 'Again, morning' except for the fifth. It ends with a couplet that counts as one unit, the two lines both marked ('Now ..., Now ...'), but together equivalent ways of making the same point. Notice that unlike the preceding four stanzas, what he caught is not stated. That is held over to be the subject of an entire scene in itself. (I call such holding over 'extraposition'.) What we do learn in this ending casts what has preceded in a new light. Using his meagre resources resourcefully, step by step the boy has become a man.

The second scene is ordinary at the level of number of stanzas and verses: three stanzas, five, three and three verses, respectively. In content it swells, with what Russo (1974: 374) has called 'epic fullness.'

The first stanza describes the boy catching, not fish, but a delicacy prepared for winter, a mixture of huckleberries and salmon. He sings because he knows that a spirit power has given it to him. Saving himself, he has been blessed. The people across the river who had deserted him watched and ask what he has become.

The second stanza is devoted to intensifying particles and the boy's song. The song can be repeated as long as desired. The food has come to him from the daughter of a being in the river, a being who causes whirlpools.

The third stanza swells its three verses with catalogues in the second and third (more 'epic fullness'). The first verse locates the occasion — he sleeps a fifth time. The second verse expatiates on the woman he awakes to find with him, her beauty and ornament, the house they are now within, the blanket covering them both. The third verse itemizes the kinds of food she has brought, embracing four kinds of fish in two lines of generalization (had given him food, plenty of everything she had brought).

In the third scene the tempo changes yet again. There are five verses, but none of them has 'then' to indicate a succeeding step. The verses are for the staying together of the man and woman, each marked only with 'now.'

In sum, the act has three scenes, and each scene has three or five stanzas, or (in the last) five verses. Yet each of the parts is strikingly different in pace. The act of fishing is detailed in precise, parallel, incremental steps, day by day, only for its culmination to put the hearer on hold. The next scene reiterates a song in one stanza, and swells with catalogues in another. The culminating scene suspends progression of time.

Such a *lyric moment* occurs also in the centre of Charles Cultee's 'Sun's Myth' (Kathlamet Chinook), and its wording and form suggest a sense of shared pattern. (For the whole, see Hymes [1994b].)If the passage is taken to be prose, and Englished as prose sentences, then it is understandable that recurrent relations might not be quite apparent. Here is how the published running translation appears (Boas 1901: 29): 'He asked about all those things, and thought: "I will take them." When it was evening, the old woman came home. She hung up something that pleased him. It was shining. Every morning the old woman disappeared. At night she came back. She brought home all kinds of things. She brought home arrows. Sometimes she brought mountain-goat blankets and elk-skin shirts. She did so every day. He stayed there a long time; then he grew homesick. He stayed there a long time; then he grew homesick ...'

The last line above begins a new scene, and in fact a new act and the second half of the myth. The scene in question is itself an act, completing the first half. The relations of the scene in question are as follows:

A long time he stayed there;
  now he took that young girl.
They stayed there.
In the early light,
  already that old woman was gone.
In the evening,
    she would come home;
  she would bring things,
    she would bring arrows;
  sometimes mountain goat blankets she would bring,
    sometimes elkskin armors she would bring.
Every day like this.

Notice the suspension of change in the first pair of verses (stayed, stayed there), departure and return in the second (was gone, came home ... bring), and absence of any verb in the fifth, last verse. The corresponding scene in 'The Deserted Boy' (Wishram / Wasco Chinook) also pairs morning and the rest of a day (lines 118, 119), and has 'stayed there' twice (119, 120). There is perhaps another parallel, a woman providing (goods in 'Sun's Myth,' food in 'The Deserted Boy').[5]

Stumbling Blocks?

Now that one can see such possibilities, one wonders why they were not seen by Boas or his students. What seems not to have happened is overcoming the received dichotomy of song and narrative as equivalent to poetry and prose. Some of this writing occurred in a time of experimentation in poetic form, experiments in the alignment of lines on the page. It is probably not surprising that what was put forward as highly modern in our own civilization would not be applied to what was studied as unwritten tradition in an ancient culture.

What *is* surprising is that no connection was made between the presentation of conversation in plays and conversation in oral narratives. It would have seemed an obvious convenience, and clarification, to distinguish turns at talk on the page. The turns themselves are there in the story, not an intervention from without. Seeing turns at talk might have suggested other relations and recurrences within a text.

Perhaps there was a feeling that any change in the record of what had been dictated was an imposition; that once a text was taken down as carefully as possible, that written record took the place of the original speaking as guarantor of authenticity. Of course one might notice slips of hearing or transcription, or even, it might seem, of speaking. But change beyond scrupulous editing smacked of lack of rigour, of scientific observation.

The practice of alphabetizing the words of Native American languages in terms of the phonetic alphabet, instead of the standard alphabet, suggests such an attitude. The phonetic alphabet, of course, was no more a part of the Native American language than was the European alphabet. And if Native Americans used materials written by outsiders about their own language, the European alphabet would be familiar.

This is speculation, although I have encountered attitudes that suggest it. Perhaps an element of caution was involved. Everyone knows that songs have form, no intrusion there. Narrative form is another matter. There was no awareness of a single kind of patterning for that, then or for the most part now. Still, in some texts the recurrence of certain initial elements is constant and might have been taken as a mark of recurrence. But the past cannot fairly be criticized for not discovering what many today decline to recognize even when pointed out.

On Irony

There is irony here, and an implicit contradiction. The Boasian goal was to represent languages in their own terms, free from distortion and overlay from the preconceptions of another culture. Nowhere are texts excluded from this goal. Texts, indeed, are explicitly included as indispensable to reaching the goal. In a letter of 1905 to W.H. Holmes, urging that all of Swanton's Haida texts be published, Boas stresses the connection: 'I do not think that anyone would advocate the study of antique civilizations or, let me say, of the Turks or the Russians, without a thorough knowledge of their languages and of the literary documents in these languages; and contributions not based on such material would not be considered as adequate. In regard to our American Indians we are in the position that practically no such literary material is available for study, and it appears to me as one of the essential things that we have to do, to make such material accessible. My own published work shows, that I let this kind of work take precedence of practically everything else, knowing it is the foundation of all future researches.'

The necessity of a mode of treatment appropriate to the features of the material is remarked: 'The fact is nowhere more apparent than in our studies based on the old missionary grammars. In these the characteristic features of the languages treated are so entirely obscured by the mode of treatment, that without new and ample texts our understanding of the languages will always remain inadequate.'

'The characteristic features of the languages': disclosing those became the starting point of an American tradition of synchronic grammar preceding and independent of European structuralism. If traditions were consistent, the texts that contributed to the linguistics ought themselves to have become the starting point of a tradition of analysis of narrative form. But 'the characteristic features' of the texts were obscured by mode of treatment, a mode of treatment that persisted. Texts that are a kind of poetry in having an organization of lines were treated as prose and published as paragraphs. The ethos of an 'analytic' approach, and indeed concepts central to the grammatical work, might have been extended into work with texts, but were not.

Irony in Time Perspective (1)

If this is ironic, it is an irony that Boas helped provide a basis for overcoming. Arnold Krupat (1988, 1992) has written of such irony with regard to Boas, focusing on an apparent contradiction between anthropology's goal of being a science, concerned with laws, yet postponing the formulation of laws until a time when all (or enough) was known. Let me put that contradiction in the perspective of the long term.

First, it is not quite true that Boas was a positivist for whom the facts are 'simply out there' (Krupat 1992: 90). It is fairer to say that he was an empiricist who had to overcome the ways in which cultural assumptions could distort perception and interpretation. Of that there was abundant evidence, from racial and cultural prejudice, and in particular from failure to see that unwritten languages and cultures could have patterns of their own. (See Stocking 1968: 59; 1974a: 58–9.)

Second, the laws that Boas thought it possible to find were in important part laws of the human mind, common to all, yet accessible only through the diverse outcomes of specific cultural and linguistic histories. Such laws would not simply present themselves, but require informed comparison and sifting of many such outcomes.

In effect, three kinds of 'laws,' or generalizations, were involved. One kind was not far to seek: the respects in which human beings, as such, were creatures with certain common potentialities in regard to language and culture. Negative critique of evolutionary and racial theories had this positive result from early on in Boas's work.

A second kind of 'law' would predict the course and development of an individual case. It may be worth clarifying what Boas actually said on this point, since Krupat has drawn attention to his 1932 presidential address to the American Association for the Advancement of Science, and in an otherwise valuable book Jonaitis (1995: 35) claims that Krupat says that 'Boas explicitly asserts that laws governing culture cannot be found.' But Krupat does not so assert. In his original article (1988: 113) Boas's statement that '[t]he phenomena of our science are so individualized, so exposed to outer accident that no set of laws could explain them' (RLC 257) is given as the last of a series of partial quotations, intended to show pervasive scepticism. In the later version in his own book, it is again the last of a long series of such phrases, a series Krupat is careful to precede with the caution 'without, to be sure, providing sufficient context to understand each of his remarks in itself' (1992: 98). And he follows the list with the remark: 'For all that aporia and antiphrasis structure Boas's text, still, the doubts and negations may yet imply some positive recommendations.' For Krupat, the point is that throughout the text one finds 'irony's ability to doubt and deny; the question for science is whether the doubt and denial are, once again, in the interest of alternative affirmations or whether they go so far as to deny affirmative statements of any kind' (1992: 97).

Missing from all this is a sentence Boas puts after the one quoted to the effect that the situation of anthropology is in principle that of science as a whole. 'It is as in any other science dealing with the actual world surrounding us. For each individual case we can arrive at an understanding of its determination by inner and outer forces, but we cannot explain its individuality in the form of laws' (RLC 257). Boas cites astronomy and biology with respect to the present location of stars and the forms of individual species. On the next page he sums up his position, not denying possible general laws in anthropology, but saying that 'general laws ..., on account of the complexity of the material will be necessarily vague and, we might almost say, so self-evident that they are of little help to a real understanding' (RLC 258). A multitude of affirmative statements as to determination by inner and outer forces are possible; but not 'generalized conclusions ... that will be applicable everywhere and that will reduce the data of anthropology to a formula which may be applied to every case, explaining its past and predicting its future' (257). Even so, Boas concludes his address with a universalizing goal: 'It is our task to discover among all the varieties of human behavior those that are common to all humanity. By a study of the universality and variety of cultures anthropology may help us to shape the future course of mankind.'

This third kind of positive finding seems always to have been in Boas's mind with regard to language. At the time he wrote, generalizations valid for all languages and cultures in terms of how they became what they are were far to seek. It is fair to say that they are closer now. Shortly after Boas's death, indeed, a renewed concern for universals (in the sense of universal implications in the relations among features) was initiated by Joseph Greenberg while at Boas's institution, Columbia University. The concern for universals has been influential, and together with much other work in language typology, is directly in keeping with what Boas would have considered desirable (cf. Greenberg 1954, 1963, 1978). A generation and more of renewed work by many scholars can be said to have done much to carry forward what Boas (and his student, Sapir) began. Indeed, although much work in generative grammar and cognitive linguistics sets cultural considerations aside, the methodological principle of seeking in language what could not be culturally motivated can be said to be Boasian. Boas more than once said that language was basic to the discovery of such laws, because, being out of awareness, it was not subject to secondary manipulation (e.g., 1911: 63).

Work in 'ethnopoetics' can be seen in this light as well. It can particularly be said to honour and justify the argument Boas made to Holmes, in the letter of 1905, when he wrote (Stocking 1974a: 123): 'As we require a new point of view, so future times will require new points of view, and for them the texts, and ample texts, must be available.'

Boas's own Kathlamet texts, such as 'Swan's Myth,' 'Salmon's Myth, and 'Sun's Myth,' all written down a century ago, are examples. (Cf. Hymes 1985, 1995.) They disclose organization that links particulars and general principles. They are part of the evidence for possibilities of form, which, if not innate, still are likely to prove universal (Hymes 1991). They link such possibilities with ways of shaping specific to cultures, with resources that serve individual expression. As with universals of language, so with narrative form: materials preserved by the Boasian tradition, and the ethos of its work, connect the general and the particular. These discoveries are consistent with his own belief in the universality of 'the craving to produce things that are felt as satisfying through their form and ... the capability of man to enjoy them' (1927: 9). That the implicit form is felt but often out of awareness may be part of its contribution to a sense of what is said as inherently warranted (cf. Urban 1996: 183–6, 204). Ultimately there is no irony, only the fact that more than one lifetime is required.

Irony in Time Perspective (2)

One still can wonder further as to what may have conditioned the timing of a recognition of ethnopoetic form. I suspect that Boas himself was reasonably satisfied to assert that rhythmic repetition is fundamental in narrative art. He had found it in visual art, and believed it to be present in all art. About the time he wrote 'Stylistic Aspects of Primitive Literature,' his classic book, *Primitive Art* (1927) asserted symmetry, rhythmic repetition, and form as foundations of aesthetic activity (cf. Jonaitis 1995: 23, 28, 301, 304), and included similar pages on verbal art (chap. 7, 'Primitive Literature, Music, and Dance,' pp. 299–340). Certainly Boas saw esthetic form as potentially universal in human life: 'The very existence of song, dance, painting and sculpture among all the tribes known to us is proof of the craving to produce things that are felt as satisfying through their form, and of the capability of man to enjoy them. All human activities may assume forms that give them esthetic values' (1927: 9). One can imagine what he concluded about mastery of the means of decorative art being extended to mastery of words: 'From this we conclude that a fundamental, esthetic formal interest is essential; and also that art, in its simple forms, is not necessarily expressive of purposive action, but is rather based upon our reactions to forms that develop through mastery of technique.'

Still, this did not happen. There is no study of narrative by Boas that pursues these properties with thoroughness, perhaps because for Boas the key trait of rhythm was after all close to music, when it came to narrative, rhythm was not considered to be an aspect of linguistics. He remarks (1925): 'It is not easy to form a correct opinion regarding the rhythmic character of the formal prose; in part because the rhythmic sense of primitive people is much more highly developed than our own. The simplification of the rhythm of modern folk song, and of the poetry intended to appeal to popular taste, has dulled our feeling for rhythmic form' (RLC 492). Recall the statement quoted earlier about form apart from music (1927: 301): 'Poetry without music, that is to say forms of literary expressions of fixed rhythmic form, are found only in civilized communities, except perhaps in chanted formulas. In simpler cultural forms the music of language alone does not seem to be felt as an artistic expression, while fixed rhythms that are sung occur everywhere.' Presumably 'in civilized communities' alludes to explicitly written and taught forms, such as sonnets, sestinas, and the like. The irony here is that what was not yet recognized in preliterate communities was equally unrecognized in literate communities. The kind of organization of oral narrative considered here is present all around us, and commonly as invisible. (See the last two chapters of Hymes 1996 on narratives from New York and Philadelphia.)

Some of Boas's students certainly carried on his concern with style in the sense of characterizing in close detail the various aspects of a narrative tradition (cf. Reichard 1930, 1947; and Jacobs 1959, 1960, 1972). Correspondence with students and others may illuminate this continuity.

None of the work, so far as I know, suggests analysing a text throughout for formal relations. None suggests that relationships of form might run throughout a text. None suggests that recurrent elements may stand in relations to each other that indicate points of equivalence in organization (cf. Jakobson 1960: 358).

Recurrence and equivalence are at the heart of the kind of work in question and illustrated here. Perhaps there is a fundamental practical difference between recognizing rhythmic repetition in visual art and in oral narrative. The object of art – a box, a basket – a blanket, shows its formal repetition. One can walk around it to confirm one's sense of that. A narrative text, written in a notebook, framed by the pages of the notebook, begins and ends and proceeds in terms of an arbitrary external frame. Turns at talk, recurrent particles, expressions of change of time or location, do not stand out against the rest of which they are a part. When such a text is typed and printed, it is paragraphed, but not on an analytic principle, and little else about it is presented so as to disclose recurrent relationships. Some persons may have an eye and visual imagination able to reconstruct such a text in their minds. Most of us need to put it on a page, and indeed experiment with ways of showing what recurs and succeeds.

I am not aware that any in the Boasian tradition experimented with modes of presentation alternative to paragraphs of prose. That may be a key to why there was a delay in being as 'analytic' about narrative as about grammar. I can only suggest some enabling circumstances that may have helped a recognition of narrative as poetry defined by relations of equivalence, in keeping with Jakobson's generalization, make sense and take root in some Americanist work – circumstances not present for Boas, and perhaps not for those who followed him.

(a) During the 1920s and 1930s, and certainly after the Second World War, the notion of poetic form changed for many. Contemporary poetry experimented with a wide variety of kinds of line and relations among lines. Lines with internal metrics (as with lines in songs) were far from the only kinds. The boundary between prose and poetry became far less definite. (Early in the century contemporary poetics affected the translation of Native American song texts, but not, so far as I know, of texts considered to be prose.)

(b) The dominance after the Second World War of the 'New Criticism' encouraged intense examination of poems, and other works of literature, for internal structure.

(c) In the same period, a thoroughgoing distributional perspective became familiar to American linguists, and approaches to the formal study of discourse emerged.

By 1960, then, the time of publication of Jakobson's essay, it would not to some seem strange to consider as poetry lines that were not metrical, but were connected to each other externally. It would not seem strange to trace the distribution of a grammatical element, say, a particle, and to suspect its recurrence of having an organizing function.

These are suggestions. In any case, looking back, one can see that the notion of grammatical process, as 'composition in definite order' (Boas 1911: 27) could have been extended to the relations of phonetic groups such as 'lines' or 'verses' (intonation contours), or their syntactic equivalent. An example would be the 'Chinookan triplet' illustrated above, and the relations of succession that emerge in Native American narratives, understood as sequences of lines.

As said, one could imagine the notion of grammatical categories, as ideas expressed by processes, extended to recurrent constituents of narratives. A number of them have been noticed by those writing about 'style' (e.g., Jacobs 1972), as kinds of content, but not always as significant for organization. Change of location, change of time, change of participant, for example, are regularly indications of change at a formal level, such as change of scene.

No Boasian, so far as I know, analysed a narrative throughout as a sequence of such units, from introduction through scenes and turns at talk to, say, concluding pronouncement or remonstrance. Ends and beginnings got attention, but not much of what came between.

It is particularly striking that turns at talk were not set out as units. Even Jacobs, who considered Clackamas narratives dramas, did not set the turns at talk of the characters separately. Perhaps there was unwillingness to adapt a mode of presentation from our culture (separation of turns in printed plays). Yet one needs to *see* such things in order to recognize and think about their relations to each other. Often enough ritual acts were obscured by failure to set them out as such, and by failure to translate the same words the same way. Identity of words is often an essential part of larger organization (e.g., initial particles).

I cannot avoid the thought that most of all an inherited sense of what poetry must be, as against prose, persisted, even though people might not have the same sense. Poetry had quotable lines, prose had sensible paragraphs. If this is true, then it is a deep irony indeed.

In any case, we do have what has been preserved, and because it was preserved, much of its internal form as narrative, and as grammar, can still be discovered. Transcending the irony requires that collections be redone. The original manuscripts and notebooks must be used if possible. (Cf. the discussion of changes introduced by Sapir into the printed text of Louis Simpson's 'The Deserted Boy' in Hymes 1981, chap. 4, and that and other points in Hymes 1994a; and the indications of intention in unpublished details of Boas's Kathlamet notebooks for two versions of 'Salmon's Myth' [Hymes 1985].)

New editions, concerned with presentation as well as preservation, are one way in which scholarship can fulfil the tradition's ideal of taking Native American languages as seriously as texts in European languages are taken.

Boas was of course right in putting first the need to preserve texts for the future, texts that the future would not be able to obtain. We are now able to recover and repatriate them, as it were, in more adequate form. Thanks to preservation, we can explore presentation, and help to realize a conception of the Americanist Tradition as governed by the demands of its materials (cf. Hymes 1976). In the long term we are able to adapt Boas's well-known statement about the grammars of the languages (1911: 81): 'the psychological groupings which are given depend entirely upon the inner form of each ...,' substituting 'narrative' for 'language' at the end. We can do work of which it can be said that the narrative 'has been treated as though an intelligent Indian was going to develop the forms of his own thoughts by an analysis of his own form of speech' (ibid.).

NOTES

1 I am grateful to Bruce Mannheim for calling my attention to Reichard's work.

2 These pages are cited with regard to Boas above. The example for 'Rhythmic Repetition of Contents and Form is Found Commonly in Primitive Narrative' has to do with repetition of incidents five times in Chinook tales. Relations of form within incidents or throughout a narrative are not mentioned.

3 For ease of printing, I adopt the conventions followed in Hymes (1981) of using C for alveolar affricate, G for velar g, L for voiceless lateral fricative, S for shibilant, and X for velar x.

4 Boas indeed analysed the elements in the Chinook verb in terms of categories expressed and their order relative to each other, recognizing nouns as what would today be called adjuncts to the person-markers in the verb that mark relations of transitive subject, transitive object / intransive subject, and indirect object, in successive positions. The first person singular n- could occur in any of the three positions, but not in the same word. A person acting on himself or herself would be indicated by an occurrence of the marker followed by a reflexive element. But all three positions may occur in one word.

5 Cultee's Kathlamet 'Swan's Myth,' the example from Boas noted by Stocking, also exemplifies nicely the dual aspect of ethnopoetic form, grounding in a recurrent kind of relation, on the one hand, here three and five, and on the other hand, change of actual rhythms from part to part.

I hope to include the myth in a book on the dialectic of relations between genders in the treatment of Salmon in Chinookan myths. Cultee's 'Swan's Myth' is an inversion of his development of 'Salmon's Myth' (Hymes 1985). In the first a woman guarantees winter food from the river, while banishing from the river creatures who have mocked her (swans). In the second a man guarantees winter food from the river (flounder), while banishing those who have mocked him (Bluejay, Crow).

REFERENCES

Berman, Judith. 1991. *The Seal's Sleeping Cave. The Interpretation of Boas's Kwak'wala Texts.* Ph.D. dissertation, University of Pennsylvania, Department of Anthropology.

Bernstein, Michael André. 1994. *Foregone Conclusions. Against Apocalyptic History.* Berkeley & Los Angeles: University of California Press.

Boas, Franz. 1887a. 'Poetry and Music of Some North American Tribes.' *Science* 9: 383–5.

– 1887b. 'A Year among the Eskimo.' *Bulletin of the American Geographical Society* 19: 383–402. (In Stocking 1974a: 45–55).

– 1901. *Kathlamet Texts.* Bureau of American Ethnology, Bulletin 26. Washington: Government Printing Office. (The introduction, the English translation of 'Myth of the Swan,' the first printed page of the interlinear text, and the first page of the field notebook on which the text begins, are reproduced in Stocking 1974a: 116–22.)

– 1905. Letter to W.H. Holmes of 24 July. In Stocking 1974a: 122–3, with the heading 'The Documentary Function of the Text.'

– 1911. Introduction to *Handbook of American Indian Languages* (Bureau of American Ethnology, Bulletin 40, Part 1). Washington, DC: Government Printing Office.

– 1914. 'Mythology and Folk-Tales of the North American Indians.' *Journal of American Folk-Lore* 27: 374–410. (RLC 451–90).

– 1917. Introduction to *International Journal of American Linguistics* 1: 1–8. (RLC 199–210).

– 1925. 'Stylistic Aspects of Primitive Literature.' *Journal of American Folk-Lore* 38: 329–39. (RLC 491–502).

– 1927. *Primitive Art.* Oslo: Instituttet for Sammenlignende Kulturforskning, H. Aschehoug.

– 1940. *Race, Language and Culture.* New York: Macmillan Co. [RLC].

Fletcher, Alice. 1901. 'The Hako: A Pawnee Ceremony.' Bureau of American Ethnology, Annual Report 22, 282–368. Washington: Government Printing Office.

Gill, Sam D. 1981. *Sacred Words. A Study of Navajo Religion and Prayer.* Westport, CT: Greenwood Press.

Greenberg, Joseph. 1954. 'A Quantitative Approach to the Morphological Typology of Language.' In R. Spencer, ed., *Methods and Perspectives in Anthropology*, 192–220. Minneapolis: University of Minnesota Press.

– 1963. 'Some Universals of Grammar with Particular Reference to the Order of Meaningful Elements.' In J. Greenberg, ed., *Universals of Language*, 58–90. Cambridge, MA: MIT Press.

– 1978. *Universals of Human Language. Vol. 1: Method and Theory.* Stanford: Stanford University Press.

Hymes, Dell, ed. 1974. *Studies in the History of Linguistics: Traditions and Paradigms.* Bloomington: Indiana University Press.

– 1976. 'The Americanist Tradition in Linguistics.' In Wallace L. Chafe, ed., *American Indian Languages and American Indian Linguistics (The Second Golden Anniversary Symposium of the Linguistic Society of America)*, 11–33. Lisse: Peter de Ridder Press. [EHLA 115–35 (with additional references)].
– 1981. *'In vain I tried to tell you.'* Philadelphia: University of Pennsylvania Press.
– 1983. [1976] *Essays on the History of Linguistic Anthropology*. Amsterdam and Philadelphia: John Benjamins. [EHLA].
– 1985. 'Language, Memory, and Selective Performance: Cultee's 'Salmon's Myth' as Twice Told to Boas.' *Journal of American Folk-Lore* 98: 391–434.
– 1991. 'Is Poetics Original and Functional?' *Language & Communication* 11(1/2): 49–51. (Issue of peer commentary on F.J. Newmeyer, 'Functional Explanation in Linguistics and the Origins of Language' [3–28]).
– 1992. 'Use All There Is to Use.' In Brian Swann, ed., *On the Translation of Native American Literatures*, 83–124. Washington: Smithsonian Institution.
– 1994a. 'Ethnopoetics, Oral Formulaic Theory, and Editing Texts.' *Oral Tradition* 9(2): 330–70.
– 1994b. Verse Translation with Preface for 'Sun's Myth' in Brian Swann, ed., *Coming to Light: Contemporary Translations of Native American Literatures of North America*, 273–85. New York: Random House & Vintage Press. [Copyright 1994, released early 1995].
– 1996. *Ethnography, Linguistics, Narrative Inequality*. London: Falmer Press.
Hymes, Dell, and John Fought. 1975. 'American Structuralism.' In T.A. Sebeok et al., eds, *Historiography of Linguistics* (Current trends in linguistics, vol. 13), 903–1176. The Hague: Mouton. (Reprinted, augmented, as separate volume, 1981).
Jonaitis, Aldona, ed. 1995. *A Wealth of Thought. Franz Boas on Native American Art*. Seattle: University of Washington Press.
Jacobs, Melville. 1959. *Content and Style of an Oral Literature*. Chicago: University of Chicago Press.
– 1960. *The People Are Coming Soon*. Seattle: University of Washington Press.
– 1972. 'Areal Spread of Indian Oral Genre Features in the Northwest States.' *Journal of the Folklore Institute*. 9(1): 10–17.
Jakobson, Roman. 1960. 'Closing Statement: Linguistics and Poetics.' In Thomas A. Sebeok, ed., *Style in Language*, 350–77. Cambridge: The Technology Press.
Krupat, Arnold. 1988. 'Anthropology In the Ironic Mode: The Work of Franz Boas.' *Social Text* 19/20: 105–18. Later versions in Marc Manganaro, ed., *Modernist Anthropology: From Fieldwork to Text* (Princeton: Princeton University Press, 1990), and A. Krupat, *Ethnocriticism: Ethnography, History, Literature* (Berkeley and Los Angeles: University of California Press, 1992), 81–100.
Musil, Robert. 1995. *The Man Without Qualities*. Translated by Sophie Wilkins and Burton Pike. 2 vols. New York: Knopf. [Cf. *The Man Without Qualities*, trans. Eithne Wilkins and Ernst Kaiser. 3 vols. London: Secker & Warburg, 1966; *Der Mann ohne Eigenschaften*, ed. Adolf Frisé. Reinbek bei Hamburg: Rowohlt, 1978. The unfinished work was first published in three volumes in 1930, 1933, and 1943. Cf. Bernstein 1994: 164n22].
Reichard, Gladys. 1922. 'The Complexity of Rhythm in Decorative Art.' *American Anthropologist* 24: 183–207.
– 1930. 'The Style of Coeur d'Alêne Mythology.' *International Congress of Americanists* (Hamburg) 24: 243–53.
– 1944. *Prayer: The Compulsive Word*. (Monographs of the American Ethnological Society 7). New York: J.J. Augustin.

– 1947. *An Analysis of Coeur d'Alêne Indian Myths.* (Memoirs American Folklore Society 41). Philadelphia AFS.

– 1990 [1974, 1950]. *Navaho Religion. A Study in Symbolism.* (Bollingen Series 18). Princeton, NJ: Princeton University Press.

Russo, Joseph. 1994. 'Homer's Style: Non-formulaic Features of an Oral Aesthetic.' *Oral Tradition* 9(2): 371–89.

Stocking, George W., Jr. 1962. 'Matthew Arnold, E.B. Tylor, and the Uses of Invention, with an Appendix on Evolutionary Ethnology and the Growth of Cultural Relativism, 1871–1915: From Culture to Cultures.' Prepared for 'Conference on the History of Anthropology,' New York, Social Science Research Council, 12–14 April. [Cf. Stocking 1968: 69–90].

– 1968. *Race, Culture and Evolution: Essays in the History of Anthropology.* New York: Free Press.

– ed. 1974a. *The Shaping of American Anthropology, 1883–1911. A Franz Boas Reader.* New York: Basic Books.

– 1974b. 'The Basic Assumptions of Boasian Anthropology.' Prepared for the conference, 'The Nature and Function of Anthropological Traditions,' Wenner-Gren Foundation for Anthropological Research, New York, 17–21 April 1968. In Stocking 1974a: 1–20.

– 1974c. 'The Boas Plan for the Study of American Indian Languages.' Prepared for a conference on the history of linguistics at the Newberry Library, Chicago, 1968. In Hymes, ed., 1974: 454–83.

Urban, Greg. 1996. *Metaphysical Community. The Interplay of the Senses and the Intellect.* Austin: University of Texas Press.

7 Cultural Relativism in the Americanist Tradition: From Anthropological Method to Indigenous Emancipation

JOHN J. COVE

'Culture,' it seems, is in the twilight of its career, and anthropology with it.

Marshall Sahlins, *How 'Natives' Think about Captain Cook*

It was only in the early 1980s that I began to think of myself as a cultural anthropologist. The transition was gradual and began when my French structuralist interests in mythology led me to the Tsimshian and thus Boas. He had been largely ignored in my sociological and social anthropological training and had no relevancy to my initial research in 'formalist' economic anthropology. I was therefore surprised to discover that Boas was a sophisticated methodologist who spoke to contemporary issues in anthropology, philosophy, religious studies, and sociology (Cove 1987: 13–41).

My study of Tsimshian mythology led me to do fieldwork among the Gitxsan at a time when their land claims were emerging, and I became involved in that process for a number of years. This applied research focus made me more appreciative of an ideological, historical, and relativistic view of culture. It facilitated a different kind of relationship with indigenous peoples than I had previously experienced.

As a consequence, I became more appreciative of the Americanist Tradition, and the concept that particularly captured my attention was cultural relativism. Borrowing Darnell's similes (this volume), my 'groundhog' interests in the history of the discipline increasingly suggested that this concept has been central to the shaping of both the ethnographic and theoretical enterprises. My 'foxy' side has led me to do research in Australia and New Zealand as well as Canada on a variety of subjects and I concur with Darnell (this volume) that the disciplinary impact of the Americanist Tradition has not been limited to that continent. Specific to cultural relativism, I would add that it is no longer a purely anthropological concept. As will be discussed, it has provided indigenous peoples in a number of countries with a basis for political action – a factor that has had global import for anthropology. As Bidney (1968: 543–7) argues, cultural relativism is a theory, method, basis of moral evaluation, and guide for action.

This paper explores those meanings and changes in them. Attention will be given to (1) the shift in emphasis from the methodological and theoretical aspects of cultural relativism to its evaluative and action-oriented dimensions, (2) the appropriation of cultural relativism by indigenes to serve their political ends, and (3) the practical and ethical implications raised by these changes for contemporary cultural anthropology.

Cultural Relativism as Theory and Method

The theoretical elements of cultural relativism have their roots in seventeenth- and eighteenth-century Western epistemological discourse. The emergence of culture within German idealism had a characteristic distinct from its British counterpart. The former reflected the assumptions that 'all reality *as known* is cultural reality, all human experience is culturally mediated' (Bidney 1968: 544). Relativism was built into this view of culture, one that was distinctly German in origin – serving as a means of countering the growing political, economic, and intellectual dominance of France and England (Sahlins 1995: 10–13).

From the outset, the German emphasis on cultural relativism was anti-universalistic and defined a particular trajectory for the development of the human sciences. In contrast to Anglo-French positivism, German cultural sciences were more phenomenological. This orientation confronted a problem best stated by the sociologist Max Weber (1949: 81–2): 'All knowledge of *cultural* reality ... is always knowledge from *particular points of view*' (emphases mine). For Weber, the human sciences provided one such point of view. It could not be the same as those of a culture's members because the purposes of scientific and non-scientific understandings differed.

Following Dilthey, Weber adopted *verstehen* as the methodological solution to this fundamental incompatibility, one allowing for a scientific engagement with cultural realities approximating those of culture members, that is, as meaningful. For Weber, actual meanings are, however, inappropriate for achieving scientific objectives since such meanings are individual and never fully conscious, shared, or accessible (Weber 1947: 91–5). From a Weberian perspective, specific cultures could only be adequately understood through hypothetical constructs, and the more important goal of creating general theory relied on even more abstract ones (for example, ideal types) that necessarily distorted actual cultures.

Working from the same intellectual tradition as Weber (Bunzl 1996), his contemporary Franz Boas took a somewhat different position. Boas held that an anthropologist could come to know a culture through first-hand experience with living peoples and how they understood their conditions of existence (Boas 1901: 2–3; Stocking 1968: 114–15). At the same time, he was careful to point out that indigenous understandings did not 'represent a systematic description of the ethnology of a people, but had the merit of bringing out those points which are of interest to the people themselves' (Boas 1916: 393).

It is worth noting that Boas was committed to a 'natural history approach' (Smith 1959: 46) involving the detailed examination of all facets of native ways of life. Ideational data had special import, but were not exhaustive of disciplinary interests. At the same time, those data constituted the core of any culture (Stocking 1968: 225), representing the 'uniqueness and genius' of a people that was central to Boas's vision of cultural anthropology.

Boas couched his view of cultural relativism in terms of research concerns: 'As long as we do not overstep the limits of one culture we are able to classify its features in clear and definite terminology ... If it is our serious purpose to understand the thoughts of a people the whole analysis must be based on their concepts, not ours' (Boas 1943: 314).

Boasian cultural relativism more generally meant understanding a culture in its own terms – one form of which was native informants' concepts and interpretations. Boas excluded 'esoteric' knowledge because it was culturally unrepresentative, and he recognized the importance of unconscious motives, feelings, and desires that only an anthropologist could uncover (1902; 1911: 63). Although Boas saw total reliance on informants as problematic, existing scientific theories were more so.

Boas asserted the 'relative autonomy' of cultures to avoid distortions inherent in applying a priori theoretical approaches like evolution (Lesser 1981: 6). Two qualifications should be remembered. Boas's concerns with general theory were neither exclusive to an ideological view of culture (Bidney 1968: 544; Mulvaney 1959: 52–4) nor were they anti-theoretical; he took an inductive rather than deductive stance to theory construction. Consistent with the aforementioned notion of *verstehen* as the most appropriate form of understanding for the cultural sciences, Boas held that mythology could be engaged directly by anthropologists independent of how myths were interpreted by native informants. He saw mythology as a means used by many cultures to transmit their history and accrued knowledge to future generations – what had collectively been deemed to be important, thoughts and feelings about those matters, and frames of reference for meeting the changing exigencies of existence. Given the transformations of non-Western cultures caused by European contact, mythology was especially relevant to Boas since it constituted a key means of reconstructing so-called traditional cultures (Cove 1987: 13–18). So too could mythologies from different cultures be compared in order to determine the origin, diffusion, and transformation of ideas – questions important to anthropology, but unlikely to be systematically considered by indigenous peoples. Myths as a source of data also served the discipline in a different sense: 'in this way a picture of their way of thinking and feeling will appear that renders their ideas as free from the bias of the European observer as is possible' (Boas 1935: v).

In an earlier quotation, Boas used 'if' to qualify what might be meant by the anthropological objective of understanding other cultures. He recognized that ethnography was only one component of cultural anthropology, and that cultures could be described without necessarily giving primacy to indigenous understandings. Some of his North American colleagues were seemingly less eclectic. For example, Sapir stated that '*the native's categorization of behaviour is the only correct one*' (Pelto and Pelto 1978: 55–6).

Boas's 'if' anticipated a methodological debate that began to crystallize within the Americanist Tradition during the 1960s. Borrowing from linguistics, Harris (1964) discussed this controversy in terms of the emic/etic distinction. Among the myriad meanings that have subsequently been given to these concepts was the definition of emics as subjective knowledge of the cultural insider as opposed to etics as the objective knowledge of the anthropological outsider (Headland et al. 1990). At issue were the epistemological basis of cultural anthropology and its objectives. Although Boas's cultural relativism was not entirely closed to etic approaches, among Americanists it was typically associated with emic arguments. In turn, the Boasians were subject to serious etic criticisms, namely that emics had (1) made minimal contributions to the development of anthropological theory, (2) tended to result in idealized conceptions of culture, and (3) provided an inadequate basis for solving the social, economic, and political problems faced by cultural Others (Harris 1990: 50–1; Pelto and Pelto 1978: 54). As will be seen next, it is this last point that would become central to the contemporary importance of emics and cultural relativism.

Cultural Relativism as a Basis for Evaluation and Action

Park (1988) asserts that the founders of sociology and anthropology saw those disciplines as emancipatory. Knowledge for its own sake, however, was deemed a self-evident good; with applied research having lower status because it was not disinterested and hence lacked objectivity (Poovey 1993).

Before the Second World War, applied anthropology was done almost exclusively for colonial/state governments. Australia provides an interesting illustration of this connection. A university program in applied anthropology was established in 1926. Less than a decade later, its chairperson made the following comments: (1) government needed anthropologists to more effectively apply its assimilation policies, (2) anthropologists were committed as 'good members of a higher and trustee race' to that goal, and (3) the discipline was being erroneously stigmatized as wanting to preserve Aboriginal cultures as objects of study (Elkin 1934). The last point suggests that anthropology had its own interests that were not always identical to those of the state or concerned with the welfare of indigenous peoples.

Within the Americanist Tradition, applied anthropology had little professional recognition until the Second World War, when understanding of cultural Others took on military and political significance (Ferraro et al. 1994: 41–2). Applied research declined with the end of hostilities, and the gap between basic and applied anthropology increased with expanding opportunities in the academic market place and 'disenchantment' with government service created by the McCarthy era (ibid.: 42–3).

At the same time, academic research that did not address socially relevant issues came to be increasingly questioned – ethnography being an exemplar. This change in emphasis articulated with what Darnell (this volume) calls the 'person-focused' Americanist sense of field research. It could no longer ignore the plight of indigenous peoples and recognition that assimilationist efforts had not only failed but were a source of those problems. Whereas Elkin continued to speak *for* Aborigines in Australia after the Second World War, and attempted to deny them a direct political voice, Tax in a distinctly Americanist sense asserted the need for 'action anthropology' that spoke both *to* and *with* indigenous peoples (Rubenstein 1986).

Action anthropology was overtly emancipatory, a deliberate form of 'participant interference' into relations with dominant institutions on the side of indigenous peoples (Tax 1958: 17–19). In order to make action research empowering, the classic observer/subject dichotomy was rejected in favour of a fusion between what would later be called emics and etics. Indigenous values, knowledge, and personnel were brought into partnership with their anthropological equivalents. Action anthropology also was defined as contributing to the development of theory, not merely applying it (Tax 1952).

Implicit in action anthropology were a number of ethical questions about the research enterprise. Before considering them, a broader contextualization is necessary. Anthropology was changing in other ways. The discipline no longer was taught just in elite universities, and professionals came from a broader range of class and ethnic backgrounds. These factors had contributed to the demise of cultural evolutionary theory (Harris 1968: 297) and to the post-1950s attacks on consensual assumptions in functionalism.

The above developments articulated with post-war changes in liberal democracy. In the emergent pluralistic model (Macpherson 1977), the state was an arena in which interest groups competed for recognition and scarce resources. Ethnic and racial cleavages took on greater prominence as sources of political identity and mobilization – a multicultural conception of society being one of the long-term results that laid the basis for indigenous peoples to assert the legitimacy of their cultural distinctiveness and to use culture to achieve political ends.

The politics of culture had an impact on the anthropological study of indigenous peoples and their relations with the discipline. Cultural relativism became relevant to indigenous-rights movements, and emically oriented ethnographic research acquired a new significance. These changes are best illustrated in Australian and Canadian aboriginal land claims that began in the early 1970s. Ethnographers were brought into courts as expert witnesses for indigenous plaintiffs to scientifically validate culturally specific views of title and challenge the ethnocentrism of Western legal definitions.

It is the use of cultural relativism to serve indigenous political ends that is important. The value of this concept to aborigines derives from its centrality to anthropology as *the* Western scientific discipline specializing in cultural Others. While anthropology provided scientific legitimacy for cultural relativism, the politics of culture emphasized emic views of it. As a consequence, with etics put on the defensive, the previously discussed inadequacies of emics to solve practical problems and contribute to the development of theory lost credibility.

This reversal had particular significance for global anthropology. The original emic-etic debate was almost exclusively Americanist; pre-1970s British and French social anthropology were solidly etic in orientation. Aboriginal political objectives, however, defined a different type of relationship to the discipline. As one Australian Aborigine stated in the early 1970s: 'We'll hire our own anthropologist and one on whom we can rely to prepare a report favourable to ourselves ... [W]e'll tell you [anthropologists] only as much as we think might be necessary to support our claims' (English 1975: 258).

Not only did Aboriginal communities form a new clientele for applied anthropology, they increasingly determined whether or not field research could even be done. Knowledge for its own sake was not necessarily deemed a self-evident good. Using a personal example, in British Columbia, the Gitxsan-Witsuwit'en Tribal Council initially refused me permission to research their myths, a ban that was only lifted when it became evident that these traditions were central to the land claim. Further, I was bound by a contract in which the Tribal Council not only owned the data but could veto publications drawing on those findings.

While applied research may have use-value for Native groups achieving political goals, it also has been problematic by virtue of a building in of dependency (Garneau 1988). A number of solutions have been tried in which anthropologists speak *with* rather than *for* aboriginal clients. In the most recent landmark Canadian court case, *Delgamuukw v. the Crown*, anthropological expert witnesses acted as 'cultural translators whose job it was to assist the court to understand the view of the plaintiffs' (Mills 1994: 11). This form of advocacy seemed to be shared within the discipline; no anthropologists – even those working for provincial and federal agencies – were willing to testify for the Crown. One of the anthropological expert witnesses in this trial presented emic cultural relativism as a professional ethical commitment (British Columbia 1991: 50).

Before considering the linkage between emics and ethics, the global nature of the dependency dilemma will be further explored using New Zealand as an illustration – one highlighting the importance of the Americanist Tradition. Webster (1995: 385) argues that since the 1970s, British social anthropology has adopted an Americanist view of culture because of its political saliency in all post-colonial situations. Like their counterparts elsewhere, however, Maori have raised the issue of cultural appropriation by anthropologists and 'effectively discouraged anthropological research on contemporary Maori society' (ibid.: 389).

While there has been a marked decline in anthropological fieldwork on Maori, other arrangements have occurred. The most successful has been for anthropologists to be 'ghostwriters,' that is, to assist Maori in framing their understandings in effective ways when dealing with dominant Western institutions (Cleave 1992). The Centre for Maori Studies and Research at the University of Waikato (which also serves as the research arm of the Tainui tribe), has adopted this approach. Interestingly, the Centre drew directly on Americanist action anthropology to establish its relations to all researchers irrespective of discipline.

Such an accommodation has not entirely overcome the aforementioned dependency problem or insured a continuing role for anthropology (Cove 1994). During the 1970s, Maori studies in universities became a focus of political action. More was at stake than establishing such programs; at issue was how they would be defined and explored. Assertions that only Maori perspectives were appropriate required them to distinguish these perspectives from anthropology to avoid their field being appropriated (Mead 1983: 335; Webster 1992:

41). At the same time, the Americanist emphasis on cultural relativism and emics provided a source of legitimacy that Maori academics employed. Maori religious beliefs, however, also made it possible to deny non-Maori access (Manihera et al. 1975: 11–20).

By the mid-1980s, Maori claimed to have their own science and were successful in gaining government recognition of it (Cove 1994: 12–18). Not incidentally, the etic and universalistic orientations of Western sciences were attacked on relativist epistemological grounds. So too did Maori science claimants reject any view that their scientific knowledge was valid only for their own Maori culture – Maori science was not just ethnographic. It was asserted to be theoretical and more comprehensive than its Western counterpart in so far as the former included a spiritual dimension, denied the validity of human/non-human and nature/culture distinctions, and fully integrated basic and applied research.

In all of the above efforts, Maori had support from some New Zealand anthropologists, and, for reasons that may have included ideological commitments and fears of being labelled racist, none challenged Maori critiques of the discipline (Webster 1989: 46). What did occur were 'cultural wars' (Biolsi and Zimmerman 1997: 6) within New Zealand anthropology similar to those happening in the United States fuelled by ongoing Indian/non-Indian relations (ibid.).

Returning to the theme of anthropological ethics, what is striking is both the degree of attention paid to the topic and the notion that the discipline should empower cultural Others. To make sense of those emphases requires a return to the previous discussion of the pluralistic state. Fabian (1971: 230) has argued that ethics were previously less problematic, involving little more than 'conformity with the norms of the society which sponsors the scientific enterprise.'

The growing post-war recognition of competing interests, and associated tensions over value consensus, has made the above conformity impossible, including any idea of the research enterprise as appropriately 'disinterested' and self-evidentially having positive consequences for all parties. The need for a code of ethics governing anthropological research first occurred within the Americanist Tradition. Although originally specific to applied research (Ember and Ember 1990: 492), a little over two decades later, the American Anthropological Association established an ethical code for the entire discipline (1970: 46–8). Issues raised over the military use of anthropology by the U.S. government in Latin America and Southeast Asia in the 1960s contributed to the emergence of this code, as did ongoing discussions between anthropologists and American Indians (Biolsi and Zimmerman 1997: 4).

The AAA statement of ethical principles recognized a range of obligations and the possibilities for conflict among them, but gave priority to not harming the subjects of research. That obligation was framed individualistically and addressed concerns such as protecting the confidentiality of informants. As far as indigenous peoples are concerned, avoiding harm to individual subjects was not the same as benefiting them, and indigenous communities began to increasingly involve collective interests – some of which have been antithetical to those of anthropology. The controversy over ownership of skeletal remains and artefacts is one expression. So too is the matter of historical and cultural interpretation involving the discipline speaking about Others (Cove 1995: 101–95). As we have seen in the New Zealand example, cultural relativism can put the discipline into the ambiguous situation of denying itself. The current equation of ethics with the advocating of aboriginal interests – either speaking along with indigenous voices or affirming their validity – can be seen as a form of adaptation. It is firmly tied to emancipatory knowledge and cultural politics. A New Zealand anthropologist has put it best: 'Anthropologists' primary responsibility is to the powerless who may be harmed by anthropological research, not only just to prevent harm but also with a view of empowering those people where possible' (Goldsmith 1987).

Practical and Ethical Implications

Geertz (1968) has talked about the discipline operating in an 'altered moral climate.' Cultural relativism not only survived that alteration, but has been revitalized by it. As Sahlins (1995: 13) notes, parallels exist between the historic situation of Germany and that of contemporary indigenous peoples. Both have had to deal with external dominance, one form being intellectual, and they have done so using a relativistic and ideological conception of culture.

In a similar vein, cultural relativism is one of the few modernist concepts to have flourished in the postmodernist era. Seidman (1994: 5) refers to the shifts between modernism and postmodernism as 'from metanarratives to local narratives, and from general theories to pragmatic strategies.' Each of these so-called shifts have been part of the Americanist anthropological discourse long before the advent of postmodernism. Attention to 'local narratives' has been a central feature since Boas, as have concerns with universalistic theories. The phenomenological and humanistic orientations of the Americanist Tradition have been critical of at least positivist 'metanarratives,' but without rejecting the possibility of a cultural science.

To refer back to two points raised earlier, Boas's emphasis on the 'uniqueness and genius' of a people and Darnell's observation about the 'person-focused' nature of Americanist research have contributed to anthropology so far managing to avoid a major postmodernist dilemma: being for cultural Others 'an empty alterity, providing a standpoint of critique of Western logocentrism, but one vacant of specificity' (Poster 1992: 577–8).

Not to be ignored is that postmodernism has agendas that can be at odds with 'pragmatic strategies.' Hanson (1989) was subject to a series of attacks from his colleagues – including charges of ethical misconduct – for using Maori as a case to illustrate that cultures are invented. Those critics held that his analysis undermined the authenticity of contemporary Maori culture and their efforts at empowerment. Hanson's (1991) reply was that this consequence was unintentional and only derivable from a misreading of his thesis, which stemmed from postmodernist conceptions of culture. Not discussed by either Hanson or his adversaries was the postmodernist position that defines ethical decision making about research as impossible by virtue of its tendency to relativize all political interests (Slack and Whitt 1992).

The Hanson example brings us back to the ambiguities about what constitutes ethical research. Anthropologists are not alone in either affirming that research has an ethical dimension or equating it with an exclusive type of advocacy. The interdisciplinary field of cultural studies defines itself as ethical by virtue of supporting those who are 'subjugated, silenced, repressed, oppressed, and discriminated against' (Slack and Whitt 1992: 573).

Herskovits (1973: 37) once said that cultural relativism is a 'tough-minded philosophy,' which Barrett (1984: 8) concluded had only one minor flaw – the tendency to 'idealize' cultures – which was less important than the alternative of ethnocentrically 'misrepresenting them.' My experience has been that indigenous political voices typically do present highly idealized representations of their cultures. Anthropologists have confronted inconsistencies concerning matters of fact with regard to such constructions (Keesing 1989: 18–19), and as any fieldworker knows, intercultural differences in interests and interpretation are part of social reality. As old-fashioned as it may be, a commitment to truth is sometimes at odds with that of empowering cultural Others, whoever they might *individually* be. To return to anthropologists as cultural translators in the *Delgamuukw* case, their emically oriented testimony was treated by the judge as biased (British Columbia 1991: 47–51). Although it is doubtful that a different form of anthropological testimony would have significantly changed the ultimate decision, no worse strategy could have occurred for the Native plaintiffs.

Since a number of Canadian and Australian courts have made a point of saying why they have rejected anthropological testimony, a rethinking of what is meant by effective advocacy is in order. The present intersection of indigenous and anthropological interests, emics being the vector, may be comfortable for both, but not necessarily empowering to either.

Western courts are ethnocentric (Asch 1992; Mills 1994; Ridington 1992), and appropriately should be challenged by anthropologists in these terms. At the same time, disciplinary refusal to consider the legal system as a culture with its own values, procedures, rules, and roles makes little practical or ethical sense. I would argue that anthropologists also are obligated to inform Native clients that an uncritical support of their constructs is unlikely to be effective.

Sahlins (1995: 14) has worried about anthropology's 'loss of control' over the concept of culture brought about by broader intellectual and political discourses, resulting in the discipline's demise, and he was not the first to predict that outcome (Hymes 1969). I would counter such concerns by referring to Sir Raymond Firth's statement (1981: 198) that anthropology has always been 'the uncomfortable discipline.' New uses of cultural relativism from outside the discipline have challenged anthropology to rethink and transform itself. At the same time, by virtue of the Americanist Tradition, anthropology is in a position to address the problems that currently surround the concept.

REFERENCES

American Anthropological Association. 1970. 'Principles of Professional Responsibility.' *AAA Newsletter* 11(9): 46–8.

Asch, Michael. 1992. 'Errors in *Delgamuukw*: An Anthropological Perspective.' In F. Cassidy, ed., *Aboriginal Title in British Columbia: Delgamuukw v. the Queen.* Lantzville: Oolichan Press.

Barrett, Richard. 1984. *Culture and Conduct: An Excursion into Anthropology.* Belmont, WA: Wadsworth.

Bidney, David. 1968. 'Cultural Relativism.' In D. Sills, ed., *International Encyclopedia of Social Science.* New York: Macmillan.

Biolsi, Thomas, and Larry Zimmerman. 1997. 'Introduction: What's Changed, What Hasn't.' In T. Biolsi and L. Zimmerman, eds, *Indians & Anthropologists: Vine Deloria Jr. and the Critique of Anthropology.* Tucson: University of Arizona Press.

Boas, Franz. 1901. 'The Mind of Primitive Man.' *Journal of American Folklore* 14: 1–11.

– 1902. 'The Ethnological Significance of Esoteric Doctrines.' *Science* 16(43): 872–4.

– 1911. 'Introduction.' In Franz Boas, ed., *Handbook of American Indian Languages.* Washington: Government Printing Office.

– 1916. *Tsimshian Mythology.* Annual Report of the Bureau of American Ethnology, 1909–10. Washington: Government Printing Office.

– 1935. *Kwakiutl Culture as Reflected in Mythology.* New York: Columbia University Press.

– 1943. 'Recent Anthropology.' *Science* 98: 311–14, 334–7.

British Columbia. 1991. 'Reasons for Judgment of the Honourable Chief Justice Allan McEachern in *Delgamuukw v the Queen.*' Smithers Registry no. 0843.

Bunzl, Matti. 1996. 'Franz Boas and the Humboltian Tradition: From Volkgeist and Nationalcharackter to an Anthropological Concept of Culture.' In G.W. Stocking, ed., *Volkgeist as Method and Ethic: Essays on Boasian Ethnography and the German Anthropological Tradition.* Madison: University of Wisconsin Press

Cleave, Peter. 1992. 'Mountain Claiming: The Anthropologist as Ghostwriter.' In M. Goldsmith and K. Barber, eds, *Other Sites: Social Anthropology and the Politics of Interpretation*. Palmerston North: Massey University.

Cove, John. 1987. *Shattered Images: Dialogues and Meditations on Tsimshian Narratives*. Ottawa: Carleton University Press.

– 1994. 'The Indigenisation of Science by New Zealand Maori.' Paper presented at the Canadian Anthropology Association meetings, Vancouver.

– 1995. *What the Bones Say: Tasmanian Aborigines, Science and Domination*. Ottawa: Carleton University Press.

Ember, Carol, and Marvin Ember. 1990. *Anthropology*. Englewood Cliffs, NJ: Prentice-Hall.

English, Peter. 1975. *Land Rights, Birth Rights: The Great Australian Hoax*. Bullsbrook: Veritas Publishing Co.

Fabian, Johannes. 1971. 'On Professional Ethics and Epistemological Foundations.' *Current Anthropology* 12(2): 230–1.

Ferraro, Gary, et al. 1994. *Anthropology: An Applied Perspective*. Minneapolis / St Paul: West Publishing.

Firth, Raymond. 1981. 'Engagement and Detachment: Reflections on Applying Social Anthropology to Social Affairs.' *Human Organization* 40(3): 194–202.

Gareau, Federick. 1988. 'Another Type of Third World Dependency: The Social Sciences.' *International Sociology* 3(2): 171–8.

Geertz, Clifford. 1968. 'Thinking as a Moral Act: Ethical Dimensions of Anthropological Fieldwork in the New States.' *Antioch Review* 28: 139–58.

Goldsmith, Michael. 1987. 'Power and Ethics in Social Anthropology, or Treating Anthropological Ethics and Anthropological Problems.' Discussion paper given at the NZASA Conference, Otago.

Hanson, Allan. 1989. 'The Making of the Maori: Culture Invention and Its Logic.' *American Anthropologist* 91(4): 890–902.

– 1991. 'Reply to Langdon, Levin, and Linnekin.' *American Anthropologist* 93(2): 449–50.

Harris, Marvin. 1964. *The Nature of Cultural Things*. New York: Random House.

– 1990. 'Emics and Etics Revisited.' In Thomas Headland et al., eds, *Emics and Etics: The Insider/Outsider Debate*. Newbury Park: Sage Publications.

Headland, Thomas, et al. 1990. *Emics and Etics: The Insider/Outsider Debate*. Newbury Park: Sage Publications.

Herskovits, Melville. 1973. *Cultural Relativism*. Ed. Frances Herskovits. New York: Vintage Books.

Hymes, Dell. 1969. *Reinventing Anthropology*. New York: Pantheon.

Keesing, Roger, 1989. 'Creating the Past: Custom and Identity in the Contemporary Pacific.' *Contemporary Pacific* 1: 19–42.

Lesser, Alexander. 1981. 'Franz Boas.' In Sydel Silverman, ed., *Totems and Teachers: Perspectives on the History of Anthropology*. New York: Columbia University Press.

Macpherson, C.B. 1977. *The Life and Times of Liberal Democracy*. New York: Oxford University Press.

Manihera, Te Uira, et al. 1975. 'Forward: Learning and Tapu.' In M. King, ed., *Te ao Hurihuri*. Birkenhead: Reed Books.

Mead, S.M. 1983. 'Te Toi Matauranga Maori Mo Nga Ra Kei Mau: Maori Studies Tomorrow.' *Journal of the Polynesian Society* 92: 333–51.

Mills, Antonia. 1994. *Eagle Down Is Our Law: Witsuwit'en Law, Feasts, and Land Claims*. Vancouver: UBC Press.

Mulvaney, D.J. 1959. 'The Australian Aborigines 1606–1929: Opinion and Fieldwork.' *Historical Studies Australia and New Zealand* 8: 1–56.

Park, Peter. 1988. 'Towards an Emancipatory Sociology: Abandoning Universalism for True Indigenisation.' *International Sociology* 3(2): 161–9.
Pelto, Pertti, and Gretel Pelto. 1978. *Anthropological Research: The Structure of Inquiry*. Cambridge: Cambridge University Press.
Poovey, Mary. 1993. 'Figures in Arithmetic, Figures of Speech: The Discourse of Statistics in the 1830s.' *Critical Inquiry* 19(2): 256–76.
Poster, Mark. 1992. 'Postmodernity and the Politics of Multiculturalism: The Lyotard-Habermas Debate over Social Theory.' *Modern Fiction Studies* 38(3): 567–80.
Ridington, Robin. 1992. 'Fieldwork in Courtroom 53: A Witness to *Delgamuukw*.' In F. Cassidy, ed., *Aboriginal Title in British Columbia: Delgamuukw v. the Queen*. Lantzville: Oolichan Press.
Rubenstein, Robert. 1986. 'Reflections on Action Anthropology: Some Developmental Dynamics of an Anthropological Tradition.' *Human Organization* 45(3): 270–8.
Sahlins, Marshall. 1995. *How 'Natives' Think about Captain Cook, for Example*. Chicago: University of Chicago Press.
Seidman, Steven. 1994. 'Introduction.' In S. Seidman, ed., *The Postmodern Turn*. Cambridge: Cambridge University Press.
Slack, Jennifer, and Laurie Whitt. 1992. 'Ethics in Cultural Studies.' In L. Grossberg et al., eds, *Cultural Studies*. London: Routledge.
Smith, Marian. 1959. 'Boas' "Natural History" Approach to Field Method.' In W. Goldschmidt, ed., *The Anthropology of Franz Boas*. Washington: American Anthropological Association Memoir 89, 61(5/2).
Stocking, George. 1968. *Race, Culture and Language*. New York: Free Press.
Tax, Sol. 1952. 'Action Anthropology.' *American Indigenia* 12: 103–9.
– 1958. 'The Fox Project.' *Human Organization* 17: 17–19.
Weber, Max. 1947. *The Theory of Social and Economic Action*. New York: Free Press.
– 1949. *The Methodology of the Social Sciences*. New York: Free Press.
Webster, Steven. 1989. 'Maori Studies and the Expert Definition of Maori Culture: A Critical History.' *Sites* 18: 35–6.
– 1992. 'Theories of Maoritanga in the 1920s.' In M. Goldsmith and K. Barber, eds, *Other Sites: Social Anthropology and the Politics of Interpretation*. Palmerston North: Massey University.
– 1995. 'Escaping Post-Cultural Tribes.' *Critique of Anthropology* 15(4): 381–413.

8 Authenticity and *Aggiornamento* in Spoken Texts and Their Critical Edition

H.C. WOLFART

As we slide and stumble towards the millennium, awash in cyberbabble and hubris yet as fearful (with civil society threatening to collapse around us) as the scribes and sages of the previous cycle, the place of texts in the Americanist Tradition seems an arcane question, properly part of a glass-bead game.

The very notion of a critical edition appears to have become a quaint anachronism at a moment when (subject mainly to fiscal limitations) we could presumably put the performance of a text on a multimedia CD-ROM, with the original soundtrack matched by a printed presentation emerging from the speaker's mouth in a continuously stretching and contracting bubble (depending on the length of successive words, for example) and in a typeface expressing, say, some scale of mood, with pitch and volume reflected by orientation and point size.

On the recording side, too, the kitchen table which defined my field recordings has given way to conference rooms (e.g., Whitecalf 1993) and even sound studios (e.g., Vandall and Douquette 1987) as normal and accepted sites for the telling of myths or histories.

As the means of (re-)production have changed, and the physical and social setting along with them, we should not be surprised at changes in the texts themselves, both in content and form.

The most striking aspect of the 'new' texts that Freda Ahenakew and I have begun to publish over the last few years[1] is, of course, the identity of the narrators. Practically for the first time in the study of Cree literature and ethnography, these are women speaking, telling us about life as it is lived by women.

Rather than belabour individual subject areas or explore the question of the female perspective in Cree narration (cf. Wolfart 1989, 1992, 1997), this essay concentrates on the form of these texts, which is quite different from that of the myth texts of Bloomfield's *Sacred Stories of the Sweet Grass Cree* (1930) or the equally formal accounts of historical incidents in his *Plains Cree Texts* (1934). Many of the texts collected by Freda Ahenakew are either public speeches addressed to various councils and conferences, or rather more intimate discussions held at small workshops – and also back in the kitchen, with dialogue amongst two or more Cree speakers gaining its rightful place beside declamatory prose.

Authority

Even under fundamentally new conditions, it seems self-evident that the seat of authenticity is to be sought in the text itself. Although the context of its production is, in principle, an important attribute of the text, it has traditionally been ignored as being ultimately inaccessible. The ethnography of communication remains in its infancy where non-Western societies are concerned, and the effect upon their audience of traditional Cree storytellers remains obscure despite the efforts of Darnell (1974), Valentine (1995), and others.

With the exception only of the last few centuries (and despite the fashionable interest in *Rezeptionsgeschichte* or 'reader-response theory'), the same is true for much of Western literature as well. We know very little, for example, about what the Athenian audiences of the golden age thought of the Theban plays of Sophocles. The plots were known to all, and for the prototypical tragedy, *Oedipus Tyrannos*, it has recently been argued (e.g., Steiner 1985, drawing on the close textual study of Vellacott 1971) that the text itself suggests a much more ambiguous protagonist than the modern tradition would have us believe – and thus a tension between blissful ignorance and expedient half-suppression on which it would be tantalizing to know the reaction of the audience.

For any text, in short, our knowledge is inherently limited, despite all the hermeneutical games one might play. The fundamental issue is epistemological, a question of defining what we know and of stating the basis on which we claim knowledge; and the most painful instance is that of representation: what is authentic, in any ordinary sense of the term, about reducing a *viva voce* delivery with all its voice qualities, dramatic effects, and gestures, with its knowing and expectant audience, to cold print?

At the same time – with the high-art, cutting-edge options remaining beyond the reach of increasingly disestablished university scholars – a critical edition of a text is still the best approximation to which we can realistically aspire.

At the opposite extreme, some will settle for the plot alone, and some will go further and call it translation. In this domain, the range of variation is enormous, from an actual translation, whether literal or free, to the plot summaries that

Skinner and his contemporaries used to publish in the *Journal of American Folklore* – and a limitless gradation in between, including those printed on cream paper and in fancy typography. (This is also the context for the extraordinary phenomenon, first documented in Nichols 1989, of the latter-day literati who seem to crave authenticity and claim translation status for what is evidently a new creation.)

The aesthetic quality of the book, alas, is immaterial: a paraphrase, a redaction, a retelling, a rewrite, a version – they all amount to the same thing, eloquently rendered, once more in the realm of Athenian tragedy, by the plain declaration (Hadas 1950: 306, emphasis added) that 'the beautiful and widely read versions of Gilbert Murray, the reader must be warned, *are not Euripides*.'

But at least Gilbert Murray knew his Greek while, for the languages of North America, those who play with the translation without reference to the original text merely produce 're-expressions,' as an eminent Algonquianist (Nichols 1991: 114, emphasis added) put it gently but succinctly, which are 'often *called* new translations.'

This insistence on the original text should not be confused – despite the aspersions of the literary profiteers and their attempts to gloss over the truism that translation presupposes *two* languages – with antiquarianism. The value of a text in one of the indigenous languages of North America lies not in its antiquity nor, let it be stressed, in some fancied purity; nor, indeed, in the exotic, sort-of-oriental strangeness of such texts (what has fashionably been called *otherness* in recent years). All of these are red herrings. Texts demand our attention because they are distinct expressions of the human mind – simply because, like mountains, they are there.

The 'new' texts recorded by Freda Ahenakew reveal entire realms of experience that have rarely if ever been touched upon by an outsider, either because no stranger would be admitted or because the novice might not even know of their existence. But they also offer another kind of authenticity – encountered all too rarely in the history of Americanist scholarship – that manifests itself both in the performance and in the text.

There is a world of difference between an outsider arriving and promptly but awkwardly asking for stories, evidently innocent of both language and culture, and someone of Freda Ahenakew's status (with respect to membership in the group, family ties, social status, and age) expressing her interest.

The first situation is, of course, that in which I found myself a generation ago, as I began my fieldwork among the Plains Cree of central Alberta in 1967. I ended up being told, during my first few months and by at least some storytellers, extremely simple versions of, say, the trickster cycle – simple enough in language and content, the narrator must have thought, to match my infantile level of comprehension. (And even that judgment, in truth, amounted to flattery!)

As I became more established, the narrators' confidence in my abilities (and at least in my seriousness and the respect I continued to show) must have grown, for I was told increasingly complex texts. But only when I had finally made enough progress with the philological and comparative study of the texts that the same small group of storytellers had given me over a period of ten years did it become obvious, from the evidence of multiple recordings of the same historical text (cf. Wolfart 1982b), that it was not just a matter of simplification or truncation, but that the earlier versions had omitted precisely the key parts without which the text would have remained incomprehensible – that is, the parts dealing with supernatural matters that some stray outsider could not have been expected to understand or respect.

The texts that Freda Ahenakew has been recording over the past decade and a half show no such progression. They are told in settings where everyone speaks Cree.

The kind of authenticity we seek is a matter of demonstration (rather than persuasion) and inheres in the text (rather than in the mind of the critic).

The first kind of evidence is an explicit authorship attribution. Since Cree texts are proprietary – in the inimitable phrase of Bloomfield (1928: 23), 'the following story was his for having lived and told it' – it might be more appropriate to think of it as a title deed.

It is a characteristic sign of communal property that myths, which constitute a well-defined genre of Cree texts, do not normally include a statement of ownership. This is true even in the case of a modern and, in the technical sense, definitely literary product such as the aetiological account of how rubber overshoes came to be and have their name.

There are also grammatical means of marking the authenticity of individual statements, such as the dubitative paradigm and the various evidential particles, for instance, *êtokwê* 'apparently,' *êsa* 'reportedly,' etc. (cf. Whitecalf 1993: 84), but we will here concentrate on overt authorship attributions.

To the outside observer, the most striking expression of authority is the use of quotative *itwêw* in historical accounts told at a remove; for instance, in this paragraph from John Beaverbone's story as retold by Joseph Tootoosis (Ahenakew and Wolfart 1991: 8–9):

â, kêtahtawê, **itwêw**, *ê-ati-wâpaniyik*, **itwêw**, *kâ-wâwâstaminaw-~ kâ-wâwâstinamawât ôhi pêyak*, **itwêw**, *ê-nitomât*, **itwêw**; *kîkway ka-minihkwêsit ê-nitawêyihtahk*, **itwêw**, *sêmâk*, **itwêw**, *mîcimâpoy*, **itwêw**, *ê-mâh-minahiht*, **itwêw**; *êkwa ê-sêsâwiniht ôhi wiyawihk*, **itwêw**, *wâskikanihk*, **itwêw**.

Well, suddenly, **he said**, when dawn was approaching, **he said**, he waved at one of them, **he said**, beckoning him to come, **he said**; he wanted something to drink, **he said**, and right away, **he said**, he was given sips of soup, **he said**, to drink, **he said**; and then he had his limbs exercised, **he said**, on his body, on his chest, **he said**.

All such texts have the original narrator-*cum*-owner of the text explicitly acknowledged, but once that is done, the text may continue with the current performer simply slipping into that role. Alternatively, the text may be framed by an unceasing series of quotative verbs that are highly obtrusive to an English reader but seem to be almost unnoticeable, being spoken at a lower pitch and volume than the reported text, in oral performance. (Sustained examples are plentiful in almost all our text editions; only the typographical presentation varies, e.g., Vandall and Douquette 1987, chap. 5, 8, 9, 10; Ahenakew and Wolfart 1991; Bear et al. 1992, chap. 2; Whitecalf 1993, lecture 3, sect. 10; cf. also Ahenakew and Wolfart 1987: xiii–xiv, 1991: 12; Wolfart 1992: 362–3.)

Most traditional Cree narrators will explicitly state the genre of their text, and in the case of historical texts this is typically accompanied by the statement of attribution. Just as the genre can be specified either at the beginning or at the end of the text, and sometimes both first and last, so the authorship attribution may be given in either place or both.

In introducing a performer from her home reserve, about to relate an account of a snake overpowered by a thunderbird, Freda Ahenakew jumps the gun and tells us,

... ê-wî-ât-~ ê-wî-âcimot, wiy [?sic] ôhkomipana ê-kî-âcimostâkot âcimowin.
... he is going to tell a story, having been told the story by his late grandmother.

The genre definition, to which three of these four words are devoted, is repeated twice more by the narrator:

âha, tâpwê anima, ê-kî-âcimot nôhkom, êwak ôm ôtâcimowin ôma –
Yes, it is true that my grandmother had told this story, this is her story –

The genre is mentioned several more times in the conclusion, and it is also noteworthy that the original author is once again referred to as *nôhkomipan* 'my late grandmother,' rather than merely as *nôhkom* 'my grandmother':

êkos ôm ê-kî-itâcimostawit nôhkomipan, 'wâpasinîwiskwêw' kî-isiyîhkâsow nôhkom.

That is the story my late grandmother had told me, *wâpasinîwiskwêw* my grandmother had been called.

More important, his grandmother is further identified by her proper name, *wâpasinîwiskwêw*.

There is further confirmation of the truth value of the account, and it comes in two parts: at the very end of the text, there is an explicit protestation, echoing the exordial *tâpwê* 'truly':

â, êkota isko kâ-kî-âcimostawit êwako, namôy wiy êwako kakiyâskiwin, êwako.
Well, that is as far as she had told me this story, it is not a tall tale, this one.

In the context of storytelling, the stem *kiyâski-* VAI and its derivatives, which ordinarily mean 'to lie,' have the additional meaning 'to exaggerate, to tell tall tales,' and this is the interpretation that is here explicitly excluded.

There is, however, also a further, though less explicit, device to affirm the authenticity of the text. The two excerpts just cited in fact bracket the following, which to the outside observer may seem quite out of place:

mistahi kî-cakahki-nôcikwêsîwiw, kî-miyohtwâw, kî-kisêwâtisiw; êwakw âwa kâ-kî-âcimostawit ôma.
She had been a wonderful old lady, she had been good-natured and she had been kind; she had been the one who told me this story.

This is not, of course, merely a pious testimonial for a sweet old lady. Rather, it corroborates the truth of the account by establishing a definite and overt link between narrator and author.

This personal link is functionally equivalent to the physical link often invoked in historical texts in both Cree and Ojibwe (and probably in other traditions as well). The most striking case I can think of, which I regard as defining, is that cited by John Nichols (1982, 1996: 312,316) of the supernatural protection accorded an Ojibwe widow by her husband's bundle when her camp was massacred by the Sioux; in both the published versions of the text (Kegg 1990: 42–3 [cited below], 46–7), the evidentiary statement turns on the physical presence of the hatchet marks still visible on the trees:

«mii go geyaabi ezhi-wawijiishigiwaad ingiw mitigoog,» gii-ikido.
«The trees still have the scars on them,» she said.

In the case of our Cree story, there is yet a further layer of corroboration. When Freda Ahenakew and I were working on this text and came to the mention of the old lady's name, which singles her out from the large set of individuals who might be referred to as *nôhkom*, Freda Ahenakew immediately pointed out that she remembered her well – another overt, definite, and personal link. (The original author herself is cited as remarking that she was fifteen years old at the time when the treaties were concluded, and a birthdate around 1860 is compatible with Freda Ahenakew's recollection of having seen her as a very old woman, circa 1940.)

The most common form for a narrator to establish such a personal evidentiary link is the phrase

nikî-otisâpamâwak kisêyinîpanak, ... (PO33)
I have lived long enough to have seen the old men who are now dead, ...

but such a general statement is presumably weaker than the more detailed declaration cited earlier.

Like the multiple negatives of Homeric Greek, the confirmation cannot be too strong. In another text from Freda Ahenakew's home reserve, first told to her in 1989 and since recorded a second time, the narrator relates the horrible fate of a young man who was cursed by an old woman for taking away her granddaughter. Within a matter of weeks he had become insane, ultimately being driven to unman himself. The narrator, who was a young girl at the time, was present at the elopement and also sat in church one day, trembling with fear, when the crazed young man came in and sat down immediately behind her; taking a hymnal even though he could not read and holding it upside down, he sang a completely distorted version of a standard hymn, and both tellings of the text include a rendition of his song. But the crucial point, again in both versions, comes at the end, when the narrator introduces the child of this ill-fated union and declares:

êkosi, pêyak an[a] îhtakow, pâskac ê-okosisîhkâyân, ê-kî-tahkonak ê-sîkahahtâht, ...
And so this person exists, on top of which he is my god-child and I held him in baptism, ...

As if, in a story where the narrator was present at two key events, physical authentication were needed! But here it is, as Cree narrative culture demands.

Presentation

The 'hard sheen of authenticity' (as Carol Shields puts it in *The Stone Diaries*) is not tarnished by the countless foreign bodies that have intruded into the Plains Cree world.

It is hardly surprising, in view of the massive changes to which Plains Cree life has been subjected over the past century, that narratives about the golden age (whether it is thought to end with the treaties, the opening of the bars, or the advance of the evangelicals upon the High Church) are found side by side, especially in the reminiscences of women, with accounts of deprivation, of a marginal existence at the very edge of the wage-labour economy, of techniques of soap-making and tales of boarding-school life. These are analogous to the gradual infiltration of English loanwords that can be observed in various stages of integration, or to the emergence of calques, loan-translations that range from single roots or words to complex lexemes or idioms and, perhaps, entire syntactic constructions.

This is not the place to expand on the interplay between High Christianity and pre-colonial religion (cf. Wolfart 1992), but the evidence is ubiquitous in the texts, and it would take a brave etymologist to disentangle the Christian and pre-Christian skeins that jointly define the meaning of *pâstâhowin-* NI 'breach of the natural order, transgression; sin' (cf. Wolfart and Ahenakew 1991; Wolfart 1992; cf. also Ellis in Scott et al. 1995).

Nor need we be surprised that tales of the Arabian Nights or from the collections of the Brothers Grimm (cf. Wolfart 1990) have been incorporated into the virtual library of Cree literature, or to find aetiological stories that go beyond the stripes of the birch tree to deal with the bizarre shape (and the equally alien name) of rubber overshoes (Wolfart 1982a). Individual motifs, entire stories, and even particular words as the key element in a just-so story (such as the word *rubbers* spoken with equal stress on both syllables by a frog with a heavy Cree accent) may have begun their existence as foreign bodies, but they have gradually been integrated into the fabric of Cree literature along with the rest of the colonial experience.

It is a recurrent theme in Cree *âcimowina* that some momentous event was prophesied well in advance of its actual occurrence. In 1925 Bloomfield recorded a text where an old man had dreamt of the impending arrival of the Whites, which had duly happened; in 1982 Freda Ahenakew recorded a similar text (Vandall and Douquette 1987) about an old man who had predicted that one day the Whites would even leave the earth and learn to fly.

As authenticity depends above all on the form of the text, the integrity of the presentation is not merely a matter of taste.

Philologically, the problems that arise in the presentation of spoken texts in the languages of North America do not differ in any significant respect from those which have been debated for centuries à propos of manuscripts in Greek, Latin, and Hebrew.

The shape of a text edition is largely determined by the intellectual and fiscal context. Very few North American publishers have treated text editions in the indigenous languages with the care and respect that European institutions have lavished on the texts of Greece and Rome and all the other cultures of their world (or that which even North Americans are prepared to squander on the ephemera, comparatively speaking, of interpretation and literary criticism).

Text editions vary widely in scope, purpose, audience, and in the presentation of the text itself. The two collections of Plains Cree texts published by Bloomfield, for example, differ even in their physical arrangement; in the first the translation follows the text, in the second they are printed *en regard*.

In representing the spoken form of the language, Bloomfield used a phonemic orthography but preserved a great deal of surface variation, presumably on the grounds that many aspects of the phonological system were yet to be properly analysed. This is the pattern further elaborated in the current series of text editions being prepared at Manitoba (and discussed in some detail in Wolfart 1992), notably the texts of Bear et al. 1992.

It may seem ironic, therefore, that all the Cree volumes that have so far appeared in the Publications of the Algonquian Text Society deviate from this model on one side or the other. The Plains Cree texts of Vandall and Douquette (1987) and the La Ronge Lectures of Sarah Whitecalf (1993) are presented in a heavily standardized form, with all surface variation and the effects of both external sandhi and of the special sandhi operating at compound (and, especially, preverb) boundaries restored; in short, the orthography used in these texts is identical in all but the shape of the actual letters to the rules of syllabic orthography. With the omission of false starts, slips of the tongue, and corrections or asides (as well as editorial annotations), and with syntactic adjustments made as and where required, these are *reading versions*, meant to present themselves as smoothly as standard literary prose in English. (Let me hasten to add that the collected works of Sarah Whitecalf, currently in preparation, will include a critical edition in the narrower orthography of Bear et al. 1992.)

A third approach has been taken by C. Douglas Ellis in his massive volume of texts from the west coast of James Bay (Scott et al. 1995). With the printed transcript closely hugging the phonetic ground, Ellis has produced an edition that, in its profusion of diacritical marks, seems reminiscent of the Boasian volumes and their *Augenpulver*. Yet Ellis also gets closer than most of his contemporaries to the new world of multimedia presentation by including every last text both in print and on audiotape.

The higher levels of textual organization present thorny issues of their own, ranging from practical problems of paragraphing to questions that are, ultimately, ideological: for example, whether the ethnopoetic interpretation of a text might be incorporated into the *editio princeps* of a spoken text, or whether the fundamental function of a critical edition should be kept distinct and pristine.

The register of the translation offers a parallel case. In one recent project Freda Ahenakew and I had produced a translation that was intended to keep to the middle ground between literal and free but that, nonetheless, echoed the rather formal register of the Cree original. When we sent it to the narrator, we were surprised by the vituperative tone of her objections – recall Euripides and Gilbert Murray – that this was evidently someone else speaking. Once we had regained our composure, we realized that the point at issue was the discrepancy between the formality of the Cree used in narration – which we had endeavoured to render by formal English, very much in the tradition of Bloomfield's King Jamesian diction – and the informality of the speaker's own English vernacular.

Discrepancies in style or register are not, of course, limited to the English translation. A recently recorded text centres on an eye-witness account, related at second hand, of a group of Plains Cree returning from a foray south of the Missouri River who, at the *peripeteia* of the text, watch the struggle between a thunderbird and a snake, raging up and down before their eyes and ultimately resolved when the snake is overpowered and carried ever higher into the sky. It is a dramatic scene and of religious significance, and its force and power, it appears, is neither broken nor diminished by the yardstick used to confirm the diameter of the snake:

«wahwâ, koskwêyihtâkwan ê-isi-wâpahtamihk,» itwêw. «ôki nika-mân-âna-~-tipahâkân, nôsisim,» itwêw; («'mitâtaht-kosikwanak' kî-itâwak mâna, mitâtaht-kosikwan mâna pimiy, mâna – ~, wâpiski-pimiy ê-kî-asiwatêk,» itwêw), «êwakoyikohk nânitaw ê-ispihtâskosit awa kinêpik,» itwêw.

«Oh my, it was amazing to see,» she said. «I will use these [*sc.* pails] as a measure, my grandchild,» she said; («'ten-pounders' they used to be called, ten pounds of grease, of lard, used to be inside them,» she said), «about that big around was the snake,» she said.

To an outside observer, this reference to the mundane triviality of an industrial lard-pail, painted in red with a silver lid and the words *Burns Lard* imprinted upon it, might seem jarring – but that would be an error of interpretation, a puristic excess.

The lard-pail, in other words, is entirely authentic, and a text that relates a buffalo hunt, or a combat scene in which bow and arrow are the weapons, is no more authentic as a text than one that tells of life in a Catholic boarding-school or depicts the manufacture of black woollen stockings.

While the editorial and typographical presentation of a text is a complex task, requiring attention to many interrelated issues of great subtlety, it is in the domain of translation that the skein of authenticity is most often carelessly broken.

In many of the autobiographical narratives that Freda Ahenakew and I have been transcribing, analysing, and translating, the speaker refers to her mother not by a single term but by two, the formal *nikâwiy* and the informal *nimâmâ*. In loosely paraphrasing such passages in English, Cree speakers tend to ignore the distinction that we conventionally (and by no means ideally) render by 'my mother' and 'my mom' (cf. also Wolfart 1992: 387–91).

Instead of two nouns, the analogous pair

nôhkomipan 'my late grandmother'
kâ-kî-oyôhkomiyân 'the one I used to have for my grandmother'
(cf. *nôhkom* 'my grandmother')

consists of a noun with a preterite ending (cf. Wolfart 1992: 405–6) and a periphrastic verb form for which we have not been able to find a suitable rendition into English.

Even in the translation of contemporary texts, ethnological and genealogical accuracy are sometimes in conflict with the requirements of fluency. In the reminiscences of Emma Minde, for example, we felt compelled to translate *nisikos* as 'my mother-in-law' when it refers to Mary-Jane Minde, the stepmother of Emma Minde's husband, but as 'my aunt' when it refers to Jane Minde, the wife of her husband's paternal uncle.

The problem is acute when the term appears in the plural, as in

... *ôki nisikosak nîs ôki kâ-mâmiskômakik*. (EM68)
... these two *nisikosak* about whom I am speaking.

A literal translation, 'these two mothers-in-law,' would be confusing; the only practical solution is to use a conjunction in English and refer to the two individuals who are combinable in Cree but not in English as 'both my mother-in-law and the wife of my father-in-law's brother.'

In the parallel case of the term *nisis* ('my mother's brother, my father's sister's husband; my father-in-law, my father-in-law's brother'), the text provides an instance of both the noun (*nisisak*, literally 'my fathers-in-law') and the verb (*kî-nîsiwak* 'they were two') appearing in the plural – and the verb stem itself expressing a specific number:

kî-nîsiwak ôki nisisak, ... (EM45)
These *nisisak* were two in number, ...

Since a direct translation of these Cree plurals into English plurals would be unacceptable (and an insensitive translation might even give offence), a fairly free rendition is called for (and, in the event, less awkward than in the previous case): 'My father-in-law was one of two brothers, ...'

The conundrums of presenting an appropriate translation are not restricted to lexical matters. A classic instance of the discrepancy between bare reference and the fuller meaning that a proper translation ought to capture is provided by the rapid shift between agentive and inagentive verb forms (following the victory of the thunderbird):

«êkota ohci namôy kakêtihk iyikohk kî-miyawâcikâtêw,	**indef**
ayisiyiniwak kî-miyawâtamwak;	**3p**
ê-isi-wâpahtamâhk ôma, êkwa mîna ê-iskwâhtâyâhk nipiy,	**1p, 1p**
ôm ê-wî-nipahâpâkwêhk ôm,» îtwêw.	**indef**

«From that point on there was great rejoicing,
the people rejoiced;
both at what we had seen and also that we had an abundance of water,
because one had faced death for lack of water,» she said.

To ignore such details might make for smoother English prose but would result in a much less adequate translation and presentation of the text.

While most casual readers might be oblivious to details at this level, it is striking that Emma Minde in her reminiscences (1997) makes a point of commenting almost every time she refers to her husband as *niwîkimâkan*, 'my husband,' in a context where they either were not yet married or when he had already died; to her, this is clearly not a trivial matter.

In the historiography of Americanist editorial practice, we regard the Plains Cree editions of Bloomfield as unexceptional in not including the names of the narrators on the title-page; instead, the volume issued by the National Museum of Canada uses the remarkable phrase '*by* Leonard Bloomfield.'

To blame this lapse on Bloomfield would be anachronistic, even if we were to assume that he had been in a position to influence the form and content of the title-page – a rare favour with any publisher and perhaps more so in a government bureaucracy where we know from Bloomfield's correspondence (Jenness to Bloomfield, 11 September 1928) that the manuscript had to go through the Director of the National Museum and the Deputy Minister of the Department of Mines before it could reach the departmental editor and, finally, the King's Printer. There can be no question of Bloomfield dressing himself in other people's intellectual property; each individual text is meticulously identified by its author's name, both in English and in Cree.

It also seems noteworthy today, but much less so in the contemporary context, that Bloomfield was so parsimonious (indeed, stingy) in his introductions and annotations. Not a word about Aladdin and Ali Baba, not a whisper about the European antecedents of a story that appears among the Ojibwe texts of Angeline Williams (1990) and that clearly echoes one published a hundred years earlier by the Grimm Brothers and recently recorded in a Plains Cree version in Saskatchewan (cf. Wolfart 1990) – but Bloomfield evidently recognized it for he gave it the title familiar from the Grimm tradition, 'The Two Brothers.'

Only once did Bloomfield write an interpretive essay on one of his texts, 'The Story of Bad-Owl' (1928), but even in those palaeo-congressional days, the principles of David Lodge's small world may have been at play already, and perhaps that manuscript was his ticket to the Americanist Congress at Rome. Speculation aside, the printed paper consists of half a page of introduction, a retelling of the tale as seen through the eyes of an imaginary HBC trader (and, as we would expect from a writer of Bloomfield's literary skills and sensitivity, a minor masterpiece), and then simply a translation of the text itself.

Syncretism

The 'new' texts recorded since 1981 by Freda Ahenakew remind us, even as the corpus is greatly augmented, that our knowledge of Cree literature remains uneven and shallow.

While they offer a welcome focus on the women's perspective, they still omit whole realms of existence (cf. Wolfart 1989) and are highly selective in their representation of others.

There is a special interest in obsolete technology, for example, with Rosa Longneck's account of soap-making (Bear et al. 1992: 312–19) the prize exhibit: a mundane undertaking, to be sure, but an extraordinarily lively and well-presented narrative of how it is done and how she herself used to do it. Emma Minde (1997) offers a parallel description of how the inmates of a Roman Catholic boarding school in the 1920s would produce woollen stockings, and it seems ironic that these reports of innovative technologies are more detailed and more engaging than the rather cursory invocations of the beauty of beaded clothes made from scratch – and there is very little detail of the harsh physical demands made by the task of hide preparation.

Evaluative comments are rare in Cree texts, and overt expression of emotion even rarer. The exceptions to this rule, on the other hand, are powerful. One is the lament of old women about the fate of their daughters and the abuse they suffer while the older generation can only watch – to meddle would be unacceptable and might well bring down on them the retributions of *pâstâhowin*. The other is the force of the feelings expressed by old women about their experience of being given into arranged marriages. The only emotion that is openly discussed is the overwhelming horror of a husband and a family the young girl has not even met.

This is a recurrent theme. In Emma Minde's narrative, it almost sounds like a refrain, first invoked at the very beginning:

kî-âyiman ..., êkâ ê-nisitawêyimakik ayisiyiniwak. (EM1)
It was difficult ..., because I did not know the people.

mâk âyiwâk kî-âyiman ..., môy âhpô cêskwa ê-nisitawêyimak. (EM3)
But it was worse ..., for I did not even know him yet [the young man whom I was to marry].

kî-âyiman pimâtisiwin osâm, namôy âya, môy sêmâk ayisiyiniw ati-nakayâskawâw êkâ kâ-nisitawêyimiht, ... (EM3)
Life was difficult, for you don't get used to a person right away when you haven't known him before, ...

She then repeats the lament at the close of her own story, albeit with a slight variation:

... môya wîst ê-ohci-nisitawêyimit, êkwa môy nîst ê-ohci-nisitawêyimak. (EM40)
... he did not know me, and I did not know him.

... osâm êkâ cêskw âhpô ohkwâkan ê-wâpahtamwak, kî-âyiman aya, ... (EM40)
... for I had not yet even seen his face, it was difficult ...

kî-âyiman ...; nikî-miskamâkawin niya nâpêw ka-wîcêwak, êkosi môy ê-ohci-nisitawêyimak, ... (EM40)
It was difficult ...; a man had been found for me to marry, and so I did not know him, ...

It is remarkable that *nêhiyaw* / Glecia Bear uses almost the same words (Bear et al. 1992: 210–12):

môy ôm âhpô ê-nisitawêyimak awa nâpêw, kâ-wîkihtahikawiyân. (GB8–10)
I did not even know the man whom it was arranged that I would marry.

..., êkâ ê-nisitawêyimak aw âwiyak kâ-miyiht niya, ka-wîkimak. (GB8–10)
... since I did not even know this person to whom I had been given, for me to be married to him.

The parallels range from the overall sentiment all the way to the choice of words and, indeed, of the grammatical constructions with their preference for indefinite agent forms.

For Mary-Jane Minde, too, speaking to us from the previous generation through Emma Minde, the salient point being repeated is that she did not know the man she was to marry:

wîsta namôy ê-ohci-nakayâskawât ôhi nâpêwa, ... (EM43)
she, too, had not been familiar with that man, ...

In Emma Minde's own story, the whole issue of being married to a stranger culminates in the dramatic scene of her arrival: at midnight, coming into a strange house, to have her sleeping husband pointed out to her by an eleven-year-old sister-in-law:

«aw îta ...!» (EM41)
«There he is ...!»

Given Emma Minde's rhetorical exuberance on many other occasions, it is remarkable that she treats this crucial scene with climactic understatement.

The anguish that, even after a lifetime, permeates these narratives is almost palpable. In listening to them on the eve of the millennium, we may find a measure of relief in the more joyous emotions that, in retrospect at least, were also part of Emma Minde's new life:

pêyakwan mistah âya nikî-miyawâtên, nikî-miywêyihtên –~ (EM42)
All the same I had lots of fun and I was happy –~

This remark concludes the report of the church wedding, attended only by the couple, two witnesses, and the priest.

Emotions or evaluations from a personal point of view are rare in Cree texts, including autobiographical ones, but in a woman's life history – even when viewed from the contented perspective of a ripe old age – the experience of being given away in marriage is evidently unique. Who could fail to be moved by Glecia Bear's lament (Bear et al. 1992: 212):

... *iyikohk ê-pakwâtamân ê-mâtoyân*, ... (GB8–11)
... I hated it so much and I was crying, ...

or by Emma Minde's eloquent echo:

ê-kî-mâtoyâhk anima nikâwiy aya, ... (EM41)
We did cry, my mother and I, ...

Arranged marriages clearly constitute a major theme of the autobiographical narrative of Emma Minde (1997), a volume of heavily Catholic inspiration.

While some of her terminology is also unmistakeably that of the Roman Catholic tradition, Emma Minde's reminiscences are classical in their literary form. She alternates between two major genres, the autobiographical text, or *âcimisowin*, and the counselling text, or *kakêskihkêmowin* (cf. Ahenakew and Wolfart 1987: xii). Her texts are redolent of Roman Catholic doctrine, but the virtues she extols all belong to that domain where even the most dedicated philologist would fail in the attempt to disentangle the intertwined threads of pre-Christian Cree theology and the teachings of Roman Catholicism. There is an overwhelming emphasis on teaching the young, on works of charity towards the weak and, especially, the old, and on advocacy.

The lexicon of terms for advice and counsel, for teaching and parental control is profusely illustrated:

sîhkim- VTA 'urge s.o. by speech'
sîhkiskaw- VTA 'urge s.o. bodily'

kitahamaw- VTA 'advise s.o. against (it/him)'

kakêskim- VTA 'counsel s.o., preach s.o.'
kakêskimiso- VAI 'counsel oneself'
kakêskihkêmo- VAI 'counsel people, preach at people'
miyo-kakêskihkêmowin- NI 'good counselling, good preaching'

kiskinohamaw- VTA 'teach s.o., teach (it) to s.o.'
kiskinohamâkê- VAI 'teach things'
kiskinohamâso- VAI 'teach oneself'
kiskinohamâto- VAI 'teach one another'

kiskinowâpam- VTA 'watch s.o.'s example'
kiskinowâpahtih- VTA 'teach s.o. by example'
kiskinowâpahtihiwê- VAI 'teach people by example'

As is typical of traditional narrative, there is also a densely woven texture of etymologically related stems; for instance,

wîkim- VTA 'live with s.o.; be married to s.o.'
kihci-wîkim- VTA 'be formally married to s.o.'
wîkihto- VAI 'live with one another, be married to one another'
kihci-wîkihto- VAI 'be formally married to one another';

all of the above stems occur with great frequency.

Emma Minde's discourse is remarkable, in stylistic terms, for the high proportion of nouns as opposed to verbs; for instance,

iyisâhowin- NI 'resisting temptation'
kihci-wîkihtowin- NI 'formal marriage.'

It it not surprising that there are also various turns of phrase that appear to be based on English models; for example,

... *namôy kiskêyihtamwak tânitê k-êsi-kwêskîcik anima miyawâtamowin ê-nitonahkik.* (EM9)
... they don't know where to turn next in their search for amusement.

namôy ôhci-nakîw ka-mâh-minihkwêt, kîsikâwa ka-wanihtât, ... (EM28)
He did not stop [in his work] to go drinking around, to lose whole days, ...

but such calques are, of course, part of an endless continuum that ranges from derived stems such as

sôniyâhkê- VAI 'make money'

to ancient borrowings, such as

sôniyâw- NA 'gold, silver; money'
môniyâw- NA 'Montrealer, Canadian; White'

and from well-integrated ones (here with the final *-âpiskw-* 'of stone or similarly hard and brittle consistency'), *môtêyâpiskw-* NI 'bottle, glass'

to entirely unmodified English intrusions.

Despite the occasional loanword or calque, the phraseology of these reminiscences is clearly traditional, and terms with a heavy moral content and an apparently Catholic overburden such as *iyisâhowin-* NI 'resisting temptation' occur side by side with ordinary Cree expressions such as *êkâ kwayask ê-itâtisit* (EM65), 'because his character is evil.'

A truly noteworthy pattern in these autobiographical texts of a devout Roman Catholic is the reuse of ordinary and traditional terms in specifically Christian senses; for instance,

pihkoho- VAI 'escape; be saved'
pakitin- VTI 'let go of s.t., release s.t.';
cf. *pakitinâso-* VAI 'let go (of s.t.) for oneself; make a donation, give at collection'

Inevitably, such polysemic extensions are triggered by the introduction of new objects or practices; for instance,

minihkwê- VAI 'drink; use alcohol, abuse alcohol'
pîhtwâwin- NI 'smoking; smoking cannabis, cannabis abuse'

In the same fashion, some of these reused terms reflect the transfer from one religious and moral system to another; for instance,

opawâmowin- NI 'spirit power; witchcraft'
patinikê- VAI 'make a mistake; commit a transgression'
pâstâho- VAI 'have one's transgressions fall upon oneself and one's children; sin, be a sinner'

This pattern is well documented in another semantic domain, that of health and illness, where most technical terms are simply ordinary words used in a specialised sense (cf. Wolfart 1989).

Polysemous extensions with all their ambiguities and tensions are common in technical contexts, whether theological or commercial:

... *nikî-wâpahtên kisê-manitow ê-tipêyimikoyahk ê-kî-awihit êkoni anih âya, awâsisa kâw ê-kî-otinât.* (EM4)
... I saw that God in His power over us had given us this child on loan and that He had taken her back again.

âtiht nêhiyawa, âtiht môniyâwa kî-awihêw. (EM58)
Some [fields] he had rented out to Crees, some to White people.

Similarly:

... *kî-wawêyîstam ka-nakatahk askiy* ... (EM4)
... she was prepared to leave this world behind ...

nikî-miyâwak anih âya askiya nôsisimak; pêyak iskwêw, êkwa nîso nâpêwak, nôsisimak nikî-miyâwak. (EM58)
I gave the land [lit., these pieces of land] to my grandchildren; to one granddaughter and to two grandsons I gave it.

The context may be commercial, the lexical meaning may be extended well beyond its traditional realm to include divisible real estate, but in this last example the construction displays the classical form of a chiastic reversal of word order.

The rhetorical form of this text is, for the most part, entirely traditional – despite the Roman Catholic content and flavour. There are a few details, to be sure, that would be handled differently in a fully traditional context where, for example, the use of names for deceased members of the family is strictly avoided. In the present text, the narrator goes back and forth between kin terms such as *nisikos*, 'my father's sister (woman speaking), my mother-in-law,' and English appellations such as *Mrs Minde*; one reason for this usage may well be that these are public figures whose names are widely recognized in central Alberta. She rarely uses the *-pan* suffix with kin terms as would be required for those no longer living. On the other hand, she studiously comments on the anachronistic use of ordinary kin terms, as when she refers to her future husband as *niwîkimâkan* 'my spouse,' even though she reports from the perspective of the bride-to-be, and also when she uses the same term for him retrospectively even though he is no longer alive:

... *niwîkimâkan êkwa – nik-êtâhkômâw, âsay êkwa ê-kî-nakasit* – (EM41)
... and my husband – I will call him by that kin term even though he has already left me behind –

She also omits all mention of the genealogical relationship that, under the traditional Cree system of cross-cousin marriage, would have obtained for each of the three sets of spouses whose marriages she discusses.

She similary employs a distancing comment on the one occasion where her discourse might be misunderstood as involving self-aggrandizement – an unacceptable attitude in Cree society:

namôya ninôhtê-mâh-mamihcimon pimâtisiwin ohci, mâka ... (EM5)
I do not want to brag about the life I lead, but ...

Finally, she opens each section of her narrative with a self-effacing comment that shows her – an old woman of resounding rhetorical gifts having developed from the shy, even morose girl she appears to have been – as being requested to speak about her life:

awa kâ-kakwêcimit iskwêw aw ôta kâ-pîkiskwêhit; (EM7)
This woman [Freda Ahenakew] asked me, when she made me speak in here [the tape-recorder];

... *êwakw âw âya, iskwêw awa k-âcimôhit aya, êkosi ê-isi-nitawêyihtahk k-âcimostawak*, ... (EM11)
... it is this woman [Freda Ahenakew] who is making me tell about it, that is what she wants me to tell her about, ...

êkonik ôk âya, ê-nitawêyimit aw âya Mrs Ahenakew *k-âcimakik aya, nisis êkwa aya nisikos*, ... (EM43)
It is these Mrs Ahenakew wants me to tell about, my father-in-law and my mother-in-law, ...

êkwa ôk âya iskwêwak kâ-nitawêyimikawiyân aya kik-âcimakik aya, ôta maskwacîsihk, ... (EM50)
And it is these women I am expected to tell about, here at *maskwacîsihk*, ...

There is no demonstrable relaxation of traditional style, even where the subject matter may be thought of as purely Catholic. In the following sentence, for example, the general truth of the assertion is expressed by the use of the generic singular even though the verb stems are derivationally marked as reciprocal:

... *ayisiyiniw aya, kâ-kitimâkêyihtot kwayask kâ-wîkihtot.* (EM7)
... when people love one another and when they are properly married.

This is one of many instances where the translation has to be fairly free, rendering the generic singular of the reciprocal by an English plural.

If there is a shift in overall stylistic form, it seems to manifest itself in a preference for nominal rather than verbal constructions and in the use of long sequences of parallel clauses; for instance,

kîspin kâ-kisiwâhikoyahkik,
ka-pônêyihtamawâyahkik,
namôya ka--, namôya ka-kisîstawâyahkik ayisiyiniwak,
namôy mîna ka-- kîmôc ka-nôtinâyahkik,
môy k-âh-âyimômâyahkik. (EM34)
if they have angered us,
for us to forgive them,
not to --, not to stay angry with people,
not to fight them behind their backs,
not to spread gossip about them.

... *êkwa môy ê-kiskêyihtahkik ê-tôtahkik êtok ôm âya,*
kâ-tôtâsocik,
kâ-misiwanâcihisocik,
kâ-nipahisocik. (EM36)
... and they presumably do not know what they are doing
when they do this to themselves,
when they destroy themselves,
when they kill themselves.

Such constructions, when used repeatedly, tend to impart something of a hectoring tone to the homily. In their rhetorical structure, they are clearly built upon the classical form of parallelism, occasionally embellished by chiastic structures.

In summary, given the syncretic terminology and the Roman Catholic tenor of Emma Minde's text, it is all the more remarkable that its narrative and rhetorical structure is, ultimately, indistinguishable from that of any other narrative or homiletic discourse.

Innovation

With their Catholic flavour and their traditional form, the reminiscences of Emma Minde stand in stark contrast with a text from central Saskatchewan that was performed during the winter of 1994–5 by a younger speaker (ca. 45 years of age). In this text, a highly traditional subject is cast into a rhetorical form that is quite distinct from that of the traditional tellings of such accounts of mythical events and their ultimate, aetiologically grounded, outcome.

The differences are subtle, to be sure, and as we venture onto the slippery slopes of stylistics and into the quicksands of literary criticism, we should not lightly give up the solid footing of replicable linguistic analysis.

Some differences are almost palpable: there is a marked increase, for example, in the freedom of word formation. There is a notable preference for verbs derived by the discontinuous VTA affix *wîci-X-m-*, 'do X together with s.o.'; for example,

... *ê-wîci-kîskwêmât, ê-wîci-nôtinitômât, ê-wîci-wêpahotocik,* ...
... he fooled around together with them, he fought together with them, they clashed together with one another, ...

As the last verb form in this example shows, *wîci-* may also appear in verb stems with the corresponding *-m-* suffix replaced by the reciprocal suffix *-ito-* (that is, as if construed as a preverb); for instance,

ê-wîci-pîkiskwêmât
him speaking with them;

the suffix may also be omitted altogether; for example,

ê-wîci-pîkiskwâtikocik
them speaking with one another.

While the *wîci- -m-* complex typically derives stems of the VTA class from VAI stems (cf. Wolfart 1980: 288; 1989: 333; Bloomfield 1941), the greater freedom of word formation is here illustrated by its use with verb finals such as *-pahtâ-* 'run,' which are not themselves full stems. The text contains four instances of

ê-wîcipahtamât and *ê-pimi-wîcipahtamât*
him running with them *and* him running along with them

as well as one more traditional construction,

ê-wîci-pimipahtamât
him running along with them.

A less restrictive approach to the reference of individual words is illustrated by the term *otiyinîma* 'his people,' which traditionally is used of a chief's responsibility for his charges (cf. Wolfart 1997: xix–xx). In the present text, it refers to the child's family:

... *ê-pimâcihoyit, ê-âhcipiciyit, ê-âhci-kapêsiyit otiyinîma.*
... as his people travelled on, as they moved their camp, as they moved their overnight camp.

In short, the innovations of this text are not restricted to its literary form or its rhetorical implementation, but extend through the stylistic details into the actual words and their derivational patterns as well.

The plot of this text is that of an infant accidentally left behind and raised by buffaloes. At the threshold of adulthood he discovers that he is not a buffalo and sets out to 'find his roots,' as it were. In a twist reminiscent of Jean-Jacques Rousseau, he complains about the incessant noisy chatter of human society, and he also takes offence at their dependence on buffalo meat and products. When he returns, his adoptive father explains to him the grand plan that makes the buffalo the staff of life for mankind but enjoins moderation upon the latter, too – the 'green' ethic ostensibly *avant la lettre*. When the old buffalo chief is felled, the hero despairs and his dying father offers him the option of turning himself first into a buffalo and then into a rock in buffalo shape; and in this form he remains a well-known landmark – the physical evidence so important in Cree historiography – replicably visible to all (until being submerged in a recent hydroelectric project) on the Saskatchewan prairie.

The hero's emotions are part of the narrative in a way that is quite different from the monologues of traditional Cree text. The rhetorical form may still be direct speech (rather than indirect speech or internal monologue); for example,

«mâka namôy nicîhkêyihtên, nôhtâ, ê-isi-wâpahtamân.»
«But I do not like what I see, father.»

«namôya, nôhtâ, namôy niwî-tapasîn! namôy âyiwâk niwî-tapasîn!»
«No, father, I am not going to flee! I am not going to flee any more!»;

but it expresses sentiments, and it is, moreover, addressed to an audience.

The greater attention to the hero's state of mind is balanced by a striking reduction in the elaboration of the settings and a much more rapid sequence of pivotal events. Once the hero has the grand plan revealed to him, there are only two brief transitional sections. The first consists of a single sentence describing him as content with the buffalo life and two or three about a buffalo hunt – humans on horseback, flying dust, and the sound of hooves. The second also begins with a brief description of his state of mind, to be followed immediately by a tightly compressed summary of many repetitions and then an extraordinarily laconic statement that his father has been shot:

[a] *wahwâ, êwak ôma, mêtoni mâmitonêyihtamihikow, ê-pakwâtahk awa paskwâwi-mostos-awâsis.*
[b] *kêtahtawê, êkwa êkot[a] ôma, kîhtwâm êtikwê tânitahtwâw ôm ê-kî-pimâmocik ôm ê-âh-âhtâmocik, tânitahtw-âskiy, môy ê-isi-kêhtê-ayiwit awa,*
[c] *ôhtâwiya kâ-nipahimiht; ôhtâwiya.*
[a] Oh my, this really made him think, this Buffalo-Child, and he hated it.
[b] Then at one time, after they must once more have been fleeing many times, taking refuge in various places, and he was not yet many years into adulthood,
[c] his father was killed; his father.

Remarkably, it is not even made clear – as would be obligatorily indicated by one of the traditional verb stems – whether the weapon that felled him was a bullet or an arrow.

While evaluative statements with *ê-pakwâtahk* 'he found it offensive,' are common enough in traditional narratives, they rarely occur without contextual foundation or necessity. The greater attention to chronological sequence and character development manifests itself in statements of introspection that seem to be beyond the minimum requirements of the plot; for example,

sôskwâc paskwâwi-mostos ê-kî-itêyimisot ês âwa ...
He simply considered himself a buffalo, ...

môy mistahi ati-mâmitonêyihtam ôm âyisiyinîwi-pimâtisiwin ôma kîkway.
He thought less and less about the life of the humans.

On his return from the people, his report includes a statement of the hero's sexual purity in the face of human lust:

«â, tâpwê, ahpô nikî-kakwê-wâh-wîcêkwak iskwêwak. namôy mâka kîkway nitôhc-îsîhkawâwak, nikî-ma-manâcihâwak, nikî-manâcihison; âta ê-kî-sâ-sôhki-kocîcik ôk îskwêwak, ka-kiyomâhicik.»
«Well, truly, several of the women even tried to consort with me. But I did not trifle with

them in any way, I kept treating them with respect, I maintained my self-respect; even though these women tried hard on several occasions to excite me.

The hero is not the only one whose attitude or behaviour are much more fully elaborated than seems typical of traditional contexts; for example,

... piyisk awa pêyak kâ-pîkiskwâtât; ê-ohpiniskêyit, kâ-kiyâm-âyâcik ayisiyiniwak, «hâ!» ê-kâmwâtaniyik, «awîn ôma kiya?»
... finally one of them spoke to him; when he raised his arm, the people fell silent, and «Ha!», into the silence, «Who are you?»

In sum, this text in many respects echoes the *Entwicklungsroman* or *Bildungsroman* of European literature. Where traditional Cree narrative stresses externally observable events – along the lines of 'he lived there for many years, he did this and experienced that' – the innovative approach of the present narrator almost recalls the novelistic technique of stream-of-consciousness, with the narrator and the audience taking the point of view of the hero, but silently and without the shift being marked by the soliloquy common in traditional Cree texts.

A more diffuse example of an innovative distribution in emphasis combines rhetorical (that is, macro) and stylistic (micro) features. The attention to matters of language seems unprecedented, and it is matched by heavy reliance on the stem *pîkiskwê-* VAI 'use words, speak,' and the correponding omission of the more usual and much less highly marked stems *it-* VTA 'say so to s.o.,' or *itwê-* VAI 'say so,' based on the relative root *it-*, which balances the direct speech.

The rhetorical and stylistic traits of this innovative pattern of narration are also matched by grammatical effects that, for all their subtlety, are nevertheless clearly demonstrable. With respect to preverbs, for example, the narrator allows the preverb *mêkwâ* 'while, during,' to float outside the verbal complex; for instance,

ihtakon, ihtakon, ka-tihtipipiyan, mêkwâ ê-nahipayik ôma, ...
It is possible, it is possible for you to roll yourself, while the time is right, ...;

Other Cree texts typically restrict *mêkwâ* to the preverb position and exhibit *mêkwâc* outside the verbal complex.

Similarly, the distinction between proximate and obviative third-person reference is less strict; in the following example, all four verb forms refer to the hero, but only the first three are in the obviative form:

... *ê-kî-mamâhtâwisiyit, ê-kwêskîmoyit, ê-kî-ati-paskwâwi-mostosowiyit, ê-kî-at-âsinîwit.*
... that he had supernatural powers, that he changed himself, that he had gradually turned into a buffalo, that he had gradually turned into stone.

A more narrowly stylistic feature, finally, which it would be hard to overlook in this text, is an insistence on verb phrases in sets of four:

> ... *miton ê-kinwâniskwêt mîna ê-kinosit, ê-maskawâkiyawêt, ê-sôhkâkiyawêt, ê-nahâwisit;*
> ... he had very long hair and he was tall, he had a strong body, he had a forceful body, he was slim;

> *êkos ôma kitatoskêwininaw,*
> *ê-asamâyahkik iyin-âyisiyiniwak,*
> *ê-akwanahwâyahkik ê-kîsônâyahkik ayisiyiniwak,*
> *âpacihcikana ê-miyâyahkik ayisiyiniwak,*
> *kahkiyaw kîkway ê-âpacihcikaniwiyahk,*
> *ê-otâpanihowâkêcik ayisiyiniwak.*
> That is our task,
> we feed the humans,
> we clothe the humans and keep them warm,
> we give the humans tools,
> we are useful for everything,
> the humans depend on us for their livelihood.

> *êkw ân[i] êsa ayiwinisa kâ-pêtamâht êkwa,*
> *ê-kikâsiyânêpitiht êkwa,*
> *pahkêkinwêskisina êkwa ê-tâh-tipahamoht,*
> *ê-osîhtamâht pahkêkinwêskisina.*
> And then he had clothes brought for him,
> then he had a breechclout put on him,
> then he had a pair of leggings measured for him,
> leggings he had made for him.

As in several earlier illustrations, the last two lines exhibit the rhetorical flourish of chiastic reversal.

As we look back on the two texts we have examined in some detail, the discrepancies between content and form could hardly be sharper. The reminiscences of

Emma Minde are heavily Catholic in content but traditional in form, while the buffalo story is entirely traditional in content but highly innovative in form.

While some patterns seem to disappear without a trace, others appear to be recognized as markers of a particular genre or register, as is suggested by their survival and, in some cases, even increase or exaggeration.

For either text, authority and authenticity remain beyond question, but we have before us unmistakable instances of acculturation. In one of these texts, the tell-tale signs of the modern world dominate the content; in the other, it is the form of the text that bears the marks of a massive *aggiornamento.*

NOTES

1 Thanks are due first and foremost to the several narrators from whose texts, published and unpublished, the illustrations in this essay are cited and to Freda Ahenakew, to whom most of the texts in the critical edition, and translation of which she and I have been engaged in for almost two decades were given. The financial support of the Social Sciences and Humanities Research Council of Canada and the University of Manitoba Research Board is also gratefully acknowledged.

REFERENCES

Ahenakew, Freda, and H.C. Wolfart. 1987. 'The Story-Tellers and Their Stories.' In F. Ahenakew, ed., *wâskahikaniwiyiniw-âcimowina / Stories of the House People*, Told by Peter Vandall and Joe Douquette, x–xiv. Winnipeg: University of Manitoba Press.

– 1991. 'John Beaverbone's Story as Retold by Joseph Tootoosis.' Edited and translated by Freda Ahenakew and H.C. Wolfart. In H.C. Wolfart, ed., *Linguistic Studies Presented to John L. Finlay*, 1–12. Algonquian and Iroquoian Linguistics, Memoir 8. Winnipeg.

Bear, Glecia / Nêhiyaw. 1991. *wanisinwak iskwêsisak: awâsisasinahikanis / Two Little Girls Lost in the Bush: A Cree Story for Children.* Told by Nêhiyaw / Glecia Bear. Edited and translated by Freda Ahenakew and H.C. Wolfart. Illustrated by J. Whitehead. Saskatoon: Fifth House Publishers.

Bear, Glecia, et al. 1992. *kôhkominawak otâcimowiniwâwa / Our Grandmothers' Lives, As Told in Their Own Words.* Told by Glecia Bear et al. Edited and translated by Freda Ahenakew and H.C. Wolfart. Saskatoon: Fifth House Publishers.

Bloomfield, Leonard. 1928. 'The Story of Bad-Owl.' *International Congress of Americanists [Rome, 1926], Proceedings* 22(2): 23–34.

– 1930. *Sacred Stories of the Sweet Grass Cree.* National Museum of Canada, Bulletin 60. Ottawa.

– 1934. *Plains Cree Texts.* American Ethnological Society, Publication 16. New York: AES.

– 1941. 'Proto-Algonquian – i:t – "fellow."' *Language* 17: 292–7.

Darnell, Regna. 1974. 'Correlates of Cree Narrative Performance.' In Richard Bauman and Joel Sherzer, eds, *Explorations in the Ethnography of Speaking*, 315–36. Cambridge: Cambridge University Press.

Hadas, Moses. 1950. *A History of Greek Literature.* New York: Columbia University Press.

Kegg, Maude. 1990. *Nookomis Gaa-inaajimotawid / What My Grandmother Told Me. Texts in Ojibwe (Chippewa) and English, Told by Maude Kegg.* Edited, translated, and with a glossary by John D. Nichols. 2nd, rev. edition. Bemidji, MN: Indian Studies Program, Bemidji State University.

Minde, Emma. 1997. *kwayask ê-kî-pê-kiskinowâpahtihicik / Their Example Showed Me the Way: A Cree Woman's Life Shaped by Two Cultures.* Told by Emma Minde. Edited, translated, and with a glossary by Freda Ahenakew and H.C. Wolfart. Edmonton: University of Alberta Press.

Nichols, John D. 1982. 'William Warren and Ojibwe Traditional History.' Paper presented at Quatorzième Congrès des Algonquinistes, Québec.

– 1989. '"The Wishing Bone Cycle": A Cree "Ossian"?' *International Journal of American Linguistics* 55: 155–78.

– 1991. '"Chant to the Fire-fly": A Philological Problem in Ojibwe.' In H.C. Wolfart, ed., *Linguistic Studies Presented to John L. Finlay*, 113–26. Algonquian and Iroquoian Linguistics, Memoir 8. Winnipeg: Dept. of Linguistics, University of Manitoba.

– 1996. 'William W. Warren and Ojibwe Traditional History.' In J.D. Nichols and A.C. Ogg, eds, *nikotwâsik iskwâhtêm, pâskihtêpayih! Studies in Honour of H.C. Wolfart*, 309–35. Algonquian and Iroquoian Linguistics, Memoir 13. Winnipeg: Dept. of Linguistics, University of Manitoba.

Scott, Simeon, et al. 1995. *âtalôhkâna nêsta tipâcimôwina / Cree Legends and Narratives from James Bay.* Told by Xavier Sutherland et al. Edited and translated by C. Douglas Ellis. Publications of the Algonquian Text Society / Collection de la Société d'édition de textes algonquiens. Winnipeg: University of Manitoba Press.

Steiner, John. 1985. 'Turning a Blind Eye: The Cover-up for Oedipus.' *International Review of Psycho-Analysis* 12(2): 161–72.

Valentine, Lisa Philips. 1995. *Making It Their Own: Severn Ojibwe Communicative Practices.* Toronto: University of Toronto Press.

Vandall, Peter, and Joe Douquette. 1987. *wâskahikaniwiyiniw-âcimowina / Stories of the House People.* Told by Peter Vandall and Joe Douquette. Edited, translated, and with a glossary by Freda Ahenakew. Publications of the Algonquian Text Society / Collection de la Société d'édition de textes algonquiens. Winnipeg: University of Manitoba Press.

Vellacott, Philip. 1971. *Sophocles and Oedipus: A Study of 'Oedipus Tyrannus' with a New Translation.* Ann Arbor: University of Michigan Press.

Whitecalf, Sarah. 1993. *kinêhiyâwiwininaw nêhiyawêwin / The Cree Language Is Our Identity: The La Ronge Lectures of Sarah Whitecalf.* Edited and translated by H.C. Wolfart and Freda Ahenakew. Publications of the Algonquian Text Society / Collection de la Société d'édition de textes algonquiens. Winnipeg: University of Manitoba Press.

Williams, Angeline. 1990. *The Dog's Children: Anishinaabe Texts Told by Angeline Williams.* Edited and translated by Leonard Bloomfield newly edited, and with a glossary by John D. Nichols. Publications of the Algonquian Text Society / Collection de la Société d'édition de textes algonquiens. Winnipeg: University of Manitoba Press.

Wolfart, H.C. 1980. 'Marked Terms for Marginal Kin.' In W. Cowan, ed., *Papers of the Eleventh Algonquian Conference [Ottawa, 1979]*, 283–93. Ottawa: Carleton University.

– 1982a. 'Empirische Untersuchungen zur mündlichen Literatur-Überlieferung.' In E. Lämmert, ed., *Erzählforschung*, 74–97. Stuttgart: Metzler.

– 1982b. 'Patterns of Reflexion in Plains Cree Historical Texts.' Paper presented to the 44th International Congress of Americanists, Manchester.

– 1986. 'Taboo and Taste in Literary Translation.' In W. Cowan, ed., *Actes du Dix-septième Congrès des Algonquinistes [Montréal, 1985]*, 377–94. Ottawa: Carleton University.

– 1989. 'Cree Midwifery: Linguistic and Literary Observations.' In W. Cowan, ed., *Actes du Vingtième Congrès des Algonquinistes [Hull, 1988]*, 326–42. Ottawa: Carleton University.
– 1990. '1001 Nights: The Orient and the Far Northwest.' In W. Cowan, ed., *Papers of the Twenty-first Algonquian Conference [St John's, Newfoundland, 1989]*, 370–95. Ottawa: Carleton University.
– 1992. Introduction to the Texts; Notes. In Freda Ahenakew and H.C. Wolfart, eds, *kôhkominawak otâcimowiniwâwa / Our Grandmothers' Lives, As Told in Their Own Words*, Told by Glecia Bear et al., 17–37; 351–408. Saskatoon: Fifth House Publishers.
– 1997. 'The Education of a Cree Woman.' In Freda Ahenakew and H.C. Wolfart, eds, *kwayask ê-kî-pê-kiskinowâpahtihicik / Their Example Showed Me the Way: A Cree Woman's Life Shaped by Two Cultures*, lx–xliv, Told by Emma Minde. Edmonton: University of Alberta Press.

9 Reflections on Culture, History, and Authenticity

RICHARD J. PRESTON

I invite you to explore with me the problem of the reliability of knowledge, including cultural knowledge and historical knowledge, in the context of indigenous teachers and their ethnographers. Listening to what people say gives us, as ethnographers, a basis for telling you, as audience, that you can reasonably believe a narrative that we have translated from one culture – one idiom of experience – to another. I hope to go further, to show how it is also reasonable to take seriously our claim that there are deeper meanings in these narratives, moving us 'from winks to epistemology' (Geertz 1973).

Research into the reliability of knowledge in this context has something to do with replicability, but it has even more to do with authenticity and tradition. Currently the legitimacy of the concept of authentic tradition is being challenged on the basis that, because traditions are social constructions, rather than essential and enduring relationships, they are therefore ephemeral re-inventions of the past, often motivated by self-conscious boosting (Keesing 1989) or rejection (Thomas 1992) of current political goals.

I have taken a position in defence of the legitimacy of the concepts of authenticity and tradition, accepting at once that we are indeed talking about social constructions that are, in some cases, ephemeral and presentist, but holding that we humans are mostly unself-conscious of the larger historical domains of experience (tradition) and the deeper symbolic implications of experience (personality-in-culture), most of the time. Traditions are like icebergs; we only see the tip, unless we delve deeper. We can reinvent the appearance of the tip fairly easily, but all that other stuff is still attached, underneath.

The post-structuralists, then, have a good point, but they are scratching the surface. And although the depths are intuited more than they are consciously known, these authentic qualities of tradition and personality are nontheless there; they are connected to each other; and discerning them clearly and reliably matters a great deal. Each of us and all of us are individuals in social relationships in history, participants in cultural patterns 'which a given individual partly knows and directs, partly intuits and yields to, partly is unaware of and is swayed by' (Sapir 1932: 518). Access to these patterns is the hallmark of the Americanist Tradition in ethnography.

Ethnographers have for generations sought out not a representative sample but rather one or a few individuals known for unusually extensive and finely detailed memory of things and events. The methodology is at once common sense and radical. Rather than systematically developing a large sample of informants and obtaining limited-scope responses to standardized small queries (the quantitative strategy), ethnographers rotate the methodological axis 90 degrees, limiting the number of 'consultants' (earlier, 'informants') or, more aptly stated, Native teachers, to a select few, but throwing open the scope of what we are ready to hear. The amount of knowledge recorded may be very large, a substantial sample of what the teacher may have to say on the matter.

We may then add a third dimension to the methodological axis, that of the semantic depth of the teacher's cultural idiom of expression. In the most open-ended ethnographic situation, as in the recording of oral tradition, the information is selected, sequenced, and given word form by the teacher, according to his/her sense of the Native structure of knowledge (emic), rather than the (etic) structure of the ethnographer. I have done this, and in the process of discovery that ensued, understood what the remembered narratives meant in Cree terms, so that I had a good basis for deciding what it meant to me. Then I began to write ethnography.

That was over thirty years ago, and since that time I have done many other types of research in the Cree region, some of it quite quantitative. But I am still confident of the representations I made of those narratives (Preston 1975), and they remain the core of my understanding, and valuing, of Cree culture. Now I will embark on a retrospective statement that explains how you can count on what I tell you about what they told me (Geertz 1988).

This paper moves, through a reassessment of my own early ethnographic work, to engage the issue of the recognition of authentic (Selznick 1992) traditions, arguing that the anthropological conceptualization of tradition, fuzzy as it may be (Ben-Amos 1984), should be rooted in time (Trask 1991) *as well as* in social life. We know that the ongoing reinterpretation of the past draws formatively on what we are aware of at the moment. But in celebrating our ability to rewrite history, we forget that tradition takes in a great deal more than we are aware of in our individual creations, and is much more collectively, consensually created by historical drifts in cultural form (Sapir 1921). I'll begin ethnographically.

Introducing John Blackned, Cree Elder

The late John Blackned, of Waskaganish, James Bay, knew that over the course of a full life he had retained a remarkably detailed memory of things and events, and knew that his unusual remembrance of things past was widely respected. We worked together in recording stories from 1963 through 1984, most intensively during the summers of 1964 and 1965.

He was probably, at some level, aware that he was, as we now word it, *giving voice to his regional tradition of Indigenous spirituality and ecological knowledge*. But I believe that this awareness was 'in the back of his mind,' known intuitively more than self-consciously and intellectually. He simply told me the stories that he was fairly sure he knew correctly, in a sequence that suited him. In most of what he said, he aimed to maintain his sense of the authenticity of the story, and not to reinterpret it into a contemporary or relevant version. For an initial definition of *authentic* I refer to 'the experience of continuity and wholeness in thought, feeling, and moral choice' (Selznick 1992: 65), and I will develop the concept in the course of this paper. In the course of two decades John spent hundreds of hours giving me the opportunity to learn what he wanted to teach me.[1]

Similarly, I was intuitively, but not intellectually, aware that I was what we now term *a representative of the Americanist Tradition in ethnography and was appropriating Native voice.* As a fledgling anthropologist, I did not see myself in the 'big picture' of my own tradition. I simply was a graduate student off into a strange milieu (James Bay, Quebec, Canada), in search of cultural understanding. I found John to be a congenial mentor, and I found the narratives he recounted a wonderful source for my discovery of Cree culture. I had never known anyone who related the personal significance of events (Evans-Pritchard 1965) with such rich and precise detail. In response, I made a commitment to understand what he intended in recounting the events, so that I would have a good basis for deciding what it meant to me, and then, what I could say about it, in writing, to others. So, I had experientially confirmed the meaning of cultural relativism – that by understanding a facet of another culture in terms of its own context, I was then in a position to translate this idiom of experience for an audience that knew little or nothing of the Cree. The commitment became profound and has lasted over a full career. John and I shared a keen interest in our recording project. In re-recording the tapes this year, I was impressed with the quickness of our rapport and the pleasure we took in the process. We were engaged in a hermeneutical circle, both similarly increasing our grasp of the other's comprehension, moving toward a deeper mutual understanding.

Writing this paper is the first sustained occasion I have had to try intellectually to see myself and John as taking part in the Americanist Tradition. I want to believe that the result has a measure of authenticity in it, and that the larger issue of authenticity and tradition can be well served by exploring Americanist methodology as it was worked out in our particular relationship. I am aware that this relationship is itself true to a type, in the larger context of indigenous teachers like Billy Williams (Osgood 1940, 1959), William Berens (Hallowell and Brown 1992), and many others who spoke with authority and took on apprentice Americanist ethnographers, each of whom aspired to soar on cultural wings – 'from winks to epistemology' (Geertz 1973, 1988).

Of course both of us (like every human being) had ample previous experience of being mostly unaware of our personal relation to the larger scheme of things – to our selves in the context of our tradition. I premise my argument on Sapir's concept of the scope and role of tradition in the personal expression of cultural symbolisms, 'which a given individual partly knows and directs, partly intuits and yields to, partly is unaware of and is swayed by' (Sapir 1932: 518).

For example, John had been only partly aware of the general and objective context of what anthropologists term an 'optimal foraging strategy of dispersal' as the most adaptive response to scarcity of food animals (E.A. Smith 1981: 36–65). And to the extent that he was aware of it, the strategy felt intuitively wrong to him. From oral tradition and from personal experience, he felt convinced that people should stay together during periods of extreme privation. A reason he gave was that, with a larger number of hunters, there is a better chance that at least one will have some success, and then everyone will have at least a little to eat. He also knew that when hardship reaches the point of crisis, people are more likely to doubt their leader's judgment and to want to set off on their own to some other hunting area. But he was convinced that this was not the best practice.

John remembered that, as a boy, he went with his father to take food that they had just killed to relatives who, against his father's advice, had opted for dispersal and struck off on their own. He was afraid of finding them already dead. But John and his father found them barely alive, in a desperately starving condition. Their gaunt and grateful faces were clearly remembered sixty years later. John knew stories of people who had given up on their group, going off to try to avert their deaths, and then, in their desperation, losing control of their actions and ethics. For those who survive together, maintaining their personal community proves more precious than following an optimal foraging strategy.

Again I would like to point out a similarity between John and me in terms of the psychological process of personalizing events rather than objectively seeing the larger context. For my parallel instance, I was only dimly aware of the strategic politics of Cold War power relations that caused me to be in Korea in

1951–2. I had thought it was a localized 'police action' that had run into trouble, and that we were there primarily for a face-saving military recovery from the disastrous American retreat from far northern Korea to a toehold at the southern tip. The recovery succeeded, but much more than recovery was at stake. Had Truman not then summarily fired General MacArthur rather than letting him invade Manchuria, it is quite likely that I would not have written this paper and even possible that you would not be reading it. For the survivors, a successful political strategy proves to be more broadly significant than just recovering from a humiliating setback.

All humans are mostly unaware of the overall cultural structure that tangibly informs the context of their lives, most of the time. But that larger scheme is there, its meaning is primarily formed by traditions, it is primarily perceived through intuition, and it matters a great deal. And it often matters materially. More on this later, but now back to John Blackned and his Americanist apprentice.

The Ethnographer's Enculturation

It started with a bear story, near the end of my first summer's sojourn at Waskaganish, James Bay, and developed the following summer into a regular exchange of storytelling for the current daily rate of pay. This grew into a willing collaboration with an increasingly mutual understanding of what we were doing. John became aware of my sustained interest and growing understanding of what he told me, against the backdrop of the similarity I bore to other collectors he had known.[2] He said he had talked with many white men, but I was the first who wanted to hear everything he had to say.

We exchanged more than a recognition of the boundaries of our respective otherness; we exchanged a measure of our personalities and cultures. We were able to get to know each other because we shared and recognized our common human nature as a basis for communicating our personalities and cultures. And as for Bourdieu's clinical gaze, I could hardly give a clinical gaze towards John, whose own penetrating gaze carried the authority of cumulative experience and a keen mind, telling me things of which I was largely innocent in my own life experience.

I believe we had a practical, enduring friendship; I became John's scribe and tuition-paying student, and he became my teacher. For John, his knowledge was respectfully given painstaking, detailed permanence, on tape and in writing. For me, it was an opportunity to learn from John's stories to the point of pattern emergence – experiencing a portion of his culture as an emergent system.

The narratives, and John's skill in the traditional Cree narrative style of precise understatement, had a cumulative, emergent effect on me. From a beginning as a novice collector of stories, I became a somewhat too-romantic enthusiast of what I first believed to be essentially contact-traditional lore. And then, as the empathetic connection developed between what John had to teach and what I had to learn, my ethnographic maturity led to a search, not for antiquity, but for patterning in the types of events and idioms of experience expressed in the accounts. I could take the accounts into my imagination, and say with fair-minded intellectual conviction, 'That makes sense.' Making sense meant that, while it might or might not necessarily make sense to me personally, I could vicariously participate in the events of the stories – to the extent that I could appreciate that it made good sense to the persons involved. Given this particular narrative tradition, there was a positive, cognitive fitness in what was said.

And in one specific moment during my third summer at Waskaganish, I crossed a threshold, and had a rush of intuition that came with these specific words of my inner speech – 'that makes sense ... *and it really does!!!*' This was more than romantic enthusiasm and more than empathetic and intellectual insight; it was an intuitive certainty. It was also a personal epiphany, and I was finally a committed seeker after deep cultural meanings, which I believe to be an essentially spiritual perspective.[3] It was a cultural rather than a ritual conversion experience; I did not believe in the literality of some things stated in the narratives and I did not acquire a personal relationship with a *mistabeo* or attending spirit. But I had achieved a bi-cultural option of seeing with a perspective and structure of understanding that was close to that held by John. I could test it against what was coming in the next narrative; most of the time it worked, and when it didn't, the surprises were significant further openings. When the interpreter made a mistake, I knew it and asked him to check it with John.

From this experience emerged the form of my book, *Cree Narrative: Expressing the Personal Meanings of Events* (1975). My task was to craft a context that interpreted to outsiders a view of what a Cree traditional world-view looked like from the inside. This required depicting the (apparently) exotic as integral with the normal; specifically, to take the transcript of a 'shaking tent' performance – and give it the wider context of its normal place in the spiritual life of Cree hunters, as this life was expressed in the narratives. My methodology was to present a topical sequence of texts, in translation, with commentaries that led to their better, more biculturally accurate understanding. The texts could be apprehended individually, but with my contextual comments and sequence could take on a kind of narrative plot, and emerge eventually as an aesthetic representation of a traditional Cree world-view.

My specific method was not – and still is not – explicit. When one member of my dissertation committee had asked for a chapter on method, I wrote hotly to my supervisor that I could not provide a menu of how I got from the texts to my conclusions – that my method was *to think about it a lot.* I suppose this may be a persistent and perverse hubris, and that I might, if required, have been able to write a chapter. 'A method, after all, is a varying procedure, changing with the nature of the facts studied and the problems posited' (Radin 1965 [1933]: cxvi).

But I still resist the idea, even though I recognize the variability of specific methods.[4] In fact, my resistance is a part of my generic academic method (W. Smith 1975: 3). I have read several statements of method that I thought could fit quite gracefully with my work. Yet, for this interpretation of narratives,[5] it still is a task that I feel intuitively is wrong; I would be fabricating a false logic by inventing an estimation of the process that I believe emerged intuitively in my mind – of reaching a 'critical mass' of meaning in the narratives, when they so extensively gave form to each other that an inherent and authentic structure emerged (R. Preston 1966).

In summary, I was guided by my personal perspective on trying to understand the people around me, plus a preliminary internalization of the generic academic canon of 'critical, analytical, systematic, deliberate, comparative, public, cumulative ... inductive, and in some sense empirical' thinking, moderated with a readiness to revise my preconceptions (W. Smith, 1975: 3, 18). But the primary guiding of my thought was the work of the narrator and the narratives. I believe that, in a way that I am not sure that I see, I became embedded in a part of Cree tradition, or it became embedded in me – that *to some extent* an authentic, intuitive connection was achieved, in my mind – that John's version of the oral tradition became 'psychologically real' to me. If it is useful to see this as appropriation by me of Native voice, it is also in a non-trivial sense an appropriation of me *by* Native voice. It was a deep sharing, producing a discourse of two cultures, not a theft followed by a cheap resale.

Further, and more important, I believe that what John told me is a spiritually authentic tradition. '[S]piritual authenticity is not possible without fidelity to the past. 'Fidelity' here denotes not sentimentality, but a kind of deliberate *attention* to a reality that, while having 'no one version,' contains, perhaps paradoxically, emotional, psychological, and social truths that are inextricably linked with the present and future' (Hornosty 1995: 55–6; see also Sapir 1932).

When, in the early decades of this century, John's home was a series of hunting camps built or rebuilt annually in the bush, the traditions that were expressed in narratives provided tangibly meaningful guidance for living together in a personal community and hunting for a living. But today's Crees are modern townspeople, and home for the Crees in northwestern Quebec is no longer in the bush. Rather it is located in one of nine municipally governed villages within the Cree Regional Authority, on land legislatively specified for the Crees by the governments of Quebec and Canada.

Narratives of past Cree environment and culture are still potentially profound guidance, but are not now self-consciously brought out for sharing in the leisure time of the evening. If traditional guidance for hunting and travelling in the bush is of diminished interest, traditional guidance for living in community could still be very relevant (Cruikshank 1990). But adapting to the present is the main priority, and some people feel that it is time to 'let the past go.' Perhaps the next generation will be more inclined to pay deliberate attention to the community ethics imbedded in their traditional hunting ethics (Berkes, George, and Preston 1992). If that happens, John's stories will be available, and authentic.

The Theoretical Problem of Inventing Traditions

Now I want to consider a parallel problem of presentism or historical shortsightedness regarding tradition. Within the Americanist ethnographic camp, the more extreme 'post-structuralist' or 'invention of tradition' proponents would like to think that we humans are not nearly so chronically embedded in tradition as some of us have long believed. My straw persons in this argument are Richard Handler and Jocelyn Linnekin (1984, 1991), who propose that the concept of authenticity is 'a red herring' of spurious essentialism, because all culture is mere social construction, constantly re-invented to serve present purposes, in our radically polyvocal milieu. Their argument makes apparent sense if it is set in a dichotomy between (1) tradition conceived as something objective (superorganic), passively inherited, embodied, and transmitted, and (2) tradition as the purely contemporary product of human self-consciousness. But this is a desperate dichotomy of positivist and subjectivist perspectives.[6]

Perhaps, in consequence, we are now more critically, intellectually aware that people's negotiation of personal or ethnic identity or ideology often involves rapid reinvention or transformation of some small portion of tradition that they are self-consciously aware of. But this fact does not justify ignoring the larger and less conscious domains of cultural form (for instance, syntax, core personality, other cultural structures), which are not nearly so accessible to deliberate change and are much more time-bound. As Sapir told us decades ago, persons in groups in history create a 'collective art of expression' (1921: 246) whose aesthetic character drifts historically towards a type or paradigm, reaches a poise, and then decays away only to drift towards another type.

Is there now some good evidence that this conceptualization of tradition is obsolete? Is postmodern anthropology justified in turning away from both structure and history? How much of this liberation from the modernist canon is either (1) trying to stay plausibly engaged in research amidst the face-to-face conflicts of the politics of resistance, or (2) distancing ourselves from the pitfalls of rapid change through finding intellectual composure in literary explorations that are abstracted from empirical influence – turning away from our perceptions of meaningful relationships between actual human beings. We seem to be moving into a postmodern blur, even escaping headlong into subjective idealism, at a time when we need to have more empirical and systematic knowledge as a basis for rapid adaptation to globalization. I may be voicing a modernist solecism, but I believe that this is a time for renewed efforts at synthetic statements that make sense of the scope and complexity of the present, as emergent from the past. Instead, we seem to be headed back into the pre–Second World War enthusiasm for moral relativism (Wolf 1964), symptomatic of the cult of individualism (Dumont 1986) and its scientific counterpart, arbitrariness.

If authenticity can be said to be relative to 'the eye of the beholder,' then it should also be said that eyes, minds, and intuitional processes are everywhere part of a perceptual configuration that is, at a deep level, very similarly organized in all of us (human nature), and, at an intermediate level, characteristically patterned in groups of us (culture), and, at the surface level, made individually distinctive by accidents of birth and biography (personality).

Authentic Traditions as a Solution to the Problem, Not as the Problem

What is needed is a reaffirmation of Americanist ethnographic empiricism, for the interpretive goal of developing a more grounded and extensive universe of human discourse, for the practical goals of the people studied ethnographically, and for a more adequate answer to the question of how you can believe what an ethnographer says about what other people say. The empiricist perspective is stated with characteristic grace and clarity by Sapir:

> Now fantasied universes of self-contained meaning are the finest and noblest substitutes we can ever devise for that precise and loving insight into the nooks and crannies of the real that must be forever denied us. But we must not reverse the arrow of experience and claim for our experience's imaginative condensations the primacy in an appeal to our loyalty, which properly belongs to our perceptions of men and women as the ultimate units of value in our day to day view of the world. If we do not thus value the nucleii of consciousness from which all science, all art, all history, all culture, have flowed as symbolic by-products in the humble but intensely urgent business of establishing meaningful

relationships between actual human beings, we commit personal suicide. (1949 [1939]: 581)

Authenticity, I submit, refers to persons, intimate clusters of persons, communities, or societies, whose lived experience is harmonious with, or true to, their inherent or intrinsic cultural structure or historically emergent form (Sapir 1924). Authenticity is not equal to historical accuracy; tradition is not equal to truth. Instead, authentic traditions express the integrity of their cultural form/structure. Any given cultural form serves as a bridge between empirical reality, human nature, and culture. The actual processes for this bridging are found, as Sapir told us, in the interactions of specific individuals and, on the subjective side, in the world of meanings that each abstracts for himself from these interactions. Given this essentially interactional and cumulative perspective on cultural form, we can extend the concepts of authenticity applied to individuals by some of our intellectual ancestors. Where Kierkegaard, Sartre, and Simmel located primary moral agency in individuals, Sapir broadened the field of agency with his inclusive conception of the individual. Individuals exist only in groups, and only in the flux of history, and so are embedded in cultural form. And if we accept that persons are necessarily so in-formed, authenticity *is* achieved by (1) willing and doing the genuine good (Kierkegaard 1938: 202), (2) creating/choosing value (Sartre 1956: 615), and (3) cultivating the connection between fidelity to the past, forthright recognition of the tangible world of the present, and a commitment to enhancing the coherence between the two (Simmel 1968 [1911]). To put an old adage into a new context, authenticity is being true to form.[8]

In the portrayal of John's mentoring and my enculturation, I have given a specific case in point. John Blackned was an authentic elder, because his teaching about his tradition was guided by his intuitive grasp of 'continuity and wholeness in thought, feeling, and moral choice' (Selznick 1992: 65), and by his 'fidelity to the past, ... a kind of deliberate attention to a reality that, while having 'no one version,' contains, perhaps paradoxically, emotional, psychological, and social truths that are inextricably linked with the present and future' (Hornosty 1995: 55–6).

NOTES

1 Or at least as well as the person interpreting for us could translate and as well as I could listen (cf. Sapir, in his Paiute field notes on the good fortune some children have to be able to discipline their minds to listen right through to the end of the stories, rather than drifting off to sleep).

2 He did not travel out of the Cree region until a brief medical trip, quite late in his life.

3 This is treacherous ground for many social scientists, and I should explain that it refers to *a sense of primary loyalty* – to the goal of 'that precise and loving insight into the nooks and crannies of the real which must be forever denied us' (Sapir 1939: 581).

4 An understatement. I taught the graduate field method and theory course at McMaster for 20 years.

5 For other tasks I have undertaken, this is not true. It is the narratives specifically that I am concerned with here.

6 This rejection of authenticity as essentialism seems to be yet another facet of the 1960s critique of objectivity (Maquet 1964), which is in turn traceable to theorists of historiography such as Marc Bloch and E.H. Carr, and to philosophical sociology, specifically Mannheim's paradox (Geertz 1973: 194ff.). Essentialism is indeed a red herring, since for the purposes of our argument it doesn't really matter whether, or to what extent or in what ways, it is involved in tradition/cultural forms. It is the emergent forms themselves that are germane to authenticity.

The tangible world, built upon and operated on by symbolic constructions, remains essentialist in its very substance. There is culture, and then there is reality. This is not a paradox, though we can perceive it so. The bond between symbols and substance can be ignored, but at our peril.

Eric Wolf, in *Anthropology*, bases his argument on power relations, examining the effects of the Second World War: (a) on Americanist moral relativism, given the essential wrongness of the Nazi death camps; and (b) on Melanesians, who recognized the power the Japanese, American, and Australian armies had access to, and sought by whatever symbolic means to appropriate it. The means were rarely effective, but the power was essentialist – tangibly effective in the world – and the symbolic strategies were attempts to tap into it.

Clifford Geertz (1973), in 'Ideology as a Cultural System,' differentiates between cultural constructions and reality, also appealing to the Second World War, to claim that the Japanese learned that war really is hell, and not their culturally constructed mother of culture.

7 It is in this sense that we will not credit a person with genuine culture on the basis of knowedge, virtuosity, or refinements that only act as additives that come to a personality from an external realm of value (Simmel 1968 [1911], echoed by Sartre).

REFERENCES

Baxter, Brian. 1982. *Alienation and Authenticity: Some Consequences for Organized Work*. London: Tavistock

Bedard, Joanna. 1995. 'A Critical Review of the Theory Invented Tradition.' Ph.D. comprehensive exam, paper #1. Dept of Anthropology, McMaster University, Hamilton.

Ben-Amos, Dan. 1984. 'Tradition and Identity, the Seven Strands of Tradition: Varieties in Its Meaning in American Folklore Studies.' *Journal of American Folklore* 21: 97–131.

Berkes, Fikret, Peter J. George, and Richard J. Preston. 1992. 'The Cree View of Land and Resources: Indigenous Ecological Knowledge.' McMaster University (Hamilton), TASO Report, 2nd series, no. 8.

Black (Rogers), Mary B. 1967. 'An Ethnoscience Investigation into Ojibwa World View.' Ph.D. dissertation, Department of Anthropology, Stanford University.

– 1973. 'Belief Systems,' in John J. Honigmann, ed., *Handbook of Social and Cultural Anthropology*, 549. New York: Rand-McNally.

Bloch, Marc. 1954. *The Historian's Craft*. New York: A.A. Knopf.

Borofsky, Robert. 1987. *Making History: Pukapukan and Anthropological Constructions of Knowledge*. Cambridge: Cambridge University Press.

Carr, E.H. 1962. *What Is History?* New York: A.A. Knopf.

Conn, Walter E. 1981. *Conscience–Development and Self-Transcendence.* Birmingham, AL: Religious Education Press.

Cruikshank, Julie. 1990. *Life Lived Like a Story.* Vancouver: UBC Press.

Dumont, Louis. 1986. *Essays on Individualism.* Chicago: University of Chicago Press.

Evans-Pritchard, Edward E. 1965. *Theories of Primitive Religion.* Oxford: Clarendon Press.

Fox, Richard G. 1991a. 'Introduction to Working in the Present.' In R.G. Fox, ed., *Recapturing Anthropology: Working in the Present.* Santa Fe: School of American Research Press.

– 1991b. 'For a Nearly New Culture History.' In Fox, ed., *Recapturing Anthropology.*

Friere, Paulo. 1985. *The Politics of Education.* South Hadley, MA: Bergen & Garvey.

Geertz, Clifford. 1973. 'Thick Description.' In *The Interpretation of Culture.* New York: Basic Books.

– 1973. 'Ideology as a Cultural System.' In *The Interpretation of Culture.* New York: Basic Books.

– 1988. *Works and Lives.* Stanford: Stanford University Press.

Habib, Jasmin. 1995. 'On the Uses of the Past: The Politics of Representation and Representation of Politics.' Ph.D. comprehensive exam, paper #2. Dept. of Anthropology, McMaster University, Hamilton.

Hallowell, A. Irving. 1946. 'Some Psychological Characteristics of the Northeastern Indians.' In Frederick S. Johnson, ed., *Man in Northeastern North America,* 195–225. Andover, MA: Robert S. Peabody Foundation.

– and Jennifer S.H. Brown. 1992. *The Ojibwa of Berens River: Ethnography into History.* New York: Holt-Rinehart-Winston.

Handler, Richard, and Jocelyn Linnekin. 1984. 'Tradition, Genuine or Spurious.' *Journal of American Folklore* 97: 273–90.

Hornosty, Janina. 1995. 'Hunter, Adult Adolescent, and Wounded Warlock: Images of Men in English Canadian Women's Fiction (1960–1993).' Ph.D. dissertation, McMaster University, Hamilton.

Jameson, Frederic. 1991. *Postmodernism, or, the Cultural Logic of Late Capitalism.* Durham, NC: Duke University Press.

Kierkegaard, Søren. 1938. *Purity of Heart Is to Will One Thing.* New York: Harper & Row; reissued 1956.

Koenig, Edward. 1995. Ph.D. comprehensive exam, paper #1. Dept of Anthropology, McMaster University, Hamilton.

Keesing, Roger. 1989. 'Creating the Past: Custom and Identity in the Contemporary Pacific.' *Contemporary Pacific* 1(1): 19–42.

Kundera, Milan. 1986. *The Art of the Novel.* Grove Press.

Linnekin, Jocelyn. 1991. 'Cultural Invention and the Dilemma of Authenticity.' *American Anthropologist* 93: 446–9.

Maquet, J.J. 1964. 'Objectivity in Anthropology.' *Current Anthropology* 5: 47–55.

McBride, Joseph. 1992. *Albert Camus, Philosopher and Litterateur.* New York: St Martin's Press.

McCarthy, Theresa. 1995. 'Continuity, Creativity, and Change: Semantics and Politics in Studies of "Tradition."' Ph.D. comprehensive exam, paper #1. Dept of Anthropology, McMaster University, Hamilton.

Osgood, Cornelius. 1940. *Ingalik Material Culture.* New Haven: Yale University Publications in Anthropology, no. 22.

– 1959. *Ingalik Mental Culture.* New Haven: Yale University Publications in Anthropology, no. 56.

Parry, Benita. 1987. 'Problems in Current Theories of Colonial Discourse.' *Oxford Literary Review* 9(1+2): 27–58.

Preston, Richard J. 1966. 'Edward Sapir's Anthropology: Style, Structure, and Method.' *American Anthropologist* 68: 1107–28.

– 1975. *Cree Narrative: Expressing the Personal Meanings of Events*. Ottawa: National Museum of Man, Mercury Paper in Ethnology no. 30.

Preston, Sarah C. 1986. *Let the Past Go*. Ottawa: National Museum of Man, Mercury Paper in Ethnology no. 104

Radin, Paul. 1965. [1933]. *The Method and Theory of Ethnology*. New York: Basic Books

Rosenberry, William, and Jay O'Brien, eds. 1991. Introduction to *Golden Ages*. Berkeley and Los Angeles: University of California Press.

Sapir, Edward. 1921. *Language*. New York: Harcourt.

– 1924. 'Culture, Genuine and Spurious.' *American Journal of Sociology* 29: 401–29.

– 1932. 'Cultural Anthropology and Psychiatry.' *Journal of Abnormal and Social Psychology* 27: 229–42.

– 1939. 'Psychiatric and Cultural Pitfalls in the Business of Getting a Living.' *Mental Health* 9: 237–44.

Sartre, Jean-Paul. 1956. *Being and Nothingness*. New York: Philosophical Library.

Selznick, Philip. 1992. *The Moral Commonwealth: Social Theory and the Promise of Community*. Berkeley and Los Angeles: University of California Press.

Simmel, Georg. 1968 [1911]. *Georg Simmel: The Conflict in Modern Culture and Other Essays*. Translated by K. Peter Etzkorn. New York: Teachers College Press.

Smith, Eric Alden. 1981. 'The Application of Optimal Foraging Theory to the Analysis of Hunter-Gatherer Group Size.' In Bruce Winterhalder and Eric Alden Smith, eds, *Hunter-Gatherer Foraging Strategies*. Chicago: University of Chicago Press.

Smith, Wilfred Cantwell. 1975. 'Methodology and the Study of Religion: Some Misgivings.' In Robert D. Baird, ed., *Methodological Issues in Religious Studies*, 1–30. Chico, CA: New Horizons Press.

Thomas, Nicholas. 1992.'The Inversion of Tradition.' *American Ethnologist* 19(2): 213–32.

Trask, Haunani-Kay. 1991. 'Natives and Anthropologists: The Colonial Struggle.' *The Contemporary Pacific* 3: 159–67.

Trilling, Lionel. 1972. *Sincerity and Authenticity*. Cambridge, MA: Harvard University Press.

Wolf, Eric. 1964. *Anthropology*. New York: Prentice Hall.

Zimmerman, Michael. 1981. *Eclipse of the Self and Development of Heidegger's Concept of Authenticity*. Columbus: Ohio University Press.

10 Dialogues between Worlds: Mesoamerica after and before the European Invasion

DENNIS TEDLOCK

> Our margins are shared. That's where we live, and there is hope in that because in those margins nothing is strange or odd or lost or without purpose.
>
> Simon J. Ortiz

Five centuries after Europeans first invaded the Americas, it has become possible to speak of a dialogical anthropology, which is to say an anthropology whose practitioners are becoming increasingly cognizant of the dialogical potential of language not only in their fieldwork, but in their writing as well.[1] The dialogical reformulation of the writing of cultural anthropology is radical not only in the sense that it takes the discipline back to its roots in fieldwork, but in the political sense as well, since it brings to consciousness the homology between the structure of the discourse of an omniscient third-person observer and the structure of imperialism.

There may have been a time when field dialogues could be conceptualized as mere means to an end, but the contemporary critique of representations has made that position untenable. Perhaps the greatest irony of this critique, for Americanists, is that all along we have been working in an area of the world whose languages are remarkable for the degree to which they require their speakers and writers to deal with epistemological questions, using quotatives and other evidentials to identify representations for what they are (see Chafe and Nichols 1986: viii and pt 1). When New World texts are translated into European languages, their epistemological aspects are routinely reduced and even eliminated.

Here I will explore some of the earliest recorded dialogues between European invaders and the indigenous peoples of the Americas, Mesoamerica in particular. But let us begin at the beginning, with some Native American accounts of the first dialogues that ever occurred anywhere.

According to a story told in the Keresan villages of New Mexico, 'everything that has names' was beneath the earth at the beginning. The emergence of the present order began with a conversation between two gods. Here is the version Franz Boas took down from a man named Kotye in 1919, in the village of K'awaika (Laguna). Note that the discussion has a tentative, uncertain quality:

> 'How is it?' said our mother Nautsityi. 'Is it not yet done? Shall we not put out our children?' Then our father Ichtsityi spoke:
>
> 'No,' said he. 'First I shall divide the water and the land.' Then spoke our mother Nautsityi:
>
> 'Go ahead,' said she. Then our father Ichtsityi said,
>
> 'Let me try to see,' said Ichtsityi. Then to the mountain top went out our father Ichtsityi. (Boas 1928, 1: 1)

So the first words ever spoken formed a dialogue that opens with question and answer, the most fundamental form of dialogue.

Far to the south of the Keresan villages, four centuries before Boas wrote down what Kotye told him, Cristóbal Velasco and other members of the ruling house of the former K'iche' kingdom were writing in the Guatemalan highlands, creating an alphabetic version of an ancient Mayan book known as the Popol Vuh or 'Council Book.' Again in their story, the world begins with a conversation among gods of both sexes, the Bearers and the Begetters:

> 'How should the sowing be, and the dawning? Who is to be the provider, nurturer?'
>
> 'Let it be this way, think about it: this water should be removed, emptied out for the formation of the earth's own plate and platform, then should come the sowing, the dawning of the sky-earth.' (D. Tedlock 1996: 65)

Again a dialogue is opened with questions and answers, a dialogue among gods whose power is not absolute. After they raise the earth out of the water they hold further conversations that lead to experiments in the creation of human beings. Three times they fail, but on the fourth try they succeed in making beings who are able to speak when spoken to.

When Europeans invaded the Americas they brought a different story with them, different not only in its character as a story but in the claim that it was everyone's story whether they knew it or not, and not just a story by and for its European tellers. Here is that claim as it was made on the Franciscan side of the 1524 dialogue between Spanish and Mexica (Aztec) priests, as reconstructed by

Fray Bernardino de Sahagún: 'Verily, the only, the sole divine word is the one we have borne hither, the one he had us bear hither, the great speaker of divine things, the Pope, the Holy Father' (Klor de Alva 1980: 78). This 'sole divine word' began with a singular male deity who commanded the world and its forms of life into existence by speaking the monologue of absolute power. The first words of the first man were also spoken as a monologue, one in which he gave names to all the animals and then to the first woman, speaking in her presence but in the third person. Dialogues came later, all of them disastrous: the serpent tempted Eve and Eve tempted Adam, then the singular deity extracted a confession from Adam, condemning him to a life of toil and Eve to the pain of childbirth.

Many of the native peoples of the New World, among them the K'iche', have come to tell their own versions of biblical stories – or to adapt biblical characters to their own stories, as the case may be. But even after four centuries of missionization, K'iche' narrators continue to give language a fundamentally dialogical role in the primordial world, and they place a positive construction on the earliest dialogues. Mateo Uz Abaj of the town of Chi Nik'aj, speaking in 1976, cast Jesus and Mary as the joint creators of the first humans. Here is his representation of the conversation the two of them had after making Adam:

> And then she said, because the Ancient Word was spoken by this Virgin Mary,
> 'My Jesus, look at the man, my Jesus.' When she had told him, then he said,
> 'He looks-he looks all right, doesn't he?'
> 'But no-he's sighing.'
> 'What are we going to do by way of preaching to this man? Since this man is very sad.' Then she said,
> 'No. We'll make a helper.' (D. Tedlock 1997: 176)

So it is that a divine dialogue between female and male leads to the creation of Eve, a dialogue in which the female party explicitly rejects 'preaching' (a type of monologue) as the solution to Adam's loneliness. Also thoroughly revisionist is the scene in which Eve and Adam are given their respective roles as human beings. In place of the biblical monologue, in which they listen passively while angry commands come down from on high, there comes an exchange between the two of them:

> Then Adam said to her,
> 'You, Eve: you have to make a shirt. You have to make some pants, you have to make everything. And with cotton.'

'And you, Adam: You have to work. With a pickax, with a machete.' (D. Tedlock 1997: 150)

Stories like this one have long been treated as instances of European 'influence' on passive New World others, when in fact these others have actively and even radically reformulated what they heard from European sources.[2] What needs attention now, from the descendants of the invaders, is the cultural critique implied by a discourse that neither ignores European ideas nor accepts them in their original forms.

Among the most remarkable dialogues in history are the ones that took place in 1519 between Hernán Cortés and various Mexica messengers and their lords, all the way up to Motecuhzoma himself. These dialogues required the mediation of two interpreters, each of whom had become bilingual while serving as a slave to Mayan masters. One was Gerónimo de Aguilar, a shipwrecked Spaniard who had learned Yucatec Maya, and the other was Malintzin (later baptized Marina), a native speaker of Nahuatl who had learned Chontal Maya. What Cortés said in Castilian was resaid by Aguilar in Yucatec, which was then apprehended through the filter of Chontal by Malintzin, who resaid it in Nahuatl; then the sequence was reversed for what Motecuhzoma said in Nahuatl.

Cortés, in reporting his exchanges with his Mexica counterparts, makes only one passing mention of his translators, giving Aguilar's full name and referring to Malintzin as 'an Indian woman from Putunchan' (Pagden 1971: 73); otherwise he writes as if he had been engaged in direct conversations. A different story is told by Bernal Díaz del Castillo, who observed these exchanges. Again and again he calls attention to the importance of Aguilar and especially of Malintzin, and he reveals a dramatic detail that shows how strongly the conditions of the conversations were noticed on the Mexica side. The Indians gave Cortés the name Malinche, he writes, and he takes this to mean 'Marina's captain' (Díaz 1963: 172). In fact Malinche is simply the Spanish mispronunciation of Malintzin, which would seem to indicate that the Mexica were naming Cortés directly after the woman who served as his interpreter. But if they themselves were saying 'Malinche' rather than 'Malintzin' (except when talking about her), then they were also making fun of the way he pronounced her name, naming him, as birds are often named in Nahuatl (and in every other language), after a sequence of sounds they often heard him uttering. Cortés then becomes, in effect, 'he who mispronounces the name of his interpreter repeatedly.'

Whether or not Cortés writes his interpreters into a given scene, he uses indirect discourse to gloss over everything he said to them and (with two exceptions) everything they reported Mexicas as saying. Díaz sometimes quotes the Spanish side of an exchange and (more often) the Mexica side, but with one exception (Díaz 1963: 237–8) he is like Cortés in not quoting *both* sides of the same exchange. As for the various Mexica authors who wrote their accounts of the Spanish invasion in Nahuatl, they not only give an explicit role to Malintzin, but they are just as consistent in quoting both sides of dialogues as the Spaniards are consistent in not doing so (León-Portilla 1962: 26–8, 39–40, 52, 64–5, 80–1).

In each of the two Mexica quotations offered by Cortés, Motecuhzoma makes a brief speech in which (among other things) he interprets the arrival of Cortés as the return of a nameless exiled king (Pagden 1971: 85–6, 98–9, 467). Díaz also mentions the mythic theme of return, but his direct quotations of Motecuhzoma closely coincide with those of Cortés only on the following topic: 'Malinche, I know that these people of Tlascala with whom you are so friendly have told you that I am a sort of god ... But I know very well that you are too intelligent to believe this and will take it as a joke. See now, Malinche, my body is made of flesh and blood like yours' (Díaz 1963: 223–4). What Motecuhzoma was attempting to do here, as a king who had some claim to divine ancestry and was quite aware of the ceremonial aura of deification that surrounded him, was to provide Cortés with a dialogical ground on which to stand, the face-to-face ground of human communication.

Subsequent authors have preferred the story that Indians believed the Spaniards were gods to the story that Motecuhzoma denied being a god. No such believing Indians appear in the writings of Cortés, who tells only of Motecuhzoma's effort to prevent the opposite error (Pagden 1971: 86). Díaz describes Indians as circulating rumours to the effect that Spaniards were gods, but he also reports incidents in which Indian warriors answered the rumours by vowing to kill the Spaniards, Indian priests divined the rumours to be false, and Motecuhzoma himself declared the rumours to be 'childish stories' (Díaz 1963: 141, 151, 223). As for the Mexica authors, they do state that Motecuhzoma wondered whether Quetzalcoatl (or Plumed Serpent) might be among the approaching strangers. But they describe this Quetzalcoatl not as a god but as a returning king, a king named after a god (Sahagún 1950–75, book 12: 9).

According to the Mexica account, Motecuhzoma continues to consider Cortés a potential king when he actually arrives in Tenochtitlán. But at the same time Motecuhzoma raises a question about the legitimacy of Cortés right to his face, referring to 'the unknown place whence thou hast come – from among the clouds, from among the mists' (Sahagún 1950–75, book 12: 44). If we read this trope from the European side it seems to support the elevation of Cortés to the status of a god, but it reads quite differently from the other side. Among the

Mexica and throughout Mesoamerica, claims to nobility were staked on the naming of specific earthly places, usually mountains with caves in them, as places of origin. In contrast, as the Mexica authors state the matter elsewhere, those whose souls 'dropped' from the heavens were 'the common people' (Sahagún 1950–75, book 10: 169). Taken together, Motecuhzoma's speculations about the return of Quetzalcoatl and his imputation of a cloudy and misty origin to Cortés make it sound as though he was not so much wondering whether this foreigner was a god as he was questioning the legitimacy of his obvious pretensions to power.

The story of the Spanish invasion crosses over into the realm of myth when its later tellers, unlike Cortés and Díaz and unlike the Mexica authors, make Quetzalcoatl the returning king into Quetzalcoatl the returning god (see Pagden 1971: 467–8). In effect they transform Cortés into a kind of Messiah, only thinly disguised by his newly acquired Indian name. But unlike the Old World Messiah, he escapes sacrificial death. To have that part of the plot played out in a newly invaded land, Europeans would have to wait for the eighteenth century and the story of Captain Cook, whom his countrymen would construct as what Gananath Obeyesekere calls 'the avatar of Cortés' (1992: 143). In this story, as told by both Englishmen and by Christian Hawaiians, the pagan Hawaiians who kill Cook have mistaken him for Lono, one of their gods. Here again, European mythmaking requires that a native trope, whereby persons perceived as kings (in this case Cook) may be named after gods (such as Lono), be taken literally (ibid.: 76–7). Also required is the suppression of a scene in which a local ruler attempts to shift the leader of an expedition onto a ground where they can dialogue. This time the attempt takes the radical form of a name-trading ceremony (ibid.: 88), with the visitor receiving the name Kariopoo (the English rendition of Kalani'opu'u) and the host taking the name Tuute (the Hawaiian rendition of Cook).

Once constructed, the myth of what Obeyesekere calls 'the redoubtable European who is a god to savage peoples' (1992: 177) has such a powerful hold on the European imagination that even Tzvetan Todorov, in the midst of his effort to reinterpret the events in Mexico as a chapter in the history of communications, helplessly declares his belief in 'the paralyzing belief that the Spaniards are gods' and cites the case of Captain Cook as parallel evidence (Todorov 1984: 75). Meanwhile he completely suppresses the incident in which Motecuhzoma denies his own divinity in order to speak with Cortés on the level ground of dialogue.

Judging from the accounts of a wide range of Mesoamerican writers, one of the most shocking aspects of the behaviour of the first European invaders was the asymmetrical conditions they imposed on the conduct of key dialogues. In the Mexica account of the first meeting between Motecuhzoma's messengers and Cortés, on a ship anchored off the Gulf coast, the treatment of the messengers is the main topic: 'Then the Captain gave orders, and the messengers were chained by the feet and by the neck. When this had been done, the great cannon was fired off. The messengers lost their senses and fainted away' (León-Portilla 1962: 26). When they revived, Cortés had them wined and dined and then challenged them to engage in hand-to-hand martial combat with Spaniards, using Spanish equipment. They protested that they were messengers, not warriors, but he persisted in his challenge and they fled the ship at the first opportunity.

In accounts of early confrontations with Europeans that were written by Mayans, the memory of the conditions the invaders imposed on key dialogues is preserved even where the texts of the dialogues themselves are not recorded. Such is the case with the 1524 interrogation of the two K'iche' kings, Oxib' Kej and B'elejeb' Tz'i', by Pedro de Alvarado. By Alvarado's own account, he burned the kings at the stake because he suspected them of a plot against his life, his final evidence for this plot being 'their confessions' (Mackie 1924: 60, 62). According to the account written by a Kaqchikel author, Francisco Hernández Arana, the two kings 'were tortured by Tunatiuj [Alvarado],' after which they 'were burned by Tunatiuj' (Recinos and Goetz 1953: 120). Torture, of course, would be the means by which Alvarado obtained the kings' confessions of the crime for which he burned them. That he used the standard European torture of the time, which is to say hanging by the wrists, is revealed in the Popol Vuh, which states that the kings 'were hung by the Castilian people' (see D. Tedlock 1996: 334). The use of torture makes for a different story than the one European and Euroamerican historians have gone on repeating, right down to the present day. They ignore the Kaqchikel account, misinterpret the Popol Vuh as referring to hanging as a form of execution, and rule in favour of Alvarado's statement that he executed the kings by burning them (D. Tedlock 1993: 141–2). For them, the conditions of the dialogue in which Alvarado obtained the kings' confessions is not an issue. They leave their narratives blank at precisely the spot where Mayan authors focus attention on torture.

In the Popol Vuh the torture of the kings serves as the distinguishing feature of a particular period in a chronicle that is something like a Plains winter count, except that it goes by generations of kings rather than by years. European methods of interrogation also find a place in a chronicle composed by Yucatec Mayan authors, who list a period during which 'Bishop Toral arrived [and] the hangings ceased' (Roys 1967: 138). These hangings, which took place in 1562, had been ordered by Fray Diego de Landa in the name of the Holy Inquisition (Barrera Vásquez and Rendón 1948: 156n). Like the K'iche' kings tortured by Alvarado, Landa's witnesses confessed to crimes, the worst of these being blasphemous rituals that combined the supreme sacrifices of the Mayan and Christian religions. Bishop Toral reopened Landa's investigation without the use of torture and concluded that the previous testimony was largely false (Scholes and Roys 1938: 593–619).

Historians and ethnohistorians have long preferred the evidence compiled by Landa, which is far richer than Toral's. To support their use of Landa they have argued that many details in the Inquisition testimony agree with the rest of what we know about the Mayan culture of the time.[3] This is a circular argument, given that the principal source of this knowledge has long been Landa's own *Relación de las cosas de Yucatán* (Tozzer 1941), which he wrote four years after playing the role of Inquisitor. Even the most critical reader of these documents, Inga Clendinnen (1987: 188), has clung to the reality of clandestine child sacrifices in which, so the record says, Mayas combined crucifixion with heart extraction. Here we must protest that if Landa was anything like his fellow inquisitors in Europe, it was precisely when he focused on what he conceived to be diabolical rituals that he would have been most likely to distort the testimony by asking suggestive questions (see Ginzburg 1990: 158). As in Europe, the resulting narratives would have fit a model already well known to him. In the case of the alleged child crucifixions, the most obvious model is provided by the wild tales of Jewish ritual murders that circulated in Spain just before the expulsion of the Jews, especially the story of the Santo Niño de la Guardia (Kamen 1985: 15–16). The source of this story was a sensational trial in which six Jews and six Jewish converts to Christianity confessed, under torture, to having carried out a ritual in which they crucified a Christian child and then cut his heart out. The trial took place in 1491, twenty years before any Spaniard even knew of the existence of the Maya.

Landa introduces his *Relación* with an account of the geography and history of Yucatán, but his main purpose is to describe the customs of its people. It has become a tradition among Americanist ethnographers to name Sahagún rather than Landa when seeking an early predecessor, but if we are searching for a predecessor in the writing of the anthropological genre that dominated the first six or seven decades of the twentieth century, then Landa's *Relación* makes him a far better candidate than Sahagún. The genre in question is the ethnographic monograph, in which the culture of the other is presented almost entirely in the voice of an omniscient observer who writes in the third person plural and the ethnographic present.

The sequence of Landa's topics seems a bit disorganized, but their overall effect is familiar enough: house construction, food and drink, music and drama, commerce, agriculture, kinship, religion, warfare, the life cycle, the ceremonial cycle, the writing system, and native knowledge of plants and animals. He is also like many later ethnographers in the extent to which he excludes dialogues, leaving native terms as the last traces of the voices of the others. Indeed, he narrates only a single face-to-face exchange, a dialogue to which he himself was not a party. The person on the Spanish side, who is not quoted directly, was the explorer Hernández de Córdoba, on the occasion of his landing at the spot now known as Cabo Cotoche in Yucatán: 'He found some Indian fishermen and asked them what land it was and they replied "*Cotoch*," which means "our houses and our country," and from this the name was given to that point, and asking them further by signs about the character of their land, they replied "*Ci uthan*," which means, "They say so." The Spaniards called it Yucatán' (Tozzer 1941: 4). It is indicative of the low value Landa placed on dialogue as such that his sole reported example documents the production of misinformation. Worse yet, he himself missed the meaning of the statement *Ci uthan* (*Ki' u t'an*). The Maya were actually making a comment about Hernández de Córdoba, saying, 'The way he talks is funny.'[4]

The supreme irony of Landa's suppression of dialogue is that epigraphers have been able to make sense of his account of Mayan writing only by putting his examples of hieroglyphic spellings back into the context of an interview. They start from the answers he got and then reconstruct the questions he must have asked in order to get them (Schele 1992: 12–15; Coe 1992: 104–5). The four glyphs he took to be a strangely complicated spelling for *le*, the Mayan word for 'noose,' turn out to be the signs for the four syllables he actually spoke to his informant, first naming (in Spanish) the two letters of the alphabetic spelling of *le* and then pronouncing the complete word: 'Ele, e, *le*.' When he elicited what he thought was the Mayan alphabet, what he actually got was a partial syllabary corresponding to the sounds of the names of the letters of the Spanish alphabet. He asked for the letter called 'be,' for example, but never got signs for the syllables *ba*, *bi*, *bo*, and *bu*. And finally, when he asked the informant to write something of his own choosing, he got the signs for the sentence *Ma in k'ati*, which means, 'I don't want to.'[5]

Ki' u t'an and *Ma in k'ati* are the only Mayan sentences in Landa's *Relación*. It is difficult to imagine a greater contrast than the one between these two isolated utterances and the plenitude of Nahuatl discourse in Sahagún's *Historia general de las cosas de Nueva España*, an encyclopedia of Mexica culture he compiled between 1565 and 1568 (Sahagún 1950–75). But an equal contrast exists between many of the ethnographic monographs produced during the present century and the collections of native texts published by some of the same authors under separate covers. In the one genre the ethnographer speaks at great length while the natives are confined to a marginal or supplementary discourse, and in the other the natives speak at great length while the ethnographer or linguist keeps to the margins. The writers of monographs may include excerpts from native discourse, but these are removed from their original dialogical contexts and relocated in the ethnographic present, where they serve to illustrate some point the ethnographer is already making rather than taking their places in a hermeneutical dialogue between an interpreter and a text.

Ethnographic monographs and text collections both require conversations between fieldworkers and natives for their production, but quotations of what fieldworkers said to the natives are usually suppressed even in the marginal discourse of these two genres. Most text collections are made on the basis of a theory, usually implicit, that the natives are saying things they would say to one another anyway, even in the absence of a fieldworker. The texts consist mostly of myths, legends, and tales, sometimes supplemented by accounts of events that occurred within recent generations. Sahagún's *Historia general* includes some texts of these kinds, among them the account of the Spanish invasion that was quoted earlier in the present essay. But the predominant discourse is that of third-person ethnography, the difference being that the natives are producing it themselves and in their own language, with Sahagún as their immediate audience. Thus Sahagún, as a predecessor of twentieth-century anthropologists working in the Americas, has his closest relationship to those who have run the production of ethnography as a cottage industry, such as Franz Boas (1921) and Paul Radin (1923). The first anthropologist to make extensive use of this method in Mesoamerica was Ruth L. Bunzel, in *Chichicastenango: A Guatemalan Village* (1952).

Beginning with the informants of Sahagún, native writers who have been put to work describing their own worlds, topic by topic, have produced a discourse that reaches its closest resemblance to the ethnographic monograph when they write on topics that are not focused on interpersonal relationships – geography, for example, or technological procedures that can be carried out by a person working alone. But the more the interactions of persons come into play, including interactions between human persons and other beings who are treated as persons, the more native writers diverge from their professional counterparts. It is here that they turn to a narrative mode of discourse, laced with quotations of what persons say to one another. This is particularly true of accounts of rituals, which include quotations of liturgical and oratorical discourse (Sahagún 1950–75, books 1 and 2). In the sense that such accounts both quote what people say and give the contexts in which they say it, they stand in direct contrast to collections of native texts that follow academic conventions set up early in the twentieth century, and instead resemble contemporary ethnographies of speaking of the kind published by Victoria Bricker (1973) and Gary Gossen (1974) on the Tzotzil Maya. It should also be remarked that native writers, again beginning with Sahagún's informants, are far more likely than professional ones to incorporate entire myths, legends, or tales in their accounts, and that these narratives contain still further examples of what people say and the contexts in which they say it.

It is in the margins of ethnography written by natives, as in the margins of the works of anthropologists, that the authors are most likely to make statements that situate them with respect to persons who provided them with information, whether they name those persons or not. Sahagún's writers, in their introduction to a discourse on omens, simultaneously join themselves to their sources with the pronoun 'we' and distance themselves from their sources by means of time: '[This was] in olden times, when false gods were still being worshipped, thus said some of the old men, the ancient people, when we were yet concerned with nothing else, when we believed these things to be true, when still in our land we spoke of that which the departed ones testified to us – our ancestors who are no more' (Sahagún 1950–75, book 5: 151). A passage like this one may disturb readers who are hoping for direct access to pristine otherness, but if we return it to the ground of the relationship between these writers and Sahagún, we can see that it protects the writers from the suspicion of backsliding and, at the same time, protects their own best informants – practising traditionalists, that is – from unwanted attention.

In the outermost margins of the *Historia general* may be found Sahagún's direct interventions. For example, the heading of an appendix to the section on omens reads, 'Here are told the different things which God's creatures, the idolaters, wrongly believed' (Sahagún 1950–75, book 5: 182). In the appendix to the book on the gods, the reader is told that 'the idolatry described above is refuted by means of sacred scriptural texts' (ibid., book 1: 55). Such discourse has its analogues in the writings of anthropologists, but in the place of a direct denial of what natives say or write may come an analysis that reduces it, just as Sahagún's refutation does, to the terms of another discourse altogether, that of the observer. This other discourse is not theological, but whether its terms be those of diffusionism or evolutionism, political economy or social structure, unconscious emotional forces or unconscious cognitive structures, it carries with it truth claims of a universalizing nature. Such claims, like the one made for Scripture, are opposed to the particularities of native belief.

Neither Landa nor Sahagún writes in the first person, and neither narrates a scene in which he and indigenous others are together as contemporaries, talking to one another in the first and second persons. Landa, just once, acknowledges the existence of a face-to-face encounter, but he refers to himself in the third person and uses indirect discourse to represent a conversation: 'Don Juan Cocom ... was a man of great reputation, learned in their affairs, and of remarkable discernment and well acquainted with native matters. He was very intimate with the author of this book, Fray Diego de Landa, and told him many facts concerning their antiquities. He showed him a book which had belonged to his grandfather ... In this was a painting of a deer, and his grandfather had told him that when large deer of this kind should come into that country (for this is what they call cows), the worship of the gods would cease' (Tozzer 1941: 43–6). Here Landa becomes the forerunner of twentieth-century ethnographers who pay homage, if only in the margins of a monograph or else in a separate memoir, to a principal informant. But unlike the writers of memoirs he hides the ambivalence of this kind of relationship, which reached white heat in his case. Shortly after the death of Juan Cocom and four years before he wrote his *Relación*, he had found this man guilty of heresy, excommunicating him and ordering that his bones be exhumed and burned. Perhaps, while writing the present passage, he was silently thinking of Cocom as a man who had unwisely gone against his grandfather's prophecy. But if we ask ourselves why Cocom told Landa about the prophecy in the first place, and if we consider that Mayan books contained not only prophecy but liturgy, we can easily imagine that he was playing the game of humouring a missionary. The story about his grandfather would have served not only to make it seem that the worship of the gods was a thing of the past, but also to put Landa off the track of the intimate role of ancient books in continuing worship. At any rate, it would be several years before Landa assumed the role of Inquisitor and won everlasting fame as a burner of Mayan books.

During the late decades of the twentieth century the mainstream of ethnographic writing has been shifting to a narrative mode that combines aspects of the monograph and the memoir. The reporting of the results of participant observation is now combined with the observation of participation (B. Tedlock 1991). The processes by which fieldworkers and others collaborate in the construction of cultures are no longer hidden backstage. In the strongest works of this kind the voices are not limited to those of an inquiring self and an answering other, but are split among multiple moods and roles and modes of discourse on both sides. If Americanists have a sixteenth-century forerunner in such writing it is neither Landa nor Sahagún but rather Fray Diego Durán, who was raised in Mexico and whose childhood friends included speakers of Nahuatl. In his *Libro de los ritos y ceremonias* and *El calendario antiguo*, written between 1574 and 1576, he uses third-person discourse when describing ancient customs or expounding theories that reduce them to distortions of Old World customs (Durán 1967, vol. 1; 1971). But he has other voices, periodically addressing the reader in an epistolary fashion or telling first-person stories of his personal encounters with Mexica books, songs, and continuing customs.

In his work on rites Durán gives us a glimpse of the split consciousness that would later be called participant observation. No such moments occur in the works of Landa or Sahagún, who keep up the front of their correctness as missionaries. Durán's moment comes when he is in the midst of describing an ancient ceremony that honoured the god Tezcatlipoca. Suddenly he shifts the scene to his own times: 'Instead of candles they carried flowers in their hands, just as they do today on some feasts, especially on the Day of the Ascension and on Pentecost ... and on other festivals which correspond to the ancient ones. I see these things, but I am silent, since I realize that everyone feigns ignorance. So I pick up my staff of flowers like the rest and walk along' (Durán 1971: 103). His thoughts may be different from what might have occurred to a secular ethnographer, but there remains the fact of his interior alienation.

In Durán's *Historia de las Indias de Nueva España*, which he finished in 1581, his predominant mode is to merge his voice with those of his informants, retelling Mexica myth and history in his own words (Durán 1967, vol. 2; 1994). But scattered throughout this work are quotations of Mexica speeches and songs that were uttered on momentous past occasions and preserved through the combined use of pictorial manuscripts and oral transmission. In the first chapter a Mexica myth appears in direct quotation, preceded by Durán's first-person account of his encounter with the unnamed old man from Cholula who told it to him. Like Cortés and like many a twentieth-century anthropologist, he uses direct discourse only for the native side of the conversation:

> When I begged to him enlighten me about some details I wished to put into this history, he asked me what I wanted him to tell. I realized I had found an old and learned person, so I answered, all that he knew about the history of his Indian nation from the beginning of the world. He responded:
>
> 'Take pen and paper, because you will not be able to remember all that I shall tell you.' And [he] began thus:
>
> 'In the beginning, before light or sun had been created, this world lay in darkness and shadows and was void of every created thing.' (Durán 1994: 8)

The story goes on for a few more paragraphs, but once it closes there is no further passage like this one. Instead of announcing a sustained dialogical approach, this exchange serves to establish Durán's authority for what he will afterwards state as a third-person narrator. Similar moves, establishing the fact that the ethnographer was face-to-face with the natives at some time in the past, are made in the opening chapters of various twentieth-century monographs.

The scarcity of face-to-face dialogue in Durán's writings may partly reflect his preference for documentary evidence. When he brings Mexica and Spanish documents into confrontation, he takes a more judicious position than many twentieth-century scholars. In the following passage he brings a Mexica pictorial history into his discussion of the first meeting between Cortés and Motecuhzoma, at a shrine on the outskirts of Tenochtitlán: 'According to traditions and paintings kept by certain elders, it is said that Motecuhzoma left the sanctuary with his feet in chains. And I saw this in a painting that belonged to an ancient chieftain from the province of Tezcoco. Motecuhzoma was depicted in irons, wrapped up in a mantle and carried on the shoulders of his dignitaries. This seems difficult to believe, since I have never met a Spaniard who will concede this point to me. But as all of them deny other things that have always been obvious, and remain silent about them in their histories, writings, and narrations, I am sure they would also deny and omit this' (Durán 1994: 530–1). Again and again, Durán treats the recording of history as an act that did not begin with the coming of Europeans, but was already under way among the Mexica. This history did not cease the moment European writers arrived, nor is it automatically subordinated to their versions of history. Here we see an extension of the dialogical ground beyond others who can be met face-to-face to others who are absent but whose discourse, whether transmitted orally or in documents, is more than just background material for the writing of an account whose determining point of view is that of a European outsider.

From the beginning, Europeans in the Americas have placed a high value on establishing and maintaining dominance in the field of writing systems and text production. This can be seen with dramatic clarity in the Mayan case, where the invaders were confronted with native documents that had a greater resemblance to their own than anywhere else in the Americas. Landa introduces his account of what he takes to be the Mayan alphabet with these words: 'We found a large number of books in these characters, and as they contained nothing in which there were not to be seen superstition and lies of the devil, we burned them all, which they regretted to an amazing degree, and which caused them much affliction' (Tozzer 1941: 169). Here we see the imposition, from the outside, of a single (and final) theory of interpretation on the whole corpus of Mayan literature. For Landa, reconsidering the possibility of future interpretive dialogues between readers and Mayan texts would have meant reconsidering the possibility that a conversation with the devil might be constructive.

If the paradox of Landa is that he came close to being able to read Mayan writing and yet tried to foreclose any possibility of future readings of past Mayan writers, the paradox of the dominant Mayanist scholars of the first half of the twentieth century is that they came close to doing just the opposite. They retained the notion that the main import of Mayan texts was religious, but they offered extensive interpretations while rejecting the notion that the writing itself could be read phonetically. The texts themselves had become objects of conservation, but the voices encoded within them remained silent.

The actual decipherment of Mayan writing came only with the second half of the twentieth century. Important advances have continued into the 1990s, but the major breakthroughs had all been published by 1960 (see Coe 1992: chaps 6 and 7). By the middle of that decade, the news had begun to spread into textbooks on Mesoamerican civilization. It was clear that Mayan writing spelled out grammatical sentences in known Mayan languages, partly by means of logographs (signs for whole words) but mostly with phonetic signs that stand for syllables. It was also clear that the voices encoded in the monumental inscriptions of pre-Columbian times are not concerned with religious matters alone. They speak of historical events in the lives of named men and women belonging to named royal houses, located in places that can be mapped. More recently it has been revealed that some ancient texts were signed by their authors.

In some quarters there has been a remarkable reluctance to accept the news about Mayan writing. It would appear that the last line of European resistance to dialogue with the American other is at the level of texts whose voices belong to an America devoid of Europeans. Todorov, anxious to promote the possession of writing as a major factor in the victories of the European invaders of Mesoamerica, betrays a reluctance even to mention the Mayan problem when he says, 'Among the Mayas we find certain rudiments of phonetic writing' (Todorov 1984: 160). Jack Goody, who promotes a profoundly Eurocentric view of writing systems despite being an anthropologist, takes pains to deny the existence of 'true' writing anywhere outside the Old World. He is worried enough about Mesoamerican systems to mention them, but he focuses his attention on the Zapotec script, which has yet to be deciphered, and excludes the Mayan script from his list of 'phono-syllabic' systems (Goody 1987: 18–28).

There is resistance among Mesoamericanists as well, but here the focus is on the texts rather than the writing system. On the side of the texts, epigraphers such as Linda Schele and Mary Ellen Miller have proclaimed that the Maya, all the way back to a point more than a thousand years before the European invasion, are 'a people with a written history' (Schele and Miller 1986: 14). In response to such statements the archaeologist Joyce Marcus has constructed a hierarchical taxonomy that confines Mayan inscriptions to the category 'propaganda' (Marcus 1992: 444), thus leaving 'true' history on the stratigraphic level of the victorious invaders from Europe. This view, which is shared by the members of a particular faction among archaeologists, is a secularized variant of Landa's view. Where he upheld the truth of Scripture against the lies of the devil and the gullibility of Mayans, they now uphold the truth of scientific excavations against the lies of Mayans and the gullibility of epigraphers. It is as if even the texts of the long dead posed such a threat that they had to be removed to a plane below that of an interpretive dialogue before they could be discussed.

The voices of past others encounter less resistance when they have already been cast in the writing system of the invaders, whether by others who learned the use of the Roman alphabet or by fieldworkers who used it. But even with texts of this kind most of the serious attention to the art of interpretation has been recent. In a dialogical hermeneutics, readers let themselves be addressed by a text and may be led to reconsider their own positions. The opening question is not 'What pieces of data can this text contribute to current theory?' but rather 'What kind of world is theorized by this text?' In the Mesoamerican field the pioneering work of this kind is Miguel León-Portilla's *Aztec Thought and Culture* (1963). The discourse he interprets is not in a separate volume but is quoted on almost every page, so that the reader has the option of continuing the hermeneutical process by formulating a different interpretation. He does not remove the thoughts of others to a lower plane or a past stage of evolution, but finds moments of similarity and contrast in various periods of Western thought, ranging from ancient Greece to the modern period. What emerges from this process is an *alternative* human world. Many more such worlds have yet to be unfolded.

NOTES

1 For more on dialogical anthropology, see Dwyer (1982), D. Tedlock (1983: p 4), Maranhao (1990), and D. Tedlock and Mannheim (1995).

2 As B. Tedlock has pointed out (1983), studies of so-called syncretism typically treat the natives not only as passive, but as being unaware of the European elements in what outsiders perceive as cultural mixtures.

3 The first to make this argument were France V. Scholes and Ralph L. Roys (1938: 599–600); the most recent is Nancy M. Farriss (1984: 291).

4 The emendation and translation are my own, based on the entry for *ki' t'an* in Barrera Vásquez (1980).

5 The dialogical significance of this sentence was reconstructed by J. Kathryn Josserand and Nicholas A. Hopkins, as noted by Schele (1992: 14).

REFERENCES

Barrera Vásquez, Alfredo. 1980. *Diccionario maya cordemex, maya-español, español-maya.* Mérida: Ediciones Cordemex.

Barrera Vásquez, Alfredo, and Silvia Rendón. 1948. *El libro de los libros de Chilam Balam*. México: Fondo de Cultura Económica.

Boas, Franz. 1921. *Ethnology of the Kwakiutl*. Annual Report of the Bureau of American Ethnology 35.

– 1928. *Keresan Texts*. 2 vols. Publications of the American Ethnological Society 8(1). New York: G.E. Stechert.

Bricker, Victoria R. 1973. *Ritual Humor in Highland Chiapas*. Austin: University of Texas Press.

Bunzel, Ruth L. 1952. *Chichicastenango: A Guatemalan Village*. Publications of the American Ethnological Society 22.

Chafe, Wallace, and Johanna Nichols. 1986. *Evidentiality: The Linguistic Coding of Epistemology*. Advances in Discourse Processes 20. Norwood, NJ: Ablex.

Clendinnen, Inga. 1987. *Ambivalent Conquests: Maya and Spaniard in Yucatan, 1517–1570*. Cambridge: Cambridge University Press.

Coe, Michael D. 1992. *Breaking the Maya Code*. New York: Thames & Hudson.

Díaz del Castillo, Bernal. 1963. *The Conquest of New Spain*. Translated by J.M. Cohen. Harmondsworth: Penguin Books.

Durán, Diego. 1967. *Historia de las Indias de Nueva España e islas de la tierra firme*. 2 vols. Edited by Angel María Garibay K. México: Porrua.

– 1971. *Book of the Gods and Rites and the Ancient Calendar*. Translated by Fernando Horcasitas and Doris Heyden. Norman: University of Oklahoma Press.

– 1994. *The History of the Indies of New Spain*. Translated by Doris Heyden. Norman: University of Oklahoma Press.

Dwyer, Kevin. 1982. *Moroccan Dialogues: Anthropology in Question*. Baltimore: Johns Hopkins University Press.

Farriss, Nancy M. 1984. *Maya Society under Colonial Rule: The Collective Enterprise of Survival*. Princeton: Princeton University Press.

Ginzburg, Carlo. 1990. *Myths, Emblems, Clues*. Translated by John and Anne C. Tedeschi. London: Hutchinson Radius.

Goody, Jack. 1987. *The Interface between the Oral and the Written*. Cambridge: Cambridge University Press.

Gossen, Gary H. 1974. *Chamulas in the World of the Sun: Time and Space in a Maya Oral Tradition*. Cambridge: Harvard University Press.

Kamen, Henry. 1985. *Inquisition and Society in Spain in the Sixteenth and Seventeenth Centuries*. London: Weidenfeld and Nicolson.

Klor de Alva, J. Jorge. 1980. 'The Aztec-Spanish Dialogues of 1524.' *Alcheringa/Ethnopoetics* n.s. 4(2): 56–193.

León-Portilla, Miguel. 1962. *The Broken Spears: The Aztec Account of the Conquest of Mexico*. Boston: Beacon.

– 1963. *Aztec Thought and Culture: A Study of the Ancient Nahuatl Mind*. Translated by Jack Emory Davis. Norman: University of Oklahoma Press.

Mackie, Sedley J. 1924. *An Account of the Conquest of Guatemala in 1524 by Pedro de Alvarado*. New York: The Cortes Society.

Maranhao, Tullio. 1990. *The Interpretation of Dialogue*. Chicago: University of Chicago Press.

Marcus, Joyce. 1992. *Mesoamerican Writing Systems: Propaganda, Myth, and History in Four Ancient Civilizations*. Princeton: Princeton University Press.

Obeyesekere, Gananath. 1992. *The Apotheosis of Captain Cook: European Mythmaking in the Pacific*. Princeton: Princeton University Press.

Pagden, Anthony R. 1971. *Hernán Cortés: Letters from Mexico*. New York: Grossman.

Radin, Paul. 1923. *The Winnebago Tribe*. Annual Report of the Bureau of American Ethnology 37.

Recinos, Adrián, and Delia Goetz. 1953. *The Annals of the Cakchiquels*. Norman: University of Oklahoma Press.

Roys, Ralph L. 1967. *The Book of Chilam Balam of Chumayel*. Norman: University of Oklahoma Press.

Sahagún, Bernardino de. 1950–75. *Florentine Codex: General History of the Things of New Spain*. 12 vols. Translated by Arthur J.O. Anderson and Charles E. Dibble. Monographs of the School of American Research 14. Santa Fe: School of American Research.

Schele, Linda. 1992. *Workbook for the XVIth Maya Hieroglyphic Workshop at Texas*. Austin: Department of Art History, University of Texas.

Schele, Linda, and Mary Ellen Miller. 1986. *The Blood of Kings: Dynasty and Ritual in Maya Art*. Fort Worth: Kimbell Art Museum.

Scholes, France V., and Ralph L. Roys. 1938. 'Fray Diego de Landa and the Problem of Idolatry in Yucatan.' *Publications of the Carnegie Institute of Washington* 301: 585–620.

Tedlock, Barbara. 1983. 'A Phenomenological Approach to Religious Change in Highland Guatemala.' In Carl Kendall and John Hawkins, eds, *Heritage of Conquest: Thirty Years Later*, 235–46. Albuquerque: University of New Mexico Press.

– 1991. 'From Participant Observation to the Observation of Participation: The Emergence of Narrative Ethnography.' *Journal of Anthropological Research* 47: 69–94.

Tedlock, Dennis. 1983. *The Spoken Word and the Work of Interpretation*. Philadelphia: University of Pennsylvania Press.

– 1993. 'Torture in the Archives: Mayans Meet Europeans.' *American Anthropologist* 95: 139–52.

– 1996. *Popol Vuh: The Mayan Book of the Dawn of Life*. Revised and expanded edition. New York: Simon & Schuster.

– 1997. *Breath on the Mirror: Mythic Voices and Visions of the Living Maya*. Albuquerque: University of New Mexico Press.

Tedlock, Dennis, and Bruce Mannheim, eds. 1995. *The Dialogic Emergence of Culture*. Urbana: University of Illinois Press.

Todorov, Tzvetan. 1984. *The Conquest of America: The Question of the Other*. Translated by Richard Howard. New York: Harper & Row.

Tozzer, Alfred M. 1941. *Landa's Relación de las cosas de Yucatán*. Papers of the Peabody Museum of American Archaeology and Ethnology, vol. 18. Cambridge, MA.: The Peabody Museum, Harvard University.

11 The Meaning of Writing and Text in a Changing Americanist Tradition

JANE H. HILL

In 1976, Dell Hymes characterized the Americanist Tradition as 'a continuity not only of object [the American Indian languages], but also of approach ... An irreducible minimum of continuity in approach, of values and understanding, stems from the very nature of the materials with which Americanists work' (1983: [1976] 116). Yet, as is obvious from Hymes's subsequent discussion, of 'documents' and 'works' and 'old unwieldy volumes,' the Americanist Tradition is one not only of object, and of approach, but of the materiality of the written texts that are the principal artefacts of its practice.[1] And these texts do not, in fact, 'stem from the very nature of the materials with which Americanists work.' An Americanist Tradition that was in full continuity with its object would be, mostly, an oral tradition. Rather than the history of texts, we would know instead of a history of human relationships, objects of speculation and dispute, that would link ancient speakers of the languages with their descendants in the present. Our discourse would attend, not to the way in which Hymes's 'The Wife who goes out like a Man' drew on Jacobs's *Clackamas Chinook Texts*, but to matters of exchange and licensing: how many dollars measured the worth of what passed from Charles Cultee to Franz Boas, or whether Wally Chafe was interpolating materials from a new revelation of his own when he slightly altered a passage in his most recent recitation of the Good Message, or whether Miguel Léon-Portilla in fact is the true inheritor of the right, passed by gift between nobles, to perform the songs of Nezahualcoyotl. These are not far-fetched examples; precisely this sort of concern animates many contemporary speakers of Native American languages as they observe (unfortunately, often at a distance), the 'Americanist Tradition.' The amount of money that I might be paying Roscinda Nolasquez was the obsessive concern of other elderly speakers of Cupeño during my fieldwork on that language in the 1960s; they never looked over my shoulder to see if I was getting what she said down right. Many speakers of Tohono O'odham believe that Juan Gregorio died not because he was a very old man, but because his talks with Donald Bahr about the way spirit animals can be offended (Bahr, Gregorio, Lopez, and Alvarez 1974) attracted evil forces that ethnographic method is not designed to defend against. Judith Berman (1994) has shown how rejection of Kwak'wala texts compiled by George Hunt as 'incorrect' by contemporary speakers of that language may be traced in part to questions about whether Hunt had the right to recount materials that were not his by genealogical inheritance.

Obviously, it is not new to point out that the Americanist Tradition manifests a fundamentally European way of addressing the world. The classificatory and cataloguing impulses that flowered in the Renaissance were expressed in part in complex techniques for the production of written texts in vernacular languages that were fundamental tokens in political and moral economies.[2] That history shapes our textual production today. But that the Americanist Tradition is a literate tradition has been simply self-evident. Most of us give no more attention to this literacy than fish give to water. I think, though, that we should begin to reflect more carefully on the implications of the Americanist Tradition as a tradition of the production of written texts. The urgency of such an undertaking stems from the deep concern among Native American people about the future of their languages. As long as the Americanist Tradition was fundamentally oriented toward making and preserving records, written texts were highly appropriate media for this task. But as we turn to language maintenance and development as central concerns, and as communities of speakers make decisions about what kinds of technologies might provide the best media for living languages that exist in the flow of talk between speakers as much as on tape or in books, we must reflect critically on our relationship to the written word.

While there is no question that the monuments of the Americanist Tradition include texts that were collected by fraud and threat, it is hardly helpful to see all of our textual production in simplistic terms as a violent expropriation of symbolic goods from the indigenous peoples of the Americas. John Peabody Harrington, for instance, often nagged and manipulated native-language consultants, but the indigenous community at San Juan Capistrano recently expressed their gratitude for the materials that resulted from his field procedures by hosting a conference of linguists and anthropologists on his work. I think that the case made by Mühlhäusler (1990), that the 'reduction to writing' of languages of the Pacific like Maori and Hawaiian is implicated in their moribundity, is circumstantial at best. Mexicano (Nahuatl) has a very long elite alphabetic literate tradition. This tradition has obvious ties to a pre-Columbian system of written entextualization, and flourished in the first two hundred and fifty years of the Spanish colony in many genres. While some speakers believe that this written tradition has been lost, my own experience has been that a few people in almost every community can read and write the language. Mexicano today has almost 1.2 million speakers. Furthermore, it is clear from contemporary work, including studies presented at this conference (for instance, papers by DeMallie, Nichols, Cyr) that the uses and evaluations of literacy made by the peoples of the Americas are extraordinarily diverse. The rejection of writing articulated by such commentators as Russell Means (1983) and Leslie Silko (1981), and detailed in a masterful discussion by Brandt (1981) of the anti-literacy ideology of the Upper Rio Grande pueblos, is by no means universally shared in Indian communities (cf. Basso and Anderson 1977, Goddard and Bragdon 1988, McLaughlin 1992, Walker 1981, Zepeda 1982, etc.). (Interestingly, in her most recent novel, *Almanac of the Dead*, Silko modifies her Platonist horror of the written word in order to develop as a central theme the preservation by her heroines of ancient indigenous texts.) Thus, what we need is neither a simplistic advocacy of native-language literacy as an obvious component of a language-development program, nor an equally simplistic rejection of it as inherently antithetical to indigenous consciousness. We must offer instead a more nuanced approach that helps people to ask precisely what benefit or cost might be sustained, in some particular community, by some particular use of writing. Such an approach can only grow out of a deeper understanding of our own practices.

As an opening to such a project (and my contribution should be taken as barely programmatic), I would like to review in more detail earlier approaches to the problem, and contribute some of my own thoughts on the implications of the forms of literacy that are manifest in the Americanist Tradition.

Linguistics is only one of many scholarly practices that are largely organized around writing (note that many knowledge-oriented traditions such as those of photography and film, musical composition, and painting are not so shaped), so one might ask why linguistics should be the preferred site for attention. The obvious reason is that the discourses of linguistic scholarship encounter in an exacerbated form the problem of untangling medium from message, metalanguage from object language. Every student of linguistics either reads at first hand, or has repeated in the voice of her own introductory textbook, the famous dictum of Saussure: 'The linguistic object is not both the written and the spoken forms of words; the spoken forms alone constitute the object' (Saussure 1966: 23). Americanists, who almost always work in communities where there are no, or few, written texts available prior to their own work, find it especially easy to accept Saussure's dictum. Yet the usual practice of Americanists is to set in place elaborate techniques for examining their 'object' mainly through the medium of writing. An extraordinarily large proportion of 'field method' consists in producing layer after layer of text, each layer oriented toward the next. The earliest, most informal, least prestigious layer is the principal moment in which an actual dialogic relationship with a native speaker takes place; the final, most prestigious layers are notoriously in technical language, oriented toward the community of scholars who are not speakers.

Jackson (1990) has pointed out that the lowest layers, the 'fieldnotes,' have an almost sacred quality; people avoid talking about them, or make jokes about them. Consider my own practice in my first fieldwork more than thirty years ago. My interchanges with my main consultant, Roscinda Nolasquez, were recorded, in her presence, in permanent field notebooks, with the writing operating in an intricate interaction with my own repetitions out loud of what she said, and her corrections, with each moment of inscription, '[holding] the present moment ... at bay so as to create a recontextualized, portable account ... [that is] a systematic reordering' (Clifford 1990: 64). Yet, even as they 'held the present moment at bay,' these notes simultaneously constituted the main evidence that it had occurred, and that is why they were in bound notebooks, precisely like a laboratory log. Within the moment, this writing was my *raison d'être* – Roscinda Nolasquez wanted her language to have a written record, and she knew that I could do this and she could not. Every evening I wrote out these entries by hand onto 4″ × 6″ file slips, morpheme by morpheme (according to my understanding of the morphology at that point). These lonely hours provided local warranting of my status as a serious person, who spent much time in study. Texts were first tape-recorded, then transcribed into the field notebooks. The transcription was double-checked with the informant in a joint session with the tape. The checked transcription was then typed up on ditto masters; I made multiple copies of each text and cut these up into fileable pieces. I have what the authors in *Fieldnotes* find is the usual relationship with these paper artefacts – if my house was burning, I would probably try to save these before I would save the pictures of my family. New layers of text intervened between my primary written artefacts and my dissertation (Hill 1966), and the camera-ready manuscript of texts, free translations, notes, and lexicon that the Malki Museum Press turned into *Mulu'wetam* (Hill and Nolasquez 1973). Astonishingly, only these last products are known as 'write-up' (Jackson 1990).

When I consider the amount of writing I did in this body of research, I have to think of my understanding of Cupeño as principally a work of 'eyes and hands' (Latour 1986, cited in Hutchins 1995), interestingly removed from the supposed oral-aural basis of spoken language.

Text-management software has made possible immensely intricate layerings of entextualization, with seven or eight linearly aligned tiers of various kinds of mark-up and translation, making visible the fact that each stage of analysis is primarily the production of a new segmentation of the linear text along with intertextual interpolations at that layer of segmentation. Computerized text production has led to new alphabetic obsessions – font design and ethnopoetic formatting come to mind. I have probably spent almost as much time during my linguistic career worrying about how to get my printer to put a dot under Tohono O'odham retroflex consonants, or a macron over Nahuatl long vowels, as on practising my conversational skills in those languages. Most of my hours with native speakers are conducted with one eye on those crucial controls over the first stage of textual mediation, the needle on the volume indicator and the tiny red battery light on my portable tape recorder. For every hour I spend with speakers, I spend a dozen transcribing and marking up transcriptions.

Writing is virtually the only medium through which the institution that pays my salary, or the colleagues who construct my reputation, have access to my work. I do not recall, in almost thirty years of academic life, that any university administrator has ever inquired into my conversational fluency in a Native American language. Instead, my advancement through the ranks is mediated by a text, the curriculum vitae, that lists other texts published under my name! (Ordinary people, including students, do occasionally ask whether I speak these languages, and are often very surprised to learn that my competence in them is perhaps most politely described as 'discursive' rather than 'practical.')

The uses of paper and ink (and now of electronic text) that yield a linguistics of 'eyes and hands' have survived thirty years of inexpensive high-fidelity audiotape recording and the development of video. One can argue, of course, that paper text has certain advantages as a storage medium over audiotape and video, and electronic text even enhances its principal advantage, easy, rapid access to any point in the linear sequence. However, it is clear that mere technical congruity is not the exclusive constraint on the drive toward literate production of Americanist linguists. I produced all of my multiple layers of text on Cupeño with no technology more exalted than a typewriter and a ditto machine (I did use an early photocopy machine, in the Berkeley Anthropology Department, to obtain copies of texts handwritten in pencil by Paul-Louis Faye in 1920 and 1921). Instead, each layer of text is suffused with its own moral significance, and links the scholar to large systems of power and both literal and metaphorical 'authority.' This overwhelming moral force is very much evident in the early years of the Americanist Tradition. In the first decades of Spanish rule in Mexico, European paper was almost as precious as gold, yet works of scholarship on many pages of this substance were printed there as early as the 1540s. It is fascinating to read the accounts by Hanzeli (1969) of the way that the French Jesuits, working among the Montagnais and Huron in the seventeenth century under conditions of extraordinary hardship, were able to construct a 'schooled literate' approach to these languages. In the early days they were forced to take notes on birchbark instead of unobtainable paper. Hanzeli observes that at the Huron mission of Ihonatiria, the priests 'spent the day among the Indians, listening, taking notes and occasionally speaking to them; at night they compared notes, copied and discussed them. Often they held lengthy "editorial conferences"' (1969: 49). They tested materials by 'reading them back to the informants' (ibid.: 51). Like many of their successors, they taught Indians to write, to obtain additional materials for their dictionaries. Tellingly, Hanzeli comments that, once the fundamental problems had been solved and written materials were available, contact with native speakers diminished. Thus, the missionary Jerome Lalement 'reported from the Huron mission that they no longer needed indiscriminately to admit loafing Hurons to their mission house, as they had been wont to do before, just to be exposed to their speech' (ibid.: 50).

Not only was technical incongruity not a factor in the drive toward organizing linguistic practice around literacy. These Jesuits were, of course, priests, whose main work – the recitation of the mass, the delivery of sermons, instruction in the catechism, the taking of confession, and the granting of absolution – could only be conducted orally. Rafael (1993: 39), speaking of the Dominicans in the Philippines at the same period, remarks that there was 'a pervasive assumption among Spaniards that the voice has primacy over writing in the transmission of the Gospel ... [C]onversion placed special stress on the activity of speaking and listening to God's Word. The voice was systematically ascribed a privileged position in the hierarchy of signs.'

Certainly, the goal of the Jesuits in Canada as well was mastery of the oral language, yet they filtered this orality through multiple layers of written text. How much more dominated are we by our alphabets today, when the oral imperative of the evangelist is absent for most of us? There is, of course, a notion that the best grammar is done by native speakers, and some Americanists do consider conversational fluency to be among their goals. However, most of us work in communities where our oral participation is highly constrained; many speech events in the native language are closed to us except as audiences or overhearers. And, of course, if we are academics, most of our lives are conducted in environments where the language of our scholarly focus is never heard.

The alphabet-focused linguistics of 'eyes and hands' has obviously shaped the way that linguists understand language. Aronoff (1992) has pointed out the influence of a legacy of Saussure's position that he calls 'segmentalism': the idea that 'articulation ... is deceptive, because it is continuous, with no discernible breaks between segments, while auditory impressions consist of discrete sounds in a string' (79). Aronoff points out that this was 'pure speculation' on

Saussure's part, and that it was a speculation that seems to have been the result, not of a debt to prior sources, but of the self-evident nature of this fact. Aronoff argues that, since there was no instrumental phonetics or experimental psycholinguistics in Saussure's day, this self-evidence can come only from the fact that Saussure saw the sounds of language basically in terms of alphabetic imagery. In Aronoff's view, 'segmentalism,' the linear mindset imposed by alphabetic literacy, held back the development of theory in phonology for many years, in spite of the work of the London School on prosodic phonology, and continues to prevail in morphology. It is probably not an accident that, while there is much admirable phonology for Native American languages, there is vanishingly little phonetics; the materiality of the speaking voice has been of little concern. Turning to syntax, Chafe (1995) has pointed out that the 'sentences' that appear in the pages of linguistic monographs do not seem to match the sort of units that appear when one attends strictly to the materiality of spoken discourse, with the implication being that much syntax may be a syntax of writing exclusively, its implications for the general nature of the capacity for language being thereby somewhat problematic.

In the analysis of discourse, alphabetic text production is almost certainly the source of the 'text vs. context' dualism that continues to bedevil us (Duranti and Goodwin 1993). In the Americanist Tradition, the most 'textual' forms (Briggs 1993), those that are most amenable to domestication on the page, have often been the preferred object of attention over more 'contextual' ways of speaking. This is a criticism often levelled against the ethnography of communication, but it may be the result, not of the program as laid out by Hymes, but simply of intense literate bias; one can find similar approaches to discourse by scholars who are not identified by themselves or others as ethnographers of communication. Thus, for the Tohono O'odham, we have fairly good work on songs and narratives, but virtually no information on what I am beginning to suspect is the Tohono O'odham speech skill par excellence, the rapid-fire exchange of what seems to be very funny teasing. Ruth Underhill commented, in a nostalgic passage in one of her writings, that she missed the laughter of O'odham conversationalists in the same way one would long for a cool drink of water on a hot day. Yet nowhere does she talk about what their jokes are like; her great work on O'odham texts is her study of power songs (Underhill 1938). When I was teaching O'odham literacy, my classes would regularly be punctuated by bursts of laughter from the corners of the room as students teased each other. Even when I understood the words, I never understood these jokes, and when I would ask students to repeat them or explain them, they would be exasperated in the same way that anyone is exasperated when you have to explain a joke to some dolt who didn't 'get it' the first time around. Jokes are a prime case of contextualized talk, where 'you have to be there,' sharing instantly and densely in nuances of meaning and personal histories that the most complex hypertextual artefact cannot reproduce. Consider, for instance, the finest study of Native American kidding around, Keith Basso's *Portraits of the Whiteman* (1979). Such dense attention to context is required that it takes Basso almost two hundred pages of text to account for about a dozen brief performances of whiteman jokes. (Keith Basso's career is, in fact, quite exemplary in the amount of attention he has paid to what cannot be written down, such as silence, or to ephemeral moments in skilled talk, the 'wise words' and 'shooting with stories' discussed in some of his best-known publications.)

There have been some very interesting efforts by practitioners of the Americanist Tradition to try to break out of the textual straitjacket. Thus, while Dell Hymes (1981) suggested that purely oral and gestural elements of old published texts would probably never be recovered, his suggestions about measure led directly to the identification of genuinely rhythmic performance in some Native American narrative traditions. Furthermore, the emphasis on diversity of channel in the ethnography of speaking has opened the way for the so-called ideological approaches to the study of literacy (cf. Street 1985) that contest the universalizing claims of scholars like Ong and Goody. Dennis Tedlock's (1983) provocative essay on 'phonography and the problem of time in oral narrative events' points out that many linguists fail to take tape recording really seriously: 'those who deal with the spoken word ... still seem to regard phonography as little more than a device for moving the scene of alphabetic notation from the field interview to the solitude of an office with playback facilities' (195). Briggs (1993) accuses Tedlock of a 'fetishization' of tape recording as a more privileged form of entextualization, but in fact Tedlock's essay is one of the very few serious attempts in our literature to come to grips with the implications of a technology that is different from paper and writing. Students working under Peter Ladefoged in the UCLA Phonetics Laboratory are beginning to conduct phonetic studies of languages like Navajo and Tohono O'odham (cf. Dart 1993). Scholars like Allen Burns (1980) and Ellen Basso (1984) had to break out of the drive to textual linearity to understand the role of the dialogic principle in Native American narrative. Tony Woodbury, Joel Sherzer, Greg Urban, Steve Feld, and their students at the University of Texas have focused on the rich materiality of the sound of the voice, using new developments in instrumentation to explore both small-scale bursts of particular voice qualities, as in ritual wailing, and large-scale structures shaped by gradations of pitch and amplitude. But there are certainly many other scholars who consider such work frivolous, especially when conducted on languages for which we lack the classic textual triad of grammar, texts, and dictionary.

Critics have noted that literate practices may have a number of negative or, in the words of Mühlhäusler (1990), 'dyseconomic' effects on indigenous speech communities. He notes that 'literacy seems to favor single-standard languages,' so that linguistic variability is reduced, with dialect variants 'no longer being available for internal borrowing or as a source of stylistic effects.' Literacy tends to be a vehicle for 'expatriate' concepts, and may be in fundamental conflict with traditional religious values. Written words may be regarded as inherently true, such that what is merely spoken is rejected. It has been my own experience that most communities, aided and abetted by consulting non-native-speaker linguists, think immediately of language development as prototypically characterized by the production of native-language alphabetic or syllabic artefacts – wall posters, readers, curriculum guides, pedagogical grammars, dictionaries – and by instruction in literacy to gain access to these. A driving concern of many workers in language development is to provide new materials, so that native-language literates will have something to read. Even some of the Platonists of the Upper Rio Grande have overcome their horror of writing enough to submit grant proposals for the production of (eyes-only) dictionaries.[3] To the degree that an indigenous language is seen by the community to be embodied in such artefacts, associated with the classroom and with learning, the language may come to be seen as 'difficult,' suitable as a school subject along with algebra and U.S. history, rather than taken for granted as the effortless medium of vernacular socialization. To some degree the embedding of native-language literacy in the schools has been shaped by institutional constraints. Before the Native American Language Act, almost the only way to fund indigenous-language maintenance in the United States was through bilingual education programs under Title VII – and school, of course, is the repository par excellence of written text. For non-speaker linguists who are consultants to maintenance projects, a textual product may be crucial – I have refereed more than one tenure case that hinged on a dictionary, a pedagogical grammar, or a technical paper or report. However, in several communities important uses of literacy have developed that function quite outside the school system. Among the Yaqui, the principal sites of native-language writing are the journals kept by ritual leaders of sermons, hymns, prayers, and historical notes, a realm that is quite separate from schools and grant proposals. Other uses of writing may exist in explicit opposition to the schooled tradition (like graffiti by Navajo youths), or in its shadowy interstices (like the illicit classroom note-passing observed by McLaughlin [1992], who finds that Navajo literacy is par excellence a private matter, in contrast to the English writing that mediates almost all forms of public life).

In general, it is much easier to find funding for textual products that have to do with institutions than for textual products that are for personal use such as private reading. It is easier to find money for the production of any kind of text than for performance. And, finally, it is virtually impossible to find money that will permit ordinary people to interact in ordinary ways speaking their languages. This reflects an ancient European hierarchy that privileges clerical literacy, the zone of chaste and sober men, over the sexualized and dangerously immediate world of the theatre, and both over the everyday practices that Ivan Ilich has called 'shadow work.' But, however this literate bias may be shaped, it may be, in the most literal sense, 'dyseconomic.' Many people think of paper and ink as 'cheap' compared to more high-tech media, but the attempt to produce written materials very economically may lead to the characteristic black-and-white, crookedly stapled, photocopied classroom materials that unmistakably index the stigmatization and marginalization of their languages for many Native Americans. Even more significant, though, is the way that the funding of the production of texts may pull funds away from 'shadow work,' the actual conduct of human relationships in the indigenous language. Leanne Hinton has reported that the California Master-Apprentice project can fund a Master-Apprentice pair for about ten thousand dollars a year. Native-speaker day-care personnel, who could conduct native-language-immersion pre-schools while serving a function that is desperately needed by parents, would on most reservations consider $20,000 a year a wonderful wage. But a major dictionary, an artefact to which many communities aspire, can take many years of intense effort that requires highly skilled professionals, and will probably cost close to a million dollars if all expenses are figured in. The final volume, even when produced as inexpensively as possible, will in all likelihood be priced beyond the means of ordinary people in the community of speakers.

The design and choice of writing systems has in many communities been the focus of much unproductive wrangling that might be avoided if communities simply turned to other media such as videotaping. I have heard many anecdotes of bitter factionalism around writing systems, of planning meetings disrupted by hours of debate over diacritical minutiae (see, for instance, Cyr, this volume). Today in Mesoamerica the choice of Hispanic orthography (qu) or nativist orthography (k) is often taken (erroneously, in my view as a qu person) to differentiate evil baby-burning oligarchs from progressive sympathizers with indigenous aspirations.[4] Among the Tohono O'odham, the choice between dialect variants in writing becomes foregrounded for speakers, who manifest a kind of prescriptivism in their orientation toward written text that is simply not evident in their orientation to speech. Dialect differences in speech are the object of discursive attention and occasionally of teasing. Many literate O'odham (who are mostly schoolteachers), may reject written material in a dialect not their own, in the definitive language of the school, as 'incorrect' – even when they are entirely aware that a dialect difference is what is involved and can easily talk about this fact.

Just as the commitment to writing of the seventeenth-century French Jesuit missionaries to the Montagnais and the Huron was in conflict with their material circumstances and moral goals, the academic commitment to writing in language development in indigenous languages is in conflict with many trends in the larger society. The political-economic privilege of writing is, in fact, somewhat difficult to assess, and it would be very interesting to compare in detail the economic circumstances and chances of people whose work focuses around writing (say, the sort of writer who places the occasional piece in the shopping news, and does the odd book review) and members of punk bands of equivalent local reputation. I'd put my own money down on the latter. In fact, I have a strong suspicion that in the complex embeddings of orality and literacy in 'mainstream' society, the big money is circulating in the oral layers, with the literate ones being zones where salaried hired hands do the paperwork. Thus, training young people in forms of performance, in niceties of oral interaction, and in new media for the recording and reproduction of indigenous language events – film, video, sophisticated sound recording and mixing, hypermedia like CD-ROMs – may provide them with skills that are far more marketable than native-language literacy.

In conclusion, I suggest that both non-Indian and Indian scholars who are the inheritors of the Americanist Tradition will be much more effective at language development if we work to understand better what it means to be, today, 'people of the Text.' We need to develop a reflexive sensitivity toward our own scholarly practices of literacy, comparable to that produced, for instance, by Mignolo for the Spanish in the New World, by Vicente Rafael for the Spanish and the Tagalog in seventeenth-century Manila, or, to take examples closer to home, by scholars like Heath and Collins for everyday literacies in the United States. We will surely find that our ideologies of literacy are imbricated with our positioning within political economic processes, but we need to move away from simplistic vulgar Marxism – and from its contemporary descendant, vulgar Foucauldianism. We must recognize that scholarly literacy is often in conflict with indigenous ideas about the preferred processes of entextualization, but we must also resist simplistic nativist oppositions, a glamorization of the position that holds speech to be the moist breath of the true heart and writing to be the dry rattling of the bones of millions dead. I don't find the analogies of Farella (1993), who finds recording text to resemble the building of the egregious Glen Canyon Dam, or perhaps some folly of Coyote, to be especially useful (and it is clear that his ideas are not shared by many thoughtful Navajos).

Many Native Americans take much pleasure in reading and writing in their own languages. I share this pleasure, and believe that Americanist texts, from Olmos's *Arte para aprender la lengva mexicana* of 1547 down to the *Lushootseed Dictionary* of 1994, will weigh in our favour as our descendants judge what we did. But today seems to be a very good time for us to turn the new tools developed by ideological theorists of literacy more intensively on our own practices, so that we can better understand how the knowledge of language 'by hands and eyes' that is our special skill either helps or hinders language planning and development.

NOTES

1 My interest in this topic has been especially inspired by two experiences: teaching literacy to speakers of Tohono O'odham, and my surprising new role as 'last living pronouncer' of the Cupeño language. In the latter case, the Cupeño community is in possession of all of my tapes of elderly speakers, but members still want to hear a living voice saying the words. My pronunciations serve to jog the memories of elders who can then function better as living exemplars. I thank all of the students in my Tohono O'odham classes, Ofelia Zepeda, with whom I've discussed these issues, and Leroy Miranda of the Cupa Cultural Center, Pala, California, for their help in moving me toward my present level of understanding of these issues.

2 For interesting discussion of this point, see Mignolo (1992, 1994a and b, 1995). I do not share Mignolo's view that the early Spanish grammatical tradition involved the imposition of Latin grammar on the indigenous languages, but this question is beyond the scope of this paper.

3 I refer here to the point made by Derrida in *Of Grammatology*, that the notion of the primacy of speaking in Western thought can be traced to Plato's distrust of writing.

4 Among Mayan speakers in Chiapas and Guatemala, the choice of orthographic /k/ instead of /qu/ alternating with /c/, and of /w/ instead of /hu/, is an initiative that came from Mayan-speaking communities, including native-speaker linguists, that has been generally accepted by scholars working on these languages. However, some linguists seem to feel that it is politically correct to use the official Mayan orthography throughout Mesoamerica, to the distinct confusion of non-Mayan communities, some with a long tradition of alphabetic writing.

REFERENCES

Aronoff, Mark. 1992. 'Segmentalism in Linguistics: The Alphabetic Basis of Phonological Material.' In Pamela Downing, Susan D. Lima, and Michael Noonan, eds, *The Linguistics of Literacy*. Amsterdam and Philadelphia: John Benjamins.

Bahr, Donald M., Juan Gregorio, David I. Lopez, and Albert Alvarez. 1974. *Piman Shamanism and Staying Sickness (Ka:cim Mumkidag)*. Tucson: University of Arizona Press.

Basso, Ellen 1984. *A Musical View of the Universe*. Chicago: University of Chicago Press.

Basso, Keith. 1979. *Portraits of the Whiteman*. Cambridge University Press.

Basso, Keith, and Ned Anderson. 1977. 'A Western Apache Writing System: The Symbols of Silas John.' In Ben G. Blount and Mary Sanches, eds, *Sociocultural Dimensions of Language Change*, 227–52. New York: Academic Press.

Berman, Judith. 1994. 'George Hunt and the Kwak'wala Texts.' *Anthropological Linguistics* 36: 483–514.
Brandt, Elizabeth. 1981. 'Native American Attitudes Toward Literacy and Recording in the Southwest.' *Journal of the Linguistic Association of the Southwest* 4(2): 185–95.
Briggs, Charles. 1988. *Competence in Performance*. Philadelphia: University of Pennsylvania Press.
– 1993. 'Metadiscursive Practices and Scholarly Authority in Folkloristics.' *Journal of American Folklore* 106: 387–434.
Burns, Allen. 1980. 'Interactive Features in Yucatec Mayan Narratives.' *Language in Society* 9: 307–20.
Chafe, Wallace. 1995. *Discourse, Consciousness, and Time*. Chicago: University of Chicago Press.
Clifford, James. 1990. 'Notes on (Field)Notes.' In Roger Sanjek, ed., *Fieldnotes: The Makings of Anthropology*, 47–70. Ithaca, NY: Cornell University Press.
Dart, Sarah N. 1993. 'Phonetic Properties of O'odham Stop and Fricative Constraints.' *International Journal of American Linguistics* 59: 16–37.
Duranti, Alessandro, and Charles Goodwin, eds. 1993. *Rethinking Context*. Cambridge: Cambridge University Press.
Farella, John. 1993. *The Wind in a Jar*. Albuquerque: University of New Mexico.
Goddard, Ives, and Kathleen Bragdon. 1988. *Native Writing in Massachusett*. Philadelphia: Memoirs of the American Philosophical Society 185.
Hanzeli, Victor E. 1969. *Missionary Linguistics in New France*. The Hague: Mouton.
Hill, Jane. 1966. 'A Grammar of the Cupeño Language.' PhD dissertation, University of California, Los Angeles.
Hill, Jane, and Roscinda Nolasquez. 1973. *Mulu'wetam: The First People*. Banning, CA: Malki Museum Press.
Hutchins, Edward. 1995. *Cognition in the Wild*. Cambridge, MA: MIT Press.
Hymes, Dell H. 1983 [1976]. 'The Americanist Tradition in Linguistics.' In *Essays in the History of Linguistic Anthropology*, 115–34. Amsterdam: John Benjamins.
– 1981. *In Vain I Tried to Tell You*. Philadelphia: University of Pennsylvania Press.
Jackson, Jean. 1990. '"I Am a Fieldnote": Fieldnotes as Symbols of Professional Identity.' In Roger Sanjek, ed., *Fieldnotes: The Makings of Anthropology*, 3–33. Ithaca, NY: Cornell University Press.
McLaughlin, Dan. 1992. *When Literacy Empowers*. Albuquerque: University of New Mexico Press.
Means, Russell. 1983. 'The Same Old Song.' In W. Churchill, ed., *Marxism and Native Americans*. Boston: South End Press (cited in McLaughlin).
Mignolo, Walter D. 1992. 'On the Colonization of Amerindian Languages and Memories: Renaissance Theories of Writing and the Discontinuity of the Classical Tradition.' *Comparative Studies in Society and History* 34: 301–30.
– 1994a. 'Signs and Their Transmission: The Question of the Book in the New World.' In E. Boone, ed., *Writing without Words*, 220–70. Durham, NC: Duke University Press.
– 1994b. 'Afterword: Writing and Recorded Knowledge in Colonial and Postcolonial Situations.' In Boone, ed., *Writing without Words*, 292–313.
– 1995. *The Darker Side of the Renaissance: Literacy, Territoriality, and Colonization*. Ann Arbor: University of Michigan Press.
Mühlhäusler, Peter. 1990. '"Reducing" Pacific Languages to Writings.' In John E. Joseph and Talbot J. Taylor, eds, *Ideologies of Language*, 189–205. London: Routledge.
Rafael, Vicente. 1993. *Contracting Colonialism*. Durham, NC: Duke University Press.

Saussure, Ferdinand de. 1966 [1917]. *Course in General Linguistics*. New York: McGraw-Hill.

Silko, Leslie. 1981. 'Language and Literature from a Pueblo Indian Perspective.' In Leslie Fiedler and Houston A. Baker, Jr, eds, *English Literature: Opening Up the Canon*. Selected Papers from the English Institute, 1979, new series, no. 4, 54–72.

Street, Brian. 1985. *Literacy in Theory and Practice*. Cambridge University Press.

Tedlock, Dennis. 1983. *The Spoken Word and the Work of Interpretation*. Philadelphia: University of Pennsylvania Press.

Underhill, Ruth. 1938. *Singing for Power*. Berkeley: University of California Press.

Walker, Willard. 1981. 'Native American Writing Systems.' In Charles Ferguson and Shirley Brice Heath, eds, *Language in the USA*. Cambridge University Press.

Zepeda, Ofelia. 1982. 'O'odham ha-cegitodag. Pima and Papago Thought.' *International Journal of American Linguistics* 48: 320–6.

12 Continuities and Renewals in Mayan Literacy and Calendrics

BARBARA TEDLOCK

The Americanist Tradition has long been centred on written texts and other graphic documents. Comparing texts produced in Mesoamerica during the pre-Columbian, colonial, and post-colonial periods, we see a continuity in thought and culture that reaches across the grisly experiences of the Spanish invasion. By continuity I mean a dynamic process that binds a people and their shared culture together in distinctive ways throughout their history. In this process new elements are constantly being incorporated while other elements are discarded. In a living culture, continuity never implies a thoughtless unchanging preservation.

The first forms of writing that appeared in Mesoamerica were calendar day names, carved or painted on walls, monuments, containers, and books (Marcus 1976). Since the Maya script preserved in stone has the elegant and decorative appearance of calligraphy, it probably first appeared in manuscripts written on bark paper and hide (Love 1994: 3). There is no doubt that the strongly pictorial characteristics of early Mesoamerican writing enhanced its readability, so that virtually anyone could discern some level of meaning in all of the scripts, including the hieroglyphic ones. There is some evidence that the architectural placement of writing may indicate relative degrees of literacy. For example, if the text of a monument faced away from the public, then it may have been intended to address only a small and fully literate audience (Reents-Budet 1989: 196). References to the use of manuscripts are rare, but in 1674 Francisco de Burgoa reported that they were hung on the walls of palaces (Byland and Pohl 1994: 9).

By the first century AD the Maya, together with several other Mesoamerican cultures located on the Gulf Coast and in Oaxaca, had developed language-based hieroglyphic writing systems. Since we have very few textual examples from non-Mayan hieroglyphic systems, it is Maya writing that is the best known today. This system employs a combination of logograms representing entire words, phonetic signs representing syllables, and semantic qualifiers. Texts were carved and painted on pottery vessels, building and cave walls, and in painted books or 'codices,' as they have come to be called. These books contain mythic, religious, astronomical, and historic records. The pictures and texts used in these codices were developed to keep track of the cycles of the solar year, the ritual divinatory year, the cycle of fifty-two years, the cycle of Venus, and the larger cosmic cycles of creation, destruction, and re-creation of the world. There is also a rich colonial and post-colonial alphabetic tradition of entextualization that was and still is used by Native peoples for their own cultural, social, religious, legal, and political purposes.

Although hundreds of books were burned during the sixteenth century by such Roman Catholic priests as Diego de Landa and Sánchez de Aguilar, a few of these books remained in use as late as the beginning of the eighteenth century. The majority of pre-Columbian codices that survived the early years of the Spanish invasion were painted in the international Mixteca-Puebla style of central Mexico and Native intellectuals continued to produce such documents until the mid-sixteenth century (Robertson 1968; Jansen 1990).

Núñez de la Vega (1702), writing in 1692, mentioned calendar documents that he had obtained from Tzeltal-Mayan priest-shamans who were still using them. Andrés de Avendaño y Loyola (1696) saw books containing calendars and katun (twenty-year period) prophecies at the end of the seventeenth century, and he even acquired a degree of literacy in the script (Roys 1967: 184). In highland Guatemala, during the first years of the eighteenth century, the Dominican friar Francisco Ximénez wrote of diviners who 'have a source of predictions from the time of their heathenism,' indicating that they 'see things in a book where they have all the months and signs corresponding to each day, of which I have one in my possession, and each sign or signal of that day is one of the demons who figure in their stories' (Ximénez 1967: 11).

There has been some debate as to the degree of highland Mayan participation in the writing system so well documented among lowland Mayans. But according to the sixteenth-century *Annals of the Cakchikels*, highland Mayans were not mere importers of calendrical documents, but rather produced them. When they went to pay tribute at an eastern city that may well have been Copán, they brought 'green quetzal feathers, reliquaries of red feathers, along with writings, carvings; they were giving flutes, songs, days in a row, days by the score, pataxte, cacao' (D. Tedlock 1992: 230). The words 'days in a row, days by the score' refer specifically to divinatory almanacs.

Today we have only four Mayan hieroglyphic books: the Madrid, Paris, and

Dresden codices from the lowlands, and the Grolier Codex from the Chiapas highlands. The continuation of Mayan literacy and literature, however, proved to be independent of its original script. The missionaries who burned the hieroglyphic books introduced Mayans to the Latin alphabet in order to convert their pupils into scribes for Christianity. Their hope was that these alphabetically literate Mayans would submit to their will and simply translate Christian prayers, sermons, and catechisms into the various Mayan languages, so that the priests could use them as tools for religious conversion.

From a very early date Mayan scribes found their own political and religious applications for alphabetic writing. These autonomous writers have left a rich literary legacy that is far more extensive than the surviving hieroglyphic corpus. Their most important works, created as alphabetic substitutes for hieroglyphic books, include the fourteen Yucatec Mayan *Chilam Balam* or 'Books of the Speaker of the Jaguar,' the K'iche' Mayan *Popol Wuj* or 'Council Book' and the *Rab'inal Achi'* dance drama, the *Annals of the Cakchikels*, and a document I shall call the *K'iche' Codex.*[1] Among Mayans, it is the literature of the K'iche' that has the longest and most continuous mythological, historical, poetic, and dramatic tradition. It has roots that can be traced to the Middle Classic period (AD 450), and run from the Post-Classic (beginning in AD 950) and the colonial periods, all the way to the present day (Edmonson 1985: 130).

The K'iche' Codex

This colonial-period codex consists of a set of three calendar manuscripts that were written in the Latin alphabet during the early eighteenth century in the highlands of Guatemala. Since it was at this same period that Ximénez mentioned owning a pre-Columbian calendrical codex, it may be that these three texts were transcribed from such a document. Internal evidence indicates that it was written in 1722, exactly one year after the system of tribute payment and forced labour was abolished by the Spanish crown. At this time long-suppressed Mayan practices and religious institutions emerged and combined with elements of Spanish culture, taking 'a form far more satisfactory to the people than had been possible before' (La Farge 1940: 287).

The K'iche' Codex was seen long after it was written by Archbishop Cortés y Lárraz, who wrote: 'In the town of Quezaltenango I found a calendar of theirs ... The author of this calendar was jailed for being a shaman, but he broke out of jail and hasn't been seen since. I am informed that he was a choirmaster' (Berendt n.d.: iv–v). Quezaltenango, now the second largest city in Guatemala, lies in the region where the K'iche' language was and is spoken. Cortés y Lárraz arrived there early in 1770, and the date 13 March 1770 appears in the margin of the second of the two 260-day divinatory calendars included in the codex.While it seems likely that the written transcriptions of the K'iche' calendars were made by educated members of the nobility in Quezaltenango, we do not know for certain the purpose for which these calendar texts were recorded. Perhaps they were written down by a group of Mayan daykeepers (calendar priests), in order to preserve the knowledge necessary for planning rituals and training future priests. Or they may have been produced by daykeepers at the request of an interested Catholic priest. Having been produced in 1722, they may have been kept in a local convent until 18 March 1770, when they were handed over to Archbishop Cortés y Lárraz during his visit to Quezaltenango (Carmack 1973: 165–7).

It is known that between 1768 and 1770 Cortés y Lárraz sent out questionnaires to priests all over Guatemala asking about the Native languages spoken in each community, family organization, settlement patterns, production, and trade, as well as information about local 'superstitions and idolatries.' He travelled widely during this same period, gathering Mayan documents and as much ethnographic information as he could from local curates. His purpose was to confront and combat pre-Columbian religious knowledge and intellectual traditions. His published report became one of the most important historical documents to be created in Guatemala during the entire colonial period (Cortés y Lárraz 1958). The story of the modern discovery of the K'iche' Codex begins in April of 1877, when Karl Hermann Berendt visited the Museo Nacional in Guatemala City. He was looking through the papers of Archbishop Pedro Cortés y Lárraz, and he opened a volume of labelled '*Larras, Opúsculos* [Booklets].' The first item was written in K'iche', using an orthography that was introduced in 1545 by Francisco de la Parra. It began with the words *Vae chol poal ɛih maceval ɛih cohcha chi rch*, 'Here is the order of the common days, Indian days, we speak of them.'[2] Six consecutive years from the Mayan solar calendar, beginning on 2 May 1722, followed. This is the only known colonial source to give K'iche' names for each of the Mayan solar year's eighteen twenty-day divisions (Carmack 1981: 87–8; Edmonson 1988: 237).

Berendt thought highly enough of his find to create a facsimile, following the scale, layout, and holography of the original. His work subsequently passed into the hands of Daniel G. Brinton and then came to rest in the manuscript collection of the University of Pennsylvania Library. The facsimile is now the primary document, since the original manuscript mysteriously disappeared from the Museo Nacional at some time before the facsimile arrived in the United States.

The first calendar in the K'iche' Codex spans twenty-two pages and covers the six solar years already mentioned. Each year is divided into eighteen twenty-day periods, with a five-day period, called *4,api ɛih* or 'closing days,' added at the end. From time to time, the value or significance of outstanding days during the solar year is indicated. The five closing days are pointed out in each case, and the day on which the calendar begins, known as the 'year-bearer,' is indicated.

The second part of the codex, twenty-eight pages long, contains two complete calendars based on the Mayan divinatory cycle of 260 days. This cycle is created by the combination of thirteen day numbers with twenty day names: since thirteen and twenty have no common factor, this process creates 260 unique combinations. This cycle has been described as closely linked to celestial events, such as the interval between zenith transits of the sun near the latitude 15° north, or else to earthly affairs, such as agricultural practices or midwifery (B. Tedlock 1992: 93).

Each of the divinatory calendar pages contains four almanacs. These almanacs have a list of five different day names, all with the same number coefficient. The dates thus designated are fifty-two days apart. The distance from the last date back to the one at the top of the list is again fifty-two days, so that each almanac spans the full length of the divinatory calendar (5 × 52 = 260 days). To the right of each group of five dates, in a separate column, is written an augury. The first of the five dates in each almanac is one day later than the first date in the previous almanac. The almanac that introduces the first of the two divinatory calendars begins with 1 Ymox, and the last almanac, at the bottom of the thirteenth page, begins with 13 Ee and completes a set of fifty-two almanacs. The second divinatory calendar, beginning with 1 Canil, is recorded in another hand but follows the same general pattern. On folio 38 the date 5 Canil is correctly correlated with the Gregorian date 13 March 1770.

La Farge (1947: 181), who published a single page of the K'iche' text, without a translation, suggested that each augury was a condensed statement of the controlling forces hovering over the first day in each almanac. Edmonson (1971: 36n, 59n, 60n), who quotes brief passages from this document in the footnotes to his translation of the Popol Vuh, assumes that the augury for a given group of five days applies equally to each one of them. A likelier possibility, however, is that it applies to the days only as a group and that the auguries refer to a ritual to be carried out on each of the five days. In some cases the ritual reference is overt, as when a group of days is said to be 'for the giving of alms,' but in other cases it may be allusive, as when it says 'powerful teeth, powerful claws, the owl left his mark,' suggesting the possibility of sorcery. Such an interpretation is suggested by modern practice, in which ritual acts that take advantage of the character of the days always involve the use of groups of days, never a single day (B. Tedlock 1992: 190–5).

The organization of dates into clusters of five, spaced at fifty-two-day intervals, is also known from the Dresden and Madrid codices. Out of the fifty-two possible groupings, twenty-eight appear in Dresden (Thompson 1972: 2–22) and forty-three appear in Madrid (Villacorta and Villacorta 1976: 14–64 and 79–112). Madrid probably has all fifty-two groups, but in many cases the number coefficients are illegible. The difference is that the groups in both Dresden and Madrid are arranged more by the kinds of activities affected by the accompanying auguries, such as deer trapping and bee keeping, than by a systematic exposition of all fifty-two possible combinations.

In its systematicity the K'iche' Codex resembles the Borgia, Cospi, and Vaticanus B Codices (all of the so-called Borgia group) in the Mixteca-Puebla style (Seler 1902 and 1963; Nowotny 1968; Anders 1972; Boone 1992; Díaz 1993). These codices contain all fifty-two groups of five days each and follow the same order as the first of the two K'iche' divinatory calendars, starting with the Mexican day 1 Cipatli (equivalent to K'iche' 1 Imox). On the other hand, these Mexican codices place auguries above and below each vertical column of five days, whereas the K'iche' Codex follows hieroglyphic Mayan codices in placing auguries to the right of each column.

The surviving Mayan hieroglyphic books seem to have been composed according to common standards of measurement. They all have pages more than twice as high as wide, whereas the pages of Mexican codices are either close to being square or else wider than they are high. The original of the K'iche' Codex was written on paper of Spanish manufacture, but the average spacing (5 centimetres) between the horizontal lines that divide each of its pages into four registers is the same as on a four-register page in the Dresden Codex and close to the spacing (5.5 centimetres) in the Madrid Codex (see figure 12.1). This does not mean that the K'iche' Codex was transcribed from the Dresden or Madrid codices, but it does suggest that it was modelled on a hieroglyphic original that followed established Mayan rules of page proportion.

Organizing the sacred calendar into groups of five evenly spaced days has the effect of facilitating cross-references to the Mesoamerican Venus calendar, which reckons heliacal eastern rises of Venus as running in cycles of five, repeating the same five evenly spaced divinatory day names (but with changing numbers) in each complete cycle. Indeed, one of the entries in the K'iche' Codex (Berendt n.d.: 47) makes a direct reference to Venus as the morning star:

Utzilah ɛih ticbal, auexabal
    Good days for planting, sowing
sak amaɛ cauexic
    in peace one plants

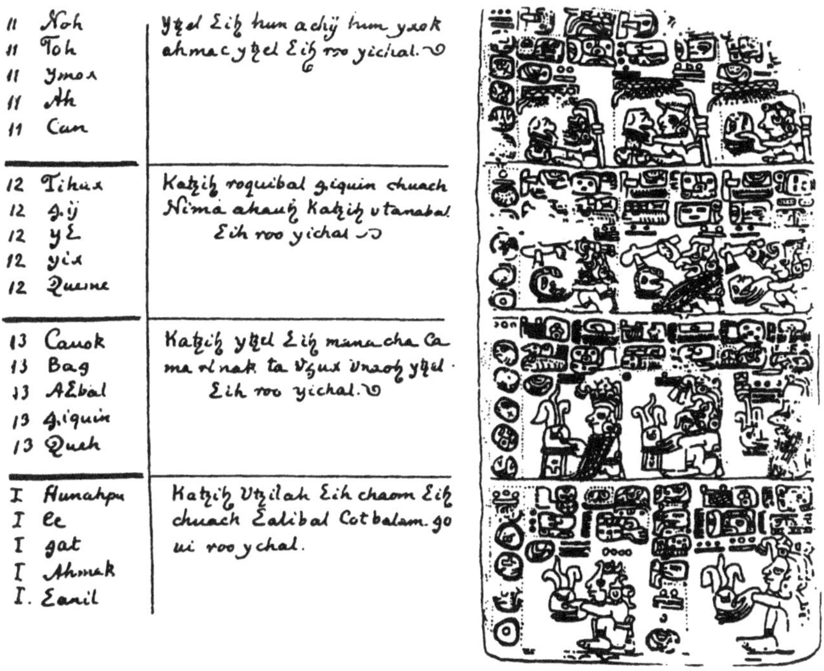

FIGURE 12.1 Page 32 of the K'iche' Codex (left) compared with page 97 of the Madrid Codex (right), proportioned as in the original. Note the similarity in the height of the four registers. The list of days in the third register of the K'iche' Codex is the same as the list in the first register of the Madrid, except that the starting day in the Madrid list is the equivalent of Queh instead of Tihax.

chaɛan nima 4humil
  the great star [Venus] rises
eko ɛih chaon ɛih.
  bringer of day [morning star], beautiful day.

This is the most recent of all evidence for systematic Venus reckoning in the Mayan world. It is the entry for 3 Toh, 3 Ymos, 3 Ah, 3 Can, and 3 Noh, and it so happens that, when this document took effect, on 3 May 1722, the most recent heliacal eastern rise of Venus had taken place on 19 June 1721, which was 3 Toh. The next eastern rise would have been expected on 24 January 1723, which was 2 Ah. Apparently the influence of this event spread its dominion beyond the actual day of its occurrence, just as the character of the first day of a new solar year reasserts itself throughout that year.

The set of five day names associated with Venus on the K'iche' Codex corresponds to the set used in the Borgia group rather than to those of the Dresden Venus table, whose K'iche' equivalents – ɛanil, Hunahpu, E, 4at, and Ahmak – run one day later in each case. It may be that the Borgia dates begin periods whereas the Dresden dates end them, so that there is no real disagreement as to the divinatory timing of Venus events. In any case, the positive value the K'iche' Codex assigns to Venus as the morning star directly contrasts with Central Mexican sources. Instead, it fits the Popol Vuh, where the first human beings yearn for the appearance of the Great Star that will announce the first rising of the sun and deliver them from darkness (D. Tedlock 1996: 64–6).

The K'iche' Codex is unrivalled among Mayan alphabetic documents, whether highland or lowland, in the directness of its resemblance to a screenfold book. This is ironic, given that it has long been customary to assign the surviving codices (except for the Grolier) to the lowland Maya.

There is a possibility that these two divinatory texts are readings from two different hieroglyphic books. This is suggested by the fact that although they largely correspond in their prognostications, they begin on different day names and disagree in their auguries more than can be accounted for by variant readings. Only the first author ends each entry with utzilah [or ytzel] ɛih roo ychal, 'good [or bad] days all five of them.' In various passages in the second calendar the scribe seems to be complaining of the difficulty of reading: 'It doesn't say anything anywhere about how they go and come,' 'It doesn't say, it doesn't really say what happens,' 'Twisted is its word.' In the first calendar there is a day named Yix, while in the second the same day is written Balam, meaning 'jaguar' in either case.

In both calendars there are day names written Nooh and Ee. Both of the words contain a vowel followed by a glottal stop, written as No'j and E' in the new official Mayan orthography. The use of a doubling of vowels to notate such sound combinations is also present in the *Chilam Balam of Chumayel* and the *Chilam Balam of Chan Kan*, where it has already been interpreted as a retention of a spelling rule used in the hieroglyphic script (Bricker 1989).

In order to compare the content of these two calendars more closely I will begin with the initial entry in the first calendar for the days 1 Yix [*Ix*], 1 Queme [*Kame*], 1 Tihax [*Tijax*], 1 4,ih [*Tz'i'*], 1 Yɛ [*Iq'*].

Katzih royoval ɛih
  Truly angry days
utiobal cumatz, utiobal balam, ca4ha
  the bite of the serpent, bite of the jaguar, it says
hun coh balam xe çivan, oher tzih.
  one puma jaguar at the bottom of the canyon, ancient words.

Here note that the use of the quotative *ca4ha* [*kach'a*], 'it says,' indicates that there is a source of knowledge other than first-hand experience. Also, the evidential noun phrase *oher tzih*, 'ancient words,' specifically indicates that the author is citing ancient tradition rather than current secular knowledge.

The same entry by the second scribe begins with the calendar day named 1 Balam equivalent to 1 Yix. It reads:

Ki royeval ɛi ucovil ɛih
  Very angry days, hard days
utiobal cumatz, balam
  the bite of the serpent, the jaguar
maui chi colo tah chutio.
  one cannot escape their bites.

This recalls a passage from the Popol Vuh: 'And then, all at once, Tohil, Auilix, and Hacauitz were turned to stone, along with the icons of the puma, jaguar, rattlesnake, fer-de-lance, which the White Sparkstriker took with him into the trees. Everywhere, all of them became stone when the sun, moon, and stars appeared. Perhaps we would have no relief from the voracious animals today – the puma, jaguar, rattlesnake, fer-de-lance – and perhaps it wouldn't even be our day today, if the original animals hadn't been turned to stone by the sun when he came up' (D. Tedlock 1996: 161).

Today, in the highlands of Guatemala, K'iche' lineages maintain thousands of stone icons and small box-shaped altars that must be fed copal and strong drink on days named Ix. Owing to the religious activities that take place at these shrines on these days, children born on Ix are considered to have the ability to become patrilineage heads. The altars visited on Ix are known as *warab'al ja* literally 'sleeping place of the house,' but with 'sleeping place' serving as a term for 'foundation' and 'house' as a metaphor for 'lineage,' in this case the ancestral members of lineage going back to its founder. That this is an example of cultural continuity is indicated by the glyphic phrase *u waybil ch'ul*, literally 'the sleeping place of the spirits,' carved on the small stone house shrines that were excavated by E. Willard Andrews V in a residential group at the Classic-period city of Copán (Freidel, Schele, and Parker 1993: 188–9).

The day Ix, as reported in the Chilam Balam books of Yucatán, has an augury similar to that given for Ix (or Balam) in the K'iche' Codex. Thus, in the list of days recorded in the Chilam Balam of Kaua (translated by Barrera Vásquez 1939) the entry for Ix reads, 'The fierce jaguar. Bloody his mouth; bloody his claws. A slayer as well. Devourer of flesh. Killer of men.' And the Chilam Balam of the Mani calendar list describes this day as pertaining to a fierce jaguar with bloody mouth and claws.

Cultural Renewal Today

The K'iche' Codex provides an important linguistic and cultural bridge between the sixteenth-century Popol Vuh and ongoing religious practices. Mayan intellectuals today are keenly interested in their own culture, history, and language.[3] They formed an organization known as the Academia de las Lenguas Mayas de Guatemala (ALMG) and voted in new orthographies for writing the twenty-six Mayan languages spoken in Guatemala (see ALMG 1988). President Vinicio Cerezo signed their decisions into law in 1987, and in 1991 the Guatemalan Congress recognized the Academia as an autonomous government ministry. It is currently directed by a group of highly educated Mayan professionals.

One of the current Mayan leaders, Demetrio Cojtí, is a Cakchiquel who earned a doctorate in communications in Belgium. He recently described the effort of the Academia to promote Maya languages: 'We Maya have always resisted our colonial situation. It used to be that we would say yes and then do the other thing, but this is the beginning of a new stage of articulated, conscious resistance. Language is the heart of it ... Maya languages have been relegated to the markets, to the servants' quarters, to the mountains, and the ravines. Who speaks Maya in the Congress? No one. On television? No one except the evangelicals. Who teaches it in the schools? No one' (Canby 1994: 337). He and other members of the Academia are also encouraging indigenous customs such as wearing distinctive hand-woven textiles, burning copal incense at outdoor shrines, and using the Mayan calendar for both ritual and secular purposes and events. A number of the leaders of the movement have also gone back to the ancient system of naming and adopted their birth dates on the 260–day sacred calendar as personal names. Thus, Demetrio Cojtí Cuxil is now also known as Waqi' Q'anil or 'Six Harvest.'

Several other all-Mayan organizations were also founded during the late 1980s: Centro de Documentación Maya, Centro de Investigación Social Maya, Coordinadora Cakchiquel de Desarrollo Integral, Asociación de Escritores Mayances de Guatemala, Mayab' Ajtz'ib' Jun Iq', and Mayahuil. Mayab' Ajtz'ib' means 'Mayan Writers,' while Jun Iq' is the date of its founding on the 260-day K'iche' calendar. The main activity of this all-Mayan organization is to publish literature written by Mayas in any Mayan language. The Mayahuil, a Mam Mayan organization, whose name means 'New Dawn,' led a 1992 protest against the celebration of the quincentennial of the so-called 'discovery' of America and has since been bringing widespread environmental destruction to public attention.

To date these organizations have published a number of books, including dictionaries and grammars in several languages, a monthly Spanish-K'iche' bulletin titled *Chatwalijoq*, and an annual appointment book titled *Cholb'al Chak: Calendario Maya*, 'Instrument for ordering one's work: Mayan Calendar,' which accurately correlates with the Gregorian calendar. A number of rural K'iche'-speaking communities have published mimeographed versions of the *Rajilb'al Q'ij Maya* (Mayan Day Count), again correlated with the Gregorian calendar.

These activities are part of an emerging highland Mayan communal culture of resistance to Western domination and control. Mayan languages, myths, and textiles, together with the sacred earth and the ancient calendar, have become key cultural values. They are also core symbols in the construction of a transnational Pan-Mayan diasporic identity. The Mayan intellectuals and professionals in this movement – physicians, dentists, lawyers, professors – have created their own discipline of Mayan Studies. They promote linguistic and anthropological research by Mayans about Mayans, and they critique Latin American racism and North American neocolonialism. Mayan peoples today are asserting their rights to their own conceptual world, their own ethnic identity, their own land – and, as always, their own time.

NOTES

The research that made this paper possible was supported, in part, by fellowship grants from the National Endowment for the Humanities (1993) and the American Council of Learned Societies

(1994). Anthony Aveni, Elizabeth Boone, James Brady, Victoria Bricker, Allan Burns, Michael Coe, Dorie Reents-Budet, Linda Schele, Andrea Stone, and Dennis Tedlock have offered excellent advice on previous versions of this essay.

1 Oliver La Farge received permission from the Archives of the University of Pennsylvania to translate and publish this document, which he never did. In a letter of 16 September 1946 to Linton Satterthwaite he proposed to call the manuscript 'A Quiché Codex in Latin Script.'

2 Here the tresillo, written as a backward 3 or 'ɛ,' indicates a glottalized back k now written as q'; the cuatrillo, or '4' the glottalized front k now written as k'; the 4 with comma, '4,' is now tz'; and the '4h' is now ch'.

3 See Colop Xec and Sam Colop 1982; Otzoy 1992, 1996; Otzoy and Sam Colop 1990; Cojtí Cuxil 1989, 1991a, 1991b, 1995, 1997; Sam Colop 1991, 1994; COMG 1991, 1995; B. Tedlock 1993; Warren 1997.

REFERENCES

Academia de las Lenguas Mayas (ALMG). 1988. *Lenguas mayas de Guatemala: Documento de referencia para la pronunciación de los nuevos alfabetos oficiales*. Guatemala: Instituto Indigenista Nacional.

Anders, Ferdinand. 1972. *Codex Vaticanus B (3773)*. Graz, Austria: Akademische Druck- und Verlaganstalt

Avendaño y Loyola, Andrés de. 1696. 'Relación de las dos entradas que hize a la conversión de los gentiles itzaex y cehaches.' Manuscript copies in the Ayer Collection, Newberry Library, Chicago, and at the Tozzer Library, Harvard University, Cambridge, MA.

Barrera Vásquez, Alfredo. 1939. 'El pronóstico de los 20 signos del tzolkin, segun los libros de Chilam Balam, de Kaua y de Maní.' *Registro de Cultura Yucateca* 6: 4–33.

Berendt, Karl Hermann. n.d. 'Calendario de los Indios de Guatemala Kiché (1722).' Berendt Collection, manuscript no. 58. Facsimile in University Museum Library, University of Pennsylvania, Philadelphia.

Boone, Elizabeth Hill. 1992. 'Pictorial Codices of Ancient Mexico.' In Richard Townsend, ed., *The Ancient Americas: Art from Sacred Landscapes*, 197–210. Chicago: The Art Institute of Chicago

Bricker, Victoria R. 1989. 'The Last Gasp of Maya Hieroglyphic Writing in the Books of Chilam Balam of Chumayel and Can Kan.' In William F. Hanks and Don S. Rice, eds, *Word and Image in Maya Culture: Explorations in Language, Writing and Representation*, 39–50. Salt Lake City: University of Utah Press.

Byland, Bruce E., and John M.D. Pohl. 1994. *In the Realm of 8 Deer: The Archaeology of the Mixtec Codices*. Norman: University of Oklahoma Press.

Canby, Peter. 1994. *The Heart of the Sky*. New York: Kodansha America.

Carmack, Robert M. 1973. *Quichean Civilization: The Ethnohistoric, Ethnographic, and Archaeological Sources*. Berkeley: University of California Press.

– 1981. *The Quiché Mayas of Utatlán*. Norman: University of Oklahoma Press.

Cojtí Cuxil, Demetrio. 1989. 'Problemas de "la identidad nacional" guatemalteca.' In Coordinadora Cakchiquel de Desarrollo Integral (COCADI), ed., *Cultura maya y políticas de desarrollo*. Chimaltenango, Guatemala: COCADI.

– 1991a. *La configuración del pensamiento político del pueblo Maya*. Quetzaltenango: Asociación de Escritores Mayances de Guatemala.

– 1991b. 'L'université contre les mayas.' In Alain Breton et Jacques Arnauld, eds, *Mayas*, 241–7. Série Monde, no. 56. Paris: Autrement.
– 1995. *Ub'aniik ri Una'ooj Uchomab'aal ri Maya' Tinamit: Configuración del pensamiento político del pueblo Maya* (2da, parte). Guatemala: Editorial Cholsamaj.
– 1997. *Ri Maya' Moloj pa Iximulew: El Movimiento Maya (En Guatemala)*. Guatemala: Editorial Cholsamaj.
Colop Xec, Isaías, and Luis E. Sam Colop. 1982. *Je ubanic le kc'aslemal: Asi es como vivimos*. Guatemala: Universidad de San Carlos de Guatemala, Centro de Aprendizaje de Lenguas.
Consejo de Organizaciones Mayas de Guatemala (COMG). 1991. *Derechos Específicos del pueblo Maya; rujunamil ri mayab' amaq'*. Guatemala: Cholsamaj.
– 1995. *Construyendo un futuro para nuestro pasado, derechos de pueblo Maya y el processo de paz*. Consejo de Organizaciones Mayas de Guatemala. Guatemala City: Cholsamaj.
Cortés y Lárraz, Pedro. 1958. *Descripción Geográfico-Moral de la Diócesis de Goathemala*. 2 vols. Biblioteca 'Goathemala,' vol. 22. Guatemala.
Díaz, Gisele, and Alan Rodgers. 1993. *The Codex Borgia*. New York: Dover.
Edmonson, Munro S. 1971. *The Book of Counsel: The Popol Vuh of the Quiche Maya of Guatemala*. Middle American Research, pub. 35. New Orleans: Tulane University Press.
– 1985. 'Quiche Literature.' In Munro S. Edmonson, ed., *Supplement to the Handbook of Middle American Indians: Literatures*, 107–32. Austin: University of Texas Press.
– 1988. *The Book of the Year: Middle American Calendrical Systems*. Salt Lake City: University of Utah Press.
Freidel, David, Linda Schele, and Joy Parker. 1993. *Maya Cosmos: Three Thousand Years on the Shaman's Path*. New York: Morrow.
Jansen, Maarten. 1990. 'The Search for History in the Mixtec Codices.' *Ancient Mesoamerica* 1: 99–112
La Farge, Oliver. 1940. 'Maya Ethnology: The Sequence of Cultures.' In Clarence L. Hay, Ralph L. Linton, Samuel K. Lothrop, Harry L. Shapiro, and George C. Vaillant, eds, *The Maya and Their Neighbors*, 281–91. New York: D. Appleton-Century.
– 1946. 'Letter of September 16th to Linton Satterthwaite.' Located in University of Pennsylvania Museum Archives, Philadelphia.
– 1947. *Santa Eulalia*. Chicago: University of Chicago Press.
Love, Bruce. 1994. *The Paris Codex: Handbook for a Maya Priest*. Austin: University of Texas Press.
Marcus, Joyce. 1976. 'The Origins of Mesoamerican Writing.' *Annual Review of Anthropology* 5: 35–67.
Nowotny, Karl Anton. 1968. *Codex Cospi*. Facsimile. Graz, Austria: Akademische Druck- und Verlaganstalt
Núñez de la Vega, F. 1702. *Constituciones diocesanas del obispado de Chiapa*. Rome.
Otzoy, Irma. 1992. 'Identidad y trajes maya.' *Mesoamérica* 23: 95–112.
– 1996. *Maya' b'anikil Maya' tzyaqb'äl: Identidad y Vestuario Maya*. Guatemala: Editorial Cholsamaj.
Otzoy, Irma, and Luis Enrique Sam Colop. 1990. 'Identidad étnica y modernización entre los mayas de Guatemala.' *Mesoamérica* 19: 97–100.
Reents-Budet, Dorie. 1989. 'Narrative in Classic Maya Art.' In William F. Hanks and Don S. Rice, eds, *Word and Image in Maya Culture: Explorations in Language, Writing, and Representation*, 189–97. Salt Lake City: University of Utah Press.
Robertson, Donald. 1968. 'The Tulum Murals: The International Style of the Late Post-Classic.' In *Verhandlungen des XXXVIII Internationalen Amerikanisten-Kongresses*, 12–18, Aug. 1968, Stuttgart-Munich, 2: 77–8. Paris: International Congress of Americanists.

Roys, Ralph L. 1967. *Ritual of the Bacabs: A Book of Maya Incantations.* Norman: University of Oklahoma Press.

Sam Colop, Luis Enrique. 1991. *Jub'aqtun omay kuchum k'aslemal: Cinco siglos de encubrimiento – a propósito de 1992.* Nab'e tijob'al wuj, Cuaderno ndm. 1. Guatemala: Ch'ob'anelab' uk'aslemal mayab' amaq', Seminario Permanente de Estudios Mayas.

– 1994. 'Maya Poetics.' Ph.D. dissertation, State University of New York, Buffalo.

Seler, Eduard. 1902. *Codex Vaticanus No. 3773 (Codex Vaticanus B).* Berlin and London.

– 1963. *Commentarios al Códice Borgia.* México: Fondo de Cultura Económica.

Tedlock, Barbara. 1992. *Time and the Highland Maya.* Revised and expanded edition. Albuquerque: University of New Mexico Press.

– 1993. 'Mayans and Mayan Studies from 2000 BC to AD 1992.' *Latin American Research Review* 28(3): 153–73.

Tedlock, Dennis. 1992. 'The Popol Vuh as a Hieroglyphic Book.' In Elin C. Danien and Robert J. Sharer, eds, *New Theories on the Ancient Maya,* 229–40. Philadelphia: The University Museum.

– 1996. *Popol Vuh.* Revised and expanded edition. New York: Simon & Schuster.

Thompson, John Eric Simpson. 1972. 'A Commentary on the Dresden Codex: A Maya Hieroglyphic Book.' *American Philosophical Society Memoirs* 93. Philadelphia.

Villacorta C., J.A., and C.A. Villacorta. 1976. *Códices Mayas.* Guatemala City: Tip. Nacional.

Warren, Kay B. 1997. 'Reading History as Resistance: Mayan Public Intellectuals in Guatemala.' In Arturo Escobar and Sonia E. Alvarez, eds, *Cultures of Politics/Politics of Cultures: Latin American Social Movements Revisited,* Boulder, CO: Westview.

Ximénez, Francisco. 1967. *Escolios a las historias del origen de los indios.* Sociedad de Geogafía e Historia de Guatemala, pub. 13. Guatemala.

13 Why Collect Texts? The Native, Evangelical, and Americanist Traditions among the Tuscaroras

BLAIR A. RUDES

Reported to have been the largest and most powerful tribe in the interior of the Carolinas at first European contact in the seventeenth century (Lawson 1709), the Tuscaroras were decimated in a war with the colonists in 1711–13 (Saunders 1886–1980). Most of the survivors fled the Carolinas and took refuge among the related Iroquois tribes in New York State and Ontario, where they were adopted as the sixth nation of the Iroquois Confederacy. By the end of the nineteenth century, the Tuscarora language could be heard primarily in two locations: on the Tuscarora Indian Reservation near the city of Niagara Falls, New York, and on the Six Nations Reserve near Brantford, Ontario. There were major dialect differences in the language as spoken in the two locations, which are described in part in Rudes (1999). The dialect spoken on the Six Nations Reserve is referred to here as the western dialect; that spoken on the Tuscarora Indian Reservation is the eastern dialect.

Since 1828 more than one hundred Tuscarora texts in the Native language and in English translations have been recorded by the Tuscaroras themselves and by academic researchers. As shown in table 13.1, these texts represent the combined effort of thirteen collectors and more than thirty speakers of the Tuscarora language and are the result of hundreds of hours of labour. The texts cover a wide range of genres and topics, including personal and tribal histories, medical practices, fables, law, and religion (see appendices 13.1 and 13.2). As such, they are a rich repository of cultural and linguistic knowledge. Given the effort that has gone into collecting and preserving this information, it is pertinent to ask what use has been made of these texts. In answering this question it is essential to distinguish between the *Native Tradition* regarding the collection and transmission of texts and the *Americanist Tradition* as practised in American anthropology and linguistics. In addition, mention needs to be made of the dissemination of Tuscarora texts within what is perhaps best labelled the

TABLE 13.1 Chronology of Tuscarora text recording

Dates	Collector	Place	Speakers
1828	David Cusick	Tuscarora Indian Reservation	David Cusick, unknown others
1875–83	Erminnie A. Smith	Tuscarora Indian Reservation	John Mt. Pleasant, J.N.B. Hewitt, unknown others
1879–81	Elias Johnson	Tuscarora Indian Reservation	Elias Johnson, unknown others
1880–1912	J.N.B. Hewitt	Tuscarora Indian Reservation	Lucinda Thompson, Joseph Henry, John Gansworth, George Williams, Joseph Williams, unknown others
1883	Albert S. Gatschet	Tuscarora Indian Reservation	Elias Johnson, Adam Williams
1946–54	Floyd G. Lounsbury	Tuscarora Indian Reservation	Nellie Gansworth
1948–49	Anthony F.C. Wallace	Tuscarora Indian Reservation	Nellie Gansworth, Jonas Green, David Hewitt, William Mt. Pleasant, Denny Printup, Clinton Rickard, Edgar Rickard, Daniel Smith
1965–66	Barbara Graymont	Tuscarora Indian Reservation	Clinton Rickard
1969	Elton Greene	Tuscarora Indian Reservation	Elton Greene
1970–present	Marianne Mithun	Tuscarora Indian Reservation	Elton Greene, Marjorie Printup
		Six Nations Reserve	Robert Mt. Pleasant
1973–present	Blair A. Rudes	Tuscarora Indian Reservation	Paul Bissell, Berdie Crogan, Dorothy Crouse, Louise Henry, Kenneth Patterson, Marjorie Printup, Amelia Williams
1974	Michael K. Foster	Six Nations Reserve	Percy Cayuga
1980–94	Marjorie Printup	Tuscarora Indian Reservation	Marjorie Printup

Evangelical Christian Tradition. Table 13.2 provides a summary of the uses made of Tuscarora texts by the individuals who collected them and others. The uses are described in greater detail below.

TABLE 13.2 Uses made of Tuscarora texts

Collector	Published				Course materials		Research input	
	Tuscarora and English		English only					
	Collector	Others	Collector	Others	Collector	Others	Collector	Others
Native Tradition								
D. Cusick			✓	✓			✓	✓
E. Johnson			✓	✓			✓	✓
Evangelical Tradition								
E. Greene								
M Printup					✓			
Americanist Tradition								
E.A. Smith			✓	✓			✓	✓
A.S. Gatschet				✓				
J.N.B. Hewitt		✓	✓	✓			✓	✓
F.G. Lounsbury					✓	✓	✓	✓
B. Graymont							✓	
A.F.C. Wallace	✓			✓	✓		✓	✓
M. Mithun	✓				✓		✓	
M.K. Foster							✓	
B.A. Rudes							✓	

The Native Text Tradition among the Tuscaroras

Traditionally, among the Iroquois legends of creation, primordial creatures, medical practices, and other topics were typically related orally during the winter months to members of the family, clan, or entire tribe. Certain of the listeners 'collected' these texts by memorizing the plot, but not necessarily the exact wording, for later transmission. While all of the texts were generally known by the adult members of the tribe, the collectors specialized in learning the plot of particular legends in sufficient detail that they could be relied upon to accurately, but creatively, reproduce them later. The emphasis here is on creativity, for the available evidence reveals that, while the plot of an Iroquois legend rarely changes in the retelling, the details often do (Chafe 1981; Day and Foster 1995). Thus, the objective of collecting texts in the Native tradition was to ensure their transmission to future generations and the motive was public service, that is, to share the message of the texts with others in the community.

The first publication of Tuscarora texts grew out of the Native tradition. In 1828, David Cusick, a Tuscarora solider in the War of 1812 who in 1816 had provided a Tuscarora vocabulary for Thomas Jefferson's collection, published a book entitled *Ancient History of the Six Nations* (Cusick 1828). The work drew heavily on traditional Tuscarora narratives about the history of the tribe, as well as the histories of the other Iroquois nations, and quoted English translations of passages from several of these texts. By relating portions of Tuscarora texts, Cusick was continuing the tradition of his ancestors of collecting and interpreting legends and transmitting them to others, albeit in the novel medium of written English and, as a result, to an audience that included non-Tuscaroras who were literate in English.

A half-century later another Tuscarora, Elias Johnson, followed in Cusick's footsteps. In 1881, Johnson published his *Legends, Traditions and Laws of the Iroquois, or Six Nations, and History of the Tuscarora Indians* (E. Johnson 1881). In this work, quite long portions of traditional narratives, many composed of several episodes, were presented in English translation.

Around the same time as Johnson's book appeared, another Tuscarora was engaged in the collection of Tuscarora texts as well as texts from other Iroquois nations. This individual was John Napoleon Brinton (J.N.B.) Hewitt, who, at the time, was working as an assistant to the educator and researcher Erminnie A. Smith (Rudes 1994b). Hewitt, however, adopted Smith's approach to recording texts and as a result worked within the Americanist rather than the Native tradition.

The Evangelical Christian Text Tradition among the Tuscaroras

In the Evangelical Christian text tradition, the concern is not with collecting texts, for the texts are fixed in the word of Jesus Christ in the Gospels. Rather, the concern is with disseminating these texts to as large an audience as possible. The efforts at disseminating texts by two Tuscaroras fall at least in part into this tradition. In 1969, Chief Elton Greene published a short pamphlet of Tuscarora vocabulary and sentences (Greene 1969). He also included a Tuscarora version of the Lord's Prayer. One motive in printing the prayer was to illustrate Tuscarora grammar and, as a result, his work might be placed within the Americanist Tradition. However, in choosing a religious tract as his example, it is also possible that Greene was using his pamphlet as a vehicle for disseminating Christian beliefs and, thus, his work was within the Evangelical Christian tradition.

The second individual was Marjorie Printup, who recorded two renderings in Tuscarora of Christian religious tracts for Gospel Recordings: Genesis and the story of Noah's Ark (Printup 1979, 1980). Her motive in producing these texts was firmly within the Evangelical Christian tradition of spreading the Gospel of Jesus Christ.

The Americanist Text Tradition among the Tuscaroras

In the Americanist Tradition, the primary objective of collecting texts is to obtain data about the language and/or culture of the population under study that will inform the collector's research. Thus, the motive of the work is personal enrichment – what may seem to be merely a matter of satisfying the individual's intellectual curiosity.[1] The earliest efforts at recording Tuscarora texts within this tradition were those of Erminnie A. Smith, an educator from New Jersey, member of the American Association for the Advancement of Science, and the first woman to give a paper before that organization in 1879.

Smith's research among the Iroquois was supported by the Bureau of Ethnology (later renamed the Bureau of American Ethnology) within the Smithsonian Institution. She conducted fieldwork in the late 1870s and early 1880s on the Tuscarora Indian Reservation, as well as other Iroquois reservations in New York State. Smith used the information from these texts to prepare an article entitled 'Myths of the Iroquois' (Smith 1883). Unfortunately, she did not identify the tribal provenance of many of the texts that she published. Thus, the texts listed from her article cited in appendix 2 are those that either can definitely be identified as of Tuscarora origin, because an untranslated Tuscarora word occurs in the text, or those that could be of Tuscarora origin, although they might also be of Mohawk, Onondaga, or Seneca origin.

Besides the published myths, it is uncertain how many other texts Smith collected. In 1880 she hired J.N.B. Hewitt to help her in her research (Pilling 1888: 82). Upon her death in 1886, Hewitt was appointed to continue her work for the Bureau of American Ethnology and the texts were turned over to him. He recopied them in his own handwriting and, ultimately, they became intermingled with and indistinguishable from the texts that Hewitt himself collected.

In 1883, another staff member of the Bureau of American Ethnology, Albert S. Gatschet, visited the Tuscarora Indian Reservation, where he recorded six texts from Elias Johnson and Adam Williams, both speakers of the western dialect of Tuscarora (Gatschet 1883). It is unclear why Gatschet made the trip and gathered this information; he made no known use of it during his lifetime.

Unquestionably, the individual responsible for collecting the most Tuscarora textual material was J.N.B. Hewitt. Including the texts collected by Erminnie A. Smith that he retranscribed and edited and the additional texts that he himself collected over the next forty years, Hewitt's Tuscarora texts numbered more than sixty, of which around forty are in Tuscarora, with and without English translations, and another twenty are in English only (Hewitt 1883–1923). Of these texts, Hewitt published only one, 'The Sun Myth and the Tree of Language of the Iroquois,' and only its English version (Hewitt 1892). In addition, he used a few pieces of information from various of the texts in his numerous articles in the *Handbook of American Indians North of Mexico* (Hodge 1907, 1910) and other publications. However, as a result of his incessant efforts at collecting new data and his ceaseless editing of material already collected, the bulk of the texts remained unused and unpublished. For example, Judd (1967: 50–1) says of Hewitt that 'he was a stickler for accuracy, and what others have called a procrastinating habit may have been an ancestral unwillingness to be judged careless and inaccurate.'

Since Hewitt's death in 1937 there have been two major publications of his Tuscarora texts. First, F. Roy Johnson published the English translations of all of Hewitt's texts for which such translations existed (F.R. Johnson 1967). Twenty years later, in collaboration with the Tuscarora speaker and retired history teacher Dorothy Crouse, I published thirty-six of Hewitt's texts in Tuscarora with English translations (Rudes and Crouse 1987). In addition to these published collections, every researcher from Hewitt's time to the present who has researched Tuscarora culture and/or language has consulted Hewitt's manuscript texts in the National Anthropological Archives of the Smithsonian Institution (successor to the Bureau of American Ethnology).

The next individual to engage in linguistic research on the Tuscarora Indian Reservation was Floyd G. Lounsbury. Beginning in 1946, Lounsbury made short visits to the reservation during stopovers on his way from his home in

Wisconsin to Yale University to attend graduate school. However, it was not until 1954 that he focused on text collection (Lounsbury 1952, 1954). During the 1954 trip he collected two texts, one of which was a retelling of the 'Crossing the Ice' migration legend earlier published by Anthony F.C. Wallace and William Reyburn (1951). While Lounsbury never published either of the texts he collected, he used them to inform his publications on general Iroquoian linguistics and as course materials in his classes at Yale University. He also provided copies of the texts to his student, Marianne Mithun (Williams), who drew examples from the texts for her 1974 doctoral dissertation (Williams 1974 [1976]).

Not long after Lounsbury began his research, another graduate student in anthropology, Anthony F.C. Wallace, made two visits to the Tuscarora Indian Reservation (Wallace 1948, 1949). During those visits Wallace made wire recordings of thirty-eight texts, a collection second in size only to that of J.N.B. Hewitt. These recordings, along with field notes, in which he provided Tuscarora transcriptions with English interlinear translations for seven of the texts, were archived at the American Philosophical Society in Philadelphia and a report of the research was published in the Society's *Proceedings* (Wallace 1949).[2] Wallace also published one of the texts in collaboration with William Reyburn (Wallace and Reyburn 1951). In addition, information from the texts provided input into Wallace's monograph *The Modal Personality Structure of the Tuscarora Indians* (Wallace 1952). Other than the one published text and data for his book, the only other use that has been made of Wallace's texts up to the present consists of citations from the English translations of seven texts recorded in his field notes in Johnson (1961).

Over the years 1965 and 1966, the historian Barbara Graymont worked with the noted Tuscarora Second World War veteran Clinton Rickard to collect personal histories and traditional beliefs (Graymont 1965, 1966). In all, she recorded nineteen texts in Tuscarora and English and another five texts in English only. Some of these were verbatim repetitions of texts recorded earlier from Clinton Rickard by Anthony F.C. Wallace. The information in six of the texts provided the primary data source for an autobiography of Clinton Rickard that was compiled and edited by Graymont (Rickard 1973). Essentially, no use has been made to date of the other texts, which remain in Graymont's possession.

The next researcher to engage in the collection of Tuscarora texts was Marianne Mithun (Williams). Having begun her work in 1970, Mithun has gathered fifteen texts from a number of speakers of Tuscarora, most importantly Chief Elton Greene at the Tuscarora Indian Reservation and Robert Mt. Pleasant on the Six Nations Reserve (Mithun 1973–present). Mention was made earlier of her doctoral dissertation (Williams 1974 [1976]), which benefited from the texts she gathered. In addition, two of the texts that she collected from Chief Greene were co-published (Mithun and Greene 1980), and data from these texts have appeared in numerous of her other publications and course materials (e.g., Mithun 1979, 1984; Williams 1973).

In addition to Mithun's work with Robert Mt. Pleasant, Michael K. Foster also recorded a short vocabulary and long life history from a Tuscarora speaker at Six Nations Reserve, Percy Cayuga (Foster 1974). While the vocabulary has been transcribed from the tapes (Rudes 1988), no progress has been made on transcribing the text.

My own work on gathering Tuscarora texts began in late 1973. From 1973 to 1976 I recorded a number of texts on everyday topics and conversations among Tuscarora speakers. These texts provided input into my doctoral dissertation (Rudes 1976) and several subsequent publications (e.g., Rudes 1981, 1985, 1994b).

Beginning in 1975, the focus of my research changed to the re-elicitation of earlier extant texts, particularly those of Gatschet, Hewitt, and Wallace (Rudes 1973–present). To date this work has resulted in the publication of Hewitt's texts in the original and re-elicited Tuscarora with English translations (Rudes and Crouse 1987). The texts have also provided data for a Tuscarora lexicon (Rudes 1988) and a dictionary (Rudes, 1999). In addition, revised English translations of two of the texts were published in a collection edited by Brian Swann (Rudes 1994a).

Convergence of Two Traditions

In the Native tradition, individual Tuscaroras learned texts for later oral transmission to the general Tuscarora public. In the Americanist Tradition, the individual collects texts for the information they provide to the individual's research on the people under study, and the texts themselves are only rarely retransmitted in their entirety.

There is another 'tradition' regarding the collection of Native texts that bridges the Native and the Americanist Traditions and that may be labelled the Convergent tradition. The practice of reciprocity – giving something back to someone who has given something – is a fundamental feature of many indigenous cultures of the Americas. Undoubtedly through contact with Native peoples during their research, the practice of reciprocity was early adopted by researchers working within the Americanist Tradition. While in the past the practice of Americanist reciprocity has more often than not involved monetary remuneration (consultant fees) or gifts of greater or lesser value to the researcher and the Native recipient, another form of reciprocity has evolved over the past few decades: the Convergent tradition of gathering and disseminating texts in which individuals immersed in the Native tradition have collaborated with individuals working within the Americanist Tradition to produce joint publications that simultaneously achieve the Native goal of disseminating the texts to an audience within the Native community and the Americanist goal of informing the researcher's studies. Two examples of the Convergent tradition with respect to Tuscarora texts are Mithun and Greene (1980) and Rudes and Crouse (1987). Both of these publications were co-authored by linguists working in the Americanist Tradition and Native speakers of the Tuscarora language operating within the Native tradition.

The benefits of this convergence of the Native and Americanist Tradition should be obvious. For the academic researcher, the collection of texts continues to provide valuable insights into the language and culture, in this case, of the Tuscarora people; for the collaborating Native speakers, the effort provides an opportunity to preserve and disseminate more widely than otherwise possible the beliefs and traditions of their people.

Conclusion

The extent to which earlier linguists and anthropologists utilized Tuscarora text data in their own research and publications does not seem to justify the considerable investment of time and effort that went into recording these texts. However, the true value of their work lies not in what they did with the texts but in the fact that, by recording them in the first place, they preserved for future generations of the Tuscarora people and academic researchers otherwise irretrievable knowledge of the Tuscarora language and culture.

I say irretrievable for two reasons. First, there are currently only two fluent speakers of Tuscarora living on the Tuscarora Indian Reservation and none at the Six Nations Reserve. However, the language situation among the Tuscaroras is not as desperate as the preceding statement might make it appear. Although there are only a couple of truly fluent speakers, there are a fair number of competent, but out-of-practice, speakers on the Six Nations Reserve and the Tuscarora Indian Reservation, as well as some living off-reservation in Washington, DC, and North Carolina, for example. In addition, significant efforts are being made to teach the language to both children and adults on the Tuscarora Indian Reservation.

Second, many of the older legends, medical practices, and histories recounted in the recorded texts are no longer remembered by the Tuscarora people. Only now, some 110 years after Erminnie A. Smith recorded her texts, are the Tuscarora people beginning to benefit from her research and later efforts by others. Similarly, the research of contemporary linguists and anthropologists continues to benefit from the work of their predecessors.

Thus, we arrive at the answer to the question posed at the the outset – why collect texts? Beyond the immediate aspirations and interests of the individual who initially hears and records a narrative, the preservation of the text – in whatever media – opens up to future generations a window to earlier knowledge that they might never have had.

Appendix 13.1: Annotated List of Extant Tuscarora-language Texts

A. Gatschet, Albert S. (1883) [Western Tuscarora texts with English word-by-word translations]
   1. Creation Myth
   2. The Migrations of the Iroquois
   3. The Thunder and His Son
   4. The Tuscaroras Leave North Carolina
   5. Johnson Meets a Dwarf While Hunting
   6. The Abandoned Baby

B. Graymont, Barbara (1965, 1966) [Eastern Tuscarora texts with running English translations]
   1. History of the Indian Defense League
   2. Climbing Mt Banahao
   3. Stopping a Philippine Funeral
   4. An Attack by Ladrones
   5. Situation of the Tuscarora Reservation upon Return from Army
   6. How a Witch Was Discovered
   7. Grandmother Sees a False Face
   8. Tale of Three Hunters and a Ghost
   9. Tuscarora Rescue of Peter B. Porter
   10. Tuscarora New Year's Festival
   11. Interview with J.N.B. Hewitt
   12. A Stranger Appears in Church
   13. Story of Corn
   14. Captain Cusick Escapes from Western Indians
   15. Grandfather Goes to Kansas
   16. How a Beaver Outwitted Two Hunters
   17. The Devil's Hole

C. Greene, Elton (1969) [Eastern Tuscarora text without translation]
   1. The Lord's Prayer

D. Foster, Michael K. (1974) [Tape recording of Western Tuscarora text with running English translation]
   1. Personal History

E. Hewitt, J.N.B. (1883–1923)
   1. Genesis Myth: A Fragment [Eastern Tuscarora text without translation]
   2. The Creator [Eastern Tuscarora text without translation]
   3. Tuskarora Cosmogony: A Tuskarora Cosmogonic Myth [Eastern Tuscarora text with partial running English translation]
   4. A Tree of Language, Tuskarora Legend [Eastern Tuscarora text with running English translation]
   5. Kaˀtárhwaht Woman: The Pythoness [Eastern Tuscarora text with running English translation]
   6. The Killing of the Mythic Reptile [Eastern Tuscarora text without translation]
   7. White Corn, Squash and Corn [Eastern Tuscarora text without translation]
   8. The Great Bird and the Hunter [Eastern Tuscarora text without translation]
   9. How Medicine Men Were Chosen [Eastern Tuscarora text without translation]
   10. A Monster [Eastern Tuscarora text with running English translation]
   11. An Uncle and His Nephew, or the Child Adopted by a Bear [Eastern Tuscarora text with running English translation]
   12. Food Offering to the Animals by a Hunter [Eastern Tuscarora text with word-by-word English translation and running English translation]
   13. A Society of Wizards Destroyed [Eastern Tuscarora text without translation]
   14. House Destroyer [Eastern Tuscarora text without translation]
   15. The Twelve Mystical Bugs [Eastern Tuscarora text with running English translation]
   16. Preventative of Smallpox, Scarlatina and Other Contagious Diseases [Eastern Tuscarora text with running English translation]
   17. Love Potion [Eastern Tuscarora text with running English translation]
   18. Dropsy [Eastern Tuscarora text with running English translation]
   19. White Ash [Eastern Tuscarora text without translation]
   20. Black Jaundice [Eastern Tuscarora text with running English translation]
   21. Medical Notes [Eastern Tuscarora text with running English translation]
   22. Dew Berry (Cure for Diarrhea) [Eastern Tuscarora text without translation]
   23. John Foxe's Seventy Dollar Medicine [Eastern Tuscarora text without translation]
   24. Akutrę̀·we [Eastern Tuscarora text without translation]
   25. The Akutrę̀·we Who Played Ball [Eastern Tuscarora text with running English translation]
   26. The Mischief Maker [Eastern Tuscarora text with running English translation]

27. The Tradition of the Elopement of a Woman with an Owl [Eastern Tuscarora text with running English translation]
28. The Mythic Flying Head [Eastern Tuscarora text without translation]
29. Uyaʔkwáher: An Old Woman [Eastern Tuscarora text with running English translation]
30. Stone Giant [Eastern Tuscarora text without translation]
31. A Man Followed by a Stone Giant [Eastern Tuscarora text without translation]
32. Rukwéhu and the Warriors: The Story of a Fabulous Saurian [Eastern Tuscarora text with running English translation]
33. Uhstrù·riʔ: The Prophetic Bird-like Being [Eastern Tuscarora text with running English translation]
34. Tobacco and the Buried Head [Eastern Tuscarora text without translation]
35. The Great Snake and the Thunder Have a Child [Eastern Tuscarora text without translation]
36. A Man Entertained by the Thunders [Eastern Tuscarora text with running English translation]
37. Tuscarora Version of a Law Prohibiting Tyrannical Conduct on the Part of Federal Chiefs [Western Tuscarora text without translation]

F. Lounsbury, Floyd G. (1952, 1954)
   1. Crossing the Ice: A Migration Legend of the Tuscarora Indians [Eastern Tuscarora with English word-by-word translation; re-elicitation of Wallace and Reyburn 1951]
   2. New Year's Celebration [Eastern Tuscarora with English word-by-word translation]

G. Mithun, Marianne (1970–present) [Eastern Tuscarora texts with running English translations]
   1. The Dinosaur
   2. The Wart
   3. Show Business
   4. Legend of the Maid of the Mist
   5. How to Make Indian Corn Bread
   6. How to Make Indian Corn Soup
   7. The Origin of the Red Man
   8. Excerpt from the New Doctrine of Handsome Lake
   9. The Lord's Prayer
   10. The Fox
   11. The Flying Head
   12. The Stone People
   13. The Fox and the Bee

14. Funereal Ceremony
15. General Porter

H. Mithun, Marianne, and Elton Greene (1980) [Texts G.1 and G.2]

I. Printup, Marjorie (1979, 1980), Gospel Recordings [Narration in Eastern Tuscarora on cassette tape with English translation]
   1. Genesis.
   2. Exegesis on Noah's Ark.

J. Rudes, Blair A. (1973–present) [Eastern Tuscarora texts with word-by-word English translations and running English translations]
   1. Conversation between Dorothy Crouse and Amelia Williams
   2. Trip to the State Park
   3. Recipe for Corn Soup

K. Rudes, Blair A., and Dorothy Crouse (1987) [Re-elicited and original Eastern Tuscarora texts collected by J.N.B. Hewitt (texts E.1 through E.36) with English translations for those for which Hewitt's translation was not preserved]

L. Wallace, Anthony F.C. (1948–9) [Eastern Tuscarora with word-by-word English translations]
   1. The Boy Who Abused the False Face
   2. The Big Snake
   3. A Medicine Vision
   4. The Strongest Animal on Earth
   5. How the Black Lizard Became Small
   6. How Dan Smith Became Interested in Herbs
   7. How the Tuscarora Came to Leave North Carolina

M. Wallace, Anthony F.C. (1948, 1949) [Eastern Tuscarora texts]
   1. The Monster Bird
   2. The Five Gifts of the Europeans to the Indians
   3. The Man Who Came with the Message of Peace
   4. A Hunter Cured by a Man in a Silvery Canoe
   5. A Ghost Story about a Hunting Party Overtaken by Nightfall
   6. A Man Who Died of Fright of a Ghost
   7. A Story about a Giant
   8. A Story about the Devil
   9. The Burning of the Village in 1812
   10. The Salt War in New York State
   11. The Tuscaroras Release General Porter from the British during the War of 1812
   12. A Party of Tuscaroras Migrates to Kansas
   13. The Origin of the White Bear Clan in North Carolina
   14. How the Tuscaroras Helped the United States during the War of 1812
   15. History of the Indian Defense League

16. Captain Cusick's Escape from an Ambush by Western Indians
17. The Migrations of the Tuscaroras
18. Crossing the Ice: A Migration Legend of the Tuscarora Indians (see Wallace and Reyburn 1952 and Lounsbury 1952, 1954)
19. History of the Temperance Society
20. Easter Monday Morning Celebrations
21. Biographical Sketch of Samuel Jacobs
22. How an Onondaga Lineage Came to Live at Tuscarora
23. Murder of a Witch
24. Massacre at Devil's Hole
25. Battle between the French and the Tuscarora
26. History of Farming on the Tuscarora Reservation
27. Contrasts between Present-Day and Traditional Methods of Child Raising
28. How a Tuscarora Boy Learned to Use English
29. A Brief Autobiography
30. How a Tuscarora Acquired His Formal Education

N. Wallace, Anthony F.C., and William Reyburn (1951) [Text M.18 as transcribed by William Reyburn]

Appendix 13.2: Annotated List of English-only Tuscarora Texts

O. Cusick, David (1828)
   1. Invasion of the Rununkue-ike
   2. That-tea-ro-skeh
   3. Invasion of the Oyahgauharh and Big Elk
   4. Great Lakes Confederacy and Emperor of South
   5. Ill-Omened Blazing Star
   6. Tarenhiawagen Returns to Help the Six Families
   7. Migrations of the Six Families
   8. Ot-ney-yar-heh
   9. The Abandoned Baby
   10. Hinen Rescues the Maiden
   11. Forming of the 'Horseshoe'

P. Graymont, Barbara (1965, 1966)
   1. Marchand Murder Trial
   2. Job Henry
   3. Rickard in Jail at Hull, Quebec
   4. Dorothy Goodwin
   5. Rickard's Army Experiences in the Philippines
   6. Division in the Council

Q. Hewitt, J.N.B. (1883–1923)
   1. Tuscaroras Migrate before Famine
   2. Kahastinens, or the Fire-Dragon
   3. The Giant Rattlesnake
   4. The Brave Warrior and the Enchanted Bear
   5. The Pygmies and the Greedy Hunter
   6. A Dwarf Man and the Hunter
   7. En-kwe-shu-i-yen, or a Dwarf Anthropoid
   8. A Visit to the Land of the Disembodied Spirits
   9. A Man-Eating Ghost
   10. Vampire Doll
   11. The Orphan and the Mastadon
   12. Making of a Stone Giant
   13. Ka-tar-hwat, in the Form of a Beautiful Woman, Marries a Man
   14. The Story of the Father, His Seven Sons, and a Daughter – 'The Acts of the Seventh Son'
   15. The Wicked Giant's Death
   16. A Duel between a Three-Legged and One-Eyed Dog and Fox
R. Hewitt, J.N.B. (1892) [English translation of text E.4]
S. Johnson, Elias (1881)
   1. Creation
   2. Origin of the Iroquois
   3. Oyahquaharh
   4. The Horned Serpent
   5. Flying Head
   6. Stonish Giants
   7. Mythic Lizard
   8. Mammoth Bear
   9. Giant Mosquito
   10. Rabbit
   11. The Hunter and Medicine Legend
T. Johnson, F. Roy (1967) [A compendium of English translations of Tuscarora texts taken from Cusick 1828, Johnson 1881, Smith 1883, and manuscript texts of Albert S. Gatschet, J.N.B. Hewitt, and Anthony F.C. Wallace. Also includes elaborations on comments about Carolina Indians in Lawson 1709. It is often difficult to specify the source of a particular text in Johnson because of his practice of amalgamating pieces of text from various researchers, often creating a wholly new tale in the process. Includes portions of the following texts: A.1–A.6; E.5–E.7, E.9–E.12, E.15, E.25–E.27, E.30, E.33, E.35; L.1–L.7; N.1, O.1–O.11, Q.1–Q.16, S.1–S.16, V.1–V.5.]

U. Rudes, Blair A. (1994) [Revised English translations of two of J.N.B. Hewitt's texts published in Rudes and Crouse 1987, specifically, E.30 and E.35]

V. Smith, Erminnie A. (1883)

1. Hinu^{n} Destroying the Giant Animals
2. The Thunderers
3. The North Wind
4. Giant Head
5. The Stone Giant's Wife
6. The Stone Giant's Challenge
7. The Warrior Saved by the Pigmies
8. The Pigmies and the Greedy Hunter
9. The Pigmies Mission
10. The Origin of Witches and Witch Charms
11. An Incantation to Bring Rain
12. A Cure for All Bodily Injuries
13. Witch Transformation
14. A Superstition about Flies
15. Origin of the Human Race
16. Formation of the Turtle Clan
17. Origin of Medicine
18. Origin of Tobacco
19. Origin of Plumage
20. Why the Chipmunk Has the Black Stripe on His Back
21. Origin of the Constellations
22. The Pole Star
23. Infants Nursed by Bears
24. The Boy and His Grandmother
25. The Dead Hunter
26. The Old Man's Lessons to His Nephew
27. The Hunter and His Faithless Wife
28. The Boy and the Corn
29. The Guilty Hunters
30. The Hunter and His Dead Wife

NOTES

I wish to thank Barbara Graymont, the late Floyd G. Lounsbury, and Marianne Mithun for providing me with information regarding the Tuscarora texts that they have collected. I also wish to thank Michael K. Foster for providing me with a copy of the Tuscarora text and vocabulary that he obtained from Percy Cayuga.

1 More explicitly, I am noting here that, in the absence of such external considerations as accessibility of the subject of study and availability of funding for the research, the individual academic researcher will set a research agenda according to personal interests rather than any higher-order considerations of the public welfare. In reality, external considerations often cause the researcher to modify the direction of research toward more 'practical' (i.e., beneficial to others) issues.

2 The American Philosophical Society has since had the recordings transferred to reel-to-reel tape.

REFERENCES

Chafe, Wallace L. 1981. 'Differences between Colloquial and Ritual Seneca, or How Oral Literature Is Literary.' In Alice Schlichter, Wallace L. Chafe, and Leanne Hinton, eds, *Reports from the Survey of California and Other Indian Languages 1*. Berkeley: Dept. of Linguistics, University of California.

Cusick, David. 1828. *Ancient History of the Six Nations*. Lewiston, NY: Tuscarora Village.

Day, Gordon M., and Michael K. Foster. 1995. 'Oral Literatures of the Northeastern Algonquians and the Northern Iroquoians.' In *The Dictionary of Native American Literatures*. New York: Greenwood Press.

Foster, Michael K. 1974. Cassette Tape Recordings of Vocabulary and Texts from Percy Cayuga. Hull, Quebec: Canadian Museum of Civilization.

Gatschet, Albert S. 1883. Tuskarora Words and Etymologies. Box 372-b. Washington: Smithsonian Institution, National Anthropological Archives.

Graymont, Barbara. 1965, 1966. Tape Recordings of Work with Chief Clinton Rickard. Ms. Lynbrook, NY: Barbara Graymont.

Greene, Elton. 1969. *The Tuscarora Language*. Murfreesboro, NC: Johnson Publishing.

Hewitt, J.N.B. 1883–1923. Hewitt Collection. Washington: Smithsonian Institution, National Anthropological Archives.

– 1892. 'The Sun Myth and the Tree of Language of the Iroquois.' *American Anthropologist* (o.s.) 5: 61–2.

Hodge, Frederick Webb. 1907, 1910. *Handbook of American Indians North of Mexico*. 2 vols. Bureau of American Ethnology Bulletin 30. Washington: Smithsonian Institution.

Johnson, Elias. 1881. *Legends, Traditions and Laws of the Iroquois, or Six Nations, and History of the Tuscarora Indians*. Lockport, NY: Union Printing and Publishing.

Johnson, F. Roy. 1961. Unpublished field notes.

– 1967. *The Tuscaroras*. Vol. I: *Mythology, Medicine, Culture*. Murfreesboro, NC: Johnson Publishing.

Judd, Neil M. 1967. *The Bureau of American Ethnology: A Partial History*. Norman: University of Oklahoma Press.

Lawson, John. 1709. *A New Voyage to Carolina*. Originally published as part of *A New Collection of Voyages and Travels: With Historical Accounts of Discoveries and Conquests in All Parts of the World*, collected by John Stevens. London: 1708–11. [1714 edition reprinted as *Lawson's History of North Carolina*, 1937, edited by F.L. Hariss, for the North Carolina Society of the Colonial Dames of America. Richmond, VA: Garrett and Massie.]

Lounsbury, Floyd G. 1952, 1954. Field notes. New Haven, CT: Floyd G. Lounsbury.

Mithun, Marianne. 1970–present. Field notes. Santa Barbara, CA: Marianne Mithun.

– 1979. 'Iroquoian.' In Lyle Campbell and Marianne Mithun, eds, *Languages of Native America*, 133–212. Austin: University of Texas Press.

– 1984. 'The Proto-Iroquoians: Cultural Reconstruction from Lexical Materials.' In Michael K.

Foster, Jack Campisi, and Marianne Mithun, eds, *Extending the Rafters: Interdisciplinary Approaches to Iroquoian Studies*, 259–82. Albany: State University of New York.

Mithun, Marianne, and Elton Greene. 1980. 'The Dinosaur, The Wart.' In Marianne Mithun and Hanni Woodbury, eds, *Northern Iroquoian Texts*, 104–9, 156–7. International Journal of American Linguistics – Native American Texts Series. Chicago: University of Chicago Press.

Pilling, James C. 1888. *Bibliography of the Iroquoian Languages*. Bureau of American Ethnology Bulletin 6. Washington: Smithsonian Institution.

Printup, Marjorie. 1979. *Genesis*. Los Angeles: Gospel Recordings.

– 1980. *Exegesis on Noah's Ark*. Los Angeles: Gospel Recordings.

Rickard, Clinton. 1973. *Fighting Tuscarora: The Autobiography of Chief Clinton Rickard*, edited by Barbara Graymont. Syracuse, NY: Syracuse University Press.

Rudes, Blair A. 1973–present. Tuscarora Field Notes. Washington: Blair A. Rudes.

– 1976. 'Historical Phonology and the Development of the Tuscarora Sound System.' Unpublished doctoral dissertation, State University of New York, Buffalo.

– 1981. 'A Sketch of the Nottoway Language from a Historical-Comparative Perspective.' *International Journal of American Linguistics* 47(1): 27–49.

– 1985. 'Reconstructing Word Order in a Polysynthetic Language: from SOV to SVO in Iroquoian.' In J. Fisiak, ed., *Historical Syntax*. The Hague: Mouton.

– 1988. Transcription of Canadian Tuscarora Vocabulary Collected in 1974 at Brantford, Ontario, from Percy Cayuga by Michael K. Foster with Equivalent Words in New York Tuscarora for Comparison. Hull, Quebec: Canadian Museum of Civilization.

– 1994a. 'The Great Snake and the Thunder Have a Child, and Stone Giants.' In Brian Swann, ed., *Coming to Light: Contemporary Translations of the Native Literatures of North America*. New York: Vintage Press.

– 1994b. 'John Napoleon Brinton Hewitt: Tuscarora Linguist.' *Anthropological Linguistics* 36(4): 466–81.

– 1999. *Tuscarora-English, English-Tuscarora Dictionary*. Toronto: University of Toronto Press.

Rudes, Blair A., and Dorothy Crouse. 1987. *The Tuscarora Legacy of J.N.B. Hewitt: Materials for the Study of the Tuscarora Language and Culture*. 2 vols. Mercury Series Paper no. 108. Hull, Quebec: Canadian Ethnological Service, Canadian Museum of Civilization.

Saunders, William L., ed. 1886–1980. *The Colonial Records of North Carolina*. 10 vols. Raleigh: North Carolina State Archives.

Smith, Erminnie A. 1883. 'Myths of the Iroquois.' *Second Annual Report of the Bureau of American Ethnology*. Washington: Government Printing Office.

Swann, Brian, ed. 1994. *Coming to Light: Contemporary Translations of the Native Literatures of North America*. New York: Vintage Press.

Wallace, Anthony F.C. 1948, 1949. Tuscarora Tape Recordings and Field Notebook. Philadelphia, PA: Archives of the American Philosophical Society.

– 1949. 'The Tuscaroras: Sixth Nation of the Iroquois Confederacy.' *Proceedings of the American Philosophical Society* 93(2): 159–65.

– 1952. *The Modal Personality Structure of the Tuscarora Indians (As Revealed by the Rorschach Test)*. Bureau of American Ethnology Bulletin 150. Washington: Smithsonian Institution.

Wallace, Anthony F.C., and William Reyburn. 1951. 'Crossing the Ice: A Migration Legend of the Tuscarora Indians.' *International Journal of American Linguistics* 17(1): 42–7.

Williams, Marianne Mithun. 1973. 'A Case of Unmarked Subordination in Tuscarora.' In Claudia Coru, T. Cedric, and Ann Weiser, eds, *You Take the High Node and I'll Take the Low Node*, 89–95. Chicago: Chicago Linguistic Society.

– 1974. 'A Grammar of Tuscarora.' PhD dissertation. New Yale University, Haven, CN: [Published by Garland Press, New York, 1976]

14 George A. Dorsey, James R. Murie, and the Textual Documentation of Skiri Pawnee

DOUGLAS R. PARKS

In June 1894 the Field Columbian Museum formally opened its doors in Chicago. The opening was in part the culmination of plans by Frederick Ward Putnam, professor of anthropology at Harvard University and director of its Peabody Museum, to establish a permanent anthropological museum in Chicago. Here and in New York City Putnam envisioned the formation of great ethnological museums – or, more precisely, great anthropological programs within the larger context of monumental public natural history museums – that would be built upon field expeditions to tribes throughout the Americas to collect prehistoric artefacts and contemporary cultural objects as well as to make ethnographic records, all designed to provide a grand panorama of human life in the New World from prehistoric times to the period of European contact. In Chicago this anthropological museum was created out of the collections that had been assembled for the World's Columbian Exposition held in the city in 1893. Putnam, who had been chief of the Department of Ethnology and Archaeology for the exposition, had planned its anthropological exhibits, and during the two years preceding the fair he had sent field workers throughout the Western Hemisphere to assemble a vast collection of material objects representing the prehistoric and contemporary Native peoples of the Americas.

Immediately after the founding of the Field Columbian Museum, Putnam resigned as curator of its anthropology department, and his resignation was soon followed by that of Franz Boas, who had been Putnam's assistant during the exposition and who was then passed over as Putnam's successor in the new museum. Nevertheless, the scientific course that Putnam had charted for the anthropology program there was subsequently carried out by his student George A. Dorsey, who in 1896 was appointed assistant curator of somatology (that is, physical anthropology) and in the following year became curator of anthropology. Dorsey was three years beyond completion of his doctorate, the first Ph.D.

in anthropology granted by Harvard University. While a student there he had devoted himself to the study of archaeology and physical anthropology. Yet, despite his primary interest in those fields and his initial appointment in somatology, Dorsey's immediate tasks in the new museum were to inventory, catalogue, and label ethnographic specimens, and reinstal them in exhibit cases. Then, in 1897, after that work was completed, he began a series of expeditions throughout North America to fill in gaps in the ethnographic coverage of the museum. That goal led him to undertake long collecting trips himself, travelling frequently to the Plains, the Southwest, and the Northwest Coast to purchase specimens and record fragmentary ethnographic data.

In 1901 and 1902, after several years of those hurried collecting trips through the Plains and the West, which left him no time for significant ethnological study, Dorsey embarked on a plan to document in detail the social and religious organization of several tribes by establishing long-term collaborative relationships with educated members of those tribes. His most important collaborators were Cleaver Warden (Arapaho), Richard Davis (Cheyenne), and James R. Murie (Skiri Pawnee), all Native speakers of their languages. His strategy was to have them collect and record ethnographic data and purchase material objects in the field, and also from time to time come to Chicago, often accompanied by elderly religious leaders, where he could work with them for extended periods. It was an approach that ultimately resulted in some of the finest ethnographic descriptions ever produced in American anthropology (see DeMallie and Parks, in press).

Like Dorsey's other collaborators, James R. Murie was a mixed-blood, the child of a Skiri mother and a white father, the latter a captain under Major Frank North who commanded a battalion of Pawnee scouts. Murie was born in 1862, when the Pawnees were still living on a reservation in their traditional territory in Nebraska, and shortly after his birth, his father abandoned the family. While a child in Nebraska, Murie and his mother lived with her brother, who 'lived like a white man' (Murie 1880) and during those early years Murie attended day school for only four months. After the Pawnees moved to Indian Territory in 1876, however, he went to day school for a year and then enrolled in the boarding school at the agency, where he lived in a room next to the agent's office and learned sufficient English to become an interpreter for the agent. In 1879 he was sent to Hampton Institute in Hampton, Virginia, and over a four-year period he received an education typical of the time. Upon earning a diploma in 1883, he returned home, the first of his tribe to graduate from an Eastern school and destined to be one of Hampton's most distinguished Indian graduates (Harlan 1973, 2: 100).

After his return, Murie, like so many Indian graduates of his generation, found it difficult to settle into an occupation for which he had been educated. Initially, his goal was to become a teacher, but he never was able to secure a position. Instead, at the outset he worked for short periods as a school disciplinarian, a clerk, and a farmer, until finally he built a home on agency land and settled into life-long employment as a translator and clerk for both the agency and the Pawnee National Bank in Pawnee, Oklahoma. It was an occupation that apparently gave him ample freedom, affording him the opportunity to assist anthropologists and others who came to Pawnee to record ethnographic information on the tribe, and ultimately to develop a career as an anthropologist himself (Murie 1981, 1: 21–8).

In 1901, when Dorsey first met Murie on one of his collecting trips to Oklahoma, Murie had already worked with George Bird Grinnell in the 1880s and was then collaborating with Alice C. Fletcher, who was studying Pawnee rituals under the auspices of the Bureau of American Ethnology (Smithsonian Institution). Hence, the goals and methods of anthropology were familiar to him; Murie was, in fact, himself engaged in ethnographic and linguistic documentation. On that trip Murie and Dorsey discussed a collaborative relationship, and the next year, after Dorsey had already employed Warden and Davis for his Arapaho and Cheyenne projects, Murie agreed to work with him as an assistant for his Pawnee studies. It was a collaboration that would extend over the next seven years and produce an exceptionally rich ethnographic and linguistic record of the Skiri Pawnee (Parks 1997; DeMallie and Parks, in press).

This paper discusses one of the projects of these two men, a project that they began almost a century ago but never completed and that is today finally coming to fruition. At the same time the paper illustrates the importance of historical native-language texts to a fundamental goal of American anthropology: to understanding American Indian cultures, and specifically here that of the Pawnees, in unique ways that subsequent anthropological studies did not and could not provide. In short, the paper illustrates how, when they exist, historical collections of native-language texts, carefully studied and explicated, are crucial to a deeper, more authentic understanding of Native American culture and thought, just as they contribute fundamentally to linguistic study.

The Dorsey Agenda

In January 1903 Dorsey submitted a proposal to the Carnegie Institution of Washington for support of a four-year project 'to carry on ethnological researches among Indian tribes of the Caddoan stock,' tribes that he considered interesting because of their intermediate position between those of the high plains and those of the Southeast. All the Caddoan groups – Arikaras, Caddos,

Pawnees, and Wichitas – had a rich material culture, distinctive domiciles (the earth lodges of the Arikaras and Pawnees and the grass lodges of the Wichitas), and complex religious rituals. His plan, broad and ambitious, had two parts. The first was to document the mythology and languages of all four Caddoan tribes. The second part was specific to the Pawnees: to document their religious rituals, including the hundreds of songs intrinsic to them. The task of documenting Pawnee religion, he argued, was an onerous one that had not yet been accomplished, both because the rituals were regarded as personal property and because securing information on them was necessarily expensive, requiring payment of goods and money. Moreover, such a project required an interpreter who was influential in the community and 'of the priesthood,' a person who had entree to religious leaders and their knowledge and who could as well record the ritual songs on a phonograph, then write out the words and translate them. Dorsey had selected Murie, a natural choice, as his collaborator, and in his proposal to the Carnegie Institution he asked for funds in two equal amounts, half to cover project expenses and the other half to pay the salary of Murie, who would work both in the field and at the museum in Chicago. Funding for the project was approved that month.

At least a decade earlier, Alice C. Fletcher had begun a similar project with the Pawnees, and at the time Dorsey began his work she intended to continue her study of Pawnee ceremonialism. Fletcher's success with her Pawnee studies, however, was completely dependent on her collaboration with Murie. When Dorsey proposed hiring Murie, Fletcher was just finishing the documentation of the Hako, the Pawnee calumet adoption ceremony. For this study, Murie had twice taken the Chawi priest of the ritual to Washington, DC, where he translated for Fletcher, and together they recorded on graphaphone cylinders the ritual songs and chants that form the bulk of the resultant monograph (Fletcher 1904). Murie had then carried out the demanding task of transcribing and translating all the song lyrics and chant texts.

When Dorsey hired Murie as a full-time assistant in 1902, he muscled Fletcher out of the Pawnee field, forcing her to give up her plans to do what he himself now intended to do. Over an ensuing seven-year period, between 1902 and 1909, the two men undertook collaboratively five major, interrelated projects that, had they all been completed, would have resulted in one of the most comprehensive anthropological studies of North American Indians at that period and even to this day. Those projects were, briefly, the following:

Narratives. The collection and publication of Pawnee and Arikara traditional narratives – myths, legends, and tales – was the earliest undertaking of Dorsey and Murie (Dorsey 1904a, 1904b, 1906). Here Murie served as the primary recorder, compiling representative collections in English for the two major Pawnee divisions, South Band and Skiri, as well as for the related Arikaras. For the two Pawnee collections Murie and Dorsey recorded stories from nearly fifty individuals – a relatively large percentage of the adult Pawnee population at that time and virtually the entire generation of storytellers. (For discussion of their collection of Pawnee narratives, see DeMallie and Parks in press.)

Ethnography. Simultaneous with the collection of traditional narratives, Murie recorded a wealth of material for another project that produced a book-length manuscript entitled 'The Pawnee: Society and Religion of the Skidi Pawnee,' written by Dorsey. This project began as a study of Skiri religion and ceremonialism, but as work on it progressed it became clear that the description of Skiri ceremonial life was inextricably interwoven with social life, and so the project broadened to encompass both general topics. (The manuscript, ostensibly finished in 1907, but not complete, was not published. Alexander Spoehr, however, published the portion on social organization as Dorsey and Murie 1940.)

Music. An integral feature of the two preceding projects was the recording of Pawnee music: the songs that accompanied traditional narratives, specifically tales, and those that were essential parts of rituals. To document these rich repertoires Murie and Dorsey relied on the technology of the day, the graphaphone and wax cylinders, to sound-record a vast inventory of songs – many hundreds, in fact – of which Murie wrote out the lyrics, accompanied by literal and free translations. For this aspect of their work, Dorsey enlisted the collaboration of the noted German ethnomusicologist Erich von Hornbostel, who in 1906 came from Berlin to Chicago and then visited the Pawnees in Oklahoma. Over several years von Hornbostel transcribed the music to the songs and prepared an analysis of Pawnee music. (The latter was also never published.)

Material culture. A fourth project, complementing the preceding ones, was the compilation of a large, representative collection of Pawnee material culture items for display and study at the Field Columbian Museum. That endeavour, which included acquisition of many religious objects such as sacred bundles and their contents, was to result in a monograph on material culture; but it was never completed.

Linguistic texts. The final project, and for this paper the most important one, was linguistic in nature: the recording on wax cylinders of texts dictated by Roaming Scout. In 1906 Murie brought to Chicago his mentor, an elderly monolingual Skiri priest named Roaming Scout, whom Dorsey characterized as 'one of the most influential and perhaps the most learned' person among the Skiri Pawnees at the turn of the century (Dorsey 1904: 329n1). While there, Roaming Scout recorded for them some seven hours of narration covering a range of ethnographic topics – discussions of life, death, the nature of mysterious power, healing, stars and constellations, and religious rituals – as well as Roaming Scout's autobiography, reminiscences, and several myths.

After they were recorded, Murie wrote out the Skiri text in his own alphabet and composed two translations, one a literal, putatively etymological interpretation, and the other a very free rendition that is, in fact, a retelling. Once that work was completed, Dorsey arranged for Murie and himself to go to New York to spend time working over the texts with Franz Boas, in the course of which Dorsey intended to learn basic techniques of linguistic transcription and analysis that would allow him not only to edit the texts for publication but to prepare a grammatical description of the language as well. Subsequently, over a two-year period, Dorsey refined Murie's transcriptions, making phonetic and sometimes phonemic distinctions that Murie had neglected, and began to analyse Pawnee linguistic structure as well. Dorsey's emendations were incorporated into a typed copy of the texts, doubled-spaced on three hundred legal-size pages (half Skiri, half English); but once he completed that work in 1909, he put the project aside, never to return to it or his other Pawnee studies.

The Roaming Scout Narratives: Subsequent History

Some time after abandoning his Pawnee studies, Dorsey turned over all the copies of the Roaming Scout narratives to Boas, who in turn gave the typed versions to his student Gene Weltfish in 1929 when she began linguistic and ethnographic fieldwork with the Pawnees. Weltfish undertook the retranscription and retranslation of the narratives, but produced mixed results. Of the thirty-six texts, there are thirteen interlinear retranscriptions with literal English translations – about half the collection, since three of the texts are the longest narratives. But, significantly, only three of the thirteen texts were re-elicited from a Skiri speaker; the other ten were re-elicited from speakers of the South Band dialect, which differs markedly from Skiri, and were retranscribed in that dialect. Moreover, Weltfish's transcriptions are also phonetic, and so in most ways they do not differ significantly from Dorsey's, since, like Dorsey, she failed to realize that both vowel and consonantal length are critical to an accurate phonemic writing system.

In 1982 I located the original handwritten versions of the narratives in the American Museum of Natural History and three years later found Dorsey's original typed versions together with Weltfish's surviving handwritten re-elicitations among Weltfish's papers (now at Indiana University). Together, the three sets of documents constitute the historical, written versions of the collection.

Meanwhile, the original 215 wax-cylinder recordings were sent first to

Columbia University and later moved to Indiana University, where they are now preserved in the Archives of Traditional Music and have been copied onto tape. The ravages of time, unfortunately, have rendered the sound quality of approximately one-quarter of the collection entirely inaudible and another quarter barely usable. But at least half of the sound recordings are sufficiently audible to be studied.

My own work with the narratives began in 1985. My collaborator, Nora Pratt, now in her late eighties, is the last truly fluent speaker of Skiri with sufficient knowledge of the language – ritual vocabulary and older grammatical usages – to assist with the project. At the outset both she and I were apprehensive about the feasibility of completing the task – specifically, whether the language in the texts would prove to be too difficult for a modern speaker. Fortunately, it did not, at least for her.

The routine that we followed thoroughout was for me to read a sentence or two from Dorsey's typed version of the Skiri text – the most accurate version. Once she understood it, she would repeat it so that I could write a correct transcription, and then she would translate it or explain what the sentence or passage meant. (Sometimes, of course, it was necessary to work with larger chunks of narrative, several sentences or even a paragraph.) Naturally, it was important to refer to Murie's translations, free and literal, in order to decipher certain passages, and occasionally the Weltfish version was also helpful in clarifying or confirming a translation.

We did not use the recordings, however, primarily because the sound quality is not adequate for Mrs Pratt to hear them. However, once we had retranscribed the entire corpus and rechecked it once, I listened to the recordings against the retranscriptions and checked the latter for accuracy. A variety of problems arose that complicated the retranscription and retranslation process.

Obsolete words and expressions. They were a recurrent problem, although almost all of them were eventually resolved. Often, repeated review would resolve translation difficulties: Mrs Pratt might not recognize a word on one occasion, but would recognize it on another. Sometimes she could figure out a word's meaning on the basis of context and morphemic constituency. Sometimes the Weltfish transcriptions helped. And, finally, on various occasions Arikara cognates helped to resolve a translation. In one text, for example, we encountered the form *hiíku',* which Mrs Pratt had never heard. Quite coincidentally that word in exactly the same form occurred in an Arikara text I had translated the preceding winter. In the Arikara story it designated a stick or wand used to whip individuals in the sweat lodge, and in the Roaming Scout narrative the context clearly indicated a coup stick. So we felt confident in identifying both this form and meaning in Skiri.

Changes in stylistic and lexical usages. Such changes were another recurrent, but minor, problem. In his narrative speech, for example, Roaming Scout uses the absolutive mode interchangeably with the indicative mode – in fact, he uses the absolutive as an indicative as frequently as he uses the indicative. This is not contemporary usage, and Mrs Pratt, feeling uncomfortable with it, would frequently try to substitute the indicative for the absolutive in verbal forms, commenting, 'We don't say it that way today.'

Similarly, Roaming Scout uses many lexical forms that are no longer current, but fortunately Mrs Pratt, who comes from a linguistically conservative family, recognized most of them. One example of a term she did not recognize is the word for a 'quiver,' which I had recorded years earlier from other Pawnee speakers and which has the same form in Arikara – the identity of which she accepted.

At the outset of our work on the texts, the most difficult problem was to convince Mrs Pratt that our task was to transcribe Roaming Scout's speech, not to alter it to conform to the way she or I thought he should have phrased something. She frequently felt that a different word should have been used here or there, or a different grammatical form – the way *she* would say something or, as she frequently said, 'the way we speak now.' Generally these opinions would be first reactions to something I read, and after discussion she would agree that Roaming Scout's form was better – or at least correct. Moreover, after she realized that I was unyielding in my insistence on fidelity to the original and after she became more acquainted with, and respectful of, Roaming Scout's style and usages, she herself became a strong proponent of maintaining the text precisely as he spoke it.

This same tendency to edit the text to conform to the collaborator's preferences clearly was a problem for Weltfish, too, who sometimes changed what Murie and Dorsey had written – despite the fact that, as I learned in the course of editorial work with the texts, Murie and Dorsey were always correct if one just worked through the problem sufficiently.

Change in attitude. What was at first another problem, but certainly became one of the most interesting aspects of the project for me, was to witness Mrs Pratt's changing attitude toward the content of Roaming Scout's narratives. Mrs Pratt has always prided herself on her knowledge of Skiri speech and traditional culture. She is a member of a socially and religiously prominent family. Her grandfather was a noted hereditary chief, and when she was a child tribal religious and political leaders were constantly a part of her homelife. Her mother, who died at the age of 103 in 1967, was a monolingual who was the last survivor of the Pawnee removal to Indian Territory from Nebraska. Mrs Pratt lived with her mother for most of her life and thus spoke Skiri everyday, unlike most contemporary Pawnees; her mother was also a medicine woman and the keeper of the Morning Star bundle, an important tribal religious shrine. In short, the family has been one of the most conservative linguistically and culturally, and today Nora Pratt is, naturally, recognized by Pawnees as an authority in traditional matters.

Nevertheless, like most Pawnees in the twentieth century, Mrs Pratt knows little of nineteenth-century Skiri ritualism, which ceased before the tribe's removal to Indian Territory in 1876 and which are central to the Roaming Scout narratives. Consequently, our work with the texts involved a topic that she thought she knew well – better than anyone else, in fact. Moreover, because she did not remember Roaming Scout from her childhood, she held no opinion of him and the authenticity of his words.

At the beginning of our work her reaction to many linguistic forms in the first texts, as well as their content, was befuddlement, leading her to suggest that the old man really didn't quite know what he was talking about all the time. In the text on the Wolf Was Fooled bundle, for example, Roaming Scout describes the four old men or star deities sitting diagonally in the western Heavens. The text begins: 'The ones sitting there in the west – those old men there in the western Heavens – are old men. I know it. Brother, I have seen those old men sitting there, and the reason for their sitting there is that He placed them there prominently since they were aged; and they are the ones, brother, who are the cause of our living here on earth and our speaking. Those old men there are the cause of it.' After describing how the old men are the source of the bundle, Roaming Scout states, 'And, brother, the station of those old men I am talking about is set diagonally there in the west.'

Except for a number of the celestial deities and the personification of the Heavens himself (*Tiráwaahat*), contemporary Pawnees know nothing about nineteenth-century conceptions of the Heavens. Moreover, the verb form in the last statement, 'their station is set diagonally there in the west,' puzzled Mrs Pratt even more. Her first reaction was to dismiss the form as a misunderstanding and suggest something else. I gently proposed to her what I thought it referred to based on a reading of Murie's description in his book *Ceremonies of the Pawnee* (1981). Still, the first time around, she was sceptical (or suspicious) of the passage and the description; but, later, after more discussion of it and the verb form, which is transparent in its morphemic constituency, she accepted it.

Then as our work progressed and Mrs Pratt realized just how much Roaming Scout knew and was revealing – some things familiar to her, many others not at all – she changed her attitude entirely and has become, as she has told me on numerous occasions, a learner, amazed at the wealth of detail in the narratives – so much so, in fact, that she no longer is critical of Roaming Scout's usages and is reluctant to suggest *any* alternatives. In fact, one of her most interesting comments, again expressed many times, is her amazement at 'how much those old people knew.'

Textual Content and Culture Historical Value

The contents of Roaming Scout's narratives vary dramatically. Representing one genre is his autobiography, presented in one long text that describes in rich detail boyhood in Pawnee society, and particularly the thinking and behaviour of a male child who was born into a leading family and who had religious inclinations. The narrative recounts, among other topics, his first religious deed and his instruction in ritual behaviour; the instruction he received to make smoke offerings to the deities; the consecration of his first buffalo to one of the leading Skiri sacred bundles; and the ritual meat offering he once made to the council of chiefs – a secular act – that was marred by the inappropriate behaviour of one chief and was then followed by a vision in which the Heavens spoke to Roaming Scout about the incident.

After describing those experiences, Roaming Scout devotes the final part of his autobiography to a long account of his first war party. Although rich in ethnographic detail, it is even more poignant for its personal perspective on this archetypical male activity, and especially revealing for its description of interpersonal relations among members of the party, particularly among the leaders of this and another war party who encounter one another during the expedition.

A set of texts that explain the Skiri concept of *waarukstii* ('holy, mysterious, powerful, awesome') represents another narrative genre in the collection. Some tell of Roaming Scout's own experiences. One narrative, for example, begins with a statement of his former power: 'Brother, the Heavens is the one who gave me my mysterious power. And, brother, I was holy when I went around while I was young. The Heavens was the reason I was powerful, and the Sun was the cause.' He then proceeds to recount an incident that illustrated his powers as well as an error in his judgment. Roaming Scout had agreed that his brother Scabby Bull would demonstrate his doctoring powers in the Medicine Lodge by slitting his stomach open. But another doctor, rather than Scabby Bull, came out of his booth and shot Roaming Scout with an arrow, rendering him unconscious and causing him to hemorrhage. From that dramatic moment, the narrative becomes an extended description of Roaming Scout's recuperation and how ultimately he was saved by a combination of various doctors' ministrations and the intercession of his own supernatural benefactors, Sun and a certain small animal.

Other texts in this genre include one entitled 'Animal Spirits' that describes how the Skiris and all animal kind were created to live impermanently on earth and how power, through animals on earth and celestial bodies above, was conveyed in dreams to favoured Skiri individuals, enabling them to perform miraculously in healing, war, and hunting. Six other narratives recount individual visions and exemplify the powers of men who had been blessed by Sun and various animals.

Two other texts expand Roaming Scout's portrayal of the Skiri conception of human life and of humankind's place in the universe. One, which has the title 'Spirit Land,' is an anecdotal affirmation of the afterlife. It tells of a man who seemed to die, who went to the after-world, where his deceased relatives told him it was not yet his time to come to them, and who then returned to life and affirmed that people do go to an after-world. The other, entitled 'Life, Death, and Burial,' is a long philosophical discussion of life and death, with descriptions of mourning customs and the burials accorded individuals from the various strata of Skiri society. In it is a long, verbatim recounting of a priest's oration delivered to the relatives of a group of young men who had been killed while on a war party. Roaming Scout repeats in detail the priest's words describing how life is impermanent for humans at every stage of their existence on earth and how death may come for anyone at any moment and for whatever reason whenever the Heavens wishes it. Later, Roaming Scout describes the interrelations between the living and spirits of the dead, and repeats at length what surviving relatives used to say when speaking to the dead before burial.

Yet another genre is a set of cosmogonic texts that derive at least in part from Roaming Scout's transfer of his Wolf Was Fooled bundle to Murie, to whom he entrusted this village religious shrine so that Murie could, in turn, place it in the Field Columbian Museum. (See 'The Star Map' section immediately below.) Included in this group of texts are numerous descriptions of individual stars and constellations, most of which were recorded when Roaming Scout and Murie were examining the map in Chicago. In the narratives Roaming Scout names the major celestial bodies known to the Skiri and tells whatever he knows about their lore. For some he remembers their explanatory stories, but for others he can provide no more than their names and perhaps only a fragment of what was once told about them.

Two exceptionally long narratives, both ethnographic in content, constitute a final genre. One, entitled 'Ethics,' is actually a concatenation of many stories of people and incidents, each illustrating Pawnee attitudes and behaviour toward such ethical issues as stealing, murder, lying, infidelity, and other forms of socially incorrect behaviour. Included with those stories are descriptions of the hunt and its regulation, childhood activities and games, and marriage, as well as anecdotes of individuals whose behaviour was abnormal and of older people's foibles. The collection concludes with a long story about a boy, a chief's son, whose speech and behaviour were socially inappropriate but who ultimately revealed himself to be endowed with supernatural power that enabled him to achieve great war deeds, institute the Children's *Hiruska* Society, and in the end become the head chief of his people.

The other narrative in this ethnographic genre is entitled 'Women's Work' and is a detailed description of women's activities organized around the seasons, beginning with their work in the fall, as well as descriptions of the manufacture of such women's crafts as bulrush mats, mortars and pestles, and beds. Integrated into the narrative are discussions of gender roles, gender relations, and kin relations.

The Star Map

For Westerners, one of the most notable and interesting religious objects of the Skiri is the star chart, a map of the Heavens drawn on soft hide that is a part of the Big Black Meteoric Star bundle. Murie obtained the bundle for Dorsey and the Field Columbian Museum, and subsequently scholars have assumed that the star map is an example of aboriginal astronomy – a Pawnee attempt to depict the Heavens – and that the map is at least several hundred years old, although it is not at all clear what the latter assumption is based upon.

Interestingly, Roaming Scout provides a rich set of narrative descriptions on both the bundle and the map. In a short text entitled 'The Star Map,' he tells the story of its origin (with the words of the Heavens printed in italics):

> And now, brother, as I say, the Heavens thought, *'I think I'll let an old man see me!'* [That is, He will come to a man on earth in a dream. The statement indicates that this is a vision story.]
>
> And He [the Heavens] said [speaking to the visionary], *'There is a particular reason for your seeing me, since you people are forgetting your ways here on earth.'* [Then the Heavens goes on to remind the visionary of the origin of the world and how life here on earth was intended to be.]

These passages are culturally and historically significant because they explain that

- the star map is the result of a vision, or dream, and is not conceptualized as based on observation; and
- its origin, and probably the origin of its bundle, was apparently the result of a religious revival.

Both are conclusions, certainly, that are not surprising.

In the much longer text entitled 'Wolf Was Fooled Bundle,' Roaming Scout describes at length the origin of the bundle and map, and repeats in minute detail the dream in which the visionary who drew the star map received his instructions. After recounting how the bundle was given him, Roaming Scout says:

And now, brother [here addressing Murie, as he recounts the narrative for him], after He [the Heavens] made various plans for the old man [i.e., the visionary], the Heavens said, *'You are going to do it: you are going to draw the Heavens on it.'*

And now, brother, right there the old man did it: he made it for the Heavens, after He [the Heavens] said, *'... You are going to consecrate a buffalo. Then you'll do this. Then you'll take the buffalo scalp off. Then you'll take off only the scalp of the top of the head. You should keep it in this bundle, our Mother, that you will have hanging in your lodge.'*

He said, *'You'll do this: you should place the Heavens in it. You should draw these various stars in the Heavens on that buffalo scalp and then you'll place it inside the bundle.'*

And now, brother, these things I am repeating were not the words of our Indian people [i.e., the men who have told the story]. They were the ones of our Father Above. That is what He said.

Then the old man did it after he was given the instructions, and then he made the map that you [i.e., Murie] now have, brother. It is the one of the Heavens with that black ring around it ... That line is the horizon, where the Heavens touch the earth. Then that is what our Father said.

Then the narrative goes on to recount in detail where each constellation or individual star was to be placed on the buffalo scalp and what it was to be named or was to represent. The following passages illustrate the narrative account:

Brother [again addressing Murie], our Father said, *'In the center of the Heavens you should mark a line that crosses the world diagonally. It will face it, and you should say of this line when you make it, "Here extends the Trail of Dust [Milky Way]."'* That was when our Father named these stars.

And our Father said, *'And here are the Chiefs In Council. Then the chief is going to be among them,'* [meaning] here among our people where we live on earth, brother; here where we live, *'You are a chief.'* He said, *'Here are the Chiefs In Council in the Heavens. You will do this: when you mark them in the center of the map, you will place them here and there in the center of the Heavens. They are stars.'*

Here Roaming Scout is telling us that when the Heavens designated this constellation the 'Chiefs In Council,' after creating humans on earth, he created at the same time the office or status of chief among the first Skiris – and that the chiefs on earth represented the stars in the constellation in the Heavens. And so, for example, the organization of the council of chiefs mirrored, or was a reflection of, that of the chiefs in the Heavens – as, in fact, most elements of Skiri social organization on earth were conceived to be reflections of the organization of the stars above.

Similarly, the Heavens instructed the visionary to draw stars representing other elements of life on earth. For example,

> And He said, *'This Bow in the north, this bow – I want to give you the bow and arrows to be here where you live on earth, and you are to mark its stars in the Heavens. Ha! These stars in the Heavens that are a bow represent this bow that I am giving you Indians so that you can chase buffalos and kill them. Now this is what you will use to kill buffalos whenever you wish to do it.'* Brother, he was referring to when a person occasionally killed an animal for himself and consecrated it. And when he killed a buffalo he would consecrate it [to the Heavens].

In another long passage, the Heavens instructs the original visionary to draw four additional stars, the four pillars of the Heavens, and says,

> *'You are going to perform a ritual. You are going to wrap up the map of the world in this bundle our Mother. Then you'll bring four poles up from the bottom land.'*

And after telling him what colours to paint each of the poles, the Heavens continues:

> *'Now, you are going to give a name to the ritual that I am telling about. You are going to make stars here in the Heavens, and this is what you are going to call them: Karikisu'. The Tree of Karikisu'. That is what you're going to call it. I have now given you an important ritual'* [the Four Pole Ceremony]. That is what the Heavens told the old man to tell my tribe, brother.

Finally, after recounting how the visionary was instructed to draw other stars and constellations in the Heavens, Roaming Scout says, 'Now, brother, these are the instructions He gave the old man, the things He told him when He gave him his knowledge.' Then after repeating in the words of the Heavens still more instructions, Roaming Scout concludes this section of the narrative with more explanation of the origin of the world and life in it:

He [the Heavens] said, *'Here is where the origin of the Heavens turning yellow is, when the Heavens become yellow. This is where the origin of childbirth is, when people bear their babies, and when all animal kind has its young. All the different kinds of animals: all the buffalos, elk, whitetail deer, mule deer, antelopes; all the animals in the woods; all those in the streams, the water animals; all these many insects.'* That is what He said. *'Right here is where life is to begin. That is good.'*

Roaming Scout then takes the narrative in another direction by describing the rituals in which the Wolf Was Fooled bundle figured. After that he repeats the lyrics of one of the bundle's songs, one that recounts in minute detail the elements of the world that the Heavens created. The final part of the narrative is a myth that recounts how Wolf deceived Holy Being and ultimately was killed and his skin placed on the bundle.

To return to the initial point of this textual illustration – the first section of the narrative, that is – the narrative is a verbatim account of the instructions that the Heavens gave the original visionary: where to depict each star or constellation on the tanned hide of a buffalo scalp, what each was to be named, and what each represented both in the Heavens and in their counterparts here on earth. Importantly, Roaming Scout makes clear that the map is a *symbolic* object, a representation of the powers of the heavens and their earthly manifestations: a guide to the Skiri religious conception of the Heavens, and ultimately a recounting of the origin of the world – of everything in the Heavens and on earth. Of the map Roaming Scout, in fact, says, 'It *is* the Heavens.' The contention that it represents someone's astronomical observations, attempting to make incipient Western astronomers of the Skiris, completely misses what was culturally important about the map: that it was a representation of the origin of the world, a mnemonic object that figured in religious rituals and served to recall in detail the creation of all things.

Conclusions

For a volume on the Americanist Tradition and its continuing importance to anthropology, the Dorsey agenda and the Roaming Scout collection in particular offer several instructive conclusions.

One is a minor historical clarification. All too frequently anthropologists and linguists today fall into the habit of speaking of the text tradition in Americanist studies as 'the Boasian tradition,' as though Boas were the only one to see the importance of native-language texts for cultural documentation. George Dorsey's agenda with the Pawnees (and other Plains tribes) clearly demonstrates that he, too, recognized the integral role of narrative recordings and that he developed a documentary plan parallel to, and not derivative from, that of Boas and the American Museum of Natural History, or the Bureau of American Ethnology. Boas himself, of course, recognized that others before him had established the text tradition and gave due credit to Stephen R. Riggs, James Owen Dorsey, and Albert S. Gatschet, as well as Daniel G. Brinton (Boas 1917: 1).

Second, what distinguishes Dorsey and Murie's text collections for the Skiri Pawnees and sets them above those of most other researchers early in the century was the utilization of the latest technology – the graphaphone and wax cylinders – to record speech, including narratives as well as songs. Dorsey and Murie were not unique in using the recorder, of course; Fletcher, who preceded Dorsey with the Pawnee, used it, and Murie, in fact, may have instigated its use in his collaboration with Dorsey. Most researchers of that period, however, recorded only songs and not texts. The exceptions are few – Waldemar Bogoras and Waldemar Jochelson, Frank Speck, Edward Sapir, Paul Radin, and Morris Swadesh – and none of them recorded the diversity or sheer quantity of material compiled by Dorsey and Murie, whose recordings number over a thousand cylinders (Seeger and Spear 1987). Most linguists and anthropologists, in contrast, were taking texts down in dictation, with the result that narrators usually had to speak slowly and they frequently (perhaps generally) abbreviated narratives, abridged descriptions, and simplified syntax. In short, their speech lacked the naturalness and consequent richness of freely told narratives.

The Roaming Scout narratives, in contrast, are invaluable because they were delivered naturally, and consequently are rich in descriptive detail, complex syntax, and all the other features that constitute nineteenth-century Skiri narrative style. Moreover, the student today has the opportunity to *listen* to the narratives as well as to read them, and students in the future will be able to study and analyse them in new ways.

The final conclusion of this paper has to do with the purpose of studying narrative texts. Over the past two decades the study of narratives has blossomed, in large part thanks to many of the contributors to this volume, but most of that study has focused on narrative structure and on performance – on texts as literary documents. In part, this focus undoubtedly derives from the nature of the texts available or studied for Native American languages: most of them are myths and tales. But those are only two genres of the American Indian oral tradition. Equally important are historical and ethnographic narratives, such as Roaming Scout's and George Sword's (discussed by Raymond J. DeMallie, this volume), which elucidate cultural conceptions, ethnographic issues, Native philosophy, historical topics, and other matters, all in the words of members of the culture. Although determination of the underlying structure of these texts is important to the editing and presentation of them, the content is no less important and demands careful study and explication – a combination of linguistic, historical, and cultural editing. The latter is a task identified well over a century ago as central to the Americanist Tradition, but it is one that has not generally been taken seriously over the ensuring years. As linguistics has developed into a separate discipline over the past half-century, the interest of linguists in texts as cultural and historical documents has dissipated; and as cultural anthropology has progressively neglected language study, especially in North America, the interest of anthropologists in texts (other than as literary documents) has by and large turned to narratives in English translation rather than in Native languages. It is, perhaps, time that this fundamental tenet of the Americanist Tradition be revived and once again become integral to the anthropological study of Native America.

NOTE

This paper in part summarizes material in other sources. For a more comprehensive discussion of Dorsey's study of Plains Indians and his collaboration with James R. Murie, see Parks and DeMallie (1992), Parks (1997), and DeMallie and Parks (in press). For Murie's biography, see Parks (1978) and Parks in Murie (1981, 1: 21–8).

Various individuals and institutions have aided my work with the Roaming Scout texts. Ms. Belinda Kaye, American Museum of Natural History, provided access to Murie's original handwritten transcriptions and translations. Mr James Frazier, librarian at Fairleigh Dickinson University, provided the photocopies from the Weltfish Collection of Dorsey's handwritten versions; these have subsequently been transferred to Indiana University. My work with the texts was generously supported by a grant from the National Endowment for the Humanities. Most important, however, is my debt of gratitude to Mrs Nora Pratt, who over the past decade and a half has been a tireless partner in the tedious work of retranscribing and translating the texts and has herself become dedicated to the goal of preserving Skiri Pawnee language and culture. Finally, in preparing translations of the Roaming Scout narratives I have benefited greatly from discussions with Raymond J. DeMallie (Indiana University).

REFERENCES

Boas, Franz. 1917. 'Introduction.' *International Journal of American Linguistics* 1: 1–8.

DeMallie, Raymond J., and Douglas R. Parks. In press. 'George A. Dorsey and the Development of Plains Indian Anthropology.' In *Anthropology, History, and American Indians: Essays in Honor of William Curtis Sturtevant*. Smithsonian Contributions to Anthropology, no [X] Washington, DC: Smithsonian Institution Press.

Dorsey, George A. 1904a. *Traditions of the Skidi Pawnee*. American Folk-Lore Society Memoir 8. Boston: Houghton, Mifflin.

– 1904b. *Traditions of the Arikara*. Carnegie Institution of Washington, pub. 17. Washington.

– 1906. *The Pawnee: Mythology (Part I)*. Carnegie Institution of Washington, pub. 59. Washington. Reprinted as *The Pawnee Mythology*. Lincoln: University of Nebraska Press, 1997.

– 1997. *The Pawnee Mythology*. Introduction to Bison Books edition by Douglas R. Parks. Lincoln: University of Nebraska Press.

Dorsey, George A., and James R. Murie. 1940. *Notes on Skidi Pawnee Society*. Edited by Alexander Spoehr. Field Museum of Natural History, Anthropological Series 27: 67–119.

Fletcher, Alice C. 1904. *The Hako: A Pawnee Ceremony*. Twenty-Second Annual Report of the Bureau of American Ethnology for the Years 1900–1901, part 2. Washington.

Harlan, Louis R., editor. 1973. *The Booker T. Washington Papers*. Vol. 2. Urbana: University of Illinois Press.

Murie, James R. 1880. [Letter.] *Southern Workman*, March 1880. Hampton, Va.: Hampton Normal and Agricultural Institute.

– 1981. *Ceremonies of the Pawnee. Part I: The Skiri. Part II: The South Bands*. Edited by Douglas R. Parks. Smithsonian Contributions to Anthropology, no. 27. Washington: Smithsonian Institution Press. Reprinted edition by University of Nebraska Press, Lincoln, 1989.

Parks, Douglas R. 1978. 'James R. Murie, Pawnee, 1862–1921.' In Margot Liberty, ed., *American Indian Intellectuals*, 75–89. 1976 Proceedings of the American Ethnological Society. St Paul, MN: West Publishing.

– 1991. *Traditional Narratives of the Arikara Indians*. 4 vols. Lincoln: University of Nebraska Press.

– 1994. 'Three Skiri Pawnee Stories.' In Brian Swann, ed., *Coming to Light: Contemporary Translations of the Native Literatures of North America*, 377–402. New York: Random House.

– 1997. Introduction to *The Pawnee Mythology* by George A. Dorsey. Lincoln: University of Nebraska Press.

Parks, Douglas R., and Raymond J. DeMallie. 1992. 'Plains Indian Native Literatures.' In *1492–1992: American Indian Persistence and Resurgence*, a special issue of *boundary 2*, ed. Karl Kroeber, pp. 105–47.

Seeger, Anthony, and Louise S. Spear, editors. 1987. *Early Field Recordings: A Catalog of Cylinder Collections at the Indiana University Archives of Traditional Music*. Bloomington: Indiana University Press.

15 'George Sword Wrote These': Lakota Culture as Lakota Text

RAYMOND J. DEMALLIE

As an anthropologist who has devoted a career to the Lakota (Teton Sioux) Indians of the Great Plains, I have centred on the presentation of historical texts – the documents essential for understanding mid-nineteenth-century culture and its subsequent development through the reservation period. Many colleagues and students alike have expressed dismay over what they perceive as my editorial obsession and have asked, with varying degrees of tact, whether I ever intend to get down to my own work. By way of inspiration I have been mindful of an admonition given to anthropologists more than a half-century ago by Paul Radin (1933: 186): 'The value of starting with a document cannot be too strongly stressed. In elucidating culture we must begin with a fixed point, but this point must be one that has been given form by a member of the group described, and not by an alien observer. This is, of course, a truism to the historian. Unfortunately, even excellent ethnologists sin against it all the time.'

Following the method of his teacher, Franz Boas, the documents Radin had in mind were dictated texts in native languages, the products of active dialogue between a group member (the informant) and an alien observer (the anthropologist). Significantly, however, for a number of Native American groups – including Radin's Winnebagos – the introduction of writing systems meant that Native peoples themselves produced documents reflecting their own interests and purposes, sometimes stimulated by the inquiries of anthropologists.

Fortunately for historical scholarship, literacy in the native language developed pervasively among the Sioux. The first systematic orthography for writing Dakota, representing the eastern dialects of the Sioux language, was devised by Christian missionaries in 1834; the first grammar and dictionary were published in 1851 by the Smithsonian Institution. Religious tracts in Dakota were circulated throughout this period, and by 1880 the entire Bible was published in Dakota (Pilling 1887). In addition, Sioux-language newspapers were published continuously from 1871 until the late 1930s, and included material written by individuals from all the widely scattered Sioux communities. Editorials and letters were printed in the dialect in which they were written, making such papers as the *Iapi Oaye* (*The Word Carrier*) and *Anpao Kin* (*The Daybreak*) historical archives that represent the diversity of Sioux dialects. It was in this atmosphere of flourishing native-language literacy that the Sioux people made their accommodations to reservation life.

Among the historical native-language documents produced by the Sioux, none has excited my interest more than those written just after the turn of the century by George Sword, an Oglala living on the Pine Ridge Reservation in South Dakota. The largest collection of his writings is contained in a worn ledger deposited in the Colorado Historical Society. Pasted inside the front cover is a small paper label that reads *George Sword lena owa*, 'George Sword wrote these.' The label, like the rest of the contents of the volume, is inscribed in a strong, sprawling hand, in heavy ink. It is obvious that the words were committed slowly and meticulously to the paper, syllable by syllable, with only occasional corrections. The manuscript attests to Sword's diligence in preserving a written record of the past as a legacy for the Lakota people.

Sword's writings, at least those preserved in archives, resulted from a dialogue with anthropologists. In 1902, under Boas's direction, Clark Wissler visited Pine Ridge on a field trip intended primarily to collect material for the American Museum of Natural History in New York City that would illustrate symbolism in Sioux art forms. There he met Dr James R. Walker, the agency physician, who had served at Pine Ridge since 1896. Walker, in fact, was an amateur anthropologist who recorded both physical anthropological data and information on traditional medicine and religion as an adjunct to his own role as a healer. Over the next fifteen years Walker provided Wissler with material for a series of scholarly publications, culminating in 'The Sun Dance and Other Ceremonies of the Oglala Division of the Teton Dakota' (Walker 1917). This work, now a classic, includes Walker's painstaking reconstruction of the Sun Dance, Adoption, and Girl's Puberty ceremonies, as well as a set of valuable texts by individual Lakotas, presented in English translation, that are fundamental to the understanding of nineteenth-century Lakota life. For this study, Walker depended heavily on the knowledge and guidance of George Sword.

Because he was a significant actor in the history of the Pine Ridge Sioux, we know a fair amount about Sword's life. Most valuable are a number of documents that record autobiographical statements by Sword, written by Walker and others, and the Colorado ledger, which includes Sword's lengthy autobiography written in Lakota. Yet there are important gaps, as well as frustrating inconsistencies in what we would like to know. The written autobiography is a detailed public autobiography: Sword as he wished to be remembered. The autobiographical statements for Walker are private: Sword's religious life in the days before the settling of his people on their reservation. The public-and-present life-telling contrasts starkly with the private-and-past. The difference is not one of oral versus written text, but rather of audience.

On the reservation, Sword used his skills in writing Lakota as a means of adapting to changing circumstances. There is no record of when he learned to write, but it seems likely to have been in conjunction with his joining the Episcopal Church, into which he was baptized in 1880. The earliest example of his writing that I have found is a letter dated 18 November 1881, printed in *Anpao Kin*, the Episcopal Sioux newspaper. The letter expresses Sword's commitment to Christian civilization and voices approval of the paper's discussion of the evils of dancing, gambling, and multiple wives. 'I am an Indian,' he wrote, 'and I know well how the Indians think.' The young men listened to him, but the old men did not. The Indians' situation, he wrote, 'is like uprooting a tree that is large and sturdy; when it is planted it does not grow well. But when a little tree is uprooted and placed, it grows well.' This generational difference was basic to Sword's thinking: the older generation could hang onto the past, but the younger generation had to change with the times.

Using Sword's autobiography and combining it with other sources of information (Walker 1917, 1980: 74–5, n.d.; Ricker 1907; Johnson 1910) allows for an accounting of the major events in his life. Sword was born in February 1847, the son of a chief named Bear Runs Fearlessly, later known as Shot in the Face after being wounded in a fight with the Pawnees. Sword's father was a renowned warrior as well as a shaman, a member of the Bear society; he died in a fight with Crow Indians about 1874. Sword's boyhood name was *Ic'íblebleca*, 'Shakes Himself.' When at the age of thirteen he sought a vision, the Bear Spirit gave him power to use in war. As a result of the vision he was ritually adopted by One Star, an old shaman, who taught him the Bear Ceremony (*Mathó Lową́pi*). At fourteen Sword chose *Tákuškąšką* (Spirit of Movement) as his guardian, and One Star prepared the sacred objects the boy would carry into battle. According to one account recorded by Walker, at fifteen Sword went on his first war party; in battle he touched the dead bodies of two Crows and stole two horses from the enemy. When the party returned One Star gave him the name *Tok'íchuwa*, 'Hunts the Enemy.' The next year, 1863, at age sixteen, he pierced his flesh in the Sun Dance, and in a vision the Sun instructed him to devote his life to serving the spirits. Sword told Walker, 'So I became a Shaman, and asked every man about the spirits. I learned all I could of the spirits' (Walker n.d.).

But Sword's life soon took a great turn. He participated in the Fetterman and

Wagon Box fights in 1866–7 near Fort Phil Kearny, Wyoming, adding coups against white soldiers to his record. But, he said to Walker, 'I was wounded twice and nearly taken prisoner. Then I thought that the Great Spirit of the white men must be greater than the Great Spirit The Sun. Takuskanskan had never taught me how to make cloth or things of metal, and the white people knew how to do this. So I became a friend of the white people' (Walker n.d.). In 1875, with many other Oglalas, Sword put aside warfare and joined Red Cloud's people at their agency in northwestern Nebraska near the military post of Fort Robinson. At this time he took the name of Sword (*Míwakhą Yuhá*, 'Sword Carrier'), the name that had belonged to an older brother who had inherited their father's chieftainship but subsequently had died. Sword enlisted as an Indian scout under General George Crook; early in 1877, in the aftermath of the Battle of the Little Big Horn, he served as emissary from the government to Crazy Horse, persuading his fellow Oglalas to come to Fort Robinson and make peace with the army.

At Red Cloud Agency Sword was appointed to be the first captain of the Indian Police, and at the time of the Ghost Dance troubles in 1890 he was promoted to major. Later he served as judge of the Court of Indian Offenses. He helped organize the first district and tribal councils on the Pine Ridge Reservation and also served his turn as president of the tribal council. He was a staunch member of the Episcopal Church, and for many years served as a deacon. Writing proved to be a tool that aided him in his success, and he became amanuensis for his community. He wrote news and editorials in Lakota and sent them in letters to be printed in Sioux-language newspapers; he wrote the police reports and kept the court records, recorded attendance and offerings at the weekly Episcopal Church services, and kept a winter count to document Oglala history. In addition, he wrote extensive records of the past that were descriptive accounts of the old ways. These he sold – some to other Lakota people (how extensively we do not know, but at least one example has survived in the form of a copy), others to Walker, who, expending money from the American Museum, paid Sword at the rate of about twenty-five cents per page.

Sword was proud of his literary abilities. At the end of his autobiography, composed a year before his death, he wrote of himself, 'He was gifted in writing the Lakota language and nobody was as skillful in that among the Oglalas as he.'

When Sword died suddenly on 17 October 1910, Walker was left with a body of his writings that he saw as providing the key to understanding Lakota religion. My collaborator in publishing the Walker manuscripts, Elaine Jahner, characterizes Sword's writings as 'transitional narratives' that represent 'literary thresholds between Lakota and Euro-American cultures' (1994: 159). Rooted in Lakota traditional styles, these texts at the same time reflect the influence and potential of writing as a means of cultural expression. Sword's texts may be considered to be of two kinds. Some were myths, perhaps recast in new narrative forms, which Walker published in English and used as the basis for writing his own creative synthesis of Oglala mythology. Not one of these original Lakota manuscripts in Sword's own hand has survived, complicating the attempt to evaluate them in terms of either written literature or tradition. Nevertheless, Jahner has devoted careful attention to understanding Sword's myth texts (see her introduction to Walker 1983 and Jahner 1994).

The second kind of text departs more sharply from traditional genres; most are descriptions of cultural practices and beliefs that are intended as records of the past. The autobiography combines the older genre of coup-counting with war stories and an innovative personal account that is clearly a concession to changing times: a true autobiography in the Western sense, though composed in the third person. The second type of text is, in my opinion, better considered written, not oral. The cultural descriptions, for example, form an innovative ethnographic genre that has no counterpart in older oral tradition.

Walker's opinion of the importance of Sword's material was not exaggerated. In 1896, when he began to teach Walker about Lakota religion, Sword made this statement:

> I know the old customs of the Lakotas, and all their ceremonies, for I was a *wicasa wakan* (holy man, or shaman), and I have conducted all the ceremonies. I have conducted the Sun Dance, which is the greatest ceremony of the Lakotas. The scars on my body show that I have danced the Sun Dance, and no Lakota will dispute my word. I was also a *pejuta wicasa* (medicine man), and belonged with the Bear medicine people. The Bear medicine men have all the medicine ceremonies that other kinds of medicine men have and much more. So I can tell all the medicine ceremonies. I was a *wakiconze* (magistrate [camp leader]) and so I know all the customs of the camp and of the march. I was also a *blota hunka* (commander of war parties) and have led many war parties against the enemy, both Indians and white men. The scars on my body show the wounds I have received in battle. So I know the ceremonies of war. I have been on the tribal chase of the buffalo, and know all the ceremonies of the chase. (Walker 1980: 74)

No better guide to the traditional ways of the Lakota people could be asked for.

Unfortunately, Walker on his own was unable to decipher the Sword texts. Nor was he satisfied with the translations he paid to have made. Clarence Three Stars translated a few of the texts but recast the Lakota and modernized the English, and, in Walker's words, 'destroyed the ethnological value of the work' (Walker 1980: 23). For example, Three Stars substituted English concepts for Lakota ones ('house' or 'room' instead of 'tipi,' 'sin' instead of 'disaster') and he translated prayers and songs with overtones of the King James Bible ('Under the sunset, sitteth the Bear,' 'Behold, eat it, thou saidst') (Three Stars [1909]). Walker found that Charles Nines, a non-Lakota but a fluent speaker of the language, did better translations, but Nines found the work tedious and frustrating, and eventually gave up on it.

In the matter of translation, Walker himself was likely a part of the problem. Sword told Walker that when he spoke, younger Oglalas ridiculed his style (Walker 1980: 75). He spoke in the old way, he claimed, as people did before their language was contaminated by Christian missionaries and the standardization imposed by writing. Sword conceptualized the language syllabically, seeing in word boundaries only the artefact of writing. Walker therefore insisted on etymological syllable-by-syllable translations, to which Nines objected as inappropriate and misleading (see Walker 1980: 20–3, 1982: x–xi).

In retirement near Denver, Walker laboured on alone until his death in 1926. Then, beginning in 1927, Franz Boas hired Ella Deloria, a Native Sioux whom he had trained in linguistics, to retranscribe the texts in the Colorado ledger and translate them into English. Her translations, however, were hurried, and there was no opportunity to edit them for publication. Like Three Stars and Nines, Deloria criticized certain features of Sword's written style. For example, because he wrote syllable by syllable, Sword did not generally anticipate morphophonemic changes; thus, the texts are written without the usual phonetic changes and elisions that occur in actual speech. Moreover, perhaps because writing was a slow and painstaking process for him, he frequently omitted the articles that are so characteristic of Lakota speech.

An even greater impediment to translation was the subject matter. Much of what Sword wrote about was esoteric, falling outside the experience of those individuals who had been born after the people settled at Pine Ridge. Many of his writings related to sacred knowledge and ceremonies, topics that the old men would not discuss with members of the younger generations, so it is little wonder that the work of translation seemed daunting.

When I began to work on the Sword texts the first task was to establish a corpus of Sword's writings. Certainly, I have not been able to find all of them that still exist, but I have about a third more than were known to Ella Deloria. Having recopied the texts and sorted out some of the problems, I began in 1981 to collaborate with an elderly Lakota speaker long renowned for his oratorical abilities, the Venerable Vine V. Deloria, Sr, a retired Episcopal priest who was the younger brother of Ella Deloria. That he would work with me on the project was fortuitous, for his speech provided access to essentially the same linguistic forms that were familiar to Ella Deloria. In short, we could pick up the project where she left off nearly a half-century before.

Combining the insights of a truly outstanding speaker of the language with an anthropologist's knowledge of the historical and cultural literature made the project seem feasible. Using what Dennis Tedlock (1983: 124–55) would later call the 'ethnopaleographic method,' Father Vine and I sat with two copies of the text. We read them aloud and I retranscribed them. Then we hammered out translations, punctuated from time to time by phone calls to other elders to solicit opinions and validate obscure points. Always the discussion circled around differences and similarities between traditional Lakota religion and Christianity. Here was an intellectual adventure that took us sometimes far afield from Sword himself, digressing to discuss perceived changes in the Lakota language and, ultimately, in 1984, to tape-record and transcribe Father Vine's own repetoire of oral traditions and songs as a means of comparing Lakota style.

Sword's writings for Walker comprise eighteen separate narrative texts plus a variety of song texts. Some of the narratives deal with camp life: a description of buffalo hunting and the appointing of police to supervise the camp and the hunters, as well as of butchering and the preparation of hides; an account of life in the winter camp; and descriptions of the moccasin game and hoop and pole game. Others deal with warfare: the rituals of war parties, the story of an expedition against the Pawnees, an account of how Bear medicine was used to heal those wounded in battle, and descriptions of the Kit Fox and Sacred Bow societies. Still others explicate the sacred: the story of the Calf Pipe and the teachings of the White Buffalo Woman, discussions of the Thunder-beings and their punishments of humans through death by lightning, a general account of vision seeking, the story of Bear visions and of the Bear ceremony, and texts on the Sun Dance and Hunka (adoption) ceremonies. Sword's autobiography names his parents and siblings, recounts his war expeditions, describes his experiences as an army scout, and talks about his life on the reservation. Taken together, Sword's writings present an ethnographic picture of the Lakota in the pre-reservation period that provides important detail on warfare and religion not to be found elsewere in the literature, and they document the Oglalas' early adaptation to the reservation.

From the perspective of translation, Sword's texts on sacred topics and on rituals prove to be the most challenging. Part of the difficulty reflects the obvious fact that the written text only begins to hint at the richness of the rituals. Sword treated basic cultural details – such as lighting, offering, and smoking the pipe; incensing; ritual gestures; drumming, rattling, and dancing – as contextual, obvious to any Lakota, and therefore not usually recorded as part of his narratives. Thus, full understanding of his texts requires exegesis by reference to the available ethnographic record of the Lakota. Nonetheless, his writings demonstrate more clearly than any other source the close interrelation of vision, song, and ceremonial action, adding new dimensions to our understanding of traditional religion. For example, the texts that describe Bear visions, the healing rituals of Bear doctors, and the performance of the Bear ceremony establish a web of interrelated symbolism reflecting Sword's personal experiences as a Bear dreamer. It was with one of these texts that Father Vine and I started our translation. It begins as follows:

Telling about medicines used to heal those wounded in war

1. When someone is wounded in war and survives, if one who has medicines for wounds arrives there, he hurries to open up the sacred medicines.

2. And he takes some of it and he says, 'Look upon the Bear who sits in the west holding medicines!

3. 'Thus you spoke: "When someone is struck by lightning, with this medicine you will hurry him to stand up and continue on,"' he says, and he gives him some and he takes some in his own mouth and he blows it on his face.

Here the dreamer first invokes the spirit of the Bear and, addressing the Bear, repeats the words that he heard in his vision. This speech is metaphorical: rather than 'wounded,' the victim is spoken of as 'struck by lightning'; rather than 'heal,' the Bear doctor is told he will hurry the man 'to stand up and continue on.' Section 3 (the numbering is by Sword himself) offers a good example of *hąblóglaka*, 'vision talk,' the ritualized speech of the holy men, a subject that has been of great interest to anthropologists, but about which little is known from other sources. These esoteric prayers and invocations, phrased metaphorically and aphoristically, recreate the vision experience and validate the dreamer's powers.

Linguistically, Sword's texts reporting 'vision talk' prove to be the least penetrable of his writings; they are frequently stilted and elliptical in style in comparison with conversational Lakota. By compiling a glossary of words and phrases in the sacred speech in his writings, and comparing the contexts of their use, we are able to reconstruct from Sword's texts one holy man's perspective on the sacred. Then, through comparison of Sword's material with other historical sources we can vastly increase our understanding of nineteenth-century Lakota prayer, the ritual coercion and manipulation of the spirits beyond knowing.

Sword clearly felt the inadequacy of the written page to represent sacred rituals, so with Walker's assistance he turned to the latest technology. Using a wax cylinder recorder, Sword and other Bear society members sang into the horn the songs of the rituals. Although the cylinders, preserved at the Archives of Traditional Music at Indiana University, are distorted with time, it is remarkable to be able to hear Sword's own voice almost ninety years after these recordings were made. As preludes to certain of the Bear songs, Sword recorded a number of examples of 'vision talk.' The speech is distinctive, the words almost shouted out in strongly declarative, rhythmic phrases.

'Vision talk' serves as a prelude to sacred songs, which were also given in the vision. The text on healing continues:

4. And then he sings this Bear song.

5. 1
Behold, eat this! you said.
Behold, eat this! you said.
Behold, eat this! You will live.
Behold, eat this! he said.

6. You were struck by lightning.
Behold, eat this! You will live.
Behold, eat this! he said.

7. Again he sings:
2
Someone sits suffering,
Behold, go to him!
Go to see him! they said to me.

Lines 1 and 2 of the first verse are addressed to the Bear, validating the dreamer's use of the medicines. Lines 3 through 7 of the first verse are addressed to the patient, assuring him of the power of the medicines. The second verse is also addressed to the patient and repeats the words of the Bear in the vision, directing the visionary to seek out those who are suffering (that is, those who have been wounded in battle). It validates the dreamer's right to doctor the patient.

In addition to the songs in the texts, Sword wrote two cycles of Bear songs, each comprising eighteen songs, most of which have two verses. He wrote the song texts in lines and verses, carefully labelling the verses 1 and 2, even when the words were identical. On the written page the song lyrics are stark and centre stage, like poetry, but in actual performance the words merged into the background. When sung, the words were not clearly articulated and obviously were not intended to be entirely intelligible to bystanders. The examples in the text just given represent one typical pattern: four lines in the first verse, three in the second. (Verse 1 in section 5 is followed by verse 2 in section 6; Sword apparently intended to indicate that verse 1 was then repeated, followed by the second verse 2 in section 7.) The recordings show that the regular loud-soft drumbeat turns into a tremolo to introduce each verse. Each text line is filled out with vocables to match the musical structure, and each verse closes with loud bear grunts. These animal noises become the dominant theme when listening to the Bear songs as a group. As they are performed, the songs have an urgency and power that the written text alone cannot convey. Sword did not attempt to reproduce performance by writing either the vocables or the animal sound; rather, he recorded the words, sacred knowledge known only to the Bear dreamers.

The text on healing continues after the Bear medicine man has completed his initial treatment of the patient:

8. Then if he has not died he is carried back home

9. and he doctors him with medicine and watches over him. He is brought back carefully and when he arrives the close relatives of the wounded one carefully put up a tipi for the healer and they carefully prepare a bed for the wounded one at the place of honour.

10. And the wounded one lies there and again the medicine man doctors him and he stays there and as long as he lies there and does not recover, so long he stays watching over him.

The patient is positioned at the place of honour, opposite the tipi door. The Bear doctor uses the medicines, sacred songs, and ritual actions given to him in the vision to heal the wounded man. Although he is personally responsible for the patient's recovery, he calls upon all the members of the Bear society living in the camp to assist him. They are men who have either themselves dreamed of the Bear or who, having been healed by Bear medicine, were taken into the society. Sword continues:

11. The place of honor in the lodge he rubs smooth and he incenses it with pine ('tree ears' [shelf fungus]).

12. At night all of the society members are invited to come there with drums and rattles and

13. they will sing Bear songs, so the holy man speaks of his vision and he says:

14. 'In the west there was a lodge high up, reaching the clouds, so there in the lodge I came to my senses. And then men who had painted themselves red were sitting in the lodge. And they showed a man with gaping holes whose mouth was red with blood.'

15. And he says this: 'They caused me to have these medicines.

16. '"Boy, human being, be of clear mind. Among your people there are men who lie suffering. With these holy medicines you will cause them to stand,"'

17. he said. 'They are the ones,' he said, 'they caused me to have these things.' Then he says this: 'They are called Bears, they are the ones, so humbly I tell their words. Alas! Without them I am nothing.'

In preparation for the ritual the Bear medicine man prepares an altar, located between the patient and the fireplace in the centre of the tipi. Again, before public performance of the healing songs, in sacred language the Bear medicine man recreates the vision experience through which he received his power. He tells of the lodge in the sky where his spirit went during the dream and where the Bears, who appeared in the guise of men painted red, directed him in the use of medicines to heal the wounded. He gives full credit to the medicines for his ability to heal: 'Without them I am nothing.'

Next the medicine man addresses the Bear spirit directly, which Sword indicates by placing 'Bear spirit' in parentheses:

18. '(Bear spirit) Come near me and attentively turn an ear. My boy who lies suffering, cause him
19. to stand! And your song I will relate but may I be free from any disaster.
20. 'These songs of yours are sacred. Consider your own sacred!'

The expression 'your song/words I will relate, but may I be free from any disaster' is a ritual phrase repeated throughout Sword's texts. The speaker recognizes that the words, which come from the spirits, have power, but that power has the potential to bring harm to anyone who misuses it. This ritual phrase apparently asks the spirits to overlook any mistake. The word here translated as 'disaster' is *wówaȟtani*, 'sudden, unseen misfortune.' Interestingly, this is the word that missionaries introduced for the concept of 'sin,' which today is its meaning in Lakota.

Sword next relates the physical act of doctoring the wound:

21. Then he stops up the blood and pus from the wounded one. Then the healer
22. rubs medicine on a bear claw and runs it around and around in the wound and then blood and also pus run out
23. and then it does not swell.

Either before or after the doctoring, the members of the Bear society apparently leave the lodge. Once again the medicine man invokes the power of the Bear through song and ritual action to enable the wounded man to sleep:

24. Now sometime during the night the wounded one will sleep and then the holy man takes up his medicine.

25. And he brings coals and places them on the altar and sprinkles medicine on them; when it smokes he takes the wounded one's robe and

26. incensing the robe he sings this song.

27. He does this so that he will sleep well without pain. This is the song he sings:

1

Grandfather, in a sacred manner it was made for me
Grandfather, in a sacred manner it was made for me
My robe, like a Bear, he made it for me.

28. 2

Grandfather, in a sacred manner it was made for me
My robe, like a Bear, he made it for me.

The structure of this song parallels the earlier ones, with the second verse shorter than the first. Like so many of the ritual songs, the referents are unclear. The first line could alternatively be translated, 'My grandfathers made it for me in a sacred manner,' but this seems inconsistent with the third line, which clearly says, 'he made it for me.' The reference seems to imply that the dreamer's robe is like a Bear, and the characteristic invoked – though this is pure speculation – may be hibernation, since the intent of this Bear ritual is to put the patient into restful sleep.

The text continues to discuss rituals that take place after the man is completely healed, culminating in his induction into the Bear society and the payment of gifts to the Bear medicine man.

The study of Sword's texts vastly enriches our understanding of Lakota religion in its cultural context. Even though Sword was a Christian, he was dedicated to the project of making a record of historical Lakota religion. According to Walker, Sword persuaded other holy men to cooperate in the project by arguing that after they were dead, 'all their sacred lore would pass with them unless they revealed it so that it could be preserved in writing; that future generations of the Oglalas should be informed as to all that their ancestors believed and practiced; that the Gods of the Oglalas would be more pleased if the holy men told of them so that they might be kept in remembrance and that all the world might know of them' (Walker 1980: 47).

Like a tree that has been many times uprooted and replanted, to reapply Sword's own metaphor, his texts have been worked over by many translators before me. Collaborating with a number of Lakota consultants as well as making systematic comparisons with other collections of historical Lakota texts will continue to resolve still-problematical narrative passages and help develop as fully as possible an understanding of the song texts. The published product will present the texts as Sword wrote them, with modern interlinear retranscriptions in Lakota and literal word-for-word translations in English. An accompanying tape or CD will include as many of the cylinder recordings as are now of sufficient quality to reproduce. This volume, and accompanying recordings, will be of special interest to Sioux people themselves, and will be studied especially in reservation colleges. As a literary figure, Sword holds a special place in Sioux history, and his writings should receive the same critical attention that we accord the early masterworks composed in European languages. The second volume will be a free English translation, arranged to reflect as faithfully as is reasonable his organization of words on paper. It will include a historical introduction and editorial matter that will help to contextualize the writings of a man whose achievements in the preservation of Lakota cultural traditions are only beginning to be appreciated.

The Sword texts exemplify, as Radin suggested, the value of studying culture by starting with a document. The work of translating them forces a rereading of the entire Lakota ethnographic record written in English. In the end, the comparison between the cultural insider's voice inscribed by Sword and the ethnographic voices inscribed by alien anthropologists reveals formerly obscured biases in the English record, which subtly reflects Euro-American cultural perspectives. This is particularly obvious in studying the 'vision talk,' songs, and accounts of prayer and ritual; Sword's writings make clear how much the ethnographic record, and contemporary Lakota practice, are shaped by intimate connection with Christianity. In other areas, notably warfare, Sword's texts address topics untouched by anthropologists, a gap largely accounted for by time and circumstances: few men who had gone on war parties against enemy tribes lived to be interviewed in depth by anthropologists. Finally, Sword's own strategic use of writing as a tool to adapt to the demands of changing reservation life suggests the value of literacy to American Indian peoples – both symbolic and practical – that has not been extensively explored by scholars. Anthropologists are not the only text makers. In the dialogue between Native texts and anthropological ones lies an invaluable tool for understanding culture. At the same time that such study perpetuates the Americanist textual tradition, it takes it in new directions and gives it renewed relevance to the core interests of the anthropological enterprise.

NOTE

This paper discusses the final part of a project designed to edit and publish the extensive manuscript collections of James R. Walker relating to the Oglala Lakotas. The project began in discussions with Elaine A. Jahner, then completing her doctoral degree in folklore at Indiana University, now professor of English at Dartmouth College; our collaboration has resulted in three volumes and a number of articles. I would like to acknowledge the formative influence that our collaboration has had on my thinking about the Sword texts. I am very pleased to acknowledge the assistance and support of the late Vine V. Deloria, Sr, with whom I worked intermittently from 1981 to 1988 on these translations. His expertise in the Lakota language and willingness to share his knowledge made this project possible. I would also like to acknowledge my indebtedness to Douglas R. Parks, my colleague at Indiana University, on whom I have depended for linguistic insight. My work on Sword's song texts has been stimulated by Erik Gooding, an ethnomusicologist, who is currently a graduate student in anthropology at Indiana. Finally, I must acknowledge my gratitude to the National Endowment for the Humanities for the financial support of my work on the Sword texts.

REFERENCES

Deloria, Ella C. 1938. Dakota Texts from the Sword Manuscript. MS. 30 (X8a.18), Franz Boas Collection, American Philosophical Society Library, Philadelphia.

Jahner, Elaine A. 1994. 'Traditional Narratives and Cultural Continuity.' In *1492–1992: American Indian Persistence and Resurgence*, a special issue of *Boundary 2*, ed. Karl Kroeber, 149–80. Durham, NC: Duke University Press.

Johnson, A.F. 1910. 'Career of Captain George Sword.' *Oglala Light* (Nov.): 21–33.

Parks, Douglas R., and Raymond J. DeMallie. 1994. 'Plains Indian Native Literatures.' In *1492–1992: American Indian Persistence and Resurgence*, a special issue of *Boundary 2*, ed. Karl Kroeber, 106–48.

Pilling, James Constantine. 1887. *Bibliography of the Siouan Languages*. Smithsonian Institution, Bureau of American Ethnology Bulletin 5. Washington.

Radin, Paul. 1933. *The Method and Theory of Ethnology: An Essay in Criticism*. New York: McGraw-Hill.

Ricker, Eli. 1907. Interview with George Sword. Ricker Collection, Nebraska State Historical Society, Lincoln.

Sword, George. In preparation. *'George Sword Wrote These': A Personal Account of Oglala Culture*. Translated and edited by Raymond J. DeMallie.

Tedlock, Dennis. 1983. *The Spoken Word and the Work of Interpretation*. Philadelphia: University of Pennsylvania Press.

Three Stars, Clarence. [1909.] Translation of texts by George Sword. Archives of the Department of Anthropology, American Museum of Natural History, New York.

Walker, James R. 1917. 'The Sun Dance and Other Ceremonies of the Oglala Division of the Teton Dakota.' American Museum of Natural History (New York) *Anthropological Papers* 16(2).

– 1980. *Lakota Belief and Ritual*. Edited by Raymond J. DeMallie and Elaine A. Jahner. Lincoln: University of Nebraska Press.

– 1982. *Lakota Society*. Edited by Raymond J. DeMallie. Lincoln: University of Nebraska Press.

– 1983. *Lakota Myth*. Edited by Elaine A. Jahner. Lincoln: University of Nebraska Press.

– n.d. Story of George Sword. MS FF108, James R. Walker Collection, Colorado Historical Society, Denver.

16 Ella Cara Deloria: Early Lakota Ethnologist (Newly Discovered Novelist)

BEA MEDICINE

> Ella Cara Deloria (1889–1971) was a Yankton Dakota woman who, with some other North American Natives, accepted the invitation of the anthropologist Franz Boas to become a linguistic informant and an ethnological entrepreneur in anthropology classes at Columbia University in 1929. This meant that she served as an emic, or native, speaker, teaching the anthropologists the various dialects of the Dakota; it also meant that she developed the skills of the anthropologist herself. The emic perspective, plus her scholarly training, made her a unique figure. In addition, as she was a Christian, educated in the 'modern' tradition, she was well-suited for the role of cultural mediator. (Medicine 1980: 23)

My views on Ella Deloria have not changed significantly since I wrote brief biographical notes about her (Medicine 1980, 1989). I practise what I teach – return your writing to your constituents for comments. The 1980 publication was approved by Vine Deloria, Sr, who said, 'When Vine wrote about anthropologists, he didn't mean you or your Aunt Ella. He meant others.' Vine, Jr, stated, 'It sounds like her.'

In this paper, I wish to present Aunt Ella as a Native woman and contextualize her life within Lakota cultural contours that shaped her life and work. She strongly identified with the 'Standing Rock people.' She once told me, 'I know more about them than the Dakota. I grew up in Wakpala' (South Dakota). Although she knew her band affiliation and her enrolment, her identity was firmly embedded as a Lakota.[1] The Deloria family was accepted in the Wakpala community. Although Ella and her sister Susie were summer visitors, their sustained visits evidenced their interest in community life and allowed Ella's linguistic interpretations.

Ella Deloria attended St Elizabeth's Mission in Wakpala, where her father, the Reverend Philip Deloria, was the first Native Episcopal missionary. She continued at All Saints School in Sioux Falls, and Oberlin College, receiving a B.S. in 1915 from Columbia University Teachers' College. Ella spent several years as Director of the St Elizabeth's Episcopal Boarding School in the 1950s. She and Susie were committed to the Christian education of a segment of the Lakota population. As the students attended the public school in Wakpala, her job was mainly administrative and church-related. Although Ella was committed to higher education, few of the high school graduates pursued this avenue.

She taught in Bureau of Indian Affairs schools and at Haskell Institute, also working for the YMCA in New York City. She began to do fieldwork around 1927, resigning from Haskell to devote time to Dakota research and to publish scholarly works with Boas until his death in 1942. She also contributed much to the work of others. Boas said of Ella's work: 'She has a thorough grasp of the grammar and spirit of the language. We have written together a grammar of the Dakota, of the Teton, Yankton, and Assiniboine dialects, and she is thoroughly conversant not only with the forms but also with the very intricate psychological background.'

Ella's letters to Boas reflected the conflict between her professional commitments and deeply felt kinship obligations. She cared for her father during his long illness and helped to support her sister Susie. She was known as 'Aunt Ella' to many younger ethnographer-colleagues, reflecting typical Lakota incorporativeness regarding kinship. This was not adoption, however, as it did not involve the whole kinship group.

My assessment of Ella Deloria's role as a Native intellectual is that she has not been appreciated by Lakota/Dakota people teaching in the tribally controlled colleges. At Standing Rock, one Lakota teacher of the Lakota language felt that *Dakota Grammar* was 'too technical.' *Speaking of Indians* was used in her Lakota culture class. A non-Lakota teaching an education class was contemplating using *Waterlily*. Two male Lakota instructors at Sinte Gleska University (Rosebud, South Dakota) appreciate the explication of the *tiospaye*[2] concept and the social-life aspect in her book *Speaking of Indians*.

While a process of reconstruction of Lakota culture seems under way at each college, there seems to be a continued disenchantment with ethnological work, although Frances Densmore's work on Lakota music is being used in some recordings of contemporary Lakota music and in the revitalization of Sun Dance songs. Thus, I was interested to read the book of Robert Warrior (Osage English Professor) and his comment on Ella Deloria. After stating that literary production changed after Matthews and McNickle's work, Warrior writes that 'literary production by Natives declined rapidly and was done primarily by anthropologists and historians. The most well known is Ella Cara Deloria, the aunt of Vine Deloria, Jr., whose posthumously published historical novel,

Waterlily, and anthropological texts have been important in the recovery of Native intellectual traditions' (1995: 24). He also refers to 'Ella Deloria's liberal ethnographic work' (1995: 42).

In assessing Ella's writings, one must place her in space and time and in her religious orientation – as well as her keen interest in her Lakota heritage. *Speaking of Indians* demonstrates this commitment. Her motivation appears to be to act as a cultural broker. She wished to convey the human character of Lakota life to a non-Native audience. Her information was collected when Lakota people spoke of a glorious Lakota past that she heard of through family histories, war exploits, orality, and pantomime and song. *Dakota Texts* reflects this tradition and the morality and ethical behaviour that were transmitted through oral traditions. Her 'informants' (and she used that term) were Patrick Shields and Joseph White Plume of Standing Rock, whose lives were oriented toward the proper functioning of kinship, which they saw as the bedrock of Lakota culture. Mrs Andrew Little Moon, mother of Sammy Red Eagle, and other persons in the Women's Auxiliary to the Brothers of Christian Unity (BCU) of the Episcopal Church appeared to be eager informants. After all, who could refuse to answer questions posed by the eldest daughter of the Reverend Deloria?

Ella's constant interest was in the writing of 'ethnographic' materials. This knowledge, however, was not presented to the people themselves. When I ask community people about her writings, they are unable to name them. Indeed, her brother, Vine Deloria, Sr, although a good informant to Ray DeMallie and others, did not know the bulk of her work. Indeed, when pressed, he told me that much of her collections were lost when she could not pay storage fees while she and Susie lived in New Jersey. I was told by a Native literature instructor at the University of Minnesota that Sam Deloria did not know that she had written a novel. In 1970, she told me, 'I have written a novel. It is not an ethnography so I don't want you to read it. I don't want it published.' This is a clue as to her view of her work. It was ethnographic and reflective of a part of her life that she cherished.

It may be that most anthropologists are unaware of Ella Deloria's ethnographic work. Siouan specialists have utilized it. Ernest Schusky had lauded her work on the dynamics of kinship that demonstrates the nuances of kin relations. He called it 'the best work on kinship!' Others, DeMallie for example, have used her as an informant, now termed 'consultant.' Her linguistic texts are excellent. Julian Rice's appropriations (1994) are finding a niche in Native American literature courses.

Ella Deloria's work as an ethnographer and an indigenous linguist was not fully recognized until the long-delayed publication of her novel, *Waterlily*, in

1988. It is ironic that she did not want it published and that it has superseded her ethnographic contributions. It is now on bibliographies in Native Women and Indian Literature courses and is read like an ethnographic text – which would have displeased her, I am sure. Although seen as 'sugary' and 'idealistic' by one Native professor teaching American Indian literature, it nonetheless is important in delineating the kinship dimension in dyadic interaction between members of the *tiospaye* (extended family). Morality, ethical behaviour, and the unifying theme of reciprocity are manifested from a feminine perspective. The articulation of male and female relationships is significant. It may be the emphasis on gender complementarity that causes some modern feminists to object to the novel.

In his assessment of *Waterlily*, anthropologist John Prater writes, 'Perhaps she did not look critically at her Christian beliefs, and the image of the Sioux she creates in *Waterlily* is not Sioux at all but a Christian image super-imposed on Sioux characters' (1995: 46). He traces their form 'from Ella Deloria's own "life myth."' He attributes her 'multi-cultural heritage' as a position to understand a 'context of varied intercourse.' My knowledge of her heritage that she manifested was definitely Lakota, not Dakota, She, like all aboriginal people, was subjected to Christianization and cultural imperialism. She mediated adaptive strategies that allowed her to function adequately in two social systems. These strategies fostered her effectiveness as she described herself – a Lakota woman and an ethnographer. I believe that we can anticipate more literary speculations and anthropological analyses (see, for example, Finn 1995) of her personhood and her contributions through the book *Waterlily*. Her ethnographic oeuvre, however, may be her lasting contribution to the Americanist Tradition.

Perhaps the most telling thing about Finn's article is her 'writing against the *in*grained' respect for 'personal dignity' (1995: 344), which typifies Ella Deloria. This overriding sense of personal autonomy confronts Finn, who feels a sense of complicity. I feel this is perhaps the major difference in writing about another culture and the intrusive quality of 'others' writing about us. Perhaps I too have fallen into this anthropological trap in this essay. Lakota women, then and now, do not separate the 'personal and political' as we must deal with issues which involve our communities. However, within the community context we are allowed to maintain our own dignity and idiosyncrasies. This was recognized by Aunt Ella and allowed her an intellectual freedom and honour for her achievements. I hope I have portrayed this quality.

Ella Deloria 'mentored' many scholars. Now called a 'consultant,' she was used as an 'informant,' as was her brother, Vine, Sr.[3] I wonder how many helped her in her impoverished years in Vermillion, South Dakota? When I drove to her motel to take her to lunch, she would scan the motel room, humming, and looking for something to give to me. There was little but stained coffee cups and a picture of Franz Boas, a typewriter, and several boxes. Her humour and her pleasure at going 'out to lunch' was sufficient.

Only one scholar, to my knowledge, aided Aunt Ella in her scholarly research. Robert Hall, while at the University of South Dakota, in the late 1960s, obtained a grant for her to accomplish her greatest desire – as she said, 'to do a proper Lakota dictionary with the psychological meanings of the words and ideas.' In this effort, she clearly shows the influence of Ruth Benedict and Margaret Mead. Dr Mead once told me that 'Ella was an asset at Columbia.'

Esther Goldfrank clearly articulated her indebtedness to Aunt Ella in her work on Sioux personality. She also stated that after Ella presented linguistic data, she turned to Franz Boas to ask, 'Is that alright, Dr. Boas?' Further, Dr Goldfrank stated, 'Ella was the main source for Jeanette Mirsky's work on the Lakota.' Therefore, I maintain that Ella Deloria was an 'ethnographic informant, par excellance.' She, however, had an abiding interest in Lakota culture and language, and this interest sustained her through the trying times of her life. Current reference to her as a 'consultant' diminishes her intellectual and communicative skills – both in Lakota and in English.

My data on Ella Deloria are the result of almost daily contact with her during the years of 1969–70 when we both lived in Vermillion, South Dakota. I was directing an oral-history project at the University of South Dakota. Because I became an 'anthro,' many people feel that Ella was a role model for me. Notions of cultural difference were part of my early socialization. As a child, I only knew that she 'lived in the East, and talked about Indians,' according to my mother. When Aunt Ella visited our home, she asked a lot of questions about Lakota life and language. When I graduated from college in 1945, she gave me her book *Speaking of Indians* and said, 'I'm proud of you!'

Upon my return to Wakpala as a retiree in 1989, I had the opportunity to contextualize her life in the community and the community view of her. I interviewed individuals who had worked with her while she managed St Elizabeth's Mission in 1955–8. The general statement was *lela ta yan Lakcol wo glake*: 'She spoke Lakota very well.' They noted that she 'went away to give speeches.' The students who attended the public school during this period liked her, but had no knowledge of her published work or her work as an ethnographer.

After I left Vermillion, in an undated letter, she wrote: 'There are two very nice Sisters in college and one drives so I have been going with them, once to Mission, and the other day I took them to the New Year's dinner and party at St Mary's and we had a great time, they enjoyed it. One is Theresa Martin[4] and the other is Sister Michael (Many Wounds) of Pine Ridge. Both full bloods and very smart girls.' Her attitudes about 'blooded-ness' and her concern for reciprocity are evident.

Non-Native people in surrounding 'border towns' very seldom state overt assessments of Lakota people. I asked a *wasicu* ('White') woman and active member of the Episcopal church if she remembered Ella Deloria. She said, 'We thought she was a wonderful woman. I wish she were here to help us decide what to do with St Elizabeth's Mission.' The Lakota pastor of the parish said, 'She was a good woman.'

Ella told me of her invitation to a Sun Dance on Pine Ridge reservation. First, she asked a female cousin and her husband (from Wakpala) to accompany her and Susie (her constant companion in the field). This was proper decorum. During the performance of the *Heyoka* ('Contrary') ceremony, the Heyoka removes, with bare hands, the parts of the ceremonial puppy from the boiling water in the pot. She was given the head – a great honour. She said, 'I ate this without any fuss.'

Her Lakota appetite was embedded in her cravings for certain, in Lakota terms, delicacies. She often asked my mother for prairie dogs – which father shot and the *women* ate with appreciation. In our home in Vermillion, where she ate dinner almost every day, she often said, '*To'zun* (Niece), is there anything else?' I would bring out raw kidney on a wooden cutting board. (My son would say, 'This is where I leave you' – he preferred his kidney cooked!) Later, after smiling with satisfaction, she would say, 'Is that all?' This was a signal to bring out Kahlua, which she dearly loved. This ritual was not a daily one! These examples show clearly her true bicultural adaptations. She was equally at home at formal receptions and in poor Lakota homes although she never mastered the household arts of Lakota food preservation and preparation, which was expected of every 'full-blood' woman.

Ella Deloria's presentation of self also heralded her mixed-blood status. She was always properly dressed – in white woman's style. She delighted in recounting the many times Lakota people spoke Lakota in her presence. She could answer them in Lakota and say, 'Maaah, I am Lakota, too.' Her 'informants' were mainly Episcopalians or '*shina ska*' (White robes). Because of the separation of churches, she seldom interviewed Catholics, who were mainly from the Sihasapa (Blackfoot) band. In interviewing older Lakota, she listened attentively, recorded the data in her car, and questioned them or another about some obscure point at a later time.

When one considers the time of Ella Deloria's work, and the space in which she operated – the old car she shared with her sister Susie and the apartment in Palisades, New Jersey – one wonders at her production. Her *Dakota Texts*, and her work on the Sun Dance and legends and folk tales were marvels of translation and interpretation. Seeing herself as an interpreter of Lakota culture and language, she chose a career that was, perhaps, happenstance. As an ethnologist/informant, she lived a precarious life in a strange culture, constantly on the economic fringes. Marriage seemed out of the question for her. As the eldest daughter of an Episcopalian minister, her marriage options were nil. Her sense of superiority and attitudes toward the ubiquitous 'full-bloods' were limiting factors. But she once told me, 'If I had met a man like [your son] Ted's father, I might have gotten married.'

This attitude was clearly articulated to me when, on one occasion, she stated, 'Poor Anna, she married a full-blood.' Angered, I said, 'But he fed your relatives.' (Many of her female cousins had married *wasicu* [White] men who arrived as bums on the railroad.) Her attitudes seemed apparent in the non-marriage of her younger sister, Susie. Susie often told my mother, 'I could have married any man I wanted,' or 'I envy you for your children.'[5] My father often left the room when the Deloria girls arrived. He never did enter into the jovial joking relationship with Ella as he did with Susie. He was well aware of not only full-blood/half-breed dimensions but also religious affiliation. Mother converted to Catholicism when she married my father. I relate these poignant instances to indicate the difficult cultural choices that women in the Lakota culture of my mother's generation faced.

It appears that Ella was quite aware of the 'blooded' distinction. I remember postcards from Palisades, New Jersey, one from Aunt Ella saying, 'I may be more closely related to Martin than you' after she had discovered a Sihasapa ancestor. Yet the full-blood, Martin Medicine (Sitting Crow, his Lakota name), was often a source for her linguistic work, as she told mother: 'Ask Martin what this word means and tell me.'

Ella's letters to Boas reveal the ubiquitous tension between these potential distinctions (even factions), especially in Pine Ridge. She once told me that some older men were speaking about her in Lakota as a *wasicu_winyan* (white woman). She answered them: '*Ee, tu wale, mishyama Lakota ki!*' 'Unbelievable! I'm a Lakota, too.' I asked, 'What did they do then?' She said, 'They stood up and shook my hand.' She was an *eyeska* (translator) or an *ah oze*, 'yellow armpit,' as the mixed-blood students at St Elizabeth's were labelled.[6]

My association with Ella Deloria was framed within a Lakota kinship nexus. She and her sister, Susie, visited us each summer. Susie and my mother, Anna Gabe, were inseparable, fun-loving culprits at St Elizabeth's Mission where all were students. *Tipi Sapa,* the Reverend Deloria, claimed relationship to my mother's father, Baptiste Gabe, who was fathered by a Frenchman from Louisiana and mothered by a Miniconjou woman. The Deloria girls and Mother said they were cousins. Mother was the same age as Susan, three years younger than

Ella. Susie was a pretty, fun-loving person. Ella, being the elder, was the authoritative figure. She was viewed as a 'killjoy' – according to Mother. She was upset when Susie and Mother chewed buttons off their blouses and threw them in the collection plate instead of the nickel coin each Protestant child received every Sunday to put in the plate. Contributing to the church was ingrained early in the Christian enculturation.

When I asked my mother, 'What kind of person was Aunt Ella?' she replied, 'She was very vain.' Subsequent experiences with her while living in Vermillion revealed this tendency. She never forgot and did not let you forget her mixed-blood origins. This badge of blood-lines was predominant in her relationships with the Lakota people of Standing Rock reservation, which she considered her home. She often told my oldest sister, Marguerite, 'Bea and I put Wakpala on the map.'

Recently, Nora Hawk, a Lakota 'elderly' (as we are called) told me an incident when she worked for Ella in 1955. Christmas was apparently a time of joy and carolling for the students at St Elizabeth's Mission. Ella was part of this Christian time of holiness. The dining room was decorated with streamers of green and red tissue paper, which is still a tradition at festive events in Wakpala. After dinner, in the 'Big Girls' Dormitory,' she said to a younger girl, '*Cepansi* (female cousin), *eyaya na, minexuasa jikala makauy ye*' (Go and tear a small piece of the red streamer and bring it to me). (Aunt Ella was always precise in using Lakota kin terms, and being a Lakota, one could not refuse any request made in the name of kinship.) '*Taku ye?*' (Why?), asked the minion. '*T'osa wani yakin kte*' (You'll see), said Ella. When the younger girl gave the scrap of red tissue paper to Ella, she moistened it with her saliva and daubed it on her cheeks to add colour, smiling as she did it.

This vanity persisted into her later years. When I sponsored a Fashion Show to establish the Ella Deloria Scholarship for Indian women at the University of South Dakota (1969), I took her to a beauty shop for a shampoo and set. She said, 'They took me way in back where no one could see me. How nice!' *Amerindian* (1969: 4) described Ella Deloria as a graduate of Columbia University who had been 'associated with the University in the field of research and with the W. H. Over Museum.' She came 'from a famous Dakota family ... and [was] famous in her own right as author and anthropologist.' 'Miss Bea Medicine, also a Dakota [*sic*] and an anthropologist, ... wrote and delivered the commentary for the performance, the first of its kind ever held at the University.' The national television coverage must have pleased Ella Deloria! Patricia Albers and I have donated my royalties from *The Hidden Half* to this scholarship, and Pat's to a scholarship for Indian women at the University of North Dakota.

NOTES

1 Once, in Vine, Jr's presence, my mother said, 'Bea wants to know how the Delorias were enrolled on Standing Rock.' Vine, Sr replied, 'You know your father [Baptiste Gabe] and your uncle, Charlie Gabe, worked to get me enrolled.' I had asked my father, who had replied, 'Ask your mother.' So, even in those days, as today, tensions regarding tribal enrolment were obvious.
2 These young men and the 'White' instructor of 'culture' do not like Julian Rice's interpretations of Ella's work. They use the four texts in his book *Buffalo People*, and nothing else.
3 Ray DeMallie presented a paper about her at the Ethnohistory Conference in November 1996. I heard the paper but have not seen it.
4 Lakota language teacher at Standing Rock, now Sitting Bull College, for eleven years.
5 Sadly, Aunt Ella related Susie's last days, which were spent removing the beads from a pair of old moccasins. 'But Susie was not right when she got older,' she said. Did she remember that we placed new moccasins on the deceased to travel the Spirit Trail?
6 I asked my mother, 'So, what did you do when they called you *ah oze*?' She said, 'We'd raise our arms and say, "We don't have yellow armpits."'

REFERENCES

Albers, Patricia, and Bea Medicine. 1983. *The Hidden Half: Studies of Plains Indian Women*. Washington: University Press of America.

– 1969. 'New Scholarship Named for Ella Deloria.' *Amerindian* 17(6): 4.

Deloria, Ella Cara. 1929. 'The Sun Dance of the Oglala Sioux.' *Journal of American Folklore* 42: 354–413.

– 1932. *Dakota Texts*. New York: G.E. Stechert and Co.

– 1944. *Speaking of Indians*. New York: Friendship Press.

– 1954. 'Short Dakota Texts, including Conversations.' *International Journal of American Linguistics* 20(1): 17–22.

– 1941. *Dakota Grammar*, with Franz Boas. Memoirs of the National Academy of Sciences 23. Washington.

– 1988. *Waterlily*. Lincoln: University of Nebraska Press.

Deloria, Ella Cara, and Franz Boas. 1933. 'Notes on the Dakota, Teton Dialect.' *International Journal of American Linguistics* 8: 97–121.

Finn, Janet L. 1995. 'Ella Cara Deloria and Mourning Dove: Writing for Cultures, Writing against the Grain.' In Ruth Behar and Deborah Gordon, eds, *Women Writing Culture*, 335–50. Berkeley: University of California Press.

Medicine, Bea. 1980. 'Ella C. Deloria, The Emic Voice.' *Melus* 7(4): 23–30.

– 1989. 'Ella Cara Deloria.' In Ute Gacs et al., eds, *Women Anthropologists: A Biographical Dictionary*, 45–40. New York: Greenwood Press.

Prater, John. 1995. 'Ella Deloria: Varied Intercourse.' *WICAZO SA Review* 11(2): 40–6.

Rice, Julian. 1994. *Ella Deloria's* The Buffalo People. Albuquerque: University of New Mexico Press.

Warrior, Robert Allen. 1995. *Tribal Secrets: Recovering American Indian Intellectual Traditions*. Minneapolis: University of Minnesota Press.

17 Past and New Directions for Fieldwork in Ethnolinguistics: The Case of Micmac (Northern Dialects)

DANIELLE E. CYR

In Genesis, the Judaeo-Christian God separated humans from animals by way of language and later, in the Babel episode, made language the source of mutual misunderstanding between human groups whose collective plottings had been facilitated by a shared language. Interestingly, the Montagnais Algonquian present the story exactly the other way around. Savard (1972: 107) tells us that after Carcajou, the cultural hero/trickster, and Woman Muskrat procreate, all kinds of beings were born from their union. Carcajou left to hunt and Woman Muskrat gave birth to numerous offspring who populate the Earth. On his arrival back home, Carcajou discovered a great number of dwellings and asked his wife who these peoples were. She reported they were his sons and daughters. 'After having hugged them all, he decrees they will have to speak different languages, that they will, in the future, have to divide into groups unable to communicate. If they all spoke the same language, Carcajou says, all they would do would be to fight and struggle!'

This myth illustrates how cultures assign different interpretations to language diversity. Based on such differences, we can only imagine how the whole enterprise of the Western ethnographic description of languages might have crossed into the Other's universe. While, on the one hand, we can quite easily assess the theoretical gains our enterprise has brought to our own scientific universe, on the other hand, it is a very different story to circumscribe and evaluate the results from the Other's point of view.

The goal of this paper is to illustrate the empirical effects of the theoretical ethno-enterprise on Others. I will not try to depict these effects as *realia*. Rather I will sketch them as percepts having an effect on the continuous relation between theorizing a phenomenon and living through it.

Historical Background

In North America, the Micmacs were among the earliest subjects of ethnographic inquiry. From *The New Relations of Gaspesia* by Father Chrestien LeClercq in 1691 to Father Maillard's *Account of the Customs and Manners of the Micmakis* in 1758, to Reverend Rand's *Micmac Tribes of Indians* in 1850 and Father Pacifique's *Quelque Traits Caractéristiques de la Tribu des Micmacs* in 1907, to name just a few, their customs and language were thoroughly described by missionaries, who were thus the first ethnographers.

Beyond their Christianizing agenda, the ethnographic interest of these missionaries among the Micmacs is revealed by the fact that the Catholic missionaries in particular did not mind letting the people continue with their nomadic practices and seasonal migration. It was hence 'the shepherd' who followed 'his flock,' not the other way around – to such an extent that in 1842, when the government of Nova Scotia took on the Indians' education, the Commissioner of Indian Affairs estimated that the Jesuit missionaries 'had done a poor job in acquainting the Micmacs with the art and industry of civilized life' (Battiste 1984: 146, from Canada D.I.A. 1847: 118). And, indeed, as Battiste wrote (ibid.): 'Despite over a hundred years of contact and cooperation with the French, Micmacs had solidly retained their traditional culture and livelihood.' At that time, the government even concluded that the only way to assimilate the Micmacs was to root out the French influence and restrict their nomadic habits. Father Pacifique, who worked in Listuguj (present-day Restigouche) during the first quarter of the twentieth century, was the last of the great ethnomissionaries to contribute to the enrichment of the Micmac literacy tradition.

Although Micmac language had been taught sporadically in mission schools across the Micmac territories, from Canadian Confederation in 1867 to the foundation of Native Cultural Education Centres throughout Canada in 1971, schooling in the Micmac language declined almost everywhere. A rare exception was Conne River in Newfoundland where, from approximately 1900 to 1914, all instruction was conducted in Micmac. Another attempt to teach elements of Micmac reading and writing during the first four grades was reported in Listuguj around 1903, under Father Pacifique. After 1914, however, Micmac was banished from the curriculum by the local priest. The Micmac language is now extinct at Conne River (Battiste 1984: 152).

After 1920 (Canada's Indian Act) English-language instruction was mandated by department policy (Battiste 1984). During the whole period from 1867 to 1971, very few Micmac children were reported as staying in school beyond the fifth grade. Yet, '[a]fter being taken out of school, Micmac parents taught their own children the traditional pursuits of survival, including how to read and write in Micmac if they wanted to learn' (ibid.: 151). In fact, the practice of teaching children how to read and write within the structures of the family had been organized at least as early as 1765, at the time of Father Maillard, and the practice seems to have continued until the 1960s. As a consequence of this ongoing tradition, Labillois (1996: 266) estimates that '[t]he Micmac situation was still fairly intact in 1968, when the aboriginal nations started to demand more control over the curriculum content.'

Short Historical Survey of Contemporary Ethnolinguistic Fieldwork in Québec and New Brunswick

In 1971, when the federal government finally approved the transfer of education to the Native Band Councils, eleven Native Cultural Centres were founded in the Micmac communities of Québec and the Atlantic provinces. Many efforts were made to develop culturally appropriate curriculum material for the teaching of Micmac in community schools. In the first period, field ethnolinguists did not seem to play a great role. Rather, the material was produced by Native teachers.

The reaction to this material was not always what was expected. In Gesgapegiag, Québec, for example, a program of complete schooling in Micmac was implemented during the 1970s from grade 1 to grade 4. This program appeared to be based on culturally appropriate curriculum material; it was considered at the time a pioneering and flourishing program. After several years, however, the program was abolished, and even traces of the material are now impossible to find on the reserve. When asked, the authorities say that the material was shipped to Listuguj after the closure of the program. Although it is hard to obtain official reasons why the program was abolished, unofficial sources say that the parents had started to withdraw their children from the reserve school to send them to white schools in the vicinity. In the eyes of these parents, the Micmac curriculum material displayed too much Micmac cultural content. Parents wanted their children to learn skills useful in the non-Micmac world.

In Listuguj, from 1971 to 1974, Romeo Labillois participated in the first Micmac program to be held there within these new Native curriculum policies. His report of the curriculum and teaching situation at the time (Labillois 1996: 266) is striking. He says that, while aboriginal people acquired the right to launch their own language programs, they did not get the appropriate funding to do so. Listuguj children were schooled at that time in the white school of the neighbouring town of Campbellton. The goal of the program was thus to test whether some Micmac curriculum could work within the white school system. When he started teaching, Labillois reports, he had no teaching material. He had to start from scratch, using his own knowledge of the language and the culture. In one paragraph (ibid.) he condenses an entire situation that was probably common to most Micmac reserves: 'The community had no input into the programme. The community did not really know what it wanted to do as far as teaching the Micmac language and culture in the schools was concerned. Many members of the community felt it was a waste of time and money to teach the Micmac language in the schools. Most parents felt that English language education was more important for their children if they were to succeed in making a living in life. Many native parents today prefer English language education for their children and the native language has no place in the school.'

Field Linguists and the Creation of Orthographic Fissions

At the same time as the Native Cultural Centres were founded, many linguists developed a tremendous interest in the scientific description of Native languages. Some of them joined with the Native Cultural Centres in their efforts to develop curriculum material. One major issue that arose from these associations was whether to produce curriculum material in the writing system of Father Pacifique or to start from zero with a new one. People promoting the traditional Pacifique system held that it was deeply rooted in the Elders' experience; maintaining that orthography would thus allow Elders to assist younger people in their task of teaching and learning Micmac. They also considered that resistance to literacy could be circumvented by using a culturally familiar form of writing. However, people promoting the creation of a new writing system held that Pacifique's system was not as widely spread among Elders as it was thought to be, that it was scientifically imperfect, that Pacifique's texts contained too many errors, and that their content was of minimal interest for contemporary readers (Battiste 1984).

From 1971 to 1975, the Micmac Association for Cultural Studies (MACS), based in Nova Scotia, undertook a consultation tour among Micmac communities to assess the language situation. The interviews were conducted by linguist Doug Smith and Micmac speaker and writer Bernie Francis. During these years, through sporadic consultation with linguist Jim Fidelholtz, they devised a new writing system (the Smith-Francis system), which they presented to the communities of Nova Scotia during 1974–5. After a first period of negative reaction on the part of Elders, and after extended discussions and debates, this new system was officially accepted by the Grand Council of (Nova Scotia) Micmacs. In 1982, the MACS staff changed. The new leadership decided to restore the Pacifique writing system, but this time Nova Scotia Elders rejected the old system in favour of the new one. This reaction led to the stabilization of the Smith-Francis writing system in Nova Scotia. After that, linguist John Hewson, conducting Micmac linguistic research at Memorial University of Newfoundland, adopted the Smith-Francis system. The spelling of words in Hewson's texts at times differs somewhat from Francis's texts, however.

During this whole process, Micmacs of other provinces, who had no representation at the Grand Council in Nova Scotia, did not participate in, nor were they consulted about, the writing system renewal. As a consequence, it was more difficult for them to understand the reasons for the change. Discussions and debates between Micmac consultants and linguists from Québec and New Brunswick went on for a while, addressing whether to adopt Nova Scotia's new system or to devise a writing system of their own that would better reflect their dialectal variety (that is, the /n/ dialect spoken north of the Miramichi). Withdrawing from that group, Mildred Millea, a Native teacher in Big Cove (NB), chose neither of the proposed solutions and worked to maintain and promote Pacifique's writing system. She, however, brought slight changes to this system, creating yet another new writing system. After getting support from her community, Millea's system spread to other New Brunswick communities.

In Québec, at the same period, only twelve persons were reported still to be literate in the Pacifique system. From 1976 on, linguist Gilles Delisle worked with Emmanuel Metallic, a Micmac technolinguist and writer, to elaborate curriculum material. Their major achievement was an exhaustive Micmac teaching grammar. While preparing this new material, they also developed a new writing system. During the same years, anthropologist Albert D. DeBlois prepared a dictionary of five thousand words (published in 1984) and a collection of texts (published in 1990). These documents display a slightly different writing system as well. Parallel to these systems, and working in the same geographic area, linguist Watson Williams, who had undertaken the translation of the Bible, elaborated a slightly different version of the DeBlois and Metallic writing system. His system was tested and used in Maria (Québec) and the North of New Brunswick.

Together with the Pacifique writing system, the Micmac nation now has six different writing systems available. Each is used to varying extents in some curriculum material or other. Aside from the Delisle and Metallic teaching grammar, the DeBlois and Metallic lexicon, and a recent translation of Pacifique's grammar into English by Hewson and Francis, none of these writing systems has produced consistent material or literature. If the Nova Scotia system seems to have definitely standardized into the Smith-Francis system, New Brunswick and Québec Micmacs, by contrast, could never reach an agreement on which system to implement once and for all in their communities. Some reserves,

Listuguj for instance, have been working with two or three different systems at the same time, letting the students choose which one they wanted. In other reserves, Eel River for example, one system is currently being used in adult education and another one in children's education. The on-going discussions around standardization throughout the 1970s and 1980s have absorbed all the energies of the participants, slowly turning into dissension and frustration. After 1989, the orthographic debate, being in a deadlock, was closed off and collaboration among reserves became practically non-existent.

Still, in recent years, Emmanuel Metallic has elaborated another writing system. While all other systems were relatively close to the Pacifique system, Metallic's new system is quite different. Based on the English perception of correspondences between sounds and letters, it reflects very closely the Listuguj younger speakers' pronunciation. As this system is used currently being in the making of an extensive dictionary, the Micmac language hence now has seven different writing systems.

During all these years, and despite all these efforts, the development of curriculum material seems to have declined along with the use of Micmac in families; the teaching of language and literacy has, in fact, practically disappeared from the sphere of the family. And the schooling in Micmac, if it has improved, is surely not sufficient to produce fluency on its own. In the best cases, it has extended to one hour per week or fifteen minutes a day from grade 1 to grade 6. Its scope does not go much beyond teaching expressions of politeness, numbers, lists of animals, the calendar, kinship terms, and so on. Labillois's remarks ring truer than ever.

One other important change through the years, in Québec and New Brunswick at least, is the attitude towards linguists and scholars, which has consistently declined. The fact is that, outside of technolinguists Bernie Francis and Emmanuel Metallic, no Micmac linguist is available yet. And aside from Dr David Schmidt in Eskasoni, no one else is officially working for any reserve at the moment.

Many linguists who were active in the field during the 1970s have, for all intents and purposes, disappeared. Some cannot be traced. The last linguist to be officially working for a band council was laid off a few years ago. Resentment towards linguists varies from one reserve to another, although the reproaches against them are of a type: people feel that linguists have passed through only in order to play with their language and to build their own careers.

The relations between the communities and the Native consultants who were serving both the linguists and the Band offices in the 1970s to 1980s seem to have deteriorated in a similar fashion. Many of them have lost contact with the linguist and resigned from their consulting positions at the Band offices; others have been laid off. In some communities, people who wish to participate in planning the future of their language have expressed the concern that these consultants held too strong a monopoly on issues involving the language and culture.

As for linguistic research, we hear of several linguists working on the language (John Hewson from Memorial University in Newfoundland, Albert D. DeBlois from the Canadian Museum of Civilization in Hull, David Schmidt from University College of Cape Breton, and myself from York University). Hewson is creating a grammar of Nova Scotia Micmac in collaboration with Bernie Francis. Schmidt, in collaboration with Murdena Marshall, recently published a book on Micmac hieroglyphs with a juxtalinear translation in Micmac alphabetic. DeBlois just published a new version of his lexicon, which includes seven thousand words. Yet, all these scholars work in isolation, and there is, so far, no consensus regarding priorities. I recently approached the field as a newcomer, on a Social Sciences and Humanities Research Council grant. The goal of my project was to develop a sociocultural grammar of modern Micmac, based on a collective network of Micmac contributors, that would reflect the actual link between language and culture in these communities. The state of the field, however, was such that it took me three years to create a new sense of partnership between the community members and the linguist. This has now been achieved and it is only now that the real work can begin.

The Situation at the Turn of the Twenty-First Century

If, as reported by Labillois (see above), the Micmac language was still considered intact in 1968, the language situation at the turn of the twenty-first century is much more problematic. Kinkade (1991: 162) speaks of Micmac as 'a viable language with a small population base,' saying that it is 'spoken in well-organized communities with strong self-awareness, and the native language is one of the important marks of identity.' This is perhaps true for one or two reserves in Nova Scotia and New Brunswick, and perhaps also for the official discourse in New Brunswick and Québec. However, if one observes the everyday reality, a huge gap is noticeable between the official discourse and what is actually occurring.

While the Ministry of Education of New Brunswick reports that '[p]arents have expressed concerns regarding language acquisition, retention and maintenance,' Culture and Education directors in each reserve reported to me that very few parents still raise their children to speak Micmac. Many traditional parents do not recognize themselves in the neo-traditional cultural content included in the Micmac curriculum material. This gap between official discourse and general attitudes reminded me of an article about Lebanon in *Courrier International* (228, 26 March 1995), which noted that after so many years of war, '[t]he relation between citizens and public affairs is practically non existent. This lack of interest comes from a generalized feeling of powerlessness.'

Indeed, in Québec, where the biggest efforts in terms of language planning have been made during the past decades, Micmac is bound to disappear after the next generation. As for New Brunswick, the Ministry of Education has recently (1993) put out an impressive Micmac Language Program, with the goal of enhancing teaching efforts and developing a full-fledged language program from K to G12 in the First Nations schools and in the provincial schools where 'significant' numbers of Micmac students are enrolled. It is hard to see when this program will be implemented, however, as Culture and Education directors in each reserve also reported to me that few materials were completed and that teachers felt disorganized, each one isolated in his/her own reserve. This sentiment was also echoed in the newspaper article about Lebanon, whose author adds: 'Behind this opaque screen lays a devastated universe which one can only defend with inflated speeches. Between the reality and what people have in their minds, the gap is total.' (See also Burnaby, this volume.)

Beside this synchronic disarray, there is also a diachronic one. Native people who were actively involved in the past decades have been pushed aside by the new people responsible for language and culture. The shadow of their banishment still has an effect on those who took over, however. When I managed to organize a first meeting for Micmacs now involved in language and culture development only a few weeks before the Americanist Tradition Conference, these Elders managed to get around the fact they had not been invited by the people in power and announced at the last moment that they would join the meeting. On hearing that, a younger teacher, who otherwise showed enthusiasm and leadership in the matter, lowered her voice and said, 'We are all scared and nervous.' And when I asked what they considered their most urgent need, one of the uninvited Elders spoke first and said, 'One thing we don't need any more: linguists! The linguist is gonna want more money again. We don't even get money!' The resentment could not have been expressed any more clearly.

This resentment does not mean that everything our predecessors did was wrong. They accomplished a lot and did what was necessary at a time when the priority of science over practical application was fundamental for the anthropologist. The expressed resentment, however, demonstrates that, in the minds of many Native Elders, the decline of the language is associated with the arrival of linguists.

With respect to this present situation, however, only a small margin of action is left for the linguist of the next generation. Organizing useful research programs that could be conducted in collaboration with communities seems almost unfeasible, because speech communities are disintegrating very quickly. Leaving the communities alone and working in the old style with one or two consultants *is* feasible, though it feels unethical given the dire need for curriculum material originating from and/or reflective of the whole community's input. What remains, between the reactionary discourse of disappointed Elders and the disarray of the teachers, is the collapse of the Micmac language and culture, which the field linguist has done little or nothing to stem.

New Directions in Ethnolinguistic Fieldwork

Because the cultural elite and the people in power in the communities are becoming increasingly desperate in their effort to save the language, I think the linguist still has a role to play. This role, however, is somehow different from that played in the past. New field linguists must be made aware, during their training, that when they approach a field site they cannot merely go and collect data in the traditional Americanist fashion. They need to realize that they will soon find themselves in the position of healers and/or engineers, that is, resource persons who will have to understand where the people come from and work in collaboration with them to help them use their own resources.

The Healer and the Engineer

The healer role demands a good blend of moral strength and sensitivity. As a broad goal, the next generation's linguist, as a healer, must strive to bring the former resource people back to work, to work together and to train future Native linguists.

To bring the former resource people back to work, one must first listen to their grievances; then one must help them to assess their achievements and the possible role they would like to play in a further round of language planning; and, finally one must create the appropriate tools for them to work with, given their assessment. Also, the field linguist must deal with the issue of community acceptance of these individuals and their work.[1]

Sometimes, the linguist has to play the role of a messenger, bridging the work of a marginal contributor with the work of the officials in place. This is a very slow process. First, it requires many visits to each person. Because some people have been in a state of conflict for many years, this work demands that you accept the need to dive into conflictual waters without loosing your bearings. Then it requires a lot of understanding and strength: you must feel what each person feels toward the contentious issues around planning for the language, but not give in to resentment and bitterness. Next, you have to turn into an engineer and examine which type of project could be appropriate for these people. After that you have to find out what would be the appropriate tools to implement the project. And, finally, you have to train people to work with these tools. This means you must be willing to design projects based on community needs rather than on scientific goals, willing to find funding over which you will not be the master, and willing to train people instead of writing papers.

This task takes a good deal of humility and a sense of adventure. It can take one year to understand a resource person's situation, one year to design a project in accordance with his or her specific capacities, another year to get funding, and yet another year to train and help the person resume working. But then, the results can be extraordinarily rewarding. The case of one former consultant who came back to work is striking: with time and understanding, he passed from intellectual depression to making a significant contribution after I understood correctly that he would work again on the language if he could work at home, on a project he had had on his mind for years, and provided he could get a computer and proper training. In six months he entered 4000 words in the computer, on a FileMaker Program, and fleshed out the entries with culturally relevant descriptions. The coming dictionary will be the first Micmac cultural reader made available to a non-academic audience. And because FileMaker can be used in an interactive way, we expect that each community school can use the dictionary as a teaching device to introduce students to a lexicon of their language, along with the relevant lexicographic techniques.

Ideally, one needs to bring back former resource people to work together. This involves another round of delicate intervention – a necessary one, however, because the collectivity seems recurrently to reject data and material produced in isolation by the ethnolinguist and his/her consultant. To encourage people to resume working together, you have to visit all the persons officially in charge in different reserves; understand what their political positions are, without interfering or getting involved; understand what their relations are to previous consultants and to the people in charge in other reserves; and, while remaining neutral, let them understand that you are connected with all these people, and in what ways. You also have to understand, and be sensitive to, the links between these people, the government, and the academic milieu. And, finally, you have to let enough time pass between each visit to give your future partners the opportunity to discuss with one another the relevance and usefulness of your presence and your projects. This too is a very slow process. Once all these steps have been taken, however, if the people in charge agree to collaborate in the project, it will be by choice, and there is a high probability they will commit themselves collectively.

My experience of gathering together a dozen people and discussing the future of Micmac has been extremely rewarding and promising. Although some of them had been in silent conflict with others over the past five or six years, they seemed to be happy to be back together around the same table. On one occasion, we had a full day's meeting of fruitful discussion. The participants agreed to record the entire content of these discussions and to have it transcribed. In such a way we can keep records of the collective planning of the future of the language, and the contribution of each and every participant can always be traced. In those transcripts we can read the same Elder who had said that he did not need any more linguists also saying joyfully, while the participants were chatting at length, 'It shows we don't meet that often; we can't shut up!'

One complaint that is more and more often expressed by Native people is the imposition of the Western frame of mind on the description of their languages. Those of us who have had the chance to participate in Finnish linguistic symposia know and appreciate how some Finnish students in linguistics can comment on linguistic theories with a unique blend of humour and criticism. As non-Indo-European linguists, some Finns are, indeed, probably the best lighthouses on a theoretical shore sprinkled with ethnocentric reefs. Along the same lines, however accurate a linguistic description may be in our positivist terms, it is rarely perceived as satisfying to the Native interpreter if it does not characterize the relation between language and socio-spiritual values. A linguistic description is considered less readable if the writing style does not intertwine both Western scientific features and Native poetic features. The following excerpt, from J.S. Henderson (1993), illustrates the content and the nature of that concern:

> Mi'gmaq reality is structured according to most of the linguistic concepts by which we describe it. The Mi'gmaq language has always been made up of forces (mntu'k) which underlie the perceived world – give rise to it, transcend it, energize it and transform it. All these forces can change their shape, their content; but collectively, they create dignity. The Mi'gmaq language, similar to most Algonquian languages, affirms this view of the world. They are building on verb phrases, that contain the action or motion of the flux, with hundreds of prefixes and suffixes to choose from, to express the panorama of energy and motion. The use of verbs rather than nouny subjects and objects is important: it means that there are very few fixed and rigid separate objects in the Mi'gmaq worldview. What they see is great flux, eternal transformation, and an interconnected space. With this fluidity of phoneme comprising the verb sounds every speaker can create new vocabulary 'on the fly,' custom-tailored to meet the experience of the moment, to express the very finest nuances of meaning.
>
> Experiences are the Mi'gmaq rules of inferences for arriving at a new truth about real-

ity. Experiencing the realms is a personal necessity, an intimate relationship. The process is more than a matter of defining phonemes or phones or words and phrases. Such experiences are focused on helping one to understand the nature and structure of particular realms: how they interchange yet remain related, how their language may create an elegant way of explicating an implicate order composed of very complex systems of relationships.

As represented by the structure of the language, in a connected world, the whole is no longer the whole when it is part of an explanation. A holistic process cannot be explained by first shattering it into its component parts and then assigning local explanations to the segments.

The question is how to get more Native youngsters to become interested in anthropolinguistic studies and, eventually, to take on the linguistic research. Solving this question, too, must be considered the task of the next generation of linguists. Since they are more and more in demand to help in the production of curriculum material, they must think of including in the material some projects that will induce especially talented youngsters to pursue linguistic studies when they grow up.

With this concern in mind, I have designed an elementary and junior high school program that may be an example of such an undertaking: 'The Peewee–Bantam Anthropolinguist.' That funny name points to the fact that, in our North American cultures, small children, from the age of five or six, are trained to become future professional hockey players. Why not apply such a pervasive cultural feature to a science like anthropology? My idea is to use the huge possibilities of our coming FileMaker Micmac dictionary to train young Native children in the abc's of anthropological linguistics. One way to do this is through assignments in language courses, asking them to go back home and collect specific sets of words and short examples from their parents and Elders. Flashcards printed from the dictionary layout would be the physical support for the home part of the assignment. Then, back at school, children would be asked to enter their words in the school version of the Micmac dictionary. The names of word collectors and of word givers would also be included in the dictionary. Later on, as these children grow up and reach junior high, they could be asked to collect small texts and trained to transcribe them, to dig new words out of them, and, in turn, to pass on these words to the younger students in elementary classes.

With such a modest school program, families may get interested and involved in the process, children and young teens may learn how to work in teams (trans- and cross-generational) and develop their talent within these frames, and teachers/counsellors may be better able to identify those who are specially gifted for anthropological linguistic research and mentor them toward university programs. At the same time, it is to be expected that these talented teens would also have been identified as such by their families and the community at large, and thus would already be considered as future professional language engineers in their own community. It is likely then that the community would support and encourage them to continue their training in that direction.

If this approach works, it may also make the language-game flourish again. Those language-games occurred among adults and Elders when the language was in a healthier condition. As in other cultures and linguistic groups, Mi'gmaq mature speakers have traditionally spent hours playing with the language, creating humour based on word creation and word combinations.[2] With the presence of peewee and bantam anthropolinguists as text collectors, something positive may happen in terms of language maintenance.

Conclusion

Theorizing the Other's languages never occurred as a pure and isolated agenda. From the triangular agenda of the first ethno-missionaries, religious-political-ethnographic, to the triangular one of the graduate students of the sixties, description-degree-job, to the triangular agenda of today's linguists, grants-description-publication (not to mention the overpowering triangular agenda of governments, distraction-education-assimilation), the Native communities have remained very patient – so patient that they are more and more in dire need of useful and practical material.

While completing this paper, I am also at the end of a two-year stay, as school principal and curriculum developer, with the Mi'gmaq community of Listuguj. My experience confirms the need for more cooperation between linguistic anthropologists and Mi'gmaq educators. On the one hand, researchers must participate in the education system at its most basic, practical, and dynamic level, that is, the classrooms, school grounds, parent-teacher meetings, etc., if they want to understand the real needs of the community they seek to investigate, and the implications of these needs. On the other hand, Native educators also need some basic linguistic training in order to be able to understand the kind of cooperation they can expect from scholars. They certainly need, as in the mid-seventies, training in morphology, phonology, morphophonology and syntax. However, beyond that, they also need to understand what language planning is, what are its costs and benefits for a linguistic group, and what the ethic of language research and planning is all about. It is equally important that any linguistic training dispensed to Native language teachers be customized to the world-views and the language philosophy of the people being trained. Otherwise, training would be nothing but another assimilating process imposed on Others (see Cyr 1996–7a, b).

Beyond the fact that funding agencies like the SSHRC often still stipulate that research funds should not be used for the development of curriculum material, linguistic anthropologists cannot just keep on crossing the Native universe for scientific purposes. At this crucial moment when so many languages lay on their death beds, theorizing without caring and immediately helping is increasingly damaging. Invoking scientific neutrality to stay out of the action, in my mind, amounts to playing a violin on the upper deck of a sinking Titanic ...

NOTES

1 Thanks to Lisa Valentine and Regna Darnell for this suggestion on community-acceptance issues.

2 Emmanuel Metallic, personal communication, 1994

REFERENCES

Battiste, Marie. 1984. *An Historical Investigation of the Social and Cultural Consequences of Micmac Literacy.* Ann Arbor: Microfilm Dissertations.

Cyr, Danielle. 1996–7a. 'L'intuition de l'enseignant de langue ou la vérité du linguiste?' *Recherches amérindiennes au Québec* 26(3–4): 37–42.

– 1996–7b. 'La lune est notre grand-mère: La notion de vérité comme principe assimilateur.' *Recherches amérindiennes au Québec* 26(3–4): 43–51.

DeBlois, Albert D. 1990. *Micmacs Texts.* Canadian Ethnology Service, Mercury series 117. Ottawa: Canadian Museum of Civilization.

DeBlois, Albert D., and Alphone Metallic. 1984. *Micmac Lexicon.* Ottawa: National Museums of Canada.

Delisle, Gilles, and Emmanuel Metallic. 1978. 'Micmac Teaching Grammar.' Listuguj: unpublished manuscript.

Henderson, James S.Y. 1993. 'Governing the Implicate Order: Self-Government and the Linguistic Development of Aboriginal Communities.' Paper given at the conference *Linguistic Rights in Canada: Collusion or Collisions?* Ottawa, 5 November 1993.

Hewson, John, and Bernie Francis. 1990. *The Micmac Grammar of Father Pacifique.* Winnipeg: Algonquian and Iroquoian Memoirs.

Kinkade, M.D. 1991. 'The Decline of Native Languages in Canada.' In R.H. Robins and E.M. Uhlenbeck, eds, *Endangered Languages.* Oxford: Berg.

Labillois, Romeo. 1996. 'Will the Micmac Survive?' in Jacques Maurais, ed., *Quebec's Aboriginal Languages – History, Planning and Development*, 262–9. Clevedon, Eng.: Multilingual Matters.

Leclercq, Chrestien. 1691 [1910]. *New Relation of Gaspesia.* Trans and ed. William Ganong. Toronto: Champlain Society.

Maillard, Pierre-Antoine. 1758. *An Account of the Customs and Manners of the Micmakis and Maricheets Savage Nations Now Dependent on the Governement of Cape Breton.* London: S. Hooper and A. Morley.

Pacifique de Valigny, Pierre. 1907. *Quelque Traits Caractéristiques de la Tribu des Micmacs*. Québec: Congrès International des Américanistes.

Rand, Silas. 1850. *Micmac Tribe of Indians*. Halifax: James Bowes & Son.

Savard, Rémi. 1972. *Carcajou et le sens du monde: Récits montagnais-naskapi*. Québec: Ministère des Affaires Culturelles, coll. Civilisation du Québec, série Cultures amérindiennes.

18 Nisg̱a'a Studies and the Americanist Tradition: Bringing First Nations Research and Teaching into the Academy

MARGARET SEGUIN ANDERSON
and DEANNA NYCE

One of the most enduring legacies of the Americanist Tradition is the body of texts produced by fluent Native speakers of aboriginal languages working in collaboration with museum-based researchers. The prominence of this part of the tradition receded when the centre of gravity of the discipline shifted from museum-based collection to university-based graduate training. Altered and reduced roles available for fluent Native people to participate in knowledge creation for the academy after the first third of the twentieth century shifted the dynamics between First Nations and Anthropology. As the end of the century nears, however, First Nations are claiming their voices and finding ways to recast the relationship and exercise a direct role in the academy by developing their own discipline(s). Nisg̱a'a Studies is now offered for university credit by the Wilp Wilx̱o'oskwhl Nisg̱a'a in partnership with the University of Northern British Columbia, which opened in August 1994 with First Nations Studies as one of its signature programs. While this represents a notable success in developing a community-based program, the process has highlighted structural barriers in the form of government funding processes as well as predictable resistance to First Nations' exercise of authority within the university's governance and administration. For the Nisg̱a'a, the issue of Nisg̱a'a control of Nisg̱a'a education is fundamental, especially in the fields of language and culture studies. The issue has been framed by all parties in terms of 'accountability.' Despite the difficulties inherent in the project, Nisg̱a'a Studies is a discipline that has a bright future in the academy. Its strength can be linked to a significant strand of the intellectual legacy of the Americanist Tradition, both flowing from and contrasting with earlier configurations of relationships between First Nations and academics.

Both Franz Boas and Edward Sapir, two of the foremost scholars in the Americanist Tradition, studied the language and culture of the Nisg̱a'a people at least briefly, and both published papers based on their research (Boas 1902; Sapir 1915). Their work is valued by Nisga'a people, as are all relatively early published documents on Nisga'a language and culture, but neither of them is a direct intellectual ancestor of the emerging discipline of Nisga'a Studies, a field of First Nations Studies being pioneered through the Wilp Wilxo'oskwhl Nisga'a in partnership with the University of Northern British Columbia. That discipline could only emerge in a context of Nisga'a ownership and control of Nisga'a education within the academy as well as outside it, a situation that is only now developing. A direct antecedent of Nisga'a Studies in the Americanist Tradition is found in the prolific but relatively obscure career of William Beynon. The intellectual affinities between Nisga'a Studies and the Americanist Tradition can be explored through a consideration of Beynon's work during the heyday of the Americanist Tradition, the hiatus in similar work by Native people in this area after his death in 1958, and the contemporary reconnection with the academy through the emergence of the new discipline of Nisga'a Studies.

Regna Darnell (this volume) has identified several features that she argues are distinctive of the Americanist Tradition, including the following: texts, produced by Native speakers in Native languages, are the database for both Americanist ethnography and linguistics; there is an Americanist commitment to preserving the knowledge encoded in oral traditions so that it shall not be lost from the permanent record of human achievement; and Native peoples are not objects to be studied – many of them are actively involved in the process as anthropologists and linguists. Certainly Beynon's career is a prime example of the pattern.

William Beynon

William Beynon (1888–1958) is one of the small group of Native people who collected texts in the Americanist Tradition, working with a number of anthropologists and linguists. The son of a Nisga'a mother and a Welsh father, Beynon was raised in Victoria, British Columbia, and moved to the north coast of Vancouver Island in the second decade of this century. He began his work with anthropologists almost immediately. 'William Beynon, Tsimshian, did ethnography for White anthropologists for over 40 years (1915–1956). Yet he is known to anthropology, and identified in its literature, as an "informant and interpreter"' (Halpin 1976: 141). In her biography of Beynon, Halpin quotes from Marius Barbeau's letter to Sapir, describing Beynon's contribution to his research: 'I am very fortunate in having gotten the services of Wm. Beynon, a very intelligent young half-breed Tsimshian,[1] who proves more useful still in working directly with informants for me. He records myths quite successfully and with good speed. He has them recited in Tsimshian and writes them down in English at once, sentence by sentence. The work could not be done any better if I were working with him. Meanwhile I work with other informants, with another interpreter' (Barbeau/Sapir correspondence as quoted in Halpin). Sapir's replied in the following fashion: 'I am very glad to see that you have found it possible to get your best interpreter to work independently, somewhat in the manner in which Alex Thomas has been working for me among the Nootka. I am sure that this is an excellent method with a really intelligent interpreter. There is, after all, no absolute reason why every bit of material that one utilizes in his work should have been personally obtained ... In other words, one should by no means underestimate the usefulness of an intelligent Native or half-breed in recording materials' (ibid.: 143).

Beynon also worked for Franz Boas, sending materials to him at Columbia University. According to Beynon's biographer:

> The relationship could well have been initiated by Beynon himself, who remained consistently eager for ethnographic work and wrote a number of anthropologists offering his services. He had a copy of Boas' Tsimshian Mythology (1916) and certainly knew of the errors and omissions in it, most assuredly he was aware of what was perhaps Boas' greatest error – his belief that it contained 'the bulk of the important traditions of the Tsimshian' (Boas 1916: 31). In any event, Beynon sent Boas some 252 narratives and ethnographic reports between 1932 and 1939 ... Beynon charged Boas 50 cents an hour for his own services in recording, translating, and rewriting his material, and 35 cents an hour for informant fees. He kept his services to about $50.00 per month at Boas' request. (ibid.: 147–8)

Beynon also collected information for Sapir's research on social organization, and later worked with Viola Garfield, who notes that Beynon was used as 'interpreter as well as informant ... He is conversant with all aspects of pre-White Native culture' (ibid.: 149). Halpin remarks on the conditions of Beynon's work: 'I keep wondering why Beynon did it for all those years. He certainly was not well paid, nor did he achieve what I would consider adequate recognition for his work. Perhaps the only answer is to be found somewhere close to that of Alfonso Ortiz (1972: 7): "Let me begin by stating flatly that I initially went into anthropology because it was the one field in which I could read about and deal with Indians, all of the time and still make a living. It was just that simple"' (Halpin: 152).

Towards the end of his career Beynon undertook to write an ethnogeography of the Tsimshian, under the guidance of Philip Drucker with funding obtained by Drucker for the purpose from the Smithsonian. Beynon's health failed before this work was completed and published, though a substantial manuscript was drafted.[2]

The museum funding base that supported (albeit meagerly) Beynon's lifelong work and monumental achievement was not available to the succeeding generation of Native intellectuals. The structure of how anthropologists worked had shifted over a few decades. Darnell has argued that Boas depended heavily on the interdependence of university instruction and museum funding of field research, but that B.A.E. anthropologists were progressively marginalized by their lack of access to universities where they could train their successors (Darnell this volume); for their Native collaborators the opportunity to train successors was not even a question – the government-sponsored agenda of acculturation and the deliberate suppression of Native languages and cultures made it impossible. These trends had profound implications for the relationship between Anthropology and First Nations. A number of Native people like William Beynon had built their own niches working with museum-based anthropologists, and the new paradigm made it difficult for them to remain active. When Beynon was no longer producing materials that entered the academy through his piecework employment by anthropologists, his mantle was not taken up. Instead, a number of anthropologists and linguists worked with several informants from various communities in the region, but no resources were available to foster a semi-independent scholarship of text collection.

Building the Nisg̲a'a Studies Program

Meanwhile, the threats to Native land and resource rights, suppression of Native cultures and languages, and the residential school systems were being resisted in many places on the continent, and the intellectual energy of the communities was focused on these struggles. One of the eventual results is the current Nisg̲a'a Studies program under the auspices of the Wilp Wilx̲o'oskwhl Nisg̲a'a. But Nisg̲a'a Studies did not just happen – it is part of what had been dreamed about, hoped for, struggled and prepared for by generations of Nisg̲a'a people during the decades of resistance. 'After receiving his teaching diploma in 1950, [Bert McKay, Nisg̲a'a educator] moved to Alert Bay on the northern tip of Vancouver Island where he taught for four years. In 1954 Bert returned to Lak̲alzap, as that community's first college-educated Nisg̲a'a teacher, to work in a tiny, two-room school ... Conditions were so bad, Bert recalls, that he and other members of the newly formed Nisg̲a'a Tribal Council made education their first priority, pressing governments so that "we could control and manage our own education." ... Today, School District 92 (Nisg̲a'a), created in 1977, is the first Native-run [provincial] school district in Canada, a landmark of cross-cultural development' (Nisg̲a'a Tribal Council 1993: 4–5).

There are interesting contrasts between Beynon's career and the work of the Nisg̲a'a faculty of the Wilp Wilx̲o'oskwhl Nisg̲a'a. In order to address this matter, however, it is necessary first to establish several layers of context surrounding the emergence of Nisg̲a'a Studies as a discipline joining the institutional academic tradition, starting with the structure of the post-secondary educational system in Canada and British Columbia.

The educational aspirations of the Nisg̲a'a, and of other First Nations did not end with a school district, even one that they control and in which their languages and cultures can flourish. The Nisg̲a'a in particular had gone through a process to gain control of education for their own people and had identified an ambitious post-secondary program as essential to their development as a nation. In implementing their goals, they have established a post-secondary institution and forged partnerships, including one with a new 'greenfields' university.

The groundwork for the academic discipline of Nisg̲a'a Studies has been built on the intellectual tradition of the Nisg̲a'a from time immemorial and brought into the academy by Nisg̲a'a scholars, working in a Nisg̲a'a institution. Considering the experience of the Nisg̲a'a and the University of Northern British Columbia may shed some light on the legacy of the Americanist Tradition and the First Nations with which it has always been so closely connected. The early flowering of Native intellectuals such as William Beynon, who were significant contributors to the Americanist Tradition, as collectors of Native language texts under the auspices of Franz Boas and others from the end of the nineteenth century through the first half of the twentieth century was followed by the marginalization of such individuals in the post-war period, during which the centre of gravity of anthropology on this continent completed its shift from museums to universities.

There had been sporadic calls for a university located in the Canadian north for years without results. In 1987 a public meeting held at the College of New Caledonia in Prince George, BC, focused on the possibility of extending degree-awarding opportunities in Prince George; a series of meetings followed, and by the fall of 1987 the Interior University Society was incorporated. During 1989, at the tail end of the mandate of the provincial Social Credit government, events allowed northern community leaders to act – in particular, unfortunate foot-in-the-mouth comments by the Minister of Advanced Education: 'In the interior ... people don't think of education beyond grade twelve. The questions they ask at the end of the day are "How many trees did you cut today?" or "How were things down in the mine?"' (Stan Hagen, Minister of Advanced Education, Training and Technology for British Columbia, *Globe and Mail*, 2 October 1989). Hagen's comments generated 3000 letters of protest to the government and led to a quick cabinet shuffle in which a member of the Legislative Assembly for the Prince George area became the new Minister of Advanced Education.

Perhaps having seen the light, or perhaps merely mindful that the 16,000 petition-signers were enough to swing the results of several constituencies, the Social Credit government voted to establish the new University of Northern British Columbia in June 1990, and by January 1991 the first president was in place. Twenty staff members were appointed in 1991, and the first academic plan was published.

The first version of the university's academic structure had First Nations Studies as one of the signature areas of the University of Northern British Columbia. The only constraint on the program was the concern of the President to avoid having First Nations Studies become 'ghettoized.' The University of Northern British Columbia was officially opened in August 1994 by Queen Elizabeth II, and the first regular classes began that September. Courses had actually begun during the two QuickStart years prior to the university's official opening, and First Nations Studies was among the initial offerings.[3]

The University of Northern British Columbia's BA and MA programs in First Nations Studies were the first such degrees in Canada. Other initiatives in the area of First Nations post-secondary education in British Columbia in the 1980s included the En'owkin Centre, the Nicola Valley Institute of Technology, the First Nations House of Learning at the University of British Columbia, and the Secwepemc Centre at Kamloops, which in 1993 established a minor in First Nations Studies through Simon Fraser University. The structure of the Secwepemc program was an important model for the University of Northern British Columbia's major in the discipline.

Through correspondence, meetings, consultations, and discussions with First Nations leaders and representatives, the process moved towards drafting courses and requirements to implement goals such as the following in the curriculum for the program:

- To bring First Nations' knowledge into the University with respect.
- To establish the point of view of First Nations people as the starting point for description and analysis, and to contextualize issues from this perspective.
- To acknowledge the stewardship of the First Nations of Northern British Columbia over their languages and cultures, and to work with them to create a context for the development of the highest level of scholarship in these fields.
- To ensure that the discipline of First Nations Studies at University of Northern British Columbia would remain open to continuing re-formation of ques-

tions, research methodologies, and teaching styles appropriate within First Nations contexts.

These goals could only be achieved in collaboration with First Nations, and by July of 1992 the discussions with the First Nations began in earnest when the university's newly elected Chancellor, Iona Campagnolo, toured part of the north with the President, Vice-President (Academic), and other new-to-Northern British Columbia administrators firmly in tow. Their visit to the Nass Valley was a pivotal moment in the university's history. The gist of the meeting seems to have been that the Nisg̲a'a graciously welcomed UNBC party to their territory, and then politely pointed out that the government seemed somehow to have erroneously given the university $2 million towards the delivery of post-secondary education for Nisg̲a'a people, and since delivery of such education was properly the role of the Nisg̲a'a, if the university would send the cheque there would be no hard feelings! This was, of course, the opening gambit in negotiations to establish a relationship between the university and the Wilp Wilx̲o'oskwhl Nisg̲a'a, the post-secondary educational body in the process of being established under the authority of the Nisg̲a'a Tribal Council.

Post-secondary education is not a new phenomenon for the Nisg̲a'a. Lifelong education has always been a part of the educational philosophy of Nisg̲a'a people. At community gatherings speakers often say that 'education is a way of life that begins at birth and ends at death.' There have been post-secondary educational courses in the Nass Valley for approximately twenty-five years, beginning with Department of Indian Affairs–sponsored workshops for community health representatives and for Nisg̲a'a housewives on nutrition skills. Change began with the formation of School District 92 under Nisg̲a'a control. The local board and administrators were Nisg̲a'a, and were directly accountable to the annual tribal conventions. In the land-claims statement the Nisg̲a'a Tribal Council established the goal of grooming Nisg̲a'a people for self-government, and an active campaign began to train people to implement the treaty that was being negotiated. Twenty years later, Nisg̲a'a people work in the valley and beyond with BA, BSc, BEd, LLB, MA, and MEd degrees. The first courses delivered locally were First Aid training, trades and technology offerings, and English and Psychology courses from Northwest Community College in 1976 and 1977.

The Nisg̲a'a Industry Adjustment Committee began discussions with numerous post-secondary institutions, including Northwest Community College, which serves the Nass Valley as part of its mandated area. Efforts were made to establish programs to train nurses and foresters (both with limited success). Under the auspices of the Nisg̲a'a Tribal Council, a needs study was conducted in 1988. Among its findings was the necessity to create an institution in order to provide on-going meaningful education programs. Negotiations with the University of Northern British Columbia began in mid-1992.

By January 1993 a preliminary agreement had been developed in which the university committed to consider the Wilp Wilx̱o'oskwhl in its planning and when this proposal was endorsed by the Interim Governing Council, the negotiations for a protocol proceeded. Deanna Nyce was hired away from her position as District Principal to become CEO in August 1993, and at the tribal assembly that fall Nisg̱a'a Economic Enterprises, Inc. presented a cheque for $100,000 to facilitate the move towards an incorporated institution. A four-pronged, client-driven plan was outlined to fulfil the mandate to bring high-quality education to adults in the valley: academic programs included a BA in Nisg̱a'a Studies, eventually expanding to include natural-resources programs to facilitate Nisg̱a'a management of resources in their territories; technical programs; vocational programs; and continuing community education (workshops).

The negotiating sessions to develop the protocol were generally lengthy (two to three days) and there were many missteps as we tried to find a way to work with a community in partnership instead of in a relationship of patron and client. By the time we had developed the interim agreement, the negotiators had realized that developing community-based programs to foster scholarship that built on local knowledge, such as we envisioned, would be the best, and possibly only, way to create a program in First Nations Studies that might actualize the principles we had aimed for, as affirmed in the agreement. In this particular case, the best way to develop the program within the university was to 'clear a space' in which scholarship and teaching could be developed on the basis of principles and practices appropriate to each of the intellectual traditions of the First Nations of this region.[4]

'Clearing a space' entails establishing an environment in which the lived experiences of First Nations people are the assumed norm and where a discourse can flourish that simultaneously is academic and allows the questions asked, the form of the discourse, and the values of the participants to be oriented to First Nations people. Within an institution that is so pervasively shaped by layers of Western assumptions and traditions as a university is, establishing and maintaining this orientation is a huge challenge that requires a critical mass of committed First Nations staff members and students as well as support and goodwill throughout the institution. Within an institution set in a First Nations community, however, the process is more natural, flowing from the "normalcy" of the First Nations–centred discourse in that context. In such a context, the identification of the questions, methods, perspectives, and approaches appropriate to First Nations Studies as a discipline emerges not as a contestation of the norms of the academy but as a grounded practice with its own intellectual trajectories.

Perhaps surprisingly, the smoothest phase of the negotiations with the Wilp Wilxo'oskwhl Nisga'a was over curriculum. The university's program in First Nations Studies had been written to be implemented in different ways as appropriate to local First Nations contexts, and despite having to re-present the case from time to time as new administrators and faculty joined the university, both sides became comfortable with that flexible approach fairly early on.

By November 1993 objectives had been defined for the programs to be offered in the Nass Valley. These included viability (sufficient resources to provide full functions); sustainability (being able to recruit a continuing cohort of students and to bring students in for institutes, etc., if required); goal-focused development (with Nisga'a Studies as the centrepiece, in a student-centred, flexible program); and accountability for excellence (measuring performance against goals in all areas). Most significantly, the Wilp Wilxo'oskwhl Nisga'a offer a First Nations Studies program that is genuinely guided and developed by the First Nation. Because the Nisga'a were not compelled to infuse Western thought or values into the process, the academy was enriched with a new perspective that brought high academic standards and a unique way of understanding the world – they are able to formulate their own questions and seek their own ways of finding answers, adapting and adding methods to their repertoire as needed. From this ground the Nisga'a were eager to engage in dialogue with scholars from other perspectives, and the Wilp Wilxo'oskwhl Nisga'a welcomed several UNBC faculty members to teach in the valley during the inaugural year.[5]

While the formation of the University of Northern British Columbia has been marked by successes in developing community-based programs – with the agreement with the Wilp Wilxo'oskwhl Nisga'a being the most notable – the process has highlighted major structural barriers in the form of government funding processes as well as predictable resistance to 'outside' control by First Nations communities within the university's governance and administration. The issue has been framed by all parties in terms of 'accountability.'

In contrast to the relative smoothness of negotiations on academic issues, the sessions in which the discussion focused on the control and movement of money were more frustrating, the primary reason being the structures for university funding, which are an impediment to First Nations such as the Nisga'a who are seeking to exercise ownership and control over post-secondary education. Provincial funding for programs is always under the control of a non–First Nations university or college, is generally 'soft' and short-term project based (rather than having the core commitments necessary to permit confident long-term planning), and the educational administrative infrastructure needed to exercise First Nations control is necessarily a duplication of the structures of the 'parent' university or college, and thus sometimes perceived as a costly and unnecessary 'extra.' For example, the courses needed for the instruction of the Nisga'a students during the first year of their program could have been delivered by the University of Northern British Columbia much less expensively than they were by the Nisga'a, but if this had been done, the Nisga'a planning, hiring, supervision, and support would not have been in place – the arrangement would have been the UNBC-on-the-Nass rather than Nisga'a Studies in partnership with the University of Northern British Columbia.

The Nisga'a were obliged to work with a provincially accredited post-secondary institution because they could not otherwise offer accredited courses and programs. Since the province does not directly fund or accredit First Nations post-secondary institutions, each one must affiliate with a college and/or university for program accreditation, and is funded either on a program basis by external 'soft' money or on a 'flow-through' of provincial funds transmitted first to the university or college (and accounted back to the Ministry by that university or college), or through some combination of these and other smaller funding programs. Such arrangements are almost always based on the cost of instruction, and allow little for overhead or the institutional infrastructure of the First Nations institutions. This relationship is difficult enough when the university or college is long established and the arrangement has evolved over time. However, the University of Northern British Columbia was a new institution when the partnership was being established, and its own funding arrangements were irregular. While most university funding is based on a formula in which the number of full-time equivalent (FTE) students is the major factor, the University of Northern British Columbia was funded with a block grant to build towards a future level of about 2500 FTEs in recognition of the fact that faculty and infrastructure had to be in place before students could be recruited. Unfortunately, no funds for the partnership with the Wilp Wilxo'oskwhl were put into the draft budgets prepared in the months during which the university waited to find out how much the provincial government would provide for the 1994–5 academic year.

During December of 1994 a delegation from the Nisga'a made a presentation to the university board convincing it to change the one-year commitment into a continuing one. It seems unlikely, however, given looming cutbacks in federal transfer funding to the provinces, that the University of Northern British Columbia can provide funding for the increased capacity that the Nisga'a aspire to in the near future. Given the structures in which we work, the Nisga'a have little recourse but to seek external soft funding for their plans. The

Nisga'a have negotiated provisions for their institution in their treaty, and the province has developed a post-secondary framework agreement for aboriginal institutions. It may be that on the eve of the twenty-first century the neo-colonialist structures will at last be updated and the universities will be able to shed the role of funding agency and all that carries with it.[6]

The most basic contradiction confronted in developing the relationship between the Nisga'a and the university was the latter's attempt to be both partner and funder. When the university is doubly empowered in this fashion, partnerships that offer benefits for both universities and First Nations run the risk of being distorted, turning from relationships of equals to those of hierarchical domination. If the money flow is one-way, ownership and control tend to be one-way as well. If the province treated First Nations as equals and provided them with direct funding, it would remove that contradiction, and the University of Northern British Columbia and other universities could join them as partners with great enthusiasm. Despite the range of post-secondary systems in Canada, the 'yellow brick road' of funding follows the same basic path across the country, with only a few exceptions.[7]

Nisga'a Studies and the Americanist Tradition

By the middle of the century, the Boasian model of university-based academic instruction (especially graduate instruction), with museum support for research and fieldwork for faculty and graduate students, was well established. Darnell (this volume) has noted the significance for the discipline of Anthropology of Boas's commitment to professionalization through graduate education. The new paradigm also impacted the process of text collection. In fact, the shift to universities as the centre of gravity of the discipline shifted the focus of research away from that of documentation, as it was when centred in museums, to that of building a training ground for the next generation of university-based academics. This shift in emphasis reconfigured the relationship to Native people – as each department and each scholarly generation needed to establish a unique identity. The emphasis on collection of the raw documentation often marked only a brief early phase of academic careers, and those who maintained long-term links to their Native informants sometimes became marginalized in favour of 'theory-builders' who reworked materials in the successive frameworks of functionalism, structuralism, cultural ecology, and eventually postmodern perspectives. Similarly, whereas in museum-based anthropology there had been a niche for Native people who submitted texts over long periods, university-based anthropology increasingly spent the bulk of the available research money on sending academics to the communities for their fieldwork and training. These neophytes often did not develop long-term relationships with the community, and little was available to sustain the efforts of Native intellectuals who did not join the academy.[8] There were few resources to train the next generation of Native scholars to work within the Native traditions, and those traditions were under assault by legislation and residential schooling; those Native scholars who did join the academy were often directed into work very similar to that of their cohort. It was assumed that they would have better access to information, but that their studies should otherwise be like those of their classmates. The primacy of the scholarly discourse of the university tradition was not questioned, and there was not yet a space cleared for other discourses and other questions to emerge. Assumptions that First Nations cultures were static and that the data of interest for modelling in anthropology and linguistics had been collected a generation earlier from informants who had precontact knowledge also shaped the changing discipline.

By the late 1950s there were few Native people who continued the sort of work that Beynon and others of his generation had done. During the middle of the twentieth century there were remarkably few members of any indigenous group engaged in the discourse with Anthropology in any fashion but as informants, and while there were many long-term relationships – such as those described by Dick Preston and Jane Hill in this volume – the contributions from these were mediated even more completely as they entered academic discourse by the academic collaborators than were those of the earlier generation.

Beynon worked from a complex perspective; Halpin argued that he was able to encompass both the cultures he studied as a member and the culture of the investigators with whom he collaborated. But while he became a respected expert on the cultures he studied, he never entered the academy directly; the questions that he sought to answer were the questions posed by his academic employers. The scholars with whom Beynon and his generation worked had little reason to bring them into the academy, as their value was their expertise in the Native world. Later in the century, the goal of many anthropologists and linguists became to bring Native students into the academy, and to shift their perspectives, at least insofar as they would seek answers to the same sorts of questions as their non-Native colleagues and use the same sorts of methods in doing so.

The 1950s saw the emergence of another group of Native intellectuals, people who bridged the chasm between cultures in other ways. One such person is Bert McKay, a Nisg̲a'a educator who has been among the founders of Nisg̲a'a Studies. McKay developed his own scholarly perspective and substance from the Nisg̲a'a experience of seeking nationhood, working over forty years in the development of the knowledge and institutions needed by the Nation; his contributions are primarily oral, and his work does not emphasize the innovations contributed by an individual, but rather the codification of the collective knowledge of the Nation. His intellectual discourse with colleagues in the communities is direct, at Nisga'a events such as feasts, deliberations over the formulation of the Ayuukhl Nisga'a, and meetings of the Annual Convention of the Nisga'a Tribal Council (the 1997 meeting was the fortieth annual gathering). McKay's speeches are scrutinized by members of the public at events such as these. Many of his contributions are oral, though he has also been active in documenting himself and others by recording and archiving their speeches and memoirs. His appointment by the Wilp Wilxo'oskwhl as acting director for language and culture studies institutionalized the local integrity of those programs. His role has been to bring the oral tradition into the academy, where it continues to grow and to be shaped by the staff and students at the Nisga'a Nation into written and multimedia form for transmission to future students.[9]

So while it is true that many texts have been produced by Native speakers in Native languages, the thread of continuity between the early practitioners of text production and their contemporary counterparts is tenuous. There are texts in Nisga'a, for example, spoken by Native people and written down by Boas and Sapir, but the bulk of the text record was produced directly by Native speakers, of whom William Beynon was the most prolific and interesting example. Beynon was hired by museum-based anthropologists to produce texts, often being paid piecework by the page. He worked over decades sending texts to Franz Boas, and to Marius Barbeau. He also worked with several of Boas's students, including Amelia Sussman and Viola Garfield. By the time of their fieldwork, however, the role of Native speakers producing texts in Native languages had become marginalized in the discipline. The work of the university-based scholars-in-training such as Garfield had moved to the centre of the stage. As Jane Hill (this volume) notes: 'An extraordinarily large proportion of "field method" consists in producing layer after layer of text, each layer oriented toward the next. The earliest, most informal, least prestigious layer is the principal moment in which an actual dialogic relationship with a Native speaker takes place; the final, most prestigious layers are notoriously in technical language, oriented toward the community of scholars who are not speakers ... [E]ach layer of text is suffused with its own moral significance, and links the scholar to large systems of power and both literal and metaphorical "authority."' The texts produced by Native speakers in Native languages are often that first, least prestigious layer referred to by Hill above. For one of the most eminent practitioners of the Americanist Tradition, however, that first layer was the best: 'I'm not particularly interested in "smoothed-over" versions of Native culture. I like the stuff in the raw, as felt and dictated by the Natives ... the genuine, difficult, confusing, primary sources. There must be presented, whatever else is done ... There are too many glib monographs, most of which time will show to be highly subjective performances' (Sapir to Cole, cited in Darnell, this volume).

Sapir might have been interested in Nisga'a Studies, drawing directly as it does on the raw resources of Nisga'a collective knowledge as it continues to grow and change. The development of the field has reinvigorated the discourse between the Nisga'a and the academy. A number of scholars have begun work in the Nass Valley in association with the Nisga'a Studies program.[10] Just as the work of Nisga'a scholars such as Bert McKay is subjected to scrutiny and critiques by Nisga'a experts in the oral tradition, the work of visiting scholars is presented to the community through Wilp Wilxo'oskwhl Nation, and the results of this scrutiny are expected to have an impact, just as the colleagial discourse does for any academic. This is a major breakthrough for scholarship in the valley, as for many years there was scant welcome for academics[11] owing to the widespread view among Nisga'a people that their culture had been misrepresented by anthropologists, and that they had little impact on what was written about them and no recourse from published errors. Looking forward, the Nisga'a are hoping for partnerships with the academy in an array of fields, and are confident that they are now on solid institutional ground. It is perhaps a fitting capstone to this account to note that Bert Mckay received an honorary doctorate at the first graduation ceremony at the University of Northern British Columbia.

NOTES

1 William Beynon's mother was of Nisga'a descent, but the family's links were to the Port Simpson Tsimshian community; furthermore, at the time that this correspondence was written, it was usual to refer to the Gitksan and Nisga'a as Tsimshian.

2 Margaret Anderson is currently working on an edited draft of this manuscript for publication as 'William Beynon's Ethnical Geography of the Tsimshian.'

3 Margaret Seguin Anderson joined the University of Northern British Columbia in the spring of 1992 as a Professor of First Nations Studies and Chair of that program, as well as Coordinator of First Nations Programs (this administrative role was subsequently retitled Director of First Nations Programs). On January 1994, after Alison McDonald was appointed Director of First Nations Programs, Anderson moved to Prince Rupert as Regional Coordinator, continuing as chair of the Program until July 1994, when Jim McDonald (no relation to Alison) took over as acting chair. Language and/or culture courses were taught with several First Nations as partners: Carrier (with the Yinka Dene Language Institute), Nisga'a (Wilp Wilxo'oskwhl Nisga'a), Haisla (Kitamaat Village), and Tsimshian (Tsimshian Tribal Council). The Wilp Wilxo'oskwhl Nisga'a identified members of their communities who were accepted as faculty members by the program in First Nations Studies, teaching in the joint program: Bert McKay (Nisga'a Culture), and Audrey McKay and Allison Nyce (Nisga'a Language). Their experience as educators, educational administrators, and Nisga'a language teachers, in the Bilingual-Bicultural program of

the School District, and as advisers and participants in Nisga'a clan and tribal activities were all relevant to their appointments. In 1997 a revised structure was approved by the board of governors, in which the interdisciplinary themes were not highlighted, but First Nations Studies retained its place.

4 The University of Northern British Columbia negotiation group always included Margaret Seguin Anderson (Director of First Nations Programs) and Dennis Macknak (Director of Regional Operations and University/College Relations). The Vice-President (Academic), Ken Coates, sometimes participated, as did University of Northern British Columbia's President, Geoffrey R. Weller. On two occasions the staff member in First Nations Studies, Ruby Baptiste, joined us at the table as part of her professional development.

5 The planning and implementation has been done by committees comprising the founders of the discipline of Nisga'a Studies (or at least those who have brought this tradition into the academy): the committees included Personnel, Facilities, Finance, and Negotiation. The Nisga'a language committee included Audrey Mckay, Verna Williams, and Rosie Robinson, all of whom had experience as Nisga'a language teachers since 1976; they were joined by Allison Nyce, who had graduated from the Nisga'a program offered by the school district with honours and had completed a degree in Anthropology at the University of British Columbia. This group was able to draw on work on the language done by linguists such as Bruce Rigsby, who had worked with Nisga'a elders such as Father Canon Hubert McMillan; Marie Lucie Tarpent's work with the school district as a linguist provided her doctoral dissertation work as well as locally valued research. Haj Ross spent 1993–4 at the UNBC and was much appreciated in delivering workshops for the language committee. In the field of culture the development of the curriculum was led by Bert McKay; that group was able to draw on the resources from the long-term project to codify the Ayuukhl Nisga'a (laws of the Nisga'a), doctoral research of Steven McNeary, and speeches by such Nisga'a leaders as James Gosnell, whose important speech 'Lock, Stock and Barrel' is a rallying cry for Nisga'a in its firm assertion of their ownership of their land. These groups rose to the challenge to produce a tremendous amount of work in a short period of time. While consultants such as John Corsiglia assisted in parts of the process, it was crucial both that it was completely planned and driven by the Nisga'a and that the authority of the Nisga'a was acknowledged by the academics at the university.

6 Nisga'a Economic Enterprises has assisted with a donation of $250,000 towards endowing the program, and the UNBC Development Office is helping to identify matching funds from foundations before the university submits the donation for a provincial matching-funds program. It is hoped the total endowment from this gift will reach $1,000,000.

7 Even exceptional cases are not exemplary. Saskatchewan Federated Indian College, which is largely funded by a special ISSP grant, is a dependent institution under the University of Regina and the School of Northern Studies at the University of Alberta offers very limited programs. Ontario's New Democratic Party government created new targeted funding to facilitate the emergence of a number of new partnerships, but with a change to a Tory government that effort was cut back drastically in the 'last in / first out' syndrome.

8 With some notable exceptions, including Sapir, who brought Alex Thomas to New Haven.

9 Some of the material collected by McKay and his intellectual predecessors and mentors such as Eli Gosnell has been used in four Ayuukhl Nisga'a volumes used as texts in culture courses: Nisga'a Origins, Nisga'a Clan Histories, Nisga'a Society, and The Land and Resources: Traditional Nisga'a Systems of Land Use and Ownership.

10 Since the 1994 inauguration of the academic program, in which several UNBC faculty such as Emmon Bach taught beside their Nisga'a colleagues in the valley, the WWN have hosted a number of researchers: John Barker of the University of British Columbia (studying missionar-

ies in the valley), Marie-Lucie Tarpent of Mount Saint Vincent University (continuing her work on the language), Mary-Ellen Kelm, a UNBC post-doctoral fellow and faculty member (studying the history of health-care delivery in the valley), Kiwako Okuma, a graduate student at the University of Northern British Columbia (researching her MA in the area of education as a tool in decolonization), and Fumiko Sasama (studying Nisga'a language while undertaking PhD research).

11 Some individuals did work during the decades just before to the establishment of the WWN, either under the sponsorship of Nisga'a institutions or in very informal relationships with individuals; the latter gradually became unacceptable as universities grappled with ethical issues involved in fieldwork with cultures other than one's own. See the Social Sciences and Humanities Research Council of Canada guidelines on ethics for funded research from about 1980 onward for examples of the shift.

REFERENCES

Boas, Franz. 1902. *Tsimshian Texts* [*Nass River Dialect*]. Bureau of American Ethnology Bulletin 27. Washington.

Halpin, Marjorie. 1976. 'William Beynon, Ethnographer: Tsimshian, 1888–1958.' In *American Indian Intellectuals*, 140–56. Proceedings of the American Ethnological Society, Robert F. Spencer, general editor, New York: West Publishing.

Nisga'a Tribal Council. 1993. *People of the Nass River*. Vancouver: Douglas & McIntyre.

Sapir, Edward. 1915. *A Sketch of the Social Organization of the Nass River Indians*. Anthropological Series 7. Ottawa: Geological Survey Bulletin 19.

19 Policy on Aboriginal Languages in Canada: Notes on Status Planning

BARBARA BURNABY

This paper addresses two themes in this volume on the Americanist Tradition. First, Americanist scholarship has resulted in a great deal of work in corpus planning (focused on making language materials available) and development of Aboriginal languages in the Americas. Several such undertakings are described in this book. As a complement to this work, I am offering some notes on status planning (focused on the political status of languages in a state) rather than corpus planning for Aboriginal languages in Canada. Second, some of the papers in this volume analyse the Americanist legacy from current politically oriented academic perspectives. Since status planning for languages is inherently a political process, I have included discussion of the role of academics, Americanist or not, in the development of policy on Aboriginal languages in Canada.

The paper begins with some background on Canada and its history, followed by a section on the history of policies related to Aboriginal peoples in Canada and to their languages in particular. In this section are comments on exemplar (but not necessarily exemplary) figures who have contributed to Aboriginal policy development in the respective eras. Finally, conclusions are drawn about Canada's record on Aboriginal language policies in the world context and about future directions for academics in the field of Aboriginal languages and cultures.

Background on Canada

At the time of initial European contact with northern North America, Aboriginal people in what is now Canada spoke an estimated 450 languages and dialects belonging to eleven different language families (Office of the Commissioner of Official Languages 1992: xiii). The Aboriginal population of

Canada circa 1500 is estimated to have been about 200,000, but by 1900 it had declined to about 100,000 (Hawthorn 1967: 2) because of factors such as new diseases and displacement. Immigration first from Great Britain and France, then from northern Europe, and finally involving many other groups has resulted in an ethnically and linguistically complex population of which Aboriginal peoples in Canada, even though their numbers have rebounded, are now only a small portion.

In 1991, 28% of the population reported having British-only origins, 23% French-only, and 31% neither British nor French. People reporting Aboriginal-only origins numbered 470,615 individuals, or less than 2% of the total population (Statistics Canada 1993a: 1). In terms of mother-tongue speakers of various languages, English claims 63% of the population, French 25%, other languages (neither English, French, nor Aboriginal) 13%, and Aboriginal languages less than 1%. In a special census of people reporting Aboriginal identity in 1991, 36% of adults and 21% of children said that they could speak an Aboriginal language well enough to carry on a conversation; an additional 6% of adults said that they used to be able to speak an Aboriginal language but cannot now (Statistics Canada 1993b: ix). These figures represent a major change from, for example, 1951, when 87% of those reporting Aboriginal ethnicity said that they had an Aboriginal language as their mother tongue (Burnaby and Beaujot 1986: 36). Despite problems with the accuracy of census figures, the trend away from the maintenance of Aboriginal language use among Aboriginal peoples in Canada is very clear.

Canada is a federal parliamentary democracy created in 1867 by an act of the British parliament called the British North America Act. It has ten provinces that cover the south of the country, and two territories north of the 60th parallel that are under direct federal jurisdiction but have gradually developed legislatures of their own. One of these, the Northwest Territories, is the only unit that has a majority Aboriginal population. In 1982, the federal government 'patriated' the constitution by passing the Constitution Act, which superseded the British North America Act, largely retaining the provisions of the latter and adding a Canadian Charter of Rights and Freedoms. For present purposes it is important to note that both the 1867 and 1982 acts divided legislative responsibilities so that, among many other things, the federal government deals with Aboriginal affairs while the provinces deal with education.

General Policy on Aboriginal Languages and Peoples, and Related Policies

In this section, an outline is provided of policies that directly relate to Aboriginal peoples and their languages in Canada or that strongly influence the way in which they were treated by governments. For each era, exemplars are given of people who affected policy, explicit or implicit, at the time.

Before Confederation in 1867

Phillipson (1992) describes the language attitudes and practices of the British and French colonial empires worldwide as 'linguicist' (in line with 'racist' and 'sexist'): 'The hegemony of the dominant colonial languages was buttressed by a linguicist ideology in both empires. Whereas the French more actively propagated a discourse of linguistic supremacy, the British, though apparently more pragmatic and *laissez-faire*, had a fundamentally similar attitude to the virtues of English and failings of other languages' (115).

Early colonial governments in what is now Canada dealt with Aboriginal issues through the military until about 1830, when civilian agencies took over. Colonial powers assumed that Aboriginal people were going to either die out or assimilate with the rest of the population. Aboriginal people were thought to need protection (and thus were increasingly confined to reserves of land) and 'advancement' through education and Christianization (Patterson 1972: 107–44). Governments and Christian mission societies since the seventeeth century provided schooling for and proselytized various Aboriginal groups (Burnaby 1980: 34–6; Tschantz 1980: 3ff.; Kirkness 1992: 7). Schooling was seen by authorities in most parts of the British empire as the way to 'civilize' indigenous peoples, and English as the medium. However, especially among missionaries, there was clearly conflict between the task of propagating Christianity effectively and teaching English as a primary goal (Phillipson 1992: 115). Tschantz (1980: 3ff.) gives examples of the use of Aboriginal languages in education and Christianization efforts in Canada, but cites many competing cases where only English was permitted. Outside of formal schooling, she notes, the Hudson's Bay Company in 1828 stated the policy that HBC factors should speak to their Aboriginal 'wives' and children in English or French and teach them literacy and catechism in one of those languages (Tschantz 1980: 3–4). In general, the use of English or French was seen by the colonizers as a major mark of civilization and the capacity to participate in civil society. The ability to speak, read, and write either English or French was the third qualification (after being male and over the age of twenty-one) for an Indian to be enfranchised and 'no longer be deemed an Indian within the meaning thereof' in an 1857 act of the combined colonies of Upper and Lower Canada 'To Encourage the Gradual Civilization of the Indian Tribes of this Province' (Canada, 20 Victoria, c.26, s.15 as quoted in Tschantz 1980: 12–13).

An exemplar of the kind of figure that influenced Aboriginal language policy during this period was Egerton Ryerson, although the impact of his views and actions were not to be fully realized until the time period discussed next. He was a Methodist who served as Superintendent of Education in Upper Canada and then Ontario from 1844 to 1876. In no small measure, his leadership created the system of largely secular, publically controlled and financed, compulsory, and universal education that exists for most Canadians today, with a curriculum and approach to teaching and learning that lasted into the 1950s (Brehaut 1984). In the early nineteenth century, education for Aboriginal peoples was about as scattered, haphazard, and non-egalitarian as it was for the lower classes of the rest of the population. In 1847, Ryerson published a report that reinforced the Legislative Assembly of Upper Canada's recommendation that industrial residential schools be adopted for the education of Aboriginal children. The core was to be 'a plain English education adapted to the working farmer and mechanic' (cited in Tschantz 1980: 6), but the daily schedule proposed for pupils in these schools meant that more time was spent on work on the school farm, the upkeep of the school residence, or in trades than in academic pursuits (ibid.). This model, which was used also for children of some other marginalized groups, persisted for Aboriginal pupils, but not necessarily for others, well into living memory. By the first third of the twentieth century, only Aboriginal children were educated under this system.

Ryerson is an exemplar of those influential in Aboriginal language policy in this period in that, as a figure who powerfully affected education, he contributed strongly to the life experiences of generations of Aboriginal youth through institutions that increasingly compelled their attendance and prohibited them from using Aboriginal languages between age six and the mid-teens. In the virtual absence of other policies on Aboriginal languages, education policy was of central importance.

Confederation to the 1940s

At Confederation in 1867, the British North America Act explicitly divided governing powers between the federal government and the provinces. The federal government was given jurisdiction over 'Indians' and Indian lands (s.91 (24)), while the provinces got jurisdiction over education (s.93). The effect of this division was that the education of Aboriginal peoples was, and is, the only educational jurisdiction the federal government officially has.

In 1876, the first Indian Act was passed federally. It defined who was an 'Indian' under the act. Over subsequent years, Indian bands were identified (largely through treaties with Aboriginal groups) and individuals assigned status hereditarily under the act. The Métis and Inuit were excluded, as were

Indian women who married non-Indian men (and their children), although non-Indian women who married Indian men got status (as did their children). There were also clauses whereby Indians could renounce their status, that is, become 'enfranchised.' The result over decades was that a considerable number of people with Aboriginal ancestry have not been covered under the act.

The act originally mentioned the provision of schools as buildings, but over time an elaborate set of statements on federal responsibility for education of 'Indians' evolved (ss.114–23). Also, all of the treaties signed since the original act have mentioned provisions for maintaining schools (MacPherson 1991: 7). Since the federal government otherwise had no responsibilities for education, it was not interested in developing its own system of education just for Indians. Thus, it discharged its responsibilities by granting funds to Christian organizations to carry out this duty, a relationship pursued until the 1950s. As noted above, over the years the form of education changed from basic literacy and numeracy in day schools on reserves to an industrial or agricultural model of residential schools, often far from the children's homes. Such forms of education reached more and more remote areas and became effectively compulsory by some time in the first half of the twentieth century, depending on the location. Current literature on the history of Aboriginal education emphasizes that children were kept away from their parents, often for years, that English was the only language permitted not only in the classroom but in the schoolyards and the dormitories, and that children were often severely punished for speaking an Aboriginal language (Burnaby 1980: 36–40; Tschantz 1980: 6–13; Kirkness 1992: 7, 10–12; MacPherson 1991: 2; and others). Precise policies about the use of language in education for Aboriginal children differed according to the organizations providing it.

The exemplar suggested here for influence on Aboriginal language policy is Edward Sapir. Although he had little documented effect on educational or other policies that impacted on administrations affecting life in Aboriginal communities in Canada, his status as ethnologist with the federal government indicates strongly the general administrative and public priorities applied to Aboriginal languages. While Ryerson's successors were working to ensure that Aboriginal children spoke English, Sapir's position in Canada was created to document Aboriginal languages as an object of study.

Sapir was the first Chief Ethnologist of the Anthropological Division of the Geological Survey of Canada, part of the Department of Mines, from 1910 to 1925. The Indian Affairs Branch, which then administered the Indian Act, was also part of the Department of Mines, suggesting an association between Aboriginal peoples and the hinterland. It was Sapir's job to conduct 'a thorough and scientific investigation of the Native races of Canada, their distribution, languages, cultures, etc., etc., and to collect and preserve the same' (correspondence from R.W. Brock to Sapir 1910, cited in Darnell 1990: 42). Sapir's perspective on the task was as follows: 'The Canadian government is to be congratulated on having established a systematic survey of aboriginal Canada. Now or never is the time in which to collect from the Natives what is still available for study. In some cases, a tribe has already practically given up its aboriginal culture and what can be obtained is merely that which the older men will remember and care to impart. With the increasing material prosperity and industrial development of Canada the demoralization or civilization of the Indians will be going on at an ever increasing rate ... What is lost now will never be recovered' (Sapir 1911, cited in Darnell, 1990: 51).

It appears that both Sapir's and the Canadian government's understanding was that the Aboriginal languages and cultures were doomed and that it was a valuable use of Canadian government funds to document them while they still existed. Without Sapir's passion for working with Canadian Aboriginal languages, rather than focusing on collecting artefacts from their material cultures as he was pressed to do by his employers, our current knowledge of Aboriginal languages in Canada would have been much the poorer. Darnell (1990: 55–60) also describes various efforts he made on behalf of Aboriginal people he worked with to improve their social conditions, to remove legislative restrictions placed on cultural practices such as potlatch ceremonies on the West Coast, and to get artefacts, culturally valuable to Aboriginal groups, returned from mainstream collections. However, his employment and interests directed him mainly to documentary pursuits rather than to activities that might have influenced the preservation of Aboriginal languages as living languages among communities of speakers. Indeed, his efforts to professionalize the study of anthropology and of Aboriginal languages probably had more social impact later on the actual use and development of Aboriginal languages in their communities than did his own work at the time.

1940s to 1970s

In the 1940s a parliamentary committee revised the Indian Act to assimilate the Indian population into generic government services rather than to isolate them through special treatment. The federal government began to make agreements with provincial governments to educate Aboriginal children who came from easily accessible reserves. Aboriginal schools were run on remote reserves directly by the federal government, and adhered to appropriate provincial curricula and standards for teacher qualification. At that time, provincial curricula permitted no languages other than English or French to be the medium of instruction, and although exceptions in Indian schools could have been permitted, they rarely were. This policy of provincially provided education (in English or French) was implemented to the extent that more than half of the Aboriginal elementary-school population was attending provincial schools by the 1960s, but not very successfully (Hawthorn 1967: 7); the federal government still had to get involved directly with Aboriginal education in remote areas. Also, it should be noted that all status Indians first received the vote in federal elections in 1960.

H.B. Hawthorn, a Canadian anthropologist, and others were commissioned in 1964 to write the extensive report, which bears his name, on Indians. The fact that this report was initiated by the Department of Citizenship and Immigration links a new federal interest in the national labour force with the increasingly complex immigrant and Aboriginal populations. The authors recommended that Indians be treated as other citizens but with special consideration for their unique needs. English-as-a-second-language methods, such as those beginning to be used with the many new immigrants, were suggested for Aboriginal children who did not speak English, but into the late 1970s there was no great evidence of this recommendation being implemented (Burnaby, Nichols, and Toohey 1980). Regarding policies on Aboriginal languages, the report states: 'The government's policy on the preservation of the Indian languages is ambiguous. It would appear that there is a general unwillingness to make open statements on this subject. However, the lack of attention in the courses of study would seem to indicate rather clearly that the Indian languages might be allowed to disappear and be replaced by either English or French (in Quebec)' (Hawthorn 1967: 37).

In the meantime, Canada was receiving large numbers of new immigrants who did not speak English or French, so their linguistic needs were demanding attention. Also, francophones in Quebec in the 1950s started the Quiet Revolution to demand real implementation of the linguistic equality they had perfunctorily been given in the British North America Act and in the governance of Quebec (Office of the Commissioner of Official Languages 1992: v–vii). In 1963, the federal government created the Royal Commission on Bilingualism and Biculturalism to study linguistic and cultural issues extensively in Canada. While most non-English and non-French groups were considered, 'Indians and Eskimos' were excluded in the term of reference of the commission since they were perceived not to form part of the 'founding races' (English and French) nor to constitute 'other ethnic groups.' 'Other bodies' (presumably Indian Affairs and Northern Development) were supposed to be responsible for indigenous peoples' issues (Royal Commission on Bilingualism and Biculturalism 1967: xxvi–xxvii).

The main result of the royal commission was the Official Languages Act (1968–9), which made English and French Canada's official languages. As a result of this act, French has taken on a major role in federal services; government-supported education of francophone children in French and anglophone children in French as a second language has expanded exponentially (Peat Marwick et al. 1987). Also, the role of French as the official language of Quebec was asserted in a wide range of ways, including outside of schooling and the civil service (Office of the Commissioner of Official Languages 1992).

In this climate of powerful French demands and increasing immigration, the assimilationist approach to Aboriginal affairs culminated in 1969 in the white paper of the Minister of Indian Affairs to Parliament, which proposed an end to the Indian Act on the grounds that it was racist. Aboriginal reaction to the white paper was swift in asserting that Aboriginal peoples did not want to give up their special relationship with the federal government; however, they also condemned past policies on residential schools and tuition agreements with provincial school boards, and called for fresh approaches with Aboriginal people in control. The most effective response to the white paper was *Indian Control of Indian Education*, a policy document issued in 1972 by the National Indian Brotherhood, at that time the relatively new national body speaking for Aboriginal, or at least status Indian, issues. This document insists that Indian parents should have control over and responsibility for the education of their children, and that Indian children should be educated in such a way as to enhance their self-esteem as Indian people as well as to develop their ability to make a good living in Canadian society. It goes on to reinforce the need for Indian children to get a good grounding in their ancestral language as a central factor in their identity development. Finally, it urges that the federal government retain fiscal responsibility for Indian education. The federal government accepted *Indian Control* as its policy several months after it was written, although its implementation has taken a long time.

When the white paper on Indian affairs was tabled in 1969, the main opposition to it came largely from status Indians through the relatively new national organization the National Indian Brotherhood. But, since the topic of the racist nature of the Indian Act had been raised, the other groups of people of Aboriginal ancestry – non-status Indians, Métis, and Inuit – began to form political organizations and demand Aboriginal rights along with status Indians. Therefore, four national Aboriginal organizations representing each of these groups were formed. The term 'Native' was adopted in the 1970s to refer to members of all of these groups.

As a result of backlash against the Official Languages Act from non-English, non-French groups, the prime minister in 1971 declared the country to be multicultural by policy as well as officially bilingual. This policy (which became legislation in 1988) has provided token support for non-official languages over the years, but Aboriginal groups have generally rejected its support on the grounds that their needs should be met separately by the federal government under its constitutional responsibility to them.

In the 1970s, the teaching of Aboriginal languages as a subject of instruction began in a number of federal schools and provincial schools with tuition agreements for the education of Aboriginal children. Training for Aboriginal language instructors was started in several centres. There were a few experiments (usually short-lived) in using Aboriginal languages as the medium of instruction either for children who already spoke the language or for those who did not (on the model of French immersion programs for anglophone children that were becoming very popular as a result of the Official Languages Act [Lambert and Tucker 1972]). Provincial governments began to create policy on Aboriginal education, at least partly because they were beginning to recognize the needs of those Aboriginal peoples who were not covered under the Indian Act. The Department of Indian Affairs made moves to transfer some federal school administrative powers to local education committees and to train Aboriginal people to administer education, and there were various struggles concerning the representation of Aboriginal parents on school boards in which there were tuition agreements with the federal government.

The exemplar chosen for this period of Canadian policy on Aboriginal languages is H.B. Hawthorn, the principal author of the Hawthorn Report. As an anthropologist he can be considered the kind of professional that Sapir set his sights on creating at the beginning of the century. Hawthorn notes that 'it is imperative that Indians be enabled to make meaningful choices between desirable alternatives' (1967: 5) and that education is the key to many such alternatives. However, he says:

> An alternative chosen by some people, who are now a large majority and will certainly be in large number for at least the near future, is to live on the reserve even if they work elsewhere. The reserve is the place of birth, of family, of friendships, of one's language and of most of the values one shares with others. To the extent that is allowed by its setting within a modern nation, those who own the reserve wish to direct its affairs.
>
> ... But schooling that is not accompanied or even preceded by some improvement in adult achievement is likely to be ineffective ... That is to say that the injunction implied above and so often given to the child as the foundation of schooling: learn now in order to become worthy and receive benefits later, is partly self-defeating, in this instance at least. Indians must receive some wider responsibilities and a fuller place in Canadian life now in order that learning can have enough meaning for their children. The child at

school needs to see while he learns that an Indian can do other things besides logging, trapping, fishing or small farming. (ibid.: 5–6)

It is clear that Hawthorn was still working in the climate of opinion that influenced Ryerson and Sapir, namely, that Aboriginal languages and cultures must inevitably give way to the forces of the new society that European immigrants brought to North America with them. However, Hawthorn made a great deal of the dilemma faced by Aboriginal people in making the transition to this society. He recognized the importance of power sources in traditional cultures, but notes that, in the face of the mainstream culture's focus on money as the basis of power, 'we emphasize the goal of power because nearly all Indians are concerned about their dependency and powerlessness, and demand an increase in their autonomy and self-reliance' (10). With this perspective, Hawthorn leads the way from total Eurocentric directions on Aboriginal language policy in education and elsewhere to a direction that includes Aboriginal viewpoints. It foreshadows *Indian Control of Indian Education* and later demands for Aboriginal sovereignty. However, language plays a minor part in Hawthorne's work, which emphasizes more the need for better teaching of English than the importance of a role for Aboriginal languages in education. The status of Aboriginal languages is not otherwise considered.

Beginning in the 1960s and 1970s, academics like Hawthorn began to be involved in Aboriginal affairs, not just as linguists and anthropologists with Aboriginal people as their object of study, but as people with specialized knowledge who could contribute to new developments in Aboriginal education and other areas of Aboriginal life. Activities such as Aboriginal-language curriculum development, teacher training, community development, and communications, among others, were taken up by academics with the intention of direct application of findings as well as scholarship.

1980s and 1990s

Since the early 1980s, Aboriginal efforts to secure policy decisions in their favour have mirrored the central political issue of the country, the struggle by Quebec for control of its sovereignty in Canada or outside it. Many francophones have turned from the language debate, which they have largely won, to the gaining of sovereignty itself. Aboriginal leaders have also mainly turned from the language and educational demands of the 1970s to the more global ones of the 1980s and 1990s of getting Canada to recognize them on a government-to-government basis and to entrench their rights to a land base. The term 'Aboriginal' began to replace 'Native' with the same reference to all people of

Aboriginal ancestry. As Aboriginal responses to federal structures developed, a central point was that the English and French did not deserve the title of 'founding nations' that they had given themselves in the linguistic and cultural debates of the 1960s. Aboriginal people insisted that their governments and social structures, which existed before European contact, took precedence. Thus, they now frequently call themselves First Nations and the National Indian Brotherhood evolved into the Assembly of First Nations.

Canadian politics since the early 1980s have been driven by divisive debates over the constitution and the role of Quebec in it. Aboriginal peoples have been very active in these matters, but since Aboriginal language issues have been sidelined in favour of land and jurisdiction matters, they will be treated only briefly here. When the Constitution Act was being discussed in the late 1970s and early 1980s, Aboriginal leaders demanded and were refused official inclusion in the talks. The act mentioned Aboriginal people effectively only to say that nothing in the act should 'abrogate or derogate' from existing Aboriginal rights and freedoms (s.25). However, the rights of francophones and anglophones to mother-tongue education were strongly entrenched.

Quebec did not sign the Constitution Act when it was passed in 1982, thus accelerating the French-English crisis in the country. In the two major efforts to get Quebec into the constitution (the Meech Lake Accord and the Charlottetown Accord, both of which failed) and in the four first ministers' conferences on Aboriginal affairs that came out of the provisions of the Constitution Act, Aboriginal leaders gained a higher profile for Aboriginal issues and greater inclusion in decision-making talks (Cairns 1991; Boldt 1993). Thus, at the present time, the Aboriginal peoples have gained a considerable foothold on the federal agenda. However, very little of this ground has been consolidated in concrete legislation or programs. In the mid-1980s, attempts by the Department of Indian Affairs to create an Aboriginal language policy failed (Shkilnyk 1986; Phillips 1985), as did various proposals to create an Aboriginal language institute.

It would appear that language issues have been almost totally submerged under the weight of constitutional and land-based matters. However, in its 1988 policy document on Aboriginal education, the Assembly of First Nations states that

> Aboriginal languages deserve official status within Canada, constitutional recognition, and accompanying legislative protection. The federal government is obligated to provide adequate resources to First Nations to ensure the development of language structures; curriculum materials; First Nations language teachers; resource centres; and immersion programs. Aboriginal language instruction is necessary from pre-school to post-

> secondary and adult education. First Nations support and protect the status of aboriginal languages as primary languages in many First Nations communities.
>
> First Nations have developed aboriginal language policies. These policies must be acknowledged and implemented in all schools serving First Nations students. (Assembly of First Nations 1988: 16)

The language of this statement reflects Aboriginal leaders' preoccupation with English and French Canadians' constitutional models, but at least the Aboriginal language issue is being kept alive.

In terms of education and language, the current situation is that 8.7 per cent of Aboriginal children attended federal schools in 1990–1, 47.3 per cent provincial schools, and 44 per cent band controlled schools (MacPherson 1991: 8). MacPherson (10–12) criticizes the federal government's policy on band-controlled schools for simply devolving on Aboriginal people the administration of federal programs for education rather than giving them jurisdictional control (see also Paquette 1986).

Two recent studies, by Kirkness (1992) of provincial schools and by the Assembly of First Nations (1990) of schools on reserves, both indicate that while Aboriginal languages are frequently taught as a subject of instruction in schools where there is a high enrolment of Aboriginal students, these programs are usually in the lower grades only (seldom beyond grade 3, much less in high school or adult education) and only for a small proportion of the school schedule. Rarely are Aboriginal languages used as the medium of instruction. Respondents in the Assembly of First Nations study were critical of the effectiveness of the programs and expressed the wish to have Aboriginal languages taught in all grades and with the status that French has in the curriculum (35). It also notes that '[w]here Aboriginal language is the primary language of instruction the goal is one of transition to the official language rather than maintenance of the mother tongue' (33), and '[t]he fact that First Nations languages are not used in most of the communities surveyed effectively negates efforts of language personnel' (37). The Kirkness book provides a useful overview of Aboriginal language policies and programs in all the provinces and territories (chap. 5). Overall, although there are many more Aboriginal language programs available now than there were in 1980, these data give the same impression as Clarke and MacKenzie got in their 1980 study of Aboriginal language programs, namely that such programs pay only lip-service to pluralist approaches and are actually assimilationist in intent.

One further situation is important to this discussion. The two territories are directly under federal jurisdiction although both have evolved their own legislatures. The language of government has been, until recently, English only. However, after the Constitution Act of 1982, the federal government anticipated a court challenge under the Charter that would have forced it to make French an official language of both territories. Strong protests arose locally resulting in separate agreements between the federal government and the Yukon and Northwest Territories. In the Northwest Territories in 1984, French was included with English as an official language, but so were seven Aboriginal languages (Inuktitut, Cree, and five Dene languages). The Yukon avoided making any language official, but agreed to make services available in English, French, and the Aboriginal languages of the territory (most of them Dene languages). The federal government allotted funds for the implementation of these provisions.

Fettes (1998) draws a powerful comparison between the approaches of the two territories. He indicates how the Northwest Territories has taken a symbolic, top-down approach, much like the effect of the Official Languages Act of Canada, with considerable expenditure on administration and services in Aboriginal languages that are little used or appreciated by speakers of Aboriginal languages in the NWT, and a minimum of control by or consultation with individual communities. He points out that the Dene languages in particular are small in their population base, functionally very different from English or French, and at various levels of risk in terms of maintenance or even survival. Therefore, the model of the Official Languages Act is a poor one for promoting their interests or meeting their needs. By contrast, the Yukon has taken a more consultative approach, developing permissive rather than restrictive policies, and encouraging community language development in the home and community rather than just in the school or government services. It supports local initiatives rather than dictating umbrella policy.

The exemplars chosen for this period are the former Assembly of First Nations' Grand Chief, Ovide Mercredi, and James MacPherson. Both are lawyers engaged in the intense discussions around the Aboriginal role in the constitution. Although legal matters around sovereignty and jurisdiction dominate in their work, Aboriginal language at least gets a mention. The teaching of Aboriginal languages in schools and the recognition of these languages in ways similar to those of the official languages are called for, but MacPherson also suggests the consideration of a community-based approach such as that of the Kohango Reo in New Zealand (1991: 44). Macpherson (1991: 12) criticizes Aboriginal education as: (1) confused in jurisdiction; (2) 'skeletal, incremental and, in many respects, lacking coherently articulated foundations or premises' with respect to federal policy; and (3) lacking a 'meaningful role *at a formal level* (including, perhaps, a constitutional level) for Indians in their own system' (emphasis in original). Aboriginal language policy, even more neglected than education policy, still suffers from the same problems.

In this era, academics, including Aboriginal academics, from many disciplines have become involved in Aboriginal issues for applied as well as theoretical purposes. Many have contracts with Aboriginal organizations to prepare reports with political agendas. Perhaps most characteristic of this time period, some have appeared as expert witnesses in court proceedings on matters of Aboriginal rights since the Charter has opened up the possibility of court challenges to legislation and policy.

Conclusions

Canada does not have a record to be proud of in terms of the way it has dealt with its Aboriginal languages. Indeed, it has neglected them and promoted English and French to an extent that supports the allegation of deliberate linguicide. There is no consolation in the fact that Canada is not alone in its treatment of the languages of its Aboriginal peoples. Churchill, in his 1986 study of the education of linguistic and cultural minorities in the Organization for Economic Co-operation and Development (OECD) countries, concludes that indigenous peoples in general have been treated much less well than the other minority groups in terms of respect for and support of their languages and cultures. 'The problems of indigenous peoples stand out as the most difficult and intractable faced by education today. Priority should be given to the study of their needs, placing emphasis on their own role in defining the needs. The tendency to deal with indigenous cultures in education as if their cultural base did not often depend upon a different language or upon a different register of the majority language raises serious issues requiring study. The relationship between language needs, indigenous cultures, and current schooling is very poorly known' (Churchill 1986: 164–5).

The concepts presented in this paper should not be new to academics involved in the study of Aboriginal languages and cultures in North America, although the details of the history of the policies may not be so well known. However, it is hoped that the emphasis on the role that we academics and other non-Aboriginal leaders have played may provoke some thoughts about our responsibilities towards the language and cultures from which we gain our livelihood. As people with specialized training in the structures and dynamics of human interaction, we have both power and privilege. In my view, we should be using that craft to undertake and promote the training of interested Aboriginal people so that they can provide leadership in the decisions that so urgently need to be taken. If, in the process, we can add to theoretical knowledge about the ways in which languages are structured and operate, so much the better, but we should also keep in mind that our training and experience are culture-bound.

Thus, we have a great deal to learn from our students even as we teach them what we know.

REFERENCES

Assembly of First Nations. 1988. *Tradition and Education: Towards a Vision of Our Future: A Declaration of First Nations Jurisdiction over Education*. Summerstown, Ont.: Assembly of First Nations.

– 1990. *Towards Linguistic Justice for First Nations*. Ottawa: Education Secretariat, Assembly of First Nations.

Boldt, M. 1993. *Surviving as Indians: The Challenge of Self-Government*. Toronto: University of Toronto Press.

Brehaut, W. 1984. 'Trends in the History of Ontario Education.' In H. Oliver, M. Holmes, and I. Winchester, eds, *The House That Ryerson Built: Essays in Education to Mark Ontario's Bicentennial*, 7–17. Toronto: OISE Press.

Burnaby, B. 1980. *Languages and Their Roles in Educating Native Children*. Toronto: OISE Press.

Burnaby, B., and R. Beaujot, 1986. *The Use of Aboriginal Languages in Canada: An Analysis of 1981 Census Data*. Ottawa: Department of the Secretary of State.

Burnaby, B., J. Nichols, and K. Toohey. 1980. *Northern Native Languages Project: Final Report*. Sioux Lookout, Ont.: Northern Nishnawbe Education Council.

Cairns, A. 1991. 'The Charter, Interest Groups, Executive Federalism, and Constitutional Reform.' In D.E. Smith, P. MacKinnon, and J.C. Courtney, eds, *After Meech Lake: Lessons for the Future*, 13–31. Saskatoon: Fifth House Publishers.

Churchill, S. 1986. *The Education of Linguistic and Cultural Minorities in OECD Countries*. Clevedon, Eng.: Multilingual Matters.

Clarke, S., and M. MacKenzie. 1980. 'Education in the Mother Tongue: Tokenism versus Cultural Autonomy in Canadian Indian Schools.' *Canadian Journal of Anthropology* 1(2): 205–17.

Darnell, R. 1990. *Edward Sapir: Linguist, Anthropologist, Humanist*. Berkley: University of California Press.

Fettes, M. 1998. 'Life on the Edge: Canada's Aboriginal Languages under Official Bilingualism.' In T. Ricento and B. Burnaby, eds, *Language and Politics in the United States and Canada: Myths and Realities*, 117–49. Mahwah, NJ: Lawrence Erlbaum Associates.

Hawthorn, H.B. 1967. *A Survey of the Contemporary Indians of Canada: Economic Political and Educational Needs and Policies*. Volume 2. Ottawa: Indian Affairs Branch..

Kirkness, V.J. 1992. *First Nations and Schools: Triumphs and Struggles*. Toronto: Canadian Education Association.

Lambert, W.E., and G.R. Tucker. 1972. *Bilingual Education of Children: The St. Lambert Experiment*. Rowley, MA: Newbury House.

MacPherson, J.C. 1991. *MacPherson Report on Tradition and Education: Towards a Vision of Our Future*. Ottawa: Indian Affairs and Northern Development.

National Indian Brotherhood. 1972. *Indian Control of Indian Education*. Ottawa: National Indian Brotherhood.

Office of the Commissioner of Official Languages. 1992. *Our Two Official Languages Over Time*. Revised edition. Ottawa: Office of the Commissioner of Official Languages.

Paquette, J. 1986. *Aboriginal Self-Government and Education in Canada*, Background Paper number 10, Aboriginal Peoples and Constitutional Reform. Kingston, Ont.: Institute of Intergovernmental Relations, Queen's University.

Patterson, E.P. 1972. *The Canadian Indian: A History Since 1500*. Don Mills, Ont.: Collier-Macmillan Canada.

Peat Marwick & Partners and Stacy Churchill. 1987. *Evaluation of the Official Languages in Education Program: Final Report*. Ottawa: Peat Marwick & Partners.

Phillips, S. 1985. *Aboriginal Languages in Canada: A Research Report*. Ottawa: Department of the Secretary of State.

Phillipson, R. 1992. *Linguistic Imperialism*. Oxford: Oxford University Press.

Royal Commission on Bilingualism and Biculturalism. 1967. *Report of the Royal Commission on Bilingualism and Biculturalism: General Introduction and Book I, The Official Languages*. Ottawa: The Queen's Printer.

Shkilnyk, A. 1986. 'Canada's Aboriginal Languages: An Overview of Current Activities in Language Retention.' Unpublished discussion paper. Ottawa: Department of the Secretary of State.

Statistics Canada. 1992. *Mother Tongue: The Nation*. Catalogue number 93-316. Ottawa: Statistics Canada.

– 1993a. *Ethnic Origin: The Nation*. Catalogue number 93–315. Ottawa: Statistics Canada.

– 1993b. *Language, Tradition, Health, Lifestyle and Social Issues*. Catalogue number 89-533, Post Censal Surveys Program. Ottawa: Statistics Canada.

Task Force on Aboriginal Languages. 1986. *The Report of the Task Force on Aboriginal Languages*. Yellowknife, NWT: Government of the Northwest Territories.

Tschantz, L. 1980. *Native Languages and Government Policies: An Historical Examination*. London, Ont.: Centre for Research and Teaching of Canadian Native Languages, University of Western Ontario.

20 'Interpersonal Relations' in a Kalapalo Shaman's Narrative

ELLEN B. BASSO

In this paper, I will be thinking through some ideas about the individual and culture originally offered to Americanist anthropology by Edward Sapir. My interest is in their utility for understanding some biographical practices in a central Brazilian community, the Carib-speaking Kalapalo. Also, I have come to see how these ideas – avoided by the culture and personality school that followed Sapir – can be reconsidered with value to contribute to more contemporary interests and questions, especially concerning psychology and language in American discourse. Ultimately, they bear on the question of culture itself.

I begin with a puzzling judgment made by Franz Boas. He, of course, when writing of mythological themes, focused almost exclusively upon historical issues of dissemination and assimilation – though not on how stories were actually told and accepted. Boas was looking for ways to understand the complex processes by means of which people integrated new themes into their storytelling practices. He aimed to show how these traditions might in turn be transformed by such historical processes.

In his essay 'Mythology and Folk-Tales of the North American Indians' Boas oriented his discussion of mythic history and function to a classification of themes. He characterized what he called North American 'human tales' as lacking the personification of individuals. These people seemed in his view to be hardly more than schematic (usually unnamed) emotional types ([1914]: 478). This remarkable statement may have had much to do with how Boas and his students collected stories. Perhaps it may well accord with Boas's interest in historical processes involving thematic changes in stories. His impersonal emphasis becomes curious because we usually understand Boas to have been strongly interested in the role of the individual in culture.

As is well known, the influence of the individual's role in culture was a central concern of Edward Sapir. The interaction of distinct personality types, and their influence on the thought and action of a community (Sapir [1938]), occupied Sapir's interest over a considerable period of time, and (stimulated by his association with Harry Stack Sullivan) became a central theoretical question for him, a direction taken from Boas's concern with how activities of the individual influence and even modify the forms of their society (Boas [1914]: 285). Like Boas, Sapir treated culture as a historical phenomenon, but, unlike Boas, he was drawn to understanding culture through the study of individuals influencing the dynamic conditions of change (Sapir [1934]).

While Sapir's original interest in the problem seems to have developed through his relationship with Paul Radin, and was first articulated in written form in response to Kroeber's idea of the superorganic (Darnell 1990: 146), Sapir's friendship with the psychiatrist Harry Stack Sullivan was particularly crucial for influencing his development of these questions. Sullivan's idea of 'interpersonal relations' is a concept that turns up repeatedly in Sapir's later writings. Nonetheless, this concept (like much of Sapir's later interests) was not elaborated in the subsequent development of culture and personality. The Sullivanian idea of the 'interpersonal' is not concerned with delimiting a psychological category or object, but is rather a developmental and language-focused idea. For Sullivan, the interpersonal is a context and a process that involves communication of one's experience. A person's information about the world of others develops in turn. Thus, a fundamental characteristic of interpersonal relations is personality processes.[1] This seems to have offered to Sapir a satisfactory language for thinking about the effects of individuals on each other as processes with historical implications. In his lectures at Yale, Sapir argued that Sullivan's idea of 'interpersonal relations' filled a gap between the 'psychological approach,' which treated individuals as isolated units, and the 'sociological approach,' which involved thinking through abstract social categories and lists of cultural traits. 'Culture' here is what emerges through interpersonal activity, rather than being 'transmitted' en bloc from one generation to another (Sapir 1994: 204).

On Sapir's part, Sullivan's 'fundamentally commonsensical and humanistic type of discourse'[2] might have provided the impetus for a far more complete program for understanding the psychology of the group (which, he wrote, 'must rest on the psychology of specific personal relations' ([1932a]: 363) without the twin burden of speculative ethnocentricity. The notion of 'interpersonal relations' offered to Sapir a way of looking at how (as he wrote in his encyclopedia article 'Group') 'different sorts of personalities enter into significant relations with each other and ... a more complete knowledge of the importance to be attached to directly purposive as contrasted with symbolic motives in human interaction' (ibid.: 363). In his more famous essay on 'Cultural Anthropology and Psychiatry' published the same year, Sapir insisted in a Sullivanesque way that '[t]he true locus of culture is in the interactions of specific individuals and, on the subjective side, in the world of meanings which each one of these individuals may unconsciously abstract for himself from his participation in these interactions' ([1932b]: 515). This 'world of meanings' coincides with Sullivan's way of understanding parataxis processes in interpersonal relations.

After Sapir's death, his much earlier 'configurationalist' models became far more important to anthropologists who survived him than these later concerns of his with interpersonal processes. While Radin and others were advocating the life-history approach and made a good deal of mythology, these particular insights of Sapir (evidence of his determination to study culture in transition) were never taken into the study of either Native American mythology or biography. The biographical interests of Radin and of the later 'culture and personality' school seem to have treated individuals in stories more as Boas did. Their explanations made use of schematic typological characteristics or else they were treated (particularly if they were human) as somehow representative of their culture. Anthropologists of the next generation came to understand such stories from the perspective of themes and characters – elements of configurations or patterns. Sapir's emphasis on the dynamics of change and individual creativity was left aside.

A Shaman's Story

I would like to suggest that in central Brazil people have taken an approach to this Sullivanian idea of interpersonal relations that I like to think would have appealed very much to Sapir's own way of thinking. In 1981, while residing in the Kalapalo settlement called Aifa, Kambe, a shaman (*fuati*) and senior hereditary leader (*anetu*), told me a story that for many years remained one of the more difficult for me to understand. This is a story one may legitimately call biographical, though not (we will see) in any European sense. It is also a story that is concerned with 'changes' in culture or, more exactly, with the introduction of some new and different forms of collective action; I imagine Boas would have found it especially interesting. Kambe named his story 'Posa,' after its chief personage, a shaman of that name. At first hearing it seemed to me to share a number of interests with other narratives: a shaman's friendship with powerful beings and animals (jaguars in this particular story), and the ceremonial knowledge the shaman brought back to his people from the world of powerful beings underwater. However, Posa's role as a curer who helped those beings on one particular occasion was unusual. Also, Posa is an exceptional human figure in Kalapalo stories, because he is repeatedly described (particularly after Kambe talks about something quite extraordinary he did with powerful beings) as 'the brother of powerful beings' (*itseke*), and once, when he described Posa curing them, as 'one of their grandfathers.' By 'brother' Kambe is asking me to consider a kind of friend who constantly validates these powerful beings (even when he disagrees with their goals); by 'grandfather' he has in mind a person who brings knowledge of transformation to them. While Posa has learned from these powerful beings (particularly ceremonial knowledge), the powerful beings benefit as well, from the fact that he is a human being curing them, not one of their own curers. If we were to think of the story following Boas's 1914 line of reasoning about mythic origins that emphasizes how activities of the individual influence and even modify the forms of their society, we might not find it too difficult to imagine how it might have been constructed from the narratives the shaman Posa told about himself, stories other people heard from him of his relationships with those powerful beings. As an instance of social memory, as a kind of Kalapalo biographical sketch, the narrative can seem fairly straightforward.

There are, though, two other central figures in this story. One is a bowmaster (*tafaku oto*) named Matëga who is inclined to hunt monkeys in the forest. The other is a Jaguar who mistakenly goes after the bowmaster thinking he is his enemy. In the story, the bowmaster seriously wounds this Jaguar. Posa's story becomes particularly intriguing at this point in Kambe's narrative, because it becomes so closely entwined with the encounter between man and jaguar deep in the forest. This narrative intertwining leads me to think of the story from the perspective of the other characters, that is, more comprehensively. This way, it appears not only as something that Posa might have told about himself, but as a narrative in which his tellings emerged in a kind of dialogue – interpersonally – with stories Matëga told people about his near escape from the Jaguar's attack.

Let's look first a bit more closely at the narrative to see how this works. Because of space constraints I will summarize events and most conversations in a schematic way, but should point out that they emerge in Kambe's discourse as a series of parallel events – simultaneous though occurring in different places, the separate worlds of human beings and of jaguars.

(a) Matëga suggests to the men of the settlement they go hunt for something to eat.

'Children, children, children, you who follow me,' Matëga called out to them.
  'Let's go look for some animals,
    let's go look for some animals.'
  'All right,' they answered.
That's how they answered Matëga the bowmaster.

Matëga, who was a bowmaster.
He was huge, a huge man.
That's what he was like.
'Where shall we go?' they asked him.
'To the forest, far away over in that direction.'

(b) A Jaguar, looking for his human 'enemy' (*imïtongoi*) comes to Posa. Seeing the men preparing themselves for the hunt, he asks Posa where Matëga is going. Posa tells him, but cautions him that this is the bowmaster, and that he isn't going to hunt 'any of your kind. He's going to find something to eat when the sun goes down.' The Jaguar does not listen carefully, and follows Matëga to the forest.

(c) Matëga, moving through the forest alone while the other men walk on together in a group, comes upon a troop of monkeys, and begins to shoot them.

(d) Finding that he has only one arrow left, a round-tipped kind that is used to stun birds perched in a tree, and hoping to kill a very large monkey, he redesigns it into a far more lethal one with a sharp point that can be shot at a moving target and which will penetrate flesh. After killing this monkey, Matëga places the game on each end of his bow and around his neck, and so laden goes to drink from a nearly creek (named and located near a certain settlement).

(e) The Jaguar and a companion travel through the forest, following Matëga's trail. They move above him, through the trees, so that when they are positioned to jump on him, he is unable to see them. The Jaguar jumps, but not before he argues with his companion, who warns him that Matëga is not his real enemy, but someone else, a bowmaster. Afraid of Matëga, the companion remains in the tree. Here is Kambe portraying the two Jaguars:

'Here he is!,' the Jaguar said.
'Here he is!' the other one answered.
'Here he is!' the other Jaguar said.
'Isn't that him?
That's him, isn't it?' the first one said.
'No. It isn't him that's the bowmaster.
The bowmaster.'
'No it's not. That's him.
That's the one we want.'
'You're wrong.
You're wrong, that man's the bowmaster. You're wrong, that's got to be the bowmaster.
I'm not going after him, I'm not.

I'm not going to try and catch him, I won't.
  That's the bowmaster there!'

(f) Matëga's companions return home before him and begin to cook their game. They ask each other why the bowmaster has not returned, deciding 'he was held up because he found so many monkeys.'

(g) Matëga takes the redesigned arrow and fixing it into his bow aims it at the Jaguar as he runs away. He shoots the arrow and it penetrates the Jaguar through his midsection. The Jaguar runs away while his companion follows.

(h) Back in the settlement, the sun is setting and the men ask themselves again why Matëga has not returned. 'Perhaps,' they say, 'he could not find any monkeys, so he's coming back slowly.' Just then, they see him entering the settlement burdened by all the monkeys he has shot. He calls to them, and they answer in greeting. Posa asks Matëga what happened, and he tells of the jaguar attack. Posa is startled, remembering his earlier conversation, and says to himself, 'I told that Jaguar, "he is the bowmaster."'

(i) Matëga resumes his role of hunt sponsor, bringing out hot manioc soup for the men to drink, and over several days distributing the pool of smoked monkeys donated by all the hunters. This is mentioned not only for completion of the hunt sequence but as an event that parallels the next occurrence so as to suggest simultaneity.

(j) The Jaguar, screaming in pain, is helped back to his settlement by his companion.

'Look. I'm sure I told you,' he said to him.
  'I know I told you, "That's the bowmaster."'
  That's what the other Jaguar said,
    the other one was speaking.
'You did.'

Unable to lie down, the wounded Jaguar can neither eat nor drink. If he needs to relieve himself, he must be supported by his companion. Curers, both powerful beings and Jaguars, try to help him, but they are unsuccessful because they cannot see the arrow. Finally, the Jaguar's father sends messengers to 'that other powerful being,' Posa. 'Come look at the arrow you people make,' they say. He agrees, goes back into his house to get his tobacco, and tells his wife what he must do. (This is important, as we will see later.) He arrives, immediately sees the arrow, and draws it out with his teeth. The pus-filled wound begins to drain, and the Jaguar recovers. Both Posa and the Jaguar's companion remind him of their earlier admonitions:

'Look,' Posa said to him.
  '"That's the bowmaster," I remember that's exactly what I was telling you.
    "That person leaving is the bowmaster" I remember telling that to you.
      "The bowmaster."'
'I tried to tell you the same thing,' the other Jaguar said to his companion,
    'I also tried to tell you that.
      I already told you that before.
  "That's really the bowmaster there," I kept telling you.'

(k) The Jaguar, now fully recovered, declares forcefully he is going to get even. He travels once again to Posa, who is not happy to see him. Here's the ensuing conversation:

'Where's the bowmaster?
I'm going to come and get even.
  Tomorrow, to get even.
    To get even.
    Tomorrow I'm going to come,' he said right away.
'Yes,' he answered.
  'You'll have to go if that's what you want to do.
  You'll come into the plaza.
    Into the plaza.
  I'll be smoking tobacco.
    As curers do.
  I'm planning to smoke tobacco in the plaza.
  If he's there, go jump on him.
    So you can eat him.
    So you can eat him.'
  He spoke angrily to him, angrily,
    angrily.

The Jaguar goes away, planning to return the next day.

(l) That morning, Posa tells Matëga the Jaguar has come.

'Your enemy was here just now.
  He was here just now.
He was asking about you.
He was asking about you.
"Where's Matëga," he asked me.

"He's still here," I said.
  That's what I told him.
Tomorrow he's going to come back here.
  In the plaza, tomorrow.
"All right."
You'd better bring your arrows outside,
  your arrows.
    Bring them outside.
You'll smear yourself with charcoal, you'll smear yourself with charcoal.
You'll bind your forehead with cotton string.
With cotton string that's been dyed red.
You'll smear yourself with charcoal.
  Here on your forehead, you'll smear yourself with charcoal.
And you'll smear yourself here, until you're covered with it.
What you'll do next is "Ho ho ho ho,"
  you'll go out to him, you'll come outside,
  you'll come outside to him in the plaza.
"Where's my enemy, my enemy, my enemy,
this is how I'm going to kill that Jaguar, I'm going to kill my enemy."
  You'll be pointing your bow all around.
  You'll be pointing your bow all around the plaza.
"Where's my enemy I'm going to kill that Jaguar."
  That's just what you'll say.'

Now Posa has given Matëga a plan.

(m) The next day the Jaguar comes up behind Posa while the men are smoking in the plaza. No one but Posa can see him. When Matëga appears outside, doing what Posa had told him to do, appearing like the fierce person he is, the Jaguar is frightened and 'remains hidden right in Posa's shadow.' Posa says to him,

'Look. That's the bowmaster over there.
This is the last time you'll want to do this,
    the last time.
  The last time.
If you try this again you're going to die.'

And so the Jaguar is frightened and leaves. Posa tells him to come back the next day. Then, when the Jaguar appears, Posa makes a long speech to him, telling him again this will be the last time he is going after the bowmaster, and that he will not run after any women, just run away from anyone he sees on the trail.

'Just run away from them,' he said to him.
'They'll tie you up *puh puh puh puh*,
puh puh puh puh,
that's what they'll do to you,
they'll tie you up.
They'll tie you up if you do that.
The others won't run after the women,
jaguars run after them.
To avoid being tied up.
Lest people carry them,
lest they be brought that way into the plaza.
Don't try to run beside the trails.
Don't.
Bum, they're thrown into the plaza.
And they die if they try that.'

And the Jaguar answered him:
'It won't happen.
That would be wrong for them to do, they won't run after them.'
This frightened him.
And again,
'All right,' he said to him.
This will have to be the last time I'll want to do this,
the last time.'

(n) And so the story ends with the statement:

The Jaguar didn't run after Matëga, no.
He frightened him.
He ran across the path of someone else [that is, animals].
So listen.
That was Posa.
He was the brother of powerful beings.

A Way of Listening to This Story

Now, suppose *we* are back there in Faukugu, the early Kalapalo settlement.

There is a powerful shaman among us, a man who has told us lots of stories about his friendship with powerful beings, with some of whom he had erotic liaisons, moreover, and who has brought to us (we Faukugu people) the knowledge of certain masks he saw them wearing, and designs on those masks that he says he saw on the faces of powerful beings. *We* never saw those powerful beings when they came into the ceremonial house where we were making the masks, but *he* told us he did, and the fact that we are now performing with masks is enough for us. They certainly aren't faces of any beings *we're* familiar with.

Now again suppose that we go to hunt. *We* ordinary men, somewhat nervous in the dense forest, walk along together, while our leader, a skilled and somewhat dangerous personage (the bowmaster) goes off by himself. He returns home much later than we do, considerably shaken, and tells us of a frightening encounter with a jaguar from which he barely escaped, thanks only to one arrow he happened to have reworked. Most of his story indexes his considerable skill. First, he changes a bird-shooting arrow to one that can kill a large animal. If any of us had to do such a thing, it would take some time and most likely we would work on it at home, where we keep our equipment. The bowmaster, though, wants to go after the last, biggest monkey, the leader of his troop. Second, Matëga is able to use this arrow to shoot the Jaguar, quite successfully in fact, although he doesn't actually kill him. And he mentioned a second jaguar who remained in the tree, who didn't jump down onto him. Is he bragging?

What do we hear next? We learn from Posa's wife several days – perhaps a week – later that he has gone to cure this same Jaguar! Indeed, he is gone. Because Posa reappears with a feather headdress, we see that someone has paid him after recovering from a serious illness.

Much later, Matëga does an unexpected thing: he comes out into the plaza where we are peacefully smoking and behaves as a warrior would, dressed to kill, so to speak. Even though we cannot see him, Posa tells us later that Matëga's Jaguar enemy was standing right behind him. So that's why Matëga suddenly displayed himself in a way no one had ever seen before. Suddenly he was the bowmaster of the time of cannibalistic feuding, of whom we had heard in stories about the great warriors of the past: Tamakafi, Wapagepundaka, and Tapoge.

What is Posa doing here? Kambe spoke of him with great admiration, frequently calling him the brother of powerful beings. Maybe Posa sensed something in the feelings of the men as they worried about Matëga, and when the bowmaster told his story about the Jaguar. Perhaps he directed Matëga to display himself in order to reassure the others, and perhaps Matëga himself. Posa is also doing the Jaguars a favour. The most fearsome animal and the one subject to all manner of sadistic narrative jokes, the Jaguar is cautioned to keep clear of human beings, lest he be trussed up and brought into the settlement as a trophy over whom people will gloat. This threat, though, is not sufficient. Since he does not listen clearly to what is said, the Jaguar has to confront his enemy again in a way that will immediately resurrect his memory of the pain of the festering arrow wound.

Matëga the bowmaster values (and has been trained for) predictable experiences, and is clearly more of an interpreter of experience than one who deliberately seeks newness. His intelligence is a technical and practical one. He *is* also clearly a believer. He never challenges Posa and he always clearly understands what is being told to him and how he must act, following directions perfectly. Considering what people told me about bowmaster training, this response (as well as most of what Matëga does in this narrative) is characteristic of those warriors. Their ability to focus intently on the most minute details of personal behaviour during puberty seclusion: diet, posture, medicinal practice; their intelligent ability to read signs; their problems with women; and their detachment from personal relationships – all index a special kind of intelligence. When coupled with the actual training and repeated practice, this intelligence effectively contributes to the making of a man called 'bowmaster.' He is a man who is both war leader and an especially successful hunter, a master of form.

The shaman, by contrast, manifests a very different intelligence. He is intuitive and trickster-like, a man who has, as Sapir wrote, 'an ability to respond to implications rather than to experiences, without [ever] attending to all elements of the situation' (1994: 169). The experiences Posa values are magical, involving unpredictable and unusual connections that lead to sudden insights. Posa is a man who plans elaborate subterfuges involving others in his community; they in turn are people who need simply to believe. Their faith in what he says, their confidence in what he has seen, the fact that he *has* seen, is reinforced as he repeatedly encourages them to participate (through ceremonial practice) in his own visions. Here, they have a chance to share in his creative artistry involving music, costuming, and performance. Posa seems also to be a man who follows the way of the idiosyncratic loner, spending many days far from his settlement in quest of further understanding, making contact with powerful beings. Posa is actually contributing his knowledge to the others in the form of ritual practice, which he can do successfully because he is something of a student of personality. He exhibits a special awareness of the consciousness of others (both human and non-human), and carefully identifies and respects them in a way that expands the awareness of all involved. In the words of Sapir, Posa has a 'feeling of responsibility for the life of those not identified with our group.'

What can we say about the Jaguar? He is a grudge-bearing creature, whose violent obsessions prevent him from listening carefully, from understanding what he is being told. He can understand only in the most literally visceral manner – through fear and pain, and through his memory of those emotions. But his memory only emerges from a direct experience of fear (when the bowmaster comes into the plaza), not from reflection or introspection. In this sense, though a powerful being (who can appear as a human, for example), the Jaguar is in essence animal, not human.

By combining the highly paratactical figure of the shaman with both the more visually and practically focused world of the bowmaster, and the single-minded, bitter teeth-gnashing grudges of the Jaguar, this particular Kalapalo narrative has been invested with a quite particular interest that ensured its popularity with one of the most eloquent Kalapalo storytellers. Kambe certainly gave his all during this particular telling, as attested to by the crowd of relatives who sat around us on all sides, listening excitedly. Each of the three personal presences has a special individual character, and it seems there is a fourth as well that the storyteller is helping to develop. This fourth presence is, of course, that of the listeners – those who heard Posa and Matëga speak of their adventures, and the listeners in the Kalapalo settlement of Aifa that fall of 1981. The perspective of these listeners involves faithful and close attention to what is said, following the intricate rhythms of interpersonal communication so as to form in their own thought just the sort of narrative that is actually heard from the storytellers. They attempt a shared imaginative intimacy with the storytellers, submerging themselves in the governing patterns of the speakers.

This narrative is about that particular kind of storytelling we call autobiography, which among the Kalapalo takes shape through interaction rather than introspection, episodically rather than with a necessary goal of completion (it is not life-historical). The stories certain people tell about themselves do not appear independently of those other people tell, but rather in complementarity, that is, they are constitutive of interpersonal action. Such interpersonal processes are effective when they move people to respond in kind, telling about themselves. By helping people to participate in one another's experiences, these stories thereby touch the most brilliant and the least savvy, the skilled and the clumsy, with a sense of mutual participation in a collective life.

It is easy to see how this very process is repeatedly portrayed in Kalapalo narratives through the convention of quoted speech. This is a conventional way of showing people constantly seeking validation and verification of one another's ideas and experiences. When successful, this kind of conversational activity is the foundation of community in both Kalapalo stories and the work of everyday life. The problem is with making that conversation work so that, as Sapir wrote, 'different personalities enter into significant relations with each other, purposively, sharing mutual goals and plans to work out those goals.'[3]

For some time now, we have been able to see how experiential worlds are in fact portrayed in vivid detail in Native American narratives like this Posa story – so much so that we may even speak of biographical and autobiographical material. While I agree with Arnold Krupat and Arthur Brumble that European literary biography – insofar as it emphasizes personal autonomy, idiosyncracy, introspection, and whole lives – may not be an appropriate model for evaluating these stories, one need not conclude (as they do), that 'biographical attitudes' outside European literature are absent. A South American perspective suggests otherwise.

My research on Kalapalo historical narratives makes clear how frequently detailed biographical accounts of action-oriented strategies of a person involving goal-oriented motivations, decisions, and choices emerge in a field of complex social realities. Distinctly individual, though not always fully unique, versions of reality are developed within and through particular social configurations (that is, interpersonal relations). Time is typically described as experienced through changes in these relations. Events of the past are very often remembered as stories about named people. Ideas about these people pertaining to their emotional agency, motivations, and special goals and powers or weaknesses, together with changes in these dimensions of their subjectivity, emerge as far more important to South American senses of history than objectified and generalized descriptions of serial events or groups of people. As I have written elsewhere, such stories therefore become especially suited to searches for implicit forms of historical consciousness (Basso 1995). Among the Kalapalo specifically, the poetic structuring of narratives – the logical relations that organize events and their narrative sequencing – depends upon the emotional quality of the relationships people develop with one another, the feelings they provoke within each other, and the motives arising from those feelings. To put it somewhat differently, using an expression familiar to readers of Harry Stack Sullivan, and of Edward Sapir, Kalapalo narratives grow out of evolving patterns of communication and understanding.

Finally, the title of this volume reminds me again of the importance of psychology and language not only in the scholarly Americanist Tradition, but in Native American traditions as well. Stories like that of Posa surely involve decisions and choices of individuals (though not necessarily descriptions of interior worlds). They are therefore excellent resources for thinking about the moral and practical implications of creatively different patterns of choices. To ponder are the processes of imaginative intimacy that shape interpersonal relationships, crossing both group boundaries and boundaries set up by differences of personality. These intimacy processes appear in the many and frequent contexts of changing worlds of human life, in which people feel themselves touching different worlds of experience (human, powerful being, animal) that exist side by side. For the Kalapalo – people who have lived as refugees on and off for centuries, travelling through many different environments and encountering fearsome strangers who responded to them in a variety of unpredictable ways – such contemplative activities, and the often tricksterish responses that ensue, have enabled them to survive and even flourish.

NOTES

I am particularly grateful to Stephen O. Murray and to Richard Preston for their helpful comments and especially the references to their own researches on Sapir. My thanks for suggestions and comments go also to Regna Darnell, Raymond Fogelson, and Jane Hill.

1 Sullivan (1938a: 28). This paper, published in the *American Journal of Sociology*, was part of a symposium on psychiatry in which Sapir's paper ([1938] 1985) also appeared. An earlier use by Sullivan of 'interpersonal' was in his 1927 paper 'The Onset of Schizophrenia,' in talking about understanding schizophrenia in 'interpersonal contexts' – the relations of a patient with others (see Perry 1956: 103). Sullivan's interest in anthropology was wide-ranging before he met Sapir, including the work of Rivers, Malinowski, Benedict, Powdermaker, Radin, and Kimball Young.

2 Which got Sullivan into trouble with more orthodox Freudians (see comment by Schafer 1976: 3).

3 Today we would develop this interest in motivation with reference to relations of power.

REFERENCES

Basso, Ellen B. 1995. *The Last Cannibals*. Austin: University of Texas Press.

Boas, Franz. [1914] 1982. 'Mythology and Folk-Tales of the North American Indians.' In *Race, Language and Culture*, 451–90. Chicago: University of Chicago Press.

– [1920] 1982. 'The Methods of Ethnology.' In *Race, Language and Culture*. 281–9. Chicago: University of Chicago Press.

Brumble, H. David, III. 1988. *American Indian Autobiography*. Berkeley: University of California Press.

Darnell, Regna. 1990. *Edward Sapir: Linguist, Anthropologist, Humanist*. Berkeley: University of California Press.

Krupat, Arnold. 1985. *For Those Who Come After*. Berkeley: University of California Press.

Murray, Stephen O. 1986. 'Edward Sapir in "The Chicago School" of Sociology.' In W. Cowan, M.K. Foster, and Konrad Koerner, eds, *New Pespectives in Language, Culture, and Personality*. Amsterdam and Philadelphia: John Benjamins.

Perry, Helen Swick. 1956. 'Commentary.' In Harry Stack Sullivan, *Schizophrenia as a Human Process* (*The Complete Works of Harry Stack Sullivan*, vol. 2). New York: Norton.

Preston, Richard J. 1966. 'Edward Sapir's Anthropology: Style, Structure and Method.' *American Anthropologist* 68: 1105–28.

Sapir, Edward. [1932a] 1985. 'Group.' In David Mandelbaum, ed., *Selected Writings in Language, Culture and Personality*. 364–7. Berkeley: University of California Press.

– [1932b] 1985. 'Cultural Anthropology and Psychiatry.' In Mandelbaum, ed., *Selected Writings in Language, Culture and Personality*, 509–21.
– [1934] 1985. 'Personality.' In Mandelbaum, ed., *Selected Writings in Language, Culture and Personality*, 560–3.
– [1938] 1985. 'Why Cultural Anthropology Needs the Psychiatrist.' In Mandelbaum, ed., *Selected Writings in Language, Culture, and Personality*, 569–77.
– 1994. *The Psychology of Culture*. Reconstructed and edited by Judith T. Irvine. New York: Mouton de Gruyter.
Schafer, Roy. 1976. *A New Language for Psychoanalysis*. New Haven: Yale University Press.
Sullivan, Harry Stack. [1927] 1956. 'The Onset of Schizophrenia.' In *Schizophrenia as a Human Process*. (*The Complete Works of Harry Stack Sullivan*, vol. 2). New York: Norton.
– 1938a. *Conceptions of Modern Psychiatry*. New York: W.W. Norton.
– 1938b. *The Interpersonal Theory of Psychiatry*. New York: W.W. Norton.

21 Sequentiality and Temporalization in the Narrative Construction of a South American Cholera Epidemic

CHARLES L. BRIGGS

Time becomes human to the extent that it is articulated through a narrative mode, and narrative attains its full meaning when it becomes a condition of temporal existence.

Paul Ricoeur, *Time and Narrative*

An aspect of Labov and Waletsky's (1967) analysis of narrative that has engendered much discussion is the emphasis they place on sequentiality as a link between narrative structure and lived experience. Writers who have commented on this formulation, of whom there have been too many to review in this brief article,[1] have largely followed Labov and Waletsky in assuming that iconic relations between narrative structures and events are immanent in and form crucial components of narratives. A number of authors have suggested, however, that narrative sequences and events do not stand in simple one-to-one relations. For example, Goffman (1974) and Goodwin (1990) show how narrative structures are sensitive to participation frameworks that emergence in social interaction. Briggs (1988) points to the way that sequentiality, including reiterations of key events, is closely tied to both back-channel cues and to power relations between narrators and audiences. Culler (1981) argues that narrators construct cause-and-effect relations through a range of poetic properties.

Two studies in particular provide points of departure for reformulations of the sequentiality framework. First, Bauman (1986) argues that events do not consist of what 'actually occurred,' as Labov and Waletsky (1967: 20) suggest; rather events are themselves created by narratives. Second, Heath (1983) urges us to see sequentiality as playing functionally distinct roles in different communities. I would like to go on to argue for the need to investigate sequential structure as forming part of the process of *temporalization* in narrative. To be sure, a host of other features, such as tense/aspect alternations and deictics, also play crucial roles in this process.

In concrete terms, I am proposing a shift away from a theoretical and methodological orientation that leads researchers to simply look for sequential structures in narratives, taking them to be immanent features that are necessarily present if the discourse is regarded as narrative. We should similarly not assume that the experiences represented in a given narrative necessarily take the form of discrete, sequentially ordered events. Rather, a major task of the analyst should be assessment of the degree to which a given body of discourse is structured sequentially and the extent to which experience is objectified as a series of bounded events. I will argue that such a perspective is crucial not only for resolving the formal questions raised in Labov and Waletsky (1967) but also in addressing Labov's equally provocative if somewhat less developed observations regarding 'a close connection between speech acts and [non-verbal physical] actions that implies a causal relation.'

Narratives from a South American Cholera Epidemic

I now turn to an example that illustrates how important temporalization is and how much variation narratives exhibit in terms of the extent to which they are ordered temporally. In 1992–3, a cholera epidemic killed some five hundred persons, who generally refer to themselves as belonging to an indigenous group known as 'the Warao,' in the Delta Amacuro of eastern Venezuela.[2] It is hard to imagine the psycho-social impact of the epidemic. Since cholera had not been present in South America for nearly a century, no one had any experience with the disease. Nevertheless, public-health officials made almost no efforts to warn the 24,000 residents of Warao communities that it was extremely likely to come to the delta. Cholera is a bacterial infection that is easily treated, but it can kill a healthy adult through dehydration in as little as eight hours, and the symptoms are horrifying. In some communities, up to one-third of the adults died in a day or two. Terrified, individuals and some entire communities fled the rain forest and began living as mendicants on city streets; some have never returned.

Narrativizing cholera formed a crucial part of the process of coping with this trauma. Narrators sought to articulate what cholera is, where it came from, and why it was killing so many indigenous people. Curers were in a particular bind in this regard. Unable to explain the disease or their inability to treat it, many curers died from cholera after trying to save patients. At the same time, the incredible success of rehydration therapy and antibiotics greatly enhanced the prestige of institutional medicine. Curers used narratives in attempting to prevent the complete de-legitimation of their authority.

I collected accounts of the cholera outbreak while it was still raging (November 1992), as it was abating (June–July 1993), and when only very sporadic cases were evident (January 1994 and June 1994–August 1995). I have recorded three and in some cases four accounts of the epidemic from a number of persons, including several curers. I am interested here in how these individuals temporalized the narratives they told at these different points in time. Given the brevity of this essay, I will only make reference to two narratives told by a healer, whom I will call Manuel Torres. I had worked with Mr Torres closely for nearly five years when the cholera epidemic began.

The first cases were reported in August 1992; I arrived in the delta in November of that year. The peak of the epidemic had just passed, and people were still dying from cholera. Mr Torres, along with hundreds of other Mariusans, was living in Barrancas, a small city on the edge of the delta. Sitting in a hotel room in nearby Tucupita, Mr Torres described the epidemic.

(1) 1992.1B, 13 November 1992, Manuel Torres (MT) and Charles Briggs (CB)

1. MT: Hebu asidaha, hebu asidaha tatuka abanae.
   A terrible disease, a terrible disease arose over there. (points toward delta)
2. Tatuka abanae kimia, dokohia mi.
   Over there arose something that causes diarrhea, vomiting, you see.
3. No, wabanaka hokokore, hokoi tamatika diana wabaya.
   No, if a person doesn't die by dawn, s/he dies by noon.
4. CB: Carajo, uhu!
   Damn, uuuf!
5. MT: Anayaha wabae.
   By the time it gets dark, s/he's dead.
6. CB: Wabae, ajo!
   S/he's dead, damn!
7. MT: Kobenahoro wabae, ha wabae.
   The Governor died, he was still Governor when he died.
8. CB: Tai hese.
   Even him.
9. MT: Tai hese, tai hese,
   Even him, even him,
10. un día araisa wabuae tuatakore.
   and the next day many others died the same way.

Cholera was initially referred to as *hebu asidaha*, 'a terrible disease'; even the expert healers could not divine the 'true' or spirit name of the disease. Similarly, Mr Torres could only spatialize cholera as existing 'over there' in the delta – he had no idea where it came from or how it reached the region. Mr Torres makes this uncertainty explicit several minutes later in the exchange: *Kasabamo naoae? Oko tamaha naminanaha mate!* 'Where did it come from? We still don't know this!'

As I have described elsewhere (Briggs 1992), curers assert that knowledge of *ahotana*, 'its origin,' constitutes a privileged evidentiary basis for presenting truth claims. A crucial means of imbuing narratives with authority is thus to describe the 'origin' of a phenomenon in an invisible spiritual-cum-geographical realm and then relate, step by step, how it made its way to a particular point in the social world. Lacking any sense of the 'origin' of cholera deprives Mr Torres of the ability to temporalize his narrative vis-à-vis events that marked the entrance of cholera into the delta or to make any causal assertions as to why it came to the delta and affected Warao communities so severely. As such, Mr Torres's narrative lacks authority. All of the narratives that I recorded in November 1992 were framed in precisely this way; even senior men who can assert substantial discursive authority and political power peppered their narratives with *oko naminanaha*, 'we don't know,' making explicit this lack of authority.

Mr Torres can only temporalize cholera in terms of the progression of symptoms that it produces in those it infects. He does succeed in isolating one key event, the death of the 'Governor,' the man who had led his community for some thirty years. The Governor's death is, however, not sequentialized in a linear fashion but is rather folded back into the broader cycle of people vomiting and having diarrhea and then dying. Mr Torres's narrative is highly representative of the narratives I recorded in November 1992 – none of the accounts was characterized by more than a rudimentary degree of temporalization in terms of their formal structures and the extent to which experience was objectified by sequential relations between discrete events.

Seven months later, Mr Torres relates the story of cholera in a rather different fashion:

(1) 1993.4A, 11 June 1993, Manuel Torres (MT) and Charles Briggs (CB)

1. MT: Tamasabamo karamunae.
   [The spirits] came to attack from over there. (points to southwest)
2. CB: Ajo! Sanamatana!
   Damn! What a catastrophe!
3. MT: Amaha Wirinoko, Wirinoko ekuya karamunae,
   The Orinoco River here, they came to attack through the Orinoco,

4. tane warubuae ote.
   that's what they said way over there.
5. CB: Ote.
   Way over there.
6. MT: Daukwaha obonae amahawitu, daukwahawitu, daukwaha, daukwaha,
   This very tree gave fruit, this very kind of fruit, fruit, fruit,
7. CB: daukwaha,
   fruit
8. MT: Daukwaha tai Wirinoko eku ho arai nakae,
   This fruit fell into the waters of the Orinoco,
9. aisiko hakanae tata,
   it came swiftly with [the river] over there,
10. ine mauba.
    in my dream.
11. CB: Aaah! Hiauba!
    Aaah! In your dream!
12. MT: Mauba, tamasatemo karamunae,
    In my dream, they came to attack from over there,
13. amaha karamunae Caroní!
    they came to attack from Caroní!

Mr Torres told this narrative to a group of men camped at Hota Kabuka in the delta, where several families were carving dugout canoes. He begins by pointing to the southwest, a region that is purportedly home to some of the most powerful spirits. He then traces the route that cholera took in reaching Warao communities and how it got there, by the spirits placing themselves in pieces of fruit and floating downstream.

By asserting that he knows the point of origin of the epidemic, Mr Torres has made a powerful claim for the authority of his narrative. He is able to relate knowledge of the symptomatology of cholera to the epistemologically privileged discourse of curers. In line 10, Mr Torres provides a powerful epistemological frame for the narrative, claiming that it was revealed in a dream – the most authoritative source of evidence. In line 13, he reveals the name of the 'home' of the spirits – Caroní. Knowing the 'origin' of the spirits enables him to name them, and this is the crucial step in learning how to treat cholera victims. Now that he knows the beginning of the cholera story, he can temporalize his narratives systematically, providing sequential formal structures and objectifying the epidemic in terms of discrete events. The narrative continues with a detailed account of how cholera attacked Warao communities, why it sought human victims, and of the pathology of the disease. Mr Torres's excitement in revealing the 'origin' of the epidemic and the evidentiary basis of his knowledge is conveyed in the excitement he expresses in lines 10 to 13. Temporalizing the epidemic launches him on the road to presenting an etiological account of why cholera struck Warao communities; by the following January, his cholera narratives contained fully integrated and wide-ranging causal assertions.

Conclusion

According to the perspective I am advocating, deeming sequential organization to be an immanent and criterial dimension of narrative imposes a number of limitations on analysts. First, Labov and Waletsky's (1967) definition would lead us to exclude a great deal of discourse from narrative analysis. The accounts that I recorded in the middle of the cholera epidemic would not be considered narratives according to their definition in that speech is not ordered sequentially through the use of temporal junctures and experience is not objectified in the form of discrete, interrelated events.

More important, seeing temporalization as immanent leads us to overlook the importance of studying not simply to what extent a given narrative is temporalized and the mechanisms used in doing so but the processes through which individuals and communities use temporalization in objectifying and ordering social life. Temporalizing the cholera epidemic played a crucial role in attempting to minimize the devastating long-term effects of the epidemic on indigenous communities by providing a host of different conceptual tools for facing questions regarding why so many people had died and what should be done. This task was particularly important in view of the prevalence of attacks on the legitimacy of cultural identities and practices that were waged against the victims' communities and the severe blow that was dealt to the authority of indigenous healers.

The cholera narratives suggest that variability in the degree to which narratives are temporalized cannot be adequately addressed simply by mapping differences between cultures or communities in terms of narrative syntax, shared orientations regarding storytelling, or ideologies of language. Mr Torres is a master storyteller, and I have recorded a wide range of different types of sequentially ordered narratives that he has told. Clearly, the structures of feeling and the cognitive horizons associated with lived experience are related in complex ways to vast differences in the extent to which narratives are temporalized. This relationship works in both directions – temporalization plays a crucial role not only in imbuing narratives and narrators with authority but also in shaping their capacity for the social construction of perception, identity, and memory. One question that this essay poses for comparative research is the special importance and complexity with which this relationship is imbued in settings, to use a term proposed by Das (1996) and others, of intense social suffering.

As the epigraph for this article indicates, Ricoeur argues that the way we experience temporality is contingent on representing time mimetically in narrative form. Ricoeur predicates the ability to temporalize experience on prior access to 'the capacity for identifying action in general by means of its structural features' and 'a supplementary competence' in 'identifying ... the symbolic mediations of action, or "symbols"' (1984: 54). I think that the equation is more useful if we read it the other way around. The progressive temporalization of the narrative representations of the epidemic that circulated through delta communities constituted a crucial means of objectifying traumatic experiences and resisting the imposition of debilitating identities and images.

As I write, in January of 1997, cholera has been reported in several areas of Venezuela, and cases of what public-health authorities are referring to as 'severe diarrhea' are emerging in the delta. If death, trauma, and racial stigmatization again threaten delta communities, these narratives will once again be called upon to aid in the struggle for survival and dignity.

NOTES

This paper was initially published in the *Journal of Narrative and Life History*, vol. 7, and is reprinted here by permission of the publisher. I gratefully acknowledge support from the American Council of Learned Societies, the John Simon Guggenheim Memorial Foundation, the Cultural Anthropology Program of the National Science Foundation, the National Endowment for the Humanities, the Social Sciences Research Council, and the Wenner-Gren Foundation for Anthropological Research, Inc. The research that is reported in this essay was conducted jointly with Clara Mantini de Briggs, MD.

1 Toolan (1988: 146–76) provides a useful review of some of these works.

2 The official death toll compiled by the Regional Epidemiologist of the Ministry of Health and Public Assistance was twelve. A survey that I conducted in 1994–5 with Clara Mantini de Briggs, MD, of the entire delta region yielded a count of 500 deaths.

REFERENCES

Bauman, R. 1986. *Story, Performance, and Event: Contextual Studies of Oral Narrative*. Cambridge: Cambridge University Press.

Briggs, C. L. 1988. *Competence in Performance: The Creativity of Tradition in Mexican Verbal Art*. Philadelphia: University of Pennsylvania Press.

– 1992. 'Linguistic Ideologies and the Naturalization of Power in Warao Discourse.' *Pragmatics* 2(3): 387–404.

Culler, J. 1981. *The Pursuit of Signs*. London: Routledge & Kegal Paul.

Das, V. 1996. 'Language and Body: Transactions in the Construction of Pain.' *Daedalus* 125(1): 67–91.

Goffman, E. 1974. *Frame Analysis*. New York: Harper & Row.

Goodwin, M.H. 1990. *He-Said-She-Said: Talk as Social Organization among Black Children*. Bloomington: Indiana University Press.

Heath, S.B. 1983. *Ways with Words: Language, Life, and Work in Communities and Classrooms*. Cambridge: Cambridge University Press.

Labov, W. 1982. 'Speech Actions and Reactions in Personal Narrative.' In Deborah Tannen, ed., *Analyzing Discourse: Text and Talk*, 219–47. Washington: Georgetown University Press.

Labov, W., and J. Waletzky. 1967. 'Narrative Analysis.' In J. Helm, ed., *Essays on the Verbal and Visual Arts*. Seattle: University of Washington Press.

Ricoeur, P. 1984. *Time and Narrative*. Vol. 1. Translated by Kathleen McLaughlin and David Pellauer. Chicago: University of Chicago Press.

Toolan, M. 1988. *Narrative: A Critical Linguistic Introduction*. London: Routledge.

22 Personal Agency in Systemic Discourse

LISA PHILIPS VALENTINE

The complex relationship between system and human agency appears to be fundamentally problematic in my reading of contemporary anthropological research. Either one level or the other is addressed and, when combined, the product most often resembles static snapshots or two-dimensional overlays. In contrast, it is in the dynamic interaction between human agency and system where the Americanist Tradition allows for a unique theoretical integration. In thinking over my past fifteen years of worrying with the challenge of simultaneous micro- and macro-level analysis in multiple, concurrent arenas, I have found that the primary source of friction lies in the region between the apparently incommensurate levels of the individual and the system.

The Americanist Tradition has opened up the understanding that language use, even on a propositional level, indexes social and individual positioning. Thus, we recognize that each text, no matter how technical (or legal, or official) remains at the same time a personal, situated statement. Indeed, even government documents that arrive with no named author must be read as the efforts of individuals with agency to represent and reinforce given systems. This is, ironically, rarely noticed and much less often addressed. Those of us working within text traditions are forced to recognize that no text emerges without a source or context. We understand that resistance is not the only dynamic game in town: hegemony takes equal or greater effort to maintain, and much of this hegemonic work can be found in institutional discourses. Agency works both ways, from the individual to the system and from the system (as embodied by individuals bolstered often by established operating procedures) to individuals.

The tools of the trade of (Americanist) discourse analysis (cf. Adams, this volume) include the work that has been done in attending to form, both in descriptive linguistics and in sociolinguistics.[1] Careful attention to form, especially through an examination of formal linguistic features, has laid the groundwork for genre and for an understanding of norms, usage and stylistic variation. Knowing the linguistic ground allows quick access to figure; the emphasis within the Americanist Tradition on genre and norms of interpretation provides us with the theoretical basis for addressing areas of contestation, areas of shared understanding – the playing field, so to speak, for both personal, individual action and for systemic reinforcement or change. Attention to linguistic detail gives us the tools that allow us to divide emergent figure from historical ground.[2]

The study of discourse (as opposed to text) is necessarily dynamic, as every instance studied both encapsulates history and anticipates the future. The only way to force it into a temporal vacuum is to study decontextualized text, a failure of formal linguistics *and* standard social-science content analysis. On the other hand, the analysis of *contextualized* discourse spotlights creativity and individual agency even within system(s). One thus moves from locating discourses within their historical, temporally bounded contexts to contemporary and future areas of negotiation and change.

Discourse is utilized in all systems and institutions, in interpersonal interactions as well as in interactions between people acting as agents, or as embodiments, of institutions. Discourse thus spans micro-level and macro-level processes. In each case, discourse works in similar ways, both as the subject and the medium of study: discourse allows for an examination of subtle and complex interactions not only through dialogues between individuals but also between individuals and institutions. This duality is well documented in multiple studies written from the perspective of an ethnography of speaking, many of which have been written by those represented in this volume. Issues of advocacy, ethnicity, statehood, nationality, and nationism may all be studied through the examination of language use, and in the presence or absence[3] of discourse at either primary or meta levels, the micro- and macro-levels. The issues raised by persons facing systems are counterbalanced in the crafting of responses of those persons speaking for the system. Again, personally and institutionally situated nuances are indexed within the text.

In the last six years (following almost ten years' work with northern Ojibwe people, language, and culture), I have studied systemic differences in the English discourses of Algonquian and Iroquoian people located in southwestern Ontario.[4] I have found that in carefully attending to such differences, my reading of any document related to Native peoples, regardless of the origin of that document (either Euro-Canadian or First Nation) has been radically altered. In my micro-level analysis of variable linguistic strategies employed by two geographically overlapping, yet culturally distinct groups, I have become attuned to areas of contestation in public discourse between and among Canadian aboriginal peoples that rarely arise to the consciousness of any of the parties involved.

When one moves to First Nations and governmental interactions, those local nuances become significant when one addresses aboriginal issues in state-related policy arenas.

In a dynamic analysis of personal/systemic relationships, language shifts signify major social and/or structural change. Communication accommodation theory (as outlined by Giles and Coupland 1991 and Giles, Coupland, and Coupland 1991) and research in convergence and divergence models that address types of linguistic style shifts provide interesting insights into this multilevelled, non-sequential (that is, non-conversational) discourse that characterizes individual/systemic negotiation. But I would argue that while communication accommodation theory has expanded its scope somewhat beyond issues of suprasegmental and segmental phonology and lexical choice (see Ferrara 1991 for evidence), current models do not yet take into account larger-scale discourse accommodation. I will combine the communication-accommodation model with the uniquely Americanist concept of 'norms of interpretation' of discourse to demonstrate how agency and system are implicated in alternative interpretations of a single English-language text. Let me explore this potential, and challenge, through the following case study.[5]

This case has a number of attractive aspects that make the analysis possible. First, the parties involved are assumed to share a single code, English, although individual members' first languages are not necessarily English. English is not being negotiated as a language of solidarity or power, but as a lingua franca. This means that phonological variables are, for the most part, nonsignificant. Second, the topic was given (or constrained) by the context: both parties are ostensibly equal partners in the ongoing discourse. The negotiations are not for topic maintenance as the topic was already established. Third, the discourse is non-conversational. That is, most of the discourse around the texts presented in this paper took the form of extended speeches (or monologues), many of which may have been formulated before presentation. And, finally, the context was the political negotiation of constitutional inclusion for First Nations peoples in Canada. The parties in these negotiations were defined and distinguished ethnically in the case of First Nations representatives and/or politically in the case of the Canadian politicians, none of whom was of First Nations heritage. Class was not an overt issue[6] and power relations in this set of Constitutional Conferences, were open for negotiation, unlike later conferences, where Canadian government officials came into the negotiations exerting authority over First Nations peoples.

Factors in accommodation theory that are most often exploited include class, social status, gender (to some extent), the negotiation of interpersonal power and solidarity, and, at a higher level of language choice in code-switching contexts, negotiation of ethnic and/or political identity. While all these factors are at play to some degree here, one cannot and must not assume that a delineation of such factors is explanatorily adequate, or even particularly interesting.

In order to address linguistic accommodation, one must be aware of community norms of language use. Once we are aware of shared genres and norms of interaction within a community, we are then better attuned to minute changes in those discourses that provide a diagnostic of potential changes within the broader society. Because norms of interaction within a given group differ sufficiently from others, the adjustments in any interlocutor's discourse may be seen as a performance, a negotiation, and a positioning that is, in turn, predicated upon one's expectations of *another's* norms of interaction. For example, members of an English-speaking Algonquian community may include symbolic uses of Ojibwe or Cree in discussions with English-speaking Iroquoian community members, predicated on their assumption that Native language use is a demonstration of aboriginal solidarity. Conversely, the same interlocutor may use more legal jargon when speaking with Euro-Canadian government officials, on the assumption that it will create another type of solidarity, and position the speaker as an equal participant in the discussion.

In such performances, one establishes both his or her own identity as a member of a given community and, conversely, a position vis-à-vis the interlocutor. This performance, in turn, informs and helps create the interlocutor's position and discourse in response (cf. Larsen 1983: 131). Such adjustments (accommodations) may or may not be recognized by those outside a given speech community (and this may include the interlocutor him or herself), but the discourse used, if in a single language, is *assumed* to be shared. That is, as in the case below, if everyone is using a version of English, everyone is assumed to be sharing a common meaning system. If one's words are echoed by an interlocutor, then one assumes the positioning is understood and the roles on both side accepted. Again, these assumptions are based on *apparently* shared discourses.

As a researcher involved with contemporary textual materials in addition to oral discourse, I have found that one cannot presume to understand the nuances without taking into account context, which involves an exploration of prior texts and synchronic issues, and a good grasp of cultural norms of interpretation. What follows is an illustration of ways in which a single document could, and would, have been read differently by different members of the same audience. Those alternative readings, at the same time, would not necessarily be recognized by either of the groups involved. In other words, the content of the 'accommodative discourse' may be assumed to have one set of referential and affective meanings by the speaker and yet have an entirely different set of referential (though perhaps not affective or emotive) meanings for the hearers based on their set of interpretive norms.[7] Given assumptions rooted in the shared lingua franca, the gulf would remain invisible.

The text addressed in this analysis was presented on 8 March 1984, during the second of four First Ministers' Conferences on Aboriginal Constitutional Matters, a uniquely Canadian forum specifically set up within the Canadian constitution to address the place of aboriginal peoples in Canada. In the First Ministers' Conference, the spokesperson for the federal government was the prime minister: in the first two conferences, the prime minister was Pierre Trudeau and in the last two conferences it was Brian Mulroney. The provincial governments were represented by premiers, seated and speaking in historically prescribed order. Aboriginal peoples were represented on the basis of categories defined within the Indian Act: there were three groups, Indians, Métis, and Inuit, seated at the table with the prime minister and premiers. Through the four conferences, the prime ministers, premiers, and representatives of the Aboriginal peoples changed, which, although not addressed in this paper, is extremely important for understanding directions that the negotiations took at different times in the conferences. Prime Minister Trudeau changed the protocol of the first two conferences to give second speaking position to the aboriginal representatives rather than to the provincial premiers – an important display of power politics where the provinces were essentially demoted, a type of action associated with Trudeau. When Prime Minister Mulroney took over, the second speaking position was once again given to the provincial premiers with aboriginal leaders in third ranking position.

The text examined here is the conclusion of Prime Minister Pierre Trudeau's opening remarks at the beginning of the second of the four conferences. The excerpt begins after an introduction of Trudeau. The text is presented in its entirety as written in the governmental transcript except for the added end note. The paragraph breaks are as indicated in the transcript.

So this is the last time that I will address this assembly from the chair and I didn't know the figure of 22[8] that our secretary has mentioned earlier in his statement but it makes me feel that I have been a Chairman who believes in a great deal of consultation and not any kind of confrontation.

If only for this reason, I would like to say a few words to the aboriginal peoples of Canada, not so much as Prime Minister or Chairman of this conference, but rather out of my own mind and heart as they talked to me this morning after the prayer which began this meeting.

Together we have embarked upon a journey that can lead you into full partnership in Canada, secure to you your own place in Canadian society with your own institutions of self-government, provide you with the infrastructure you need if you are to achieve economic success and protect and enhance your cultures and languages. I am proud to have walked the first mile of this journey with you. Others will take my place and continue upon the journey with you for there can be no turning back. The constitution guarantees you that.

But in the end your fate and the fate of your children's children are in your own hands. You are the custodians of an ancient spirituality. Your lives are rich in culture and tradition. The extended family that is the tribe or community can be your strong support.

Take advantage of all that a modern society can offer, but for your soul's sake stand on your own feet, on the sure foundation that spirituality, tradition and family have laid.

May God go with you on your long journey. (Government of Canada 1984: 24–5)

This discourse is fascinating at several levels. First, Trudeau was the initial speaker in this conference because of his office – Prime Minister of Canada. By virtue of the context, a First Ministers' Conference on Aboriginal Constitutional Matters, Trudeau's discourse held a certain weight, as evidenced by its inclusion in the proceedings transcript. This was an official event, an address given within a formal agenda. However, he immediately stepped back from his role in the conference to speak on a more 'personal' basis:

I would like to say a few words to the aboriginal peoples of Canada, *not so much as Prime Minister or Chairman of this conference, but rather out of my own mind and heart* as they talked to me this morning after the prayer which began this meeting. [emphasis mine]

As he spoke, Trudeau moved from using bureaucratic English to appropriating terms heard in many First Nations' English-language political discourses. This includes the use of terms such as *journey*, *self-government*, *walk ... this journey*, *cultures*, *children's children*, *custodians of an ancient spirituality*, *lives ... rich in culture and tradition*, *extended family*, *soul's sake*, and *sure foundation ... [of] spirituality, tradition and family*. By using these terms, he presents himself as understanding the aboriginal discourse of self-government from an unidentified but presumably homogeneous aboriginal perspective.

Trudeau's norms of interaction allow him to make a distinction between statements made as an individual that he could not make in his role as prime minister, a distinction that would not necessarily be assumed by aboriginal listeners. If we look at transcripts from the *first* constitutional conference, we find that Trudeau has modelled the form of his discourse after one from Chief David Ahenakew. In the initial conference, Chief Ahenakew began his discourse with general observations to the prime minister about the role of First Nations peoples in the meetings, making the point that despite the fact that '[t]he Constitution Act of 1867 mentions three distinct peoples, the Indians, the French and the English,' this was the first opportunity for First Nations peoples to have a central place in a constitutional conference. Several minutes into his speech, Ahenakew made the following rhetorical move:

> Permit me, Mr. Prime Minister, to digress for a moment. *I want to share a personal perspective with you,* not because I am important, but because *my experience typifies or exemplifies the experience of most Indian people* here today and all across Canada. I am a Cree. I come from Sandal Lake Reserve in Saskatchewan and I can trace my family as far back as before the treaties were ever signed and reserves established. My family fought for Canada in two World Wars and I served in Korea ... [emphasis mine]

In many First Nations' communities, a person is a leader because of personal attributes: a chief becomes one because he or she demonstrates behaviours that are consistent with the ideal of a 'chief.' One's person or ideas are not separate from one's role. This may be especially true in smaller communities where public and private are far less separable categories, so that the institutional representative and the individual are viewed as coexisting in every statement. Following such norms of interpretation, Trudeau's speaking 'out of [his] own mind and heart' would be viewed as an *official* statement, one where he was speaking as a representative of and for the whole of Euro-Canada.

Taking the other side, as one reads between Trudeau's appropriated lines, one discovers an 'official' version that fits a Euro-Canadian model of government negotiation:

> Together we have embarked upon a journey that can lead you into *full partnership in Canada,* secure to you *your own place in Canadian society* with your own *institutions of self-government,* provide you with the *infrastructure* you need if you are *to achieve economic success* and *protect and enhance* your cultures and languages ... The *constitution guarantees* you that. [emphasis mine]

For someone sharing Euro-Canadian norms of interaction, these words index potential policy statements within a general political genre; they would be heard as the core of Trudeau's public, political discourse. The lexicon of political discourse is marked by pervasive economic and institutional images (such as partnership, institution, self-government, economic success, Canada). The other images and metaphors less expected in a Euro-Canadian political discourse would be interpreted by the Euro-Canadian community as framing devices, as gilding for an audience, as pieces considered peripheral to the discourse, as accommodation for reasons of interpersonal solidarity.

In some cases, as in the evoking of God and spirituality, Trudeau offers 'religious' discourse from his own tradition as a familiar substitute for one piece of the social framework that aboriginal peoples have argued as central to their (multiply imagined) conception of government. This is anathema to Western conceptions of state, which disallow any combination of religion and human governance. The use is consistent with and a marker of Trudeau's view that he was speaking personally. However, using the aboriginal norms of interpretation, the references to spirituality serve to imbue the discourse with power[9] and legitimacy. The potential for misinterpretation of intent as found in this discourse for both sides of the audience, the aboriginal and the Euro-Canadian, is almost absolute. It appears that Trudeau himself had no idea how his words might be misread.

The problems are multiplied when one understands the cultural specificity of the appropriated discourse that Trudeau has chosen. While some of the images chosen by Trudeau have been adopted by aboriginal groups across Canada, the base metaphors are Algonquian in flavour. This includes the pervasive use of the term 'journey': Wiihsahkecaahk and Nanaboozho stories from Cree and Ojibwe traditions almost invariably begin with a journey, but other groups use quite different framing devices for their stories. The 'sure foundation that spirituality, tradition and family have laid' is a much more comfortable fit for Algonquian conceptions than it would be for Iroquoian, where ritual and ceremony define spirituality, tradition, and family. In a similar fashion, the 'extended family that is the tribe or community' is utterly appropriate for many Algonquian groups, but certainly would not be the initial construction for someone from the Six Nations (Iroquois), for example.

Other important factors in interpreting this text not addressed in detail here include the following:

1. The prior text. This discourse occurred in the second of the four conferences, and as seen above, Chief Ahenakew's speech was presented in the first of the conferences. This prior text certainly changed Trudeau's discourse, in form if not content. This interpretation follows more traditional versions of accommodation models that approach convergence on the basis of sequential discourse. '[T]here are data showing that non-familiars converge towards each other gradually across subsequent occasions (see, for example, Ferrara [1991]), thereby appearing to conserve some convergent acts as bargaining tools. In this way, the structure and process of mutual convergences can be quite negotiative and precursors to communicative innovations at the lexical, grammatical, prosodic and non-verbal levels' (Giles and Coupland 1991: 79). While it appears that such convergences as are found in Trudeau's speech might be incorporated into this emerging model, what we find is that the temporal displacement of

texts is comparatively enormous, spanning about a year between the two conferences, and the convergences are not so much grammatical elements or individual lexical choices as they are larger-scale discourse genres as marked not by phonology or intonation but by (assumed) shared verbal metaphors and apparent discourse structuring.

2. The future text. When Mulroney took over from Trudeau to preside over the final two conferences, the discourse changed drastically from apparent accommodation and conciliation to a discourse centred around a metaphor of 'horse trading,' where an overt language of labour negotiations was presented as the appropriate medium by Mulroney and, following his lead, the other provincial premiers. When this change in discourse genre occurred, the conferences were essentially relegated to formal means of fulfilling a legal obligation with no apparent intent to move towards a consensus between the government and representatives of First Nations peoples. In retrospect, this give credence to Trudeau's language use in the speech as at least surface convergence.

3. Textual representation. Representation and the editing (inclusion or non-inclusion) of texts, in this case within the official records, have been issues central to the Americanist Tradition. In researching this text, I came across a documentary that included videotaped portions of the conferences.[10] In comparing the oral and official written versions,[11] I was forcibly struck by the following example of systematic doctoring of the official documents, the textual materials.

In the official transcript of the initial First Ministers' Conference, dated 16 March 1983, 10:00 a.m., on page 174, we find the following:

> ... I would like to call first on the Chairman of last night's meeting, the Minister of Justice, Mr. MacGuigan.
>
> *Mr. David Ahenakew* (Nation Chief, Assembly of First Nations): Can we give the prayer again?
>
> *The Chairman*: Will you pray every morning in public?
>
> *Mr. David Ahenakew*: Yes, sir.
>
> *The Chairman*: Everyone should pray to his own God and we will have a moment of mediation. Chief?
>
> – (Prayer)
>
> We will hear from Mr. MacGuigan on last night's ...

However, the videotape shows a Cree elder beginning a prayer which is interrupted by Prime Minister Trudeau ('The Chairman') asking, '*Are you going to* pray every morning in public?' Chief Ahenakew answered with 'Yes, sir,' after which there was a long pause. Trudeau then stated, '*Well then*, everyone should pray to his own God and we will have a moment of mediation.' After a briefer pause, Trudeau turned to the Cree elder and said, 'Chief?' to signal him to continue. In the video we hear the Cree prayer, but in the middle of the prayer, over the voice of the elder, Trudeau begins reciting the Lord's Prayer in a loud voice, first in English and finishing in French. When Trudeau finished, he sat down. To his left was John Munro, the Minister of Indian Affairs. Munro leaned over to Trudeau and asked him audibly, 'Getting even?' Trudeau, equally audibly, replied, 'Yep,' and they both smiled.

The changes in the official transcript invariably paint a much more favourable picture of politicians than is evident in the words spoken around the table. This means that a person reading the texts would assume a much more benevolent attitude on the part of government officials than was evident on the floor. This textual editing, doctoring, is fascinating when viewed as systemic accommodation, where politeness is imposed on the records when it was not evident in the verbal interchanges. It is the spoken words to which people at the conference table responded, not to the written version, although the official written version is the one to which people respond after the event.

Taking an Americanist approach to linguistic norms, one can address issues of individual agency and systemic discourse. To interpret a discourse, one must be familiar with the genre of that discourse, with its lexico-semantic domains and its discourse markers. Trudeau's speech as an individual talking 'off the cuff' would be heard as having certain policy implications by a mainstream Euro-Canadian audience, but, because of norms of interpretation of discursive moves in an aboriginal community where there is little or no separation between leader and person, Trudeau's statements would be interpreted by its members as having quite distinctive and perhaps unimagined implications.

The Americanist Tradition provides tools to address related discourses that are discontinuous temporally, spatially, and even in terms of participants. Other models, such as communication accommodation theory, are just beginning to address extended discourse, although the modelling used is still quite local in its reliance on conversational analytic methodologies that assume an immediate conversational interchange.

In analysing this discourse, one might attempt to address the text as a simple case of miscommunication that 'has been identified in sociolinguistics (Milroy 1984), ... to relate to mismatching of intended and comprended referential meanings' (Giles and Coupland 1991: 192). But, in fact, this is not miscommunication as far as the interactants are concerned. Each side hears a coherent message, but it is one that indicates a convergence of political ideology for the First Nations audience but is intended as an affective convergence by the speaker. Addressing issues of stereotypes only gets us as far as accounting for the use of specific lexical items, and the problems with ultra- or contra- attuning get us into the same dilemma we find in the discussion of miscommunication: the intentions[12] and the readings by the audience do not match, although neither side may understand that the attunings have gone too far or have fallen short.

The Americanist interest in cross-cultural communication and in norms of interaction leads us to view this event as cross-communication, but the difficulties are not of a type that leaves either side *immediately* uncomfortable. The interactants assume each has understood the other's message. However, the apparent accommodations and convergences of form and lexical content can and did lead to later dissatisfaction at the abortion of what appeared to be – by both sides – real progress in negotiations. This is a case of simultaneous accommodation and miscommunication where neither and both were recognized.

Issues of individual agency, (social) institutions, power relations between groups, and hegemonic praxis are all implicated in this analysis – without the focus on language, we are unable to go beyond static indicators such as transfer, accumulation, or access to goods/wealth. When we question our own theoretical methods (addressing accommodation or divergence as accomplishing an intent), then we are theorizing our Americanist Tradition and moving forward to addressing issues that move well beyond 'personal face management' or linguistic description.

The adaptation of Americanist sensitivity to form in discourse, genre, norms, usage, and stylistic variation of both sides of individual/system interaction offers the potential to add breadth and depth to our analyses. At present, economic concern for the allocation of material outcome, legal constraint on form, and political preoccupation with power have dominated much analysis. Americanist concerns with context and situatedness through discourse, on the other hand, offer the potential to reintroduce 'humanity'[13] into such discussions.

NOTES

1 As noted by H. C. Wolfart, this volume, formal analysis has its roots, along with much of what has been addressed as the Americanist Tradition, in the humanistic movement of the fifteenth century.

2 See Murray 1994 for an excellent outline of the Americanist contributions from inception to the 1990s.

3 Keith Basso's (1972) paper on silence among the Western Apache is the classic citation on cultural meanings of the absence of discourse.

4 This research has been funded by three grants from the Social Science and Humanities Research Council of Canada (1991–4, 1994–7, 1997–2000), the first two held with Regna Darnell and the last one held with Regna Darnell and Allan McDougall, which are gratefully acknowledged here.

5 The case study addressed in this paper is taken from public documents brought to my attention

by Allan McDougall. This paper could not have been written without his insights and introduction to Euro-Canadian traditions of interpreting Canadian political process. As a newcomer to both Canadian politics and Canadian political discourse genres, I am deeply indebted to him for his patient and multiple readings and comments on this paper.

6 However, in the case of Prime Minister Trudeau, class was always a subtext in his discourse style. Those features are not specifically under consideration here.

7 Immediately after an incident rife with potential antagonism (recounted later in this paper), a peace pipe was offered to the participants around the negotiating table. A Native leader/elder, dressed in buckskin and feathers, walked around the table offering the pipe to each of the political leaders seated in order. In the video *Dancing around the Table*, each leader was seen, head slighted bowed taking a quick puff from the pipe. When the elder reached Quebec Prime Minister René Lévesque, a chain smoker, he jumped from his seat, grabbed the pipe and quickly took several deep drags. One can read his lips mouthing 'good tobacco!' to the elder. This incident demonstrates shared referential meanings – all members recognized the peace pipe and tobacco – but the affective meaning was utterly different. The first leaders appeared to be attempting to placate, albeit uncomfortably, the elder. Levesque, by contrast, reinterpreted the event from a spiritual cleansing (the aboriginal meaning) to an appreciated smoke break shared by fellow smokers. There are many different situations, such as this, that illustrate potential mismatches between referential and/or affective meanings.

8 This number refers to other occasions on which Trudeau chaired meetings.

9 The ambiguity in the use of the term 'power' is deliberate. Political, personal, and spiritual power coincide in many aboriginal traditions. In the Euro-Canadian traditions, the statements may be viewed as emotionally or rhetorically powerful, but as having no coercive value. This is precisely where the miscommunication lives. The same is true for the term 'legitimacy,' which can imply truth, validity, and even efficacy.

10 The National Film Board's video *Dancing around the Table* presents a collage of speeches and images from the conferences. The bias towards First Nations concerns is evident in materials chosen, but there are sufficient stretches of discourse in the video that are found also in the government transcripts to demonstrate the following point.

11 Hansard is the official record of proceedings in both the Parliaments of Canada and the UK. The traditions associated with inclusion and exclusion of materials is, in itself, a fascinating case of accommodation to ruling powers' abilities to (re)write history.

12 The definition and usefulness of the concept of 'intention' is currently under considerable scrutiny. It is used here to indicate readings or interpretations that a speaker may expect his/her audience to make.

13 See Preston's excellent use (this volume) of Sapir on the enterprise of studying interactions between human beings.

REFERENCES

Basso, Keith. 1972. 'To Give Up on Words: Silence in Western Apache Culture.' In P. Giglioli, ed., *Language in Social Context*, 67–86. Harmondsworth: Penguin.

Ferrara, Kathleen. 1991. 'Accommodation in Therapy.' In H. Giles et al., eds, *Contexts of Accommodation*. Cambridge: Cambridge University Press.

Giles, Howard, and Nikolas Coupland. 1991. *Language: Contexts and Consequences*. Pacific Grove: Brooks/Cole Publishing.

Giles, Howard, Justine Coupland, and Nikolas Coupland, eds. 1991. *Contexts of Accommodation: Developments in Applied Sociolinguistics*. Cambridge: Cambridge University Press.

Government of Canada. 1984. *First Ministers' Conference on Aboriginal Constitutional Matters, March 8 and 9, 1984.* Ottawa: Minister of Supply and Services Canada.

– 1991. *Aboriginal Peoples, Self-Government, and Constitutional Reform.* Ottawa: Minister of Supply and Services Canada.

Larsen, Tord. 1983. 'Negotiating Identity: The Micmac of Nova Scotia.' In A. Tanner, ed., *The Politics of Indianness: Case Studies of Native Ethnopolitics in Canada*, 37–136. St John's: Institute of Social and Economic Research, Memorial University of Newfoundland.

Murray, Stephen O. 1994. *Theory Groups and the Study of Language in North America: A Social History.* Amsterdam and Philadelphia: John Benjamins Publishing.

Scott, Colin. 1993. 'Custom, Tradition, and the Politics of Culture: Aboriginal Self-Government in Canada.' In N. Dyck and J.B. Waldram, eds, *Anthropology, Public Policy, and Native Peoples in Canada*, 311–33. Montreal and Kingston: McGill-Queen's University Press.

23 'Critical Linguistics': Alternative Approaches to Text in the American Tradition

KAREN L. ADAMS

In 'Speech and Language: On the Origins and Foundations of Inequality among Speakers,' Hymes states that the study of language 'first became a self-conscious activity, and to a great extent has developed since as an instrument of exclusion and domination ... all in the interest of cultural hegemony. It is only in our own century, through the decisive work of Boas, Sapir, and other anthropologically oriented linguists (as components of the general triumph of 'methodological relativism' in the human sciences), that every form of human speech has gained the 'right,' as it were, to contribute on equal footing to the general theory of human language' (1980c [1973]: 55). This relativism that values spoken and written language, standard and non-standard varieties, national languages as well as those of small communities, has also meant the opportunity to address the very issues of exclusion and domination mentioned above. As such, the Americanist Tradition has anticipated other current approaches that focus on the privileging of some voices and texts over others.

As Darnell (this volume) argues, in the Americanist Tradition, the links between anthropology and linguistics are strong. Culture has a symbolic definition and, based on the inseparability of language, thought, and reality, text is the database for ethnography and evidence of Native persons' point of view. This orientation to text, Native voices, and language's role in thought and the construction of reality resonates with the principles and methods of Critical Discourse Analysis.

'Critical Linguistics' (CL) and 'Critical Discourse Analysis' (CDA) as a field of linguistics are strongly committed to viewing language as social practice and texts as reflecting and reproducing culture and its equities and inequities in the distribution of power. CL and CDA employ systematic social-science and linguistic analyses of text, but distinct from many other approaches openly concern themselves with the voices of the dominated. Critical Discourse Analysis is often associated with European and British approaches and, more generally, with Western Marxist approaches to social science, though as Fairclough and Wodak (1997) point out, it may include research by scholars such as Foucault whose work is anti-Marxist. Among the CDA approaches to be considered here are Critical Linguistics proposed by Fowler and Kress in 1970s, the work of Fairclough, which emphasizes sociocultural change in discourse, and that of van Dijk, which focuses on socio-cognitive issues. All three of these approaches have a strong interest in the structure of the text and its linguistic form.[1]

That the treatment of language and text as social practice has become commonplace in American approaches can be seen in the papers in this volume. That work by American scholars on conversational analysis, language and gender, and metaphors, for example, has been of great use to those doing CDA can be seen in the references of a text such as Fairclough 1992. There is, though, little discussion of American traditions of Critical Linguistics. The following text discusses some of these American traditions, comparing them to the European schools for the theoretical view of language as a mechanism of social control and for the methods employed to discover these mechanisms.[2]

With the advent of the Bloomfieldian tradition, much of American linguistics outside of the Americanist Tradition in anthropology moved to a positivist and behaviouralist approach. Positivism has continued in Chomskyan linguistics and dominated the field of American linguistics. The traditions that remained tied to a social/cultural context have largely been treated as 'other' or at best as hyphenated approaches. As Gumperz and Hymes noted (1972/1986, 540), '[T]he scope of the term "linguistic theory" has come to be narrowed in practice to "theory of grammar"; works concerned with linguistic theory in this sense have by no means the scope and relevance of the books on language by Sapir and Bloomfield.' Within the Chomskyan tradition, text lost any interest, context was not relevant, and Native voices as well as others could be marginalized merely as explication of grammatical theories.[3]

Urban dialectology / Labovian sociolinguistics originated in an interest in mechanisms of language change and the observation of change in progress, but developed into studies of the speech styles of numerous vernaculars, focusing on the historical and theoretical explanations for current structures as well as their evaluation by the speakers and by society at large. Given the strong interest in style shifting and recording authentic voice, this work observes spoken varieties and their discourse strategies.

Though variation theory did not and still does not have text as social practice as its focus, sociolinguists in general have been active participants in arenas such as language policies in the schools. They have had a decisive effect on the outcome of court cases such as the Ann Arbor Decision (Chambers 1983). The theoretical recognition of inherent language variability allows for structures that can be exploited as social markers, but the grounds for arguing against language deficit theory or for the appropriateness of all dialects in context have always been that all varieties are rule-governed and analysable by the same methodological approach, the approach owing to Boas and Sapir as noted above. Discussions of institutional control through language choice, for example, are taken up on a case-by-case basis.[4]

The empirical correlational approach in sociolinguistics of variables and social categories has been criticized over the years for its limited approach to social class, gender, and other social categories. These criticisms have come from within the discipline, often from feminist scholars (see, for example, Cameron 1985 and Eckert 1989), and from outside the field, from critical-linguistics scholars and others (see, for example, Dittmar 1976 and Fairclough 1989), and have resulted in some improved discussions of social mechanisms and their relation to language variation.

Macro-level issues in sociolinguistics, especially the maintenance and revival of bilingualism in the United States and elsewhere, have been extensively considered by Joshua Fishman. While domain theory is neutral with regard to issues of social control, the social status of languages and the sociohistorical forces determining this status are crucial for issues of language planning. Moreover, Fishman argues that 'there is not only no interest-free language planning, but also no interest-free research on language planning' (1987: 421). His goals in maintaining multilingual/multicultural environments derive from his belief in the inseparability of language, thought, and reality and in the importance of the multiple viewpoints expressed in different languages. (See Adams and Brink 1991 for further discussion.) Fishman's work remains noticeably quiet about Native languages, though his intellectual debt to Whorf is firmly in the Americanist Tradition, and the inclusion in this volume of discussions on language planning in First Nation / Native communities (see Anderson and Nyce, Burnaby, and Cyr) foregrounds the importance of macro/institutional issues if Native language extinction is to be reversed.

Ethnomethodologists and conversational analysts have also looked at the construction of everyday knowledge through spoken interaction and as such are concerned with text and context. Theoretically, however, they have steadfastly argued against premature categorizing and treat social roles and identities as locally managed, affecting text only if identified in the text in question. As Schegloff argued, 'The fact that they [the conversational participants] are in fact respectively a doctor and patient does not make those characteristics ipso facto relevant' (1987: 219). This backgrounding of social role and its relationship to language structure and use in conversational analysis is not without its critics. Feminist scholars and critical linguists such as Fairclough (1989) disagree with this approach, seeing a category such as gender as always operating on the text. Since, as Leap (this volume) argues, what constitutes the creation of a social identity in a text can be very subtle, it may be that in the analysis of any specific text these two approaches are closer in their findings than might be expected. Certainly, scholars interested in the issues of language as social practice, including those using CDA, have employed methodological insights from conversational analysis, ignoring its theoretical constraints on social context.

Pragmatic theories of speech acts and conversational implicature are central to many of the approaches discussed here. H. Paul Grice and John Searle have provided units independent of the sentence that can be used to understand text in its social context, though neither of these philosophers deals explicitly with speech acts in interaction or with issues of dominance and power. Those building on their work, particularly that of Grice, include Robin Tolmach Lakoff and George Lakoff, who have both moved in their own directions. R. Lakoff developed a theory of conversational politeness and cooperation in context as a level of grammatical explanation, and G. Lakoff, most recently, is known for his work on metaphor and cognitive structure (e.g., Lakoff and Johnson 1980). G. Lakoff's 1991 piece on the metaphoric justification of the Gulf War and his 1996 *Moral Politics* are both critical-linguistic pieces focusing on metaphor, an area of analysis also taken up by Bolinger (1980), as we shall see. The general theoretical approach of G. Lakoff, however, was not oriented towards issues of social inequity, but to cognitive ones. The importance of metaphor's role in critical-linguistic analysis owes much to American researchers.

R. Lakoff has also addressed the relationship of language and social inequity in her widely read 'Language and Women's Place' (1973) and in *Talking Power: The Politics of Language* (1990). Relying on Grice and her own 1972 piece on the role of context, much of her work, especially the 1990 volume, lacks acknowledgment of extensive research by other American scholars on similar issues, and certainly contains no acknowledgment of research in Critical Linguistics by European scholars. Her own theory of pragmatics is not concerned with the status of speakers.

In contrast to the above-mentioned approaches of sociolinguistics, conversational analysis, and speech-act theory, discussions of language and power and language and dominance have flourished in the research on language and gender, as feminist theory has always had a strong emphasis on language as social practice. The scholars in this area have brought to the domain a variety of methodological approaches, the validity of which are sometimes contested. For example, the introspective approach of R. Lakoff (1973) has been criticized by quantitative sociolinguists and the literary examples in Tannen (1990) have been questioned as adequate validation of her claims.

Feminist theory has not typically affected theoretical approaches in American linguistics, though gender is a widely attended-to variable in sociolinguistic explanations of language variation.[5] In their concern for reference in gender-biased linguistic texts and examples, Cameron (1985) notes that feminists have made use of the Sapir-Whorf hypothesis found in the Americanist Tradition. But feminist models of language have just as often relied on the Ardeners' (1975, 1978) dominant/muted model, Marxist theory, semiology, and various psychoanalytic approaches.

In the area of language planning for language change, feminism brought clearly to the forefront of the discussion the political nature of language, the role of intentionality, a focus on dominated voices, and language's reflection and reproduction of social institutions. However, within the scholarship on language and gender, the role of dominance versus difference in explaining language strategies remains under discussion, as do issues of deconstruction and essentialism.

That feminist theory made it acceptable to discuss issues of language and power and also intentionality is directly reflected in the statements of Dwight Bolinger, another American scholar within the tradition of Critical Linguistics. In his critical-linguistics work, he mentions renewed interest in context and meaning and in the role of linguists as social critics, citing as examples work by R. Lakoff and Julia Stanley on language and gender as well as sociolinguistic work by Labov and Wolfram on Black Vernacular English and Harlem Spanish.

But a major source for Bolinger's own interest in Critical Linguistics appears to be war experiences. He discusses the divorce of meaning from linguistics in the 1940s and 1950s in the Bloomfieldian tradition, but notes the existence in 1941 of an Institute for Propaganda Analysis that included linguistics. He also cites the School of General Semantics as an attempt to deal with some of these issues, but clearly articulates the negative attitudes towards this work in linguistics owing to its superficial nature, a criticism also directed towards the National Council of Teachers of English (NCTE) publications on double-speak.

Bolinger's concern was to awaken linguists as well as broader audiences to the fact that language structures could be used to manipulate listeners and readers, and that these structures could be looked at in a systematic fashion as part of linguistics. His focus is mostly on the language of bureaucracies and advertising, but extends into issues of sexism, standardizing language, language attitudes, and racism. That this work topically is squarely in the field of Critical Linguistics is acknowledged in a review of *Language – The Loaded Weapon*

(1980) by Fairclough, one of the British linguists working in CDA. Other than remarks on a greater acceptability of dealing with context, Bolinger identified no other theoretical grounding for his discussion, and Fairclough (1982) notes this lack of consistent analysis of social issues in Bolinger's work.

Bolinger's work (1973, 1980) identifies one of the most thorough set of features capable of manipulating a listener's perception. This set bears strong similarities to the list of linguistic structures cited in the work of Fowler and Kress (1979) on 'Critical Linguistics,' who drew their categories from M.A.K. Halliday (1978). (See figure 23.1.) The overlaps are extensive, except for features of transitivity from Halliday and for several categories that Bolinger added, including euphemism, metaphor, presupposition, intonation, and collocation. There appears to be no influence of these scholars upon each other. (Fairclough 1989 also cites several of these features and includes other discourse considerations such as turn-taking.)

When Bolinger presented his earliest work in this area he was surely in a position to affect American approaches to text. His 1973 'Truth Is a Linguistic Question' is the forerunner of his 1980 *Language – The Loaded Weapon* and was originally given as the presidential address at the annual Linguistic Society of America meeting on 29 December 1972. The address appeared in *Language*, the pre-eminent American journal of theoretical linguistics a few months later, and was reprinted the next year in *Language and Public Policy*, a volume put out by the NCTE. However, a review of the Social Science Citation Index and the Arts and Humanities Citation Index for the reception of this article in English-language journals reveals few references to it. For the period 1973–94, there are only 13 citations, compared to 46 citations to R. Lakoff's 1972 article 'Language in Context,' which also appeared in *Language* and was the article Bolinger cited as making his interests more acceptable. The references to his later work, *Language – The Loaded Weapon* are broader (36), but far behind the 55 for Fairclough's volume, which was not published until 1989. While *Language – The Loaded Weapon* was reviewed in *Language in Society* and elsewhere, it received not so much as a book notice in *Language*, the journal of the society over which Bolinger had presided seven years earlier.

Why did this work with a such a comprehensive program in Critical Linguistics fall on so many deaf ears in spite of an increasing interest in context reflected in such activities as the 1973 Summer Linguistic Institute on language and context, which also featured Halliday teaching a class on the grammatical system that was to form the basis for Critical Linguistics?[6] First, the predominant voice in American linguistics treated such work as outside the mainstream of linguistics and distinguished linguists as professionals from linguists as social critics. Chomsky represents the canonical example of such a distinction. Also, discussing intentionality, even unintentional intentionality, appears to be taboo,

FIGURE 23.1
Linguistic features to be considered in Critical Linguistics

Fowler and Kress (1979: 199–213) (after Halliday)	Bolinger (1973/83)
The grammar of transitivity	
a) how many entities are affected?	yes, quantifier scope
b) is a new entity produced?	no
c) is the action reflexive?	no
d) who initiates the action?	yes
e) what kinds of entities are involved?	yes
The grammar of modality	
a) names/titles/personal pronouns	yes
b) speech acts, politeness	yes
c) modals	yes
d) verbs of appearance, cognition	yes
e) time & place deixis	yes
Transformations	
a) nominalizations	yes & reification
b) passivization	yes
c) negative raising	no
d) NP raising & extraposition	yes
no	tags
Classification	
a) relexification	yes & latinate vocabulary
b) overlexification	yes
c) position of adjective	yes
Coherence, order & unity of text	yes
no	euphemism & dysphemism
no	metaphor/metaphor themes
no	presupposition
no	biased adverbs/adjectives
no	unexpressed collocations
no	literalism
no	intonation
no	standard & vernaculars

as does discussing partisan political issues in some American public educational institutions. Bolinger was also known for his work on Spanish syntax and on intonation, and his publications on CL were far between and scarce, though

CL is addressed in two editions (1975, 1981) of his introductory linguistics text, a standard text at the time. Moreover, Bolinger's retirement from Harvard in 1973, the year his first CL article appeared, limited his access to students. It could also be that, unlike the work of Fowler and Kress (1979) and Fairclough (1989), the linguistic features in Bolinger are not set out in a programmatic fashion but must be sought out by the reader.

The year Bolinger was giving his presidential address, the work of Gumperz and Hymes and others coalesced in the volume *Directions in Sociolinguistics* (1972), which, unlike Bolinger's work, was widely received. These anthropological linguists and their students have been at the forefront of maintaining use and context in language study through notions of communicative competence, the articulation of the components of speech events, and a theory of interactional sociolinguistics that directly discusses issues of miscommunication and dominance.

Gumperz (1982a and 1982b) lays out the theory and issues in interactional sociolinguistics, which looks at texts created in institutional multicultural settings in order to understand the linguistic structures around which miscommunication occurs. Gumperz states that '[o]ur main goal ... is to show how ideology enters into face-to-face speaking practices to create an institutional space in which the subconscious and automatic sociolinguistic processes of interpretation and inference can generate a variety of outcomes and make interpretations subject to question' (1982b: 3). Gumperz's work acknowledges influence from other American approaches to text and context such as his collaboration with Hymes and the work of ethnomethodologists, conversational analysts, pragmaticists, and feminists, as well as from the French approach of Bourdieu (1973) with its view of language as social practice and ideology as a factor of modern life.[7]

The Gumperz and Hymes volume (1972/1986) also provides us with numerous examples of the speech-event model for comparison with Critical Linguistics. Let us focus on Hymes's model for the interaction of language and social life and on the research guide by Sherzer and Darnell, appendix 2 in Gumperz and Hymes, both of which allow for attention to political institutions and to issues of social control. While the guide has a section on the use of speech in education and social control (1973/1986: 553–4), the phrasing of the questions in this section focuses on the role of language in social control to ask whether there is 'an explicitly formulated policy of social control.' Critical Linguistics mostly looks at texts from industrialized societies where social control is frequently ideological and symbolic; for other societies, the role of language in social control may be downplayed. The more open-ended questions of the guide are appropriate for an approach that is trying to develop a taxonomy of the ethnography of speaking.

In general, the orientation of the ethnography of speaking model as outlined in 1973 is descriptive and taxonomic rather than critical. As noted above, it is broad in scope with regard to the social situations it addresses and may include issues of individual behaviour, unlike Critical Linguistics, which tends to concern itself with individuals only as social/institutional actors. However, the components that Hymes presents for analysing speech events are heavily mirrored in van Dijk (1993) and in Fairclough (1989: 146–52) on situational context. See figure 23.2. Such components as setting, genre, speech acts, and style are parallel in Hymes and van Dijk, and those with question marks may be so in some contexts. The differences in the approaches can be seen in the focus in van Dijk on issues of social role, access to discourse, social meaning, and ideological stands. Labels in Hymes such as speaker or sender, hearer or receiver, channel and code are traditional, but treat language metaphorically – more as information transmission than social transmission.

The components specified by Hymes have been employed in critical approaches to language use, often in the educational context. In the 1980 reprinting of Hymes's articles on language and education, he updates his 1973 article on inequality among speakers in reference to work by Habermas, a major figure in CDA. In the introduction to the volume (1980a: viii), he also acknowledges Halliday's model of language as one of the few to deal with the 'interdependence between the organization of discourse and features of situation.' However, given Hymes's orientation to studying the role of language in social control on a culture-by-culture basis, he finds Habermas's generalizations about issues of equality and unrestricted language use to be 'culturecentric,' and argues (1980c: 50) that 'ethnography will lead to reconstruction of the initial theories in more articulated, diversified form.' The article by Hill in this volume on the meaning of writing presents a nice example of this more diversified form.[8]

If one asks whether there is an Americanist/American Tradition of Critical Linguistics, the answer is obviously yes. The methodological tools and some of the theoretical issues are addressed in several different schools of linguistics and social theory. Some of the work, for instance that of Bolinger, even appears to be earlier and more extensive than some of the European approaches. Does it really matter whether researchers in the United States and Canada regard themselves as sharing similar goals and ideology and whether they attend much to the work of CDA scholars in Europe? In 1993 van Dijk stated: 'There are many ways to do "critical" discourse analysis ... and these may sometimes also be related to "national" differences. Unfortunately, this is also one of the reasons why there has been much mutual neglect and ignorance among these different approaches. International, theoretical and methodological integration would obviously benefit the realization of a common aim,

FIGURE 23.2
Characteristics of speech events for Critical Discourse Analysis

Discursive properties for Critical Analysis (van Dijk 1993)	Components of speech events (Hymes 1972/1986)
Access (opportunity to create different text types and audience for text)	
	Message form Channel Forms of speech (verbal resources)
Participant positions & roles	Speaker, or sender; addressor; hearer, or receiver, or audience; addressee
Setting	Setting (including key) Scene (psychological setting)
Genre	Genre
Communicative acts & social meanings (politeness strategies, referents, & interactions leading to political alliances)	(?)Key (?)Norms of utterance
Speech acts	Speech acts (level distinct from sentence & unique)
Macrosemantic topics (ideological stand)	(?)Purposes-goals Purposes-outcomes (?)Norms of interpretation (cross-cultural differences; belief system)
Superstructures: text schemata (e.g. argument structure)	Act sequence
Local meaning & coherence a) level of specificity & degree of completeness b) perspective c) implicitness: implications, presuppositions, vagueness	Key
Style: variation of syntax, lexicon, & sound a) lexical style b) syntactic style c) anaphora & deictics	Speech styles (including Key) (?)Norms of interaction & interpretation
Rhetoric a) metaphors b) rhetorical questions c) contrast	

namely to analyse, understand and combat inequality and injustice' (van Dijk 1993: 279).

Perhaps one of consequences is that theoretically the American work may not be as consistent in its view of language as social practice and of the role of language in reproducing and constructing social institutions. Fowler and Kress (1979) and Fairclough (1982) point to the lack of a systematic analysis of social and institutional structures in the much of the American work.

Second, Critical Linguistics and some other versions of CDA in the European tradition draw together a methodology derived from insights from many theories and models in linguistics, including American ones. This school makes explicit its methods and its search for methods, while in the American tradition there can be a great deal of reinvention, often ignoring useful work such as Bolinger's. As Critical Linguistics goes beyond many other approaches to text by looking at numerous types of structures on all linguistic levels, this focus and its explicit articulation is beneficial not only to linguists but to those interested in text in other fields. For example, Weir (1993) argues for the usefulness of CL over deconstruction and other approaches that do not conduct close analysis for work in the field of history.

Third, as van Dijk (1993) stated above, one can only benefit from a multinational approach to so many of the language and social issues that we now face. There has been some collaboration already on topics such as the discourse of discrimination; see the edited volume by Smitherman-Donaldson and van Dijk (1988). Others in the American universities have expressed enthusiasm for this work (see Agar et al. 1990, Pennycook 1990), though some have been critical (e.g., Dillon et al. 1993). Contact and discussion remain narrow, though the new journal *Discourse & Society*, edited by critical linguists and published by a company with an American presence, may change this situation. As van Dijk points out in his 1994 editorial, doing CL/CDA is not easy, for it requires multidisciplinarity in as much as one's skills in social explanation must be as strong as those in linguistic explanation. Moreover, the approach means serious discussion about cognitive issues of the representation of social knowledge and the nature of linguistic theory and formalism.

NOTES

Thanks to Regna Darnell, Elizabeth Horan, Michael Mackert, and Lisa Valentine for comments on drafts of this paper and to Karen Baertsch for help with library work.

1 For a brief, but useful discussion of the history of different approaches in CDA and their shared practices and key features, see Fairclough and Wodak 1997.

2 For a much fuller discussion of several of these American approaches, see Murray 1994.

3 This point is not meant to exclude the work of notable scholars in this field, including Ken Hale

and others, who have been politically active on behalf of the maintenance of Native languages. See Hale et al. 1992.

4 The structural analysis of text in a variationist approach is also theoretically devoid of issues of social control, as can be seen in Schiffrin 1994: 290–1. Mackert (1995) pointed out that the expression of variable rules also often reproduced the hierarchical status of standard and non-standard varieties, treating non-standard varients as deviating from standard ones.

5 This lack of impact of feminist theory on the field of linguistics was the topic of a panel at the 1991 LSA (Linguistic Society of America) meetings. Barrie Thorne was the presenter and Elinor Ochs, Marcyliana Morgan, and I were the respondents.

6 Halliday's class was not heavily enrolled in the institute in comparison to those of Schegloff, Labov, and others. (I was a student in Halliday's class.)

7 Erving Goffman is often included in the school of interactional sociolinguistics; see Murray 1994 and Schiffrin 1994, for example. His influence is important, as he dealt with social structure and issues of dominance in publications such as his 1976 work on gender and advertising, but as his focus on language is very general, I have chosen not to discuss his work here.

8 Though Hymes's interest in social inequity and the schools is a strong one, this does not mean that his work has always been applied in this way. Pennycook (1990) argues that Hymes's crucial concept of communicative competence has developed in second-language acquisition theory as a methodological approach that is devoid of discussion of the social issues of inequity in the development of competence and the acceptance of certain kinds of competence in different contexts.

REFERENCES

Adams, Karen L., and Daniel T. Brink. 1991. 'Joshua A. Fishman on Language Planning: "Brotherhood" Does Not Mean Uniformity.' In David F. Marshall, ed., *Language Planning: Focusschrift in Honor of Joshua A. Fishman*, vol. 3: 7–27. Amsterdam and Philadelphia: John Benjamins Publishing.

Agar, Michael, Marlys Pearson, and Paul Popernack. 1990. Review of N. Fairclough, *Language and Power. Journal of Pragmatics* 14: 988–91.

Ardener, Edwin. 1975. 'Belief and the Problem of Women.' In Shirley Ardener, ed., *Perceiving Women*, 1–27. London: Malaby Press.

Ardener, Shirley. 1978. *Defining Females*. New York: John Wiley & Sons.

Bolinger, Dwight. 1973 (1974). 'Truth Is a Linguistic Question.' *Language* 49(3): 539–50. (Reprinted in Hugh Rank, ed., *Language and Public Policy*, 161–75.)

– 1980. *Language – The Loaded Weapon: The Use and Abuse of Language Today*. London and New York: Longman.

Bolinger, Dwight, and Donald A. Sears. 1981. *Aspects of Language*. 3rd edition. New York and London: Harcourt Brace Jovanovich. (2nd edition 1975)

Bourdieu, Pierre. 1973. 'Cultural Reproduction and Social Reproduction.' In R. Brown, ed., *Knowledge, Education and Cultural Change*, 71–112. London: Tavistock.

Cameron, Deborah. 1985. *Feminism and Linguistic Theory*. London and Basingstoke: Macmillan Press.

Chambers, John Jr. 1983. *Black English: Educational Equity and the Law*. Ann Arbor, MI: Karoma Publishers.

Dillon, George, Anne Doyle, Carol Eastman, Sandra Silberstein, and Michael Toolan. 1993.

Review article: 'Language and Power in Critical Linguistics.' *International Journal of the Sociology of Language* 103: 185–96.
Dittmar, Norman. 1976. *A Critical Survey of Sociolinguistics: Theory and Application*. New York: St Martin's Press.
Eckert, Penelope. 1989. 'The Whole Woman: Sex and Gender Differences in Variation.' *Language Variation and Change* 1(3): 245–68.
Fairclough, Norman. 1982. Review of D. Bolinger, *Language – The Loaded Weapon*. *Language in Society* 11(1): 110–20.
– 1989. *Language and Power*. London and New York: Longman.
– 1992. *Discourse and Social Change*. Cambridge: Polity Press.
Fairclough, Norman, and Ruth Wodak. 1997. 'Critical Discourse Analysis.' In Teun A. van Dijk, ed., *Discourse as Social Interaction. Discourse Studies: A Multidisciplinary Introduction*, vol. 2: 258–84. London and Thousand Oaks, CA: Sage Publications.
Fishman, Joshua A. 1987. Conference comments: 'Reflections on the Current State of Language Planning.' In Lorne Laforge, ed., *Proceedings of the International Colloquium on Language Planning* (25–29 May 1986), 407–29. Ottawa and Québec: Les Presses de l'Université Laval.
Fowler, Roger, Bob Hodge, Gunther Kress, and Tony Trew, eds. 1979. *Language and Control*. London, Boston, and Henley: Routledge & Kegan Paul.
Fowler, Roger, and Gunther Kress. 1979. 'Critical Linguistics.' In Fowler et al., eds, *Language and Control*, 185–213.
Goffman, Erving. 1976. *Gender Advertisements*. New York: Harper Colophon Books.
Gumperz, John J. 1982a. *Discourse Strategies*. (Studies in Interactional Sociolinguistics 1.) Cambridge: Cambridge University Press.
– 1982b. *Language and Social Identity*. (Studies in Interactional Sociolinguistics 2.) Cambridge: Cambridge University Press.
Gumperz, John J., and Dell Hymes. 1972a (1986a). 'Background Reading: Appendix 1.' In Gumperz and Hymes, eds, *Directions in Sociolinguistics*, 539–47.
– eds. 1972b (1986b). *Directions in Sociolinguistics: The Ethnography of Communication*. New York: Holt, Rinehart, & Winston (Oxford and New York: Basil Blackwell, 1986; version cited).
Hale, Ken, Michael Krauss, Lucille Watahomigie, Akira Yamamoto, Colette Craig, LaVerne Masayesva Jeanne, and Nora England. 1992. 'Endangered Languages.' *Language* 68(1): 1–42.
Halliday, M.A.K. 1978. *Language as a Social Semiotic*. London: Edward Arnold.
Hill, Jane. 1991. Review of N. Fairclough, *Language and Power*. *Language in Society* 20(1): 131–7.
Hymes, Dell H. 1972 [1986]. 'Models of the Interaction of Language and Social Life.' In Gumperz and Hymes, eds, *Directions in Sociolinguistics*, 35–71.
– 1980a. Introduction to Hymes 1980b, v–xv.
– 1980b. *Language in Education: Ethnographic Essays*. Washington: Center for Applied Linguistics.
– 1980c. [1973]. 'Speech and Language: On the Origins and Foundations of Inequality among Speakers.' In Hymes 1980b, 19–61.
Lakoff, George. 1991. 'Metaphor and War: The Metaphor Used to Justify War in the Gulf.' *Viet-nam Generation* 3(3): 32–9.
– 1996. *Moral Politics: What Conservatives Know That Liberals Don't*. Chicago: University of Chicago Press.
Lakoff, George, and Mark Johnson. 1980. *Metaphors We Live By*. Chicago and London: University of Chicago Press.

Lakoff, Robin Tolmach. 1972. 'Language in Context.' *Language* 48: 907–27.
– 1973. 'Language and Woman's Place.' *Language in Society* 2: 45–80.
– 1990. *Talking Power: The Politics of Language*. New York: Basic Books.
Mackert, Michael. 1995. Personal communication.
Murray, Stephen O. 1994. *Theory Groups and the Study of Language in North America: A Social History*. Amsterdam and Philadephia: John Benjamins Publishing Co.
Pennycook, Alastair. 1990. 'Towards a Critical Applied Linguistics for the 1990s.' *Issues in Applied Linguistics* 1(1): 8–28.
Schiffrin, Deborah. 1994. *Approaches to Discourse Analysis*. Cambridge, MA, and Oxford, UK: Blackwell Publishers.
Schegloff, Emmanuel. 1987. 'Between Micro and Macro: Contexts and Other Connections.' In J.C. Alexander et al., eds, *The Micro-Macro Link*. Berkeley: University of California Press.
Sherzer, Joel, and Regna Darnell. 1972. 'Outline Guide for the Ethnographic Study of Speech Use.' Appendix 2 in Gumperz and Hymes, eds, *Directions in Sociolinguistics*, 548–54.
Smitherman-Donaldson, Geneva, and Teun A. van Dijk, eds. 1988. *Discourse and Discrimination*. Detroit: Wayne State University Press.
Stockwell, Robert P. 1993. 'Dwight Bolinger: Obituary.' *Language* 69(1): 99–112.
Tannen, Deborah. 1990. *You Just Don't Understand: Women and Men in Conversation*. New York: William Morrow.
van Dijk, Teun A. 1993. 'Principles of Critical Discourse Analysis.' *Discourse & Society* 4(2): 249–83.
– 1994. Editorial: 'Discourse Analysis as Social Analysis.' *Discourse & Society* 5(2): 163–4.
Weir, Lorna. 1993. Review and commentary: 'The Wanderings of the Linguistic Turn in Anglophone Historical Writing.' *Journal of Historical Sociology* 6(2): 227–45.
Zupnik, Janette Yael. 1991. Review of N. Fairclough, *Language and Power*. *Language in Society* 20(2): 265–9.

24 Current Extensions of Sapir and Whorf in Cross-Cultural Cognitive Science: Cognitive Styles and Ontological Categories

J. PETER DENNY

My experience of the theme of this volume, 'Theorizing the Americanist Tradition,' has been similar, I believe, to that of some of the other contributors; my membership in such a tradition was not very self-conscious, and I had certainly not done any theorizing about it. The editors, however, were very perspicacious in divining the theorists hidden inside us. Looking over the fields of cross-cultural cognition in which I have participated, guided by what I heard at the conference that preceded this volume, I see that much of the work, by anthropologists, linguists, and cross-cultural psychologists, realizes theoretical goals set by the pioneer Americanists. I know that my own thinking was originally shaped by the ideas of Boas, Sapir, and Whorf, as enthusiastically expounded by my undergraduate anthropology professor, Edmund Carpenter. He said, in his first lecture to us, that 'through the analysis of language one can show the viewpoint of a people' (personal communication, 20 October 1954),[1] a suggestion I have pursued for many years. Now it is a pleasure to set forth the ways in which Americanist theories have been further developed as part of the current cognitive science of cross-cultural cognition, one in which, as we will see, anthropologists, linguists, and psychologists are using each other's methods and contributing to each other's theories. I believe this is a partial achievement of the interdisciplinary science of culture that Sapir sought.

First of all, as someone committed to the relatedness of language and thought, I want to celebrate the surprising revival and successful re-establishment of the Whorfian hypothesis. It is especially delightful to me as a supporter of a unified cognitive science that this often doubted view – that language influences thought – has recently been supported by excellent studies that, in the spirit of cognitive science, have been done by anthropologists, but using psychological methods of experimentation: these are Kay and Kempton (1984) and

Lucy (1992). Coincidentally, in the usual tradition of Whorfian research, both studies involved Amerindian languages.

After discussing Whorf, I will turn to two areas of cross-cultural cognition, cognitive styles and ontological categories, in which current studies answer Sapir's call for studies of culture that are at once psychological and historical (Sapir 1994: 72). Accordingly, for my second topic I will examine the crucial role of cognitive styles in expanding the repertoire of theoretical notions about culture and thought. Cognitive styles are habitual ways of thinking developed in particular historical eras and used in culturally valued contexts. For example, Western decontextualized style developed in Classical Greece and is preferred for math and science tasks (Havelock 1963). For my third topic I will concentrate on another new theoretical notion, ontological categories, looking to see what they can tell us about the historical development of thinking, particularly in incipient agricultural societies. Ontological categories are a special class of fundamental concepts, such as 'animate,' 'long and rigid,' 'liquid,' 'state,' and 'place,' that control the formation and use of ordinary concepts. We will see that they appear in some studies, such as the Whorfian experiments of the 1950s, that predate the recent understanding of their significance.

Language Relativity

The Whorfian question has been centred in Amerindian studies from the time of Boas; from mid-century on it was realized that psychological experiments were necessary to show that it was true. If we look back now at the pioneering experiments such as Maclay (1958), we find that some of the data in them is supportive of the hypothesis. For example, Maclay found that those Navajo speakers who were more fluent in the language more often sorted objects into the ontological categories that are expressed by the Navajo classificatory verbs, for instance, 'elongated and rigid objects,' than did less fluent speakers. However, these results were not taken seriously, even by Maclay himself, because English speakers also sorted by the same categories. Nowadays we understand that comparisons of non-Western and Western participants can be uninterpretable if the task involves skills heavily emphasized in Western schooling, as is true for sorting by shape, and we are prepared to accept the findings showing differences between the Navajo groups as indicating an effect of language on thought.

In contrast to such pioneering efforts, the recent experiments that support the linguistic-relativity hypothesis are especially persuasive on the basis of their methodological strengths. Kay and Kempton (1984) showed that use by English speakers of the separate words for blue and green to label pairs of bluey-green colours increased the judged differences between those colours, compared to the judgments of Tarahumara (Uto-Aztecan) speakers, whose language did not provide separate blue and green words. The brilliant part of this study was the provision of a subsequent experimental manipulation that blocked the English speakers from using the separate words blue and green when making their judgments. Under these conditions, the judged differences shrank to become almost identical to those shown by the Tarahumara. This is exactly the sort of support for the weak Whorfian hypothesis we have been seeking – it shows that when you are using your language, it will automatically shape your thinking, and most significantly when you are not using your language, your thinking can operate free of it.

The more recent study of Lucy (1992) has further methodological improvements. First, he leaves the domain of colour cognition, which many agree is not one of our most essential skills, for another domain that all acknowledge to be fundamental, quantification. Looking at two aspects of quantification, plurality and cardinal number, he shows that when a speaker's language marks plurality on nouns for particular ontological categories of things, those are just the sorts of things for which they will involuntarily notice and remember the cardinal number. When asked to describe pictures of animate things, both speakers of Yucatec (Mayan) and of English encode plurality on the nouns referring to them, and more significantly both groups attend to and remember the cardinal number of the animate things even though the task does not require them to. For inanimate objects like tables, English pluralizes nouns whereas Yucatec (Mayan) does not, and only English speakers involuntarily notice and remember the cardinal number of such things. To date this is our most convincing evidence of the habitual shaping of thought by language.

These excellent studies of language relativity have prompted me to contribute some reanalysis of Whorf's own data, particularly the Shawnee examples that are closest to my own work in Algonquian semantics. Whorf's main work on Hopi has already been re-examined and found to be exaggerated but still in line with a weak relativity hypothesis (Gipper 1976). In considering his Shawnee analyses we will find the same to be true. I should also point out that modern semantic analysis is quite different from Whorf's 'Gestalt' technique and provides a much more accurate assessment of the Shawnee-English contrasts he described.

Perhaps most famously, Whorf compared a one-word Shawnee sentence describing the cleaning of a rifle barrel, *ni-pe:kw-a:lak-ha*, 'I dry its hole by tool,' with the English sentence *I clean it with the ramrod* (Whorf 1940). The literal English gloss I have given, 'I dry its hole by tool,' shows that English can come very close to expressing the same concepts as are found in the Shawnee. However, we would not usually describe the situation this way in English, but would prefer Whorf's normal English sentence. These, then, are pragmatic not semantic matters, which concern differences between the two languages in the preferred uses of concepts. Since such language preferences amount to the linguistic shaping of thought, the example still supports language relativity.

Whorf also presented well-known examples in which a pair of situations are similarly encoded in Shawnee but differently encoded in English (Whorf 1941). One such pair seems very different when described in English: *I pull the branch aside*, and *I have an extra toe on my foot*. However, they seem strikingly similar when encoded in Shawnee, *ni-lˀθaw-aˀko-n-a*, 'I make it, something stick like, forked by hand,' and *ni-lˀθaw-aˀko-θit-e*, 'I have a forked, sticklike, toe.'[2] The glosses I have provided are as close as I can get English to approximate the Shawnee, but they are strangely worded compared to Whorf's ordinary English sentences. The similarity in encoding the two situations in Shawnee arises from the identical second and third morphemes of the two words, expressing respectively the concepts 'forked' and 'sticklike.' The difference between the two languages as they encode these two situations again seems to be pragmatic – speakers of English have learned not to use the concepts 'forked' and 'sticklike' for these situations and speakers of Shawnee have learned the opposite. For the concept 'sticklike' it might be further argued that this is not genuinely a semantic equivalent of the Shawnee morpheme, since the latter is a noun classifier expressing the ontological category 'elongated and rigid' – no such morpheme occurs in English. If that is so, there is a semantic difference, as well as the pragmatic differences, between the conceptualizations encouraged by the two languages. What this brief re-examination of Whorf's Shawnee examples suggests is that much of the way in which language channels thought may be by pragmatic habits of language use, with semantic factors being secondary.

The establishment of the linguistic-relativity hypothesis is a contribution that is having increasing importance for theories in cognitive science, particularly those which emphasize that cognitive processes are shaped by the experiences humans have as they act in the world. One such theory, by George Lakoff (1987), treats linguistic relativity as a component of the view that basic experiences of the world, as they are encoded in high-frequency words, are the starting point for the metaphoric elaboration of much of the rest of cognition. Another such theory by Linda Smith, a cognitive developmental psychologist, emphasizes that throughout life our concepts are shaped and reshaped by processes of perception and attention (Thelen and Smith 1994). Smith has carried out her own Whorfian experiment (Smith and Sera 1992), which shows that as children acquire language, it sometimes reshapes their perceptual judgments. This conclusion is theoretically important for her position that there is a continual interdependency of conception and perception. All these recent developments I have reviewed make clear that linguistic relativity is currently a major theoretical contribution originating in Americanist studies.

Cognitive Style

I turn now to some work on cognitive style, a valuable contribution from cognitive psychology that we can use to meet one of the goals set by Sapir, namely to have an explicit account of mental processes that individuals use as carriers of their culture (Sapir 1994: 59–61). To start, I must introduce two cognitive-style dimensions. The first is differentiation-integration. A favourite task for assessing differentiation is the embedded-figures test in which one has to find a simple visual figure hidden in a complex one.

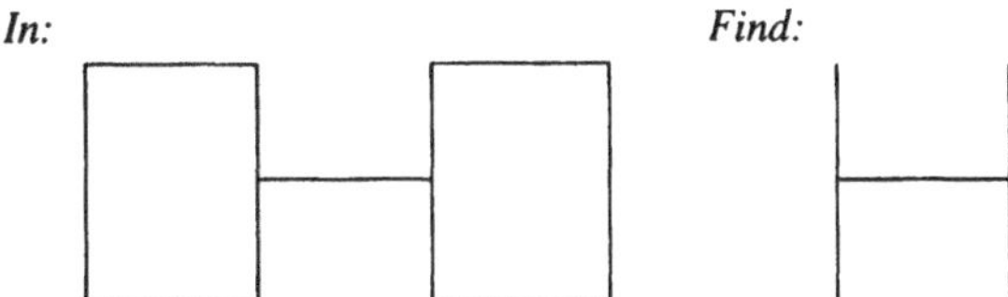

Amerindian hunters do very well at this (Berry 1976), but African agriculturalists (Berry 1976) and Australian gatherers (McIntyre 1976) do poorly.

In contrast, the closure test assesses integrative cognitive style by asking the respondent to identify objects from pictures that portray only parts of them.

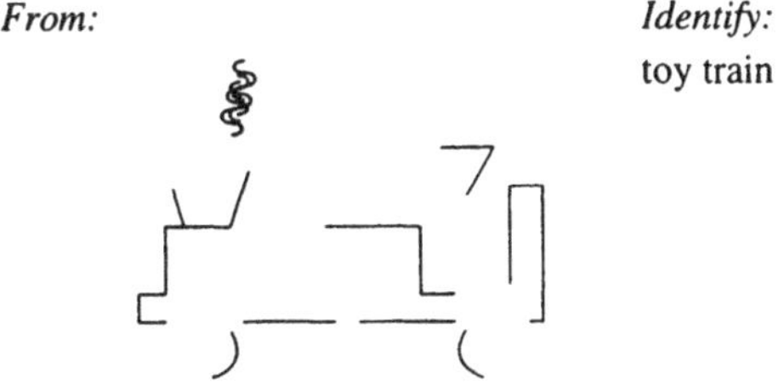

Aborigine gatherers did unusually well at this compared to Euro-Australians (TenHouten 1985). However, this test, unlike the embedded-figures test, has not been widely used and is included here mostly to illustrate integrative style.

Independently of these psychological studies, Alan Lomax (1972) discovered the differentiation-integration factor of cognitive style in his studies of song style and dance style. Lomax found that hunters in North America showed a differentiative style, which appears in song as 'individualized and unison singing organization' and in dance as 'a linear dance style.' In contrast, gatherers, especially the Bushmen, showed integrative song and dance styles characterized by 'cohesive and highly integrated singing organization and polyrhythmic, flowing, sensuous dance style' (234).

The second cognitive-style dimension is contextualization. In societies with small populations, where the audience shares a lot of background information, a very contextualized style of thought and communication is feasible, in which the audience infers a great deal of information from context. Lomax's factor analyses of song and dance styles[3] also revealed this dimension. For song style, this shows up in the high frequency of nonsense words in lyrics. Another pioneering study of this variable was carried out by Bernstein (1962), who labelled contextualization 'restricted code' because it only worked when there was shared context between sender and receiver, and decontextualization 'elaborated code' because a message had to be much fuller when the recipient was not likely to share contextual knowledge with the sender. A recent study of contextualization by Hutchins (1980) exemplifies the emergence of a unified cognitive science, since it was done by a psychologist using ethnographic field observation. He observed a very contextualized style of reasoning in a land dispute before a traditional court in the Trobriand Islands. For instance, there were times that the judge did not explain major legal points, stating instead that everyone in court knew them, nor did he give his judgment in full because he intimated that it was obvious to all present.

In contrast, in societies with large populations, strangers abound who might not share background information, so it is necessary to adopt a decontextualized style in which thoughts are fully expressed. In Lomax's studies of song style this shows up in wordy, explicit lyrics such as those of the European ballad. Chafe and Danielewicz (1987) have shown how an audience of strangers is presumed in formal and written communications and various decontextualizing devices such as passives and nominalizations appear.

Having introduced the two cognitive-style variables, we now turn to the relation between them. The main theorist of cognitive style, Herman Witkin, treated the two cognitive-style variables we have just defined as 'aspects' of one variable, field dependency (Witkin et al. 1962). Under this view, field dependence is a combination of contextualization and integration, and field independence is a combination of decontextualization and differentiation. Studies by John Berry (1976), using this single-variable theory, led to the puzzle that hunters such as the Eskimo had very high scores on the embedded-figures test just as European groups did, and this apparently meant that they had a similar field-independent cognitive style (since differentiation measured by the embedded-figures test is a component of field independence). Yet it was painfully apparent that Eskimos, like other hunters, experienced a lot of cognitive stress in adjusting to the demands of Western schooling and jobs. The solution, which I have pursued in collaboration with Berry, was to modify the theory from Witkin's one variable to the two that I have introduced above.

To show that the two aspects of field dependency were separate variables, evidence from hunters was crucial, because the two hypothesized variables are correlated in industrial groups and in mid-level agricultural groups such as those found in Africa. Western samples are both differentiative and decontextualizing, whereas African agriculturalists show the opposite value of each variable, being integrative (low differentiative) and contextualizing. Since hunters are hypothesized to be differentiative and contextualizing, as shown in the figure below, it is crucial to have data from them in order to establish the two-variable theory. Under the new theory, the high scores obtained by hunters on embedded-figures tests are interpreted as high differentiation. Therefore the first task at hand was to show that hunting groups were contextualizing. This hypothesis also applies to slash-and-burn agricultural groups who, as will be argued below, are similar to hunters in cognitive style, although different in other aspects of cognition discussed later in the paper. We chose the task most widely used by psychologists in the past, deductive reasoning, and devised a simple measure of contextualizing, counting the number of suggestions about and requests for added information. With the help of an honours student, Lori-Anne Davis, we found that Mohawk respondents made many such additions when given an unfamiliar deductive-reasoning task, whereas Euro-Canadians made almost none. More recently, in collaboration with a field anthropologist, Jo Anne Bennett, we have asked Northern Ojibway people to do both the embedded-figures test and the deductive task, and have shown that they are differentiative as measured by high scores in embedded figures, and also contextualizing as measured by requests for background information. In this way Amerindian evidence has demonstrated that two separate cognitive-style variables have to be recognized, since the values of the variables are differently combined in different kinds of societies, as shown in the figure:

	contextualizing	decontextualizing
integrative	mid-level agriculture	
differentiative	hunters	Western

With this background we can look at the theoretical status of the notion of cognitive style. One issue concerns the relative stability or flexibility of styles such as contextualization. They are regarded as more rigid if they apply across many contexts, and as more flexible if they apply to only selected contexts.

However, there can be no radical flexibility by which people are free to contextualize or decontextualize no matter what the setting. This is because all cognitive styles are sets of learned habits that must be acquired by considerable practice in particular contexts, as has been emphasized by Cook-Gumperz (1983). Therefore, when we observe fluent performance of any cognitive style there must have been past opportunities to acquire it. An interesting case of learned flexibility in contextualizing has been presented by Charles Briggs (1985). He discusses proverbs, a genre that is inherently contextualized – the point of communicating in proverbs is to use a brief, conventionalized message to elicit a great deal of other reflection from the context of the hearers' memories. Briggs shows that the Mexicanos he observed knew how, optionally, to decontextualize their proverbs when it was necessary to explain them to neophytes.

When we talk of cultures that are contextualizing or decontextualizing, this variability in the range of contexts that are approached with the one style or the other has to be recognized. It is accurate to say of industrial culture that it is decontextualized because there are very many contexts, especially highly valued ones like logic and mathematics, that call forth decontextualized thought, in which messages are fully explicit and self-contained. Nonetheless, we know from the work of Chafe and others that in informal, intimate settings people in industrial culture switch fluently to a contextualized style, constructing messages that are incomplete and require contextual interpretation.

The more complex point comes when we also recognize that some cultures are, overall, a fairly even mix of contexts that call forth one cognitive style and those that call forth its opposite. This was claimed by Lomax for some cultures in his studies of song and dance style – the irrigation agricultural societies that he called 'Old High Cultures' show a mixture of those features that are more exclusively emphasized in the more polarized societies. This is quite readily observable in dance styles. An emphatically integrative style is seen in the whole body and limb positions of African dance, and an emphatically differentiative style is seen in the detailed foot movements of European step dancing. However, the dance styles of India are a genuinely intermediate mixture with their integrative whole-body movements and their differentiative hand gestures. Evidence from cognitive studies similarly shows a mixture of cognitive styles in the irrigation agricultural societies. For instance, Japanese people show a differentiative cognitive style on tasks like the embedded-figures test (Iwawaki 1986), but an integrative style in their written communication (Harder 1984).

Overall, the attraction of cognitive style as a theoretical notion is that it simultaneously emphasizes the habitual nature of thinking and the fact that these habits are attached to contexts. Moreover, I should emphasize that these contexts are social, as seen in Hutchins's study of a Trobriand court and Cook-Gumperz's study of a classroom. The frequent use of cognitive-style concepts, whether explicitly or implicitly, in current cross-cultural cognitive science, testifies to their usefulness in partially filling the lack, which Sapir discerned, of psychological notions linking individuals to their culture. However, we must acknowledge that his further call for the study of emotional and aesthetic aspects of cognition remains largely unanswered.

Amerindian Cognition and Early Agriculture

I turn now to my third topic, studies of the cognitive associates of incipient agriculture among Amerindian groups, which constitute a present-day extension of one of Sapir's favourite themes, the connections of semantic analysis and culture history (Sapir 1916). With respect to the cognitive-style variables just discussed, Amerindian slash-and-burn agriculturalists are similar to hunters. Lonner and Sharp (1983) found that Yucatan (Mayan) villagers did well on embedded-figures tests, the favoured measure of differentiation, just as Eskimo and Cree do. A parallel similarity between Amerindian hunters and agriculturalists was observed for song and dance styles by Lomax (1972). In contrast, it is well established that mid-level agriculturalists such as African villagers lack the differentiative cognitive style as shown by poor performance on embedded-figures tests (Berry 1976). The inference I draw from this is that slash-and-burn agriculture does not take one very far along in the changes of society and mind that accompany agriculture. Nonetheless, there are particular cognitive preferences associated with early agricultural development that are revealed by Amerindian studies, and it is on these that I want to focus.

I will illustrate this first point for ontological categories. These are concepts such as 'state,' 'place,' 'animate,' 'elongated,' and 'artefact,' which, although encoded in our minds similarly to ordinary concepts, such as 'red,' 'garden,' 'bear,' and 'pencil,' in fact play special roles in forming and using the latter. They are valuable mental housekeepers because we have only 50 to 200 of them but 20,000 to 50,000 ordinary concepts – these numbers are only reasonable guesses. One indication of the separateness of ontological concepts is that, when they are encoded in language, they are expressed by their own special class of morphemes, called classifiers (Denny 1986), in contrast to the nouns, verbs, adjectives, and adverbs that express ordinary concepts. When ontological concepts are not expressed in classifiers, their presence in thought can be inferred from psycholinguistic evidence (Keil 1979).

If we look at the ontological categories expressed by classifiers in some Iroquoian languages, we see interesting signs of what gets emphasized in the early stages of agriculture: special attention is given to the distinction between 'natural kinds' and 'artefacts.' Although psychologists such as Keil (1989) and philosophers such as Putnam (1975) have argued that this is a vital distinction for all humans, many of the Iroquoian languages are unusual in marking this distinction on nouns. Gunther Michelson (1969) has shown that the noun prefix *ka-* is the classifier for artefacts, for instance, in Mohawk *kanata*, 'village' (the source for the word *Canada*), whereas the prefix *o-* is the classifier for natural things, as in *onontiara*, 'lake' (the source for *Ontario*). Some other languages have classifier systems that express the ontological concept 'artefact,' but they do so in conjunction with many other categories; Iroquoian is unusual in marking only the contrast between artefacts and natural kinds. This seems to point up one new aspect of life in incipient agricultural villages: artefacts have become much more important. Not only are the domesticated plants partly man-made, they grow in fields shaped by substantial human efforts. This new way of life was under way in the lower Great Lakes and Ohio valley by AD 900 and fully developed by AD 1300 (Ellis and Ferris 1990). By the latter date one's personal space was enclosed by the longhouse and the palisade, much bigger constructions than the teepee or the wigwam of hunting days. Not only is the agricultural life new, however, Mithun (1991) has shown that the Iroquoian classifier morphemes *ka-* and *o-* are relatively recent formations from pronouns; the degree to which they are unconsciously reinterpreted as classifiers for natural kinds and artefacts varies considerably across the languages.

To trace the development of Iroquois agriculture, and the cognitive consequences of it that we are focusing on, requires that we replace the categorization of the Iroquoians as slash-and-burn agriculturalists with a detailed culture history that makes clear where and when they became involved in corn agriculture. The usual theory since the 1950s, which hypothesized that these developments took place in the lower Great Lakes, is now doubted on linguistic and archaeological grounds. Snow (1995) has proposed that the Iroquoians came here between AD 700 and 900. Alternatively, I have proposed that they arrived only about AD 1300 (Denny 1994), having previously been part of the Monongahela tradition of the upper Ohio drainage and the Feurt phase on the middle Ohio. I mention these efforts, which are just getting under way, so that it will be understood that all the cultural categories I use in this paper – hunters, gatherers, and the rest – are convenient approximations that are to be replaced by the actual culture history of each group. This is what Sapir (1916) ardently advocated when he wrote that anthropological findings 'cannot be understood ... except as the end-points of specific sequences of events reaching back into the remote past' (Mandelbaum 1958: 391).

There is another ontological category that is emphasized in Iroquoian language, which also seems to point to the new emphasis on people making things that characterizes early agriculture. This ontological concept, 'accomplishment,' is one that concerns occurrences not objects: since it is not directly encoded in a classifier morpheme, it must be inferred from other parts of the language. My studies of this were done with Marion Johnson and M.E. O'Neail. Accomplishments are a secondary ontological category of occurrence that is sometimes developed as well as the three basic categories, 'process,' 'event,' and 'state.' The word *arrive* counts as an example of an event verb in English, because one can't say *has arrived*, using perfect aspect, until the arriving is all over, whereas *walk* is a process verb because one can say *has walked* even though walking continues. On the other hand, the process 'walk' has duration: one can say *walk for an hour*; but events do not: one cannot say *arrive for an hour* in the sense of 'spending an hour arriving.' Accomplishments such as 'build a house' are compound occurrences starting with a process and ending with an event. Therefore, like an event, one can only say *I have built the house* (using perfect aspect) when it's finished. However, like a process, one can *build the house for an hour*. This distinctive pattern of encoding establishes accomplishments as a special ontological category of occurrences in English.

In Iroquoian the category of accomplishments is larger than in English (Denny, Johnson, and O'Neail 1985). This can be seen in the fact that, in accordance with our original distinction between accomplishments and processes, many Iroquoian verbs have perfect-aspect forms that refer only to times after the action is completed, showing that they are treated as accomplishments. In contrast, the English verbs for the same occurrence allow the perfect-aspect forms to refer to times before the end of the action, showing they are treated as processes. Examples from Oneida are *thoˀsəhtu*, 'he has lowered something,' and *loyəthu*, 'he has planted' – neither of these can be used until the action is completed. In contrast, both English equivalents are process verbs, so one can say *he has lowered it for awhile and is still lowering it*, and *he has planted for an hour and is still planting*. The generality of this pattern is confirmed by Chafe's (1980) finding that another Iroquoian language, Seneca, has many accomplishment verbs that are process verbs in Japanese.

The extra emphasis on accomplishment verbs in Iroquoian languages can be more clearly associated with incipient agriculture when we observe that in the languages of neighbouring hunting groups there is no lexical category of accomplishments; all are treated as processes. In Eskimo, simple verbs allow the same two aspectual meanings, whether they are accomplishments or processes: for an accomplishment such as 'walk to the store,' *niuvirvingmut pisuktuq* can mean 'she is walking to the store' or 'she walked to the store (just now),' and similarly for the process 'walk,' *pisuktuq* can mean 'he is walking' or 'he walked (just now).' However, the contrast with event verbs remains: *tikittuq* can only mean 'she arrived (just now)' and cannot mean 'she is arriving.' Accomplishments are also lumped with processes for temporal adverbs in Eskimo, although English distinguishes them with different prepositions. The distinction is marked in English by *in* for accomplishments and *for* for processes; for instance, accomplishment: *they walked to Churchill in four days*, compared to process: *they walked for four days*. This is not marked in the Eskimo where only the bare adverb 'four days' appears: *ublunik sitamanik Kuujjuarmut pisulauqtuit*, literally 'days four Churchill-to walked-they,' and *ublunik sitamanik pisulauqtuit*, literally 'days four walked-they.'

The same is true of Cree (Algonquian); accomplishments belong to the same unmarked category as processes, whereas events have a distinctive marker *-in-* ; for instance, accomplishment *nipahaci-wak*, 'they freeze to death' and process *ma:kwaci-wak* 'they are oppressed by the cold,' but event, *takos-in-wak*, 'they arrive.'[4]

If we could add another unrelated slash-and-burn agricultural society to the Iroquoian ones, the pattern would be more strongly in evidence. Such a one is Tzeltal (Mayan) in which an exaggerated emphasis on accomplishments shows up in a quite different part of the language. Berlin (1968) reports that Tzeltal has nine noun classifiers for the ontological categories that are 'inherent states' of things, for instance, *-č'iš-* for 'elongated and rigid' things like sticks (174ff.). More important, however, the language also has hundreds of classifiers for 'temporary states' of things, most of which are the results of accomplishment actions applied to the thing in question. In many cases, it is the number of result states that is counted rather than the number of things; for instance, classifier *-puhȼ*,' 'bends,' in *ˀošpuhȼ' teˀ*, 'three bends in a tree (stem)' (ibid.: 63). Among the world's classifier systems Tzeltal presents an extraordinary emphasis on the results brought about by accomplishments.

In sum, we found no distinct treatment of accomplishments such as 'build a house' among hunters (Eskimo, Cree), exaggerated emphasis on them among incipient agriculturalists (Iroquois, Tzeltal), and continuing but lesser expression in more complex agricultural societies (English, Japanese). For the Iroquois, we saw above that this emphasis is combined with an emphasis upon artefacts provided by the classifier *ka-*; artefacts are, of course, produced by accomplishment actions. The cognitive consequences of agriculture discovered in Amerindian research seem to point to the enormously expanded load of artefact-making actions. Amerindian studies by archaeologists reveal other aspects of early agriculture, notably a decrease in nutrition and health Cohen and Armelagos 1984). It seems as though the Old Testament view (Genesis 3) of the transition to agriculture may be apt – unrelenting toil and greater mortality. Perhaps because agriculture developed slowly and recently among the native peoples of Northeastern North America, studies of their incipient agricultural societies are likely to continue to offer theoretical contributions.

Conclusion

I have set forth a number of themes from current work in cross-cultural cognition that I think continue and develop Americanist theorizing. The most straightforward of these has been the recent experimental support for the weak Whorfian hypothesis and its adoption as a part of several new theories in cognitive science. My second topic, cognitive style, is appealing because it offers a way to develop Sapir's emphasis on habitual cognition attuned to social contexts. Finally, my review of work on the historical development of the cognitive correlates of incipient agriculture shows that much more can be achieved in line with Sapir's demonstrations of culture historical changes in ideas. It seems that the Americanist Tradition is still going forward in ways that have not been much heralded.

NOTES

1 Why was he delivering his first lecture late in October? He was not snowed in up north, but rather was called in to replace an instructor retired for alcoholism.

2 These verbs exemplify Sapir's famous claim that Algonquian words are 'like tiny imagist poems' (1921: 228). The first is literally 'I-forked-sticklike-by.hand-do.to.it,' and the second is 'I-forked-sticklike-foot-do.' The second morpheme 'forked' is adverbial, although called the root or initial in Algonquian morphology. The third one 'sticklike' is a noun classifier, called by Algonquianists a classificatory medial. It expresses the ontological category 'elongated and rigid' to which the patient of the action belongs, either the branch or the toe. The remaining two elements, treated as single units called finals by Algonquianists, contain the verb morphemes. In the first word the verb is *-n-* 'do by hand,' and *-a* is a verb class marker (the meaning of which is discussed in Denny 1983). In the second word the verb is *-e* 'do a characteristic action involving something' and the something is expressed by an incorporated noun, in this case *-sit-*, 'foot, toe.' For body parts the characteristic action is usually interpreted pragmatically as 'having.' Algonquian languages are unusual in allowing the use of both a noun classifier and an incorporated noun referring to the same participant, the toe. The fusing of adverb, verb, and nominal elements in a single word is what gives the imagistic compactness. The noun classifiers and incorporated nouns of Algonquian are discussed in Denny 1989.

3 Those familiar with Lomax's work will realize that the usual terminology I am employing is cross-cut by Lomax's terms in a very confusing fashion. He calls the differentiation-integration factor 'integration,' and worse, he calls the contextualization factor 'differentiation,' alluding primarily to the decontextualized end.

4 I have argued for these and other semantic verb class markers in Denny 1985. The standard

Algonquian morphology does not always recognize them – these words would be divided into root-final-inflection: *nipah-aci-wak, tako-sin-wak.*

REFERENCES

Berlin, Brent. 1968. *Tzeltal Numeral Classifiers*. The Hague: Mouton.
Bernstein, B. 1962. 'Social Class, Linguistic Codes and Grammatical Elements.' *Language and Speech* 5: 221.
Berry, John W. 1976. *Human Ecology and Cognitive Style*. New York: Wiley.
Briggs, Charles L. 1985. 'The Pragmatics of Proverb Performances in New Mexican Spanish.' *American Anthropologist* 87: 793–810.
Chafe, Wallace. 1980. 'Consequential Verbs in Northern Iroquoian Languages and Elsewhere.' In K. Klar et al., eds, *American Indian and Indoeuropean Studies*, 43–9. The Hague: Mouton.
Chafe, W., and J. Danielewicz. 1987. 'Properties of Spoken and Written Language.' In R. Horowitz and F.J. Samuels, eds, *Comprehending Oral and Written Language*, New York: Academic Press.
Cohen, Mark N., and George J. Armelagos. 1984. *Paleopathology at the Origins of Agriculture*. New York: Academic Press.
Cook-Gumperz, Jenny. 1983. 'Socialization, Social Identity and Discourse.' In A. Jacobson-Widding, ed., *Identity: Personal and Socio-Cultural*, 123–33.
Denny, J. Peter. 1983. 'Semantics of Abstract Finals in Algonquian Transitive Inanimate Verbs.' *Canadian Journal of Linguistics* 28: 133–48.
– 1985. 'Semantic Verb Classes and Abstract Finals.' In William Cowan, ed., *Papers of the 15th Algonquian Conference*, 241–71. Ottawa: Carleton University.
– 1986. 'The Semantic Role of Noun Classifiers.' In Colette Craig, ed., *Noun Classes and Categorization*, 297–308. Amsterdam: John Benjamins.
– 1989. 'The Nature of Polysynthesis in Algonquian and Eskimo.' In Donna B. Gerdts and Karin Michelson, eds, *Theoretical Perspectives on Native American Languages*, 230–58. Albany: State University of New York Press.
– 1994. 'Archaeological Correlates for Iroquoian and Siouan.' Read at Iroquois Conference, Rensselaerville, NY.
Denny, J. Peter, Marion Johnson, and Mary Elizabeth O'Neail. 1985. 'Le concept d'accomplissement dans les langues et les cultures amérindiennes.' *Recherches Amérindiennes aux Québec* 14: 36–41.
Ellis, Chris J., and Neal Ferris. 1990. *The Archaeology of Southern Ontario to A.D. 1650*. London, Ont.: Occasional Publication of the London Chapter, Ontario Archaeological Society, No. 5.
Gipper, H. 1976. 'Is There a Linguistic Relativity Principle?' In R. Pinxten, ed., *Universalism versus Relativism in Language and Thought*, 217–28. The Hague: Mouton.
Harder, Bernhard D. 1984. 'Cultural Attitudes in Discourse Analysis.' *Canadian Journal of Linguistics* 29: 115–30.
Havelock, Eric A. 1963. *Preface to Plato*. Cambridge: Harvard University Press.
Hutchins, Edwin. 1980. *Culture and Inference: A Trobriand Case Study*. Cambridge: Harvard University Press.
Iwawaki, Saburo. 1986. 'Achievement Motivation and Socialization.' In S.E. Newstead, S.H. Irvine, and P.L. Dann, eds, *Human Assessment: Cognition and Motivation*, 341–50. Dordrecht: Nijhoff.
Kay, Paul, and Willett Kempton. 1984. 'What Is the Sapir-Whorf Hypothesis?' *American Anthropologist* 86: 65–79.

Keil, Frank C. 1979. *Semantic and Conceptual Development: An Ontological Perspective*. Cambridge: Harvard University Press.

– 1989. *Concepts, Kinds and Cognitive Development*. Cambridge, MA: MIT Press.

Lakoff, George. 1987. *Women, Fire and Dangerous Things*. Chicago: University of Chicago Press.

Lomax, Alan. 1972. 'The Evolutionary Taxonomy of Culture.' *Science* 177: 228–39.

Lonner, Walter J., and Donald W. Sharp. 1983. 'Psychological Differentiation in a Rural Yucatec Mayan Village.' In S.H. Irvine and J.W. Berry, eds, *Human Assessment and Cultural Factors*. New York: Plenum.

Lucy, John. 1992. *Grammatical Categories and Cognition*. Cambridge: Cambridge University Press.

Maclay, H. 1958. 'An Experimental Study of Language and Non-Linguistic Behaviour.' *Southwestern Journal of Anthropology* 14: 220–29.

Mandelbaum, David G. 1958. *Selected Writings of Edward Sapir*. Berkeley: University of California Press.

McIntyre, L.A. 1976. 'An Investigation of the Effect of Culture and Urbanization on Three Cognitive Styles and Their Relationship to School Performance.' In G.E. Kearney and D.W. McElwain, eds, *Aboriginal Cognition*, 231–56. Canberra: Australian Institute of Aboriginal Studies.

Michelson, Gunther. 1969. 'Einige Gedanken zur Klassifizierung von Substantiven in Mohawk.' *Abhandlung der Volkerkundlichen Arbeitsgemeinschaft* 19: 13–17.

Mithun, Marianne. 1991. 'The Nearly Opaque ka-/o- Distinction in Iroquoian Nouns.' Read at American Anthropological Asoociation, Chicago. (See also Mithun, forthcoming, 'Noun and Verb in Iroquoian.' In Bernard Comrie and Petra Vogel, eds, *An Anthology of Verb Classes*. Amsterdam: John Benjamins.)

Putnam, Hilary. 1975. 'The Meaning of "Meaning."' In *Mind, Language and Reality. Philosophical Papers*, vol. 2: 25–271. Cambridge: Cambridge University Press.

Sapir, Edward. 1916. 'Time Perspective in Aboriginal American Culture: A Study in Method.' *Geological Survey of Canada Memoir 90*. Ottawa. Reprinted 1958 in David G. Mandelbaum, ed., *Selected Writings of Edward Sapir*, 389–462. Berkeley: University of California Press.

– 1921. *Language: An Introduction to the Study of Speech*. New York: Harcourt, Brace.

– 1994. *The Psychology of Culture*. Ed. J.T. Irvine. Berlin: Mouton de Gruyter.

Smith, Linda B., and Maria D. Sera. 1992. 'A Developmental Analysis of the Polar Structure of Dimensions.' *Cognitive Psychology* 24: 99–142.

Snow, Dean R. 1995. 'Migration in Prehistory: The Northern Iroquoian Case.' *American Antiquity* 60: 59–79.

TenHouten, Warren D. 1985. 'Right Hemisphericity of Australian Aboriginal Children: Effects of Culture, Sex, and Age on Performances of Closure and Similarities Tests.' *International Journal of Neuroscience* 28: 125–46.

Thelen, Esther, and Linda B. Smith. 1994. *A Dynamic Systems Approach to the Development of Cognition and Action*. Cambridge, MA: MIT Press.

Whorf, Benjamin L. 1940. 'Science and Linguistics.' *Technology Review (MIT)* 42: 229–31, 247–8. Reprinted 1956 in J.B. Carroll, ed., *Language, Thought and Reality*, 207–19. Cambridge, MA: MIT Press.

– 1941. 'Languages and Logic.' *Technology Review (MIT)* 43: 250–2, 266, 268, 272. Repr. 1956 in Carroll, ed., *Language, Thought and Reality*, 233–45.

Witkin, H.A., R.B. Dyk, H.F. Faterson, D.R. Goodenough, and S.A. Karp. 1962. *Psychological Differentiation*. New York: Wiley.

25 Anticipating Queer Theory

WILLIAM L. LEAP

In this paper, I consider the connections between the Americanist Tradition and the set of intellectual and political claims subsumed under the inclusive label 'queer theory.'[1] I suggest here that Americanist ethnography anticipates in interesting ways queer theory's interests in lesbian/gay experience, and I use an analysis of a Gay English conversation (part of the database from my current research) to show how particular points of anticipation further a 'queer reading' of such texts.

On Queer Theory: Rethinking Gender

Other papers in this volume (Darnell, Cove, Valentine) identify key points in the Americanist concerns with language and culture. Building directly on those discussions, I begin by reviewing some of the concerns of queer theory.[2]

Queer theory is closely associated with current trends in lesbian/gay studies, though the scope of this position is much broader than that specified by either (or both) of those labels. Queer theory offers a critique of privileged forms of normativity in contemporary society. It addresses this goal by proposing a range of open-ended, self-reflexive, and often quite **[image]**inary interpretations to conditions of marginality. Queer theory uses the *border*, the *fringe*, and the native side of the *frontier*, rather than sites within the mainstream, as the starting point for those interpretations, and uses voices from the border, the fringe, and the frontier as the database for this inquiry.

With queer theory comes a reconfiguration of the categories that social scientists and humanists have traditionally used to describe social identities, since narratives from the margin do not support the distinctiveness, stability, or autonomy of these categories. Conventional gender theory holds, for example, that heterosexuality locates desire by pairing attractions between gender opposites; for instance, heterosexual men have sex with heterosexual women. Queer perspective reverses the direction of this argument. Instead of assuming that gender categories are *prediscursive* (that is, gender exists independently of the details of the social moment), queer theory assumes that gender categories are *performative* (that is, gender is a consequence of situated social practice, and not necessarily the cause); and that gender 'identity' designates a position (or stance) negotiated *out of* a particular social space, a position that may not be relevant to the social action unfolding in some other, equally particular locale.

On Queer Theory: Rethinking Identity

Queer theory is not, however, only about gender. Race, class, ethnicity, and nationalism are also performative categories under this paradigm, and need to be studied accordingly. Indeed, some of the really interesting work in queer theory involves instances where displacement, nostalgia, and/or desire have fused race, class position, ethnic background, and nationalist loyalty into multilayered claims to personal space. (*Nationalisms and Sexualities* [Parker et al. 1992] and *Displacements* [Bammer 1994] are two recent collections of papers that richly develop these themes.)

The meanings emerging from these claims to space do not always conform to the convenient gender typologies proclaimed by traditional 'identity theory,' nor do they necessarily yield to other, self-evident interpretations. Three anecdotes from recent fieldwork embellish this point:

- I asked one of the Latino men working with me on a study of 'language and gay city' to explain why he never discussed his active participation in Washington, DC's gay Hispanic community with his family and his friends. Was he afraid that other people would react negatively if they thought he was gay? 'But I'm not gay, I'm Fernando!' was his reply.
- I am listening to a forty-year-old man describe how he had just completed a sexual interaction with a twenty-six-year-old college student in a health-club sauna. I asked if he knew of other gay men who regularly came to the health club to look for male sex-partners. Immediately, he reminded me that he is not gay; he is 'married with three kids, for crissake!' Moreover, because he is not gay, his having sex with men is not 'gay sex,' so (he continued) he does not worry about conforming to 'safe sex' guidelines when he encounters a more adventurous male partner.
- A thirty-two-year-old African American man, who self-identifies as a gay African American, assured me that he does not really feel (quoting him directly) 'connected to the gay community in Washington DC at all. I just go

> two-steppin' once a week at [a DC gay bar that features Country and Western music].' He paused, then added, 'I'm really not a credit to my race or my gender.'

Understandably, queer theory responds to such claims by treating identity, like gender, as an unstable social category, something constructed in response to a particular position within the social moment, something that may be constructed quite differently as positions and moments change. Accordingly, queer research does not seek to define in some generic sense a person's claims to identity – or ethnicity, or gender – so much as it seeks to situate and deconstruct particular occurrences (or *instantiations*) of such claims. This process is termed *queer reading* (Doty 1993: xi–xii), to underscore the subjective and interpretive nature of such tasks.

On the Americanist Convergence with Queer Theory

Why discuss queer theory in a collection of papers focusing on the Americanist Tradition? Queer theorists do not claim close association with Boas, Sapir, or other of the anthropologists who helped to develop that paradigm. And, outside of occasional comments about North American 'berdache' or other liminal figures in tribal society, Americanist anthropologists have had very little to say about gender diversity and marginality.

Americanist anthropologists have, however, had a lot to say about the grand theorizing of the nineteenth-century evolutionists and other researchers whose work gave minimal attention to situational detail. As Darnell and Cove explain elsewhere in this volume, Americanists favoured context-specific descriptions of social action, particularly descriptions that foreground the 'insider perspectives' of individual social actors. Accordingly, collection and analysis of text (that is, site-specific, situated narratives) became the primary focus of Americanist data-gathering.

Queer theory, it seems to me, makes similar arguments in favour of an engaged, situated, and insider-centred exploration of human experience. Indeed, particular continuities between Americanist positions and recent claims of 'queer theory' are quite striking in this regard.

For example, Ruth Benedict's (1934) use of personality archetypes to account for cross-cultural diversity in social experience closely parallels Judith Butler's (1993) and Eve Sedgwick's (1993) appropriation of (respectively) *melancholia* and *shame* as central themes in queer experience, and Gayle Rubin's (1991) connections between same-sex erotic pleasure, bondage, dominance, and pain.

Similarly, the concerns that Boas (1920, 1929) raised regarding the incautious classification of American Indian languages into more inclusive language families show up in Martin Manalansan's (1994: esp. 61n4) reluctance to describe the sexual diversities emerging out of the Filipino diaspora in terms of Western-based *lesbian* and *gay* identities. Steve Murray's (1995, see also Murray and Arboleda 1987) argument that the worldwide diffusion of the lexical item *gay* does not necessarily coincide with a worldwide replication of a 'stigma-challenging gay community,' and Esther Newton's (1993) depiction of 'the closet' as a means of resistance to heteronormative oppression, as well as a form of accommodation to such pressure, echo similar notes of Boasian caution.

And, certainly, George Devereux's (1937) depictions of gender-crossing identity assumption and erotic practices among Mojave men anticipated Walter Williams's (1986) candid interaction with Lakota third-gendered males and Ralph Bolton's (1995) participatory studies of safe-sex practices in the Brussels bathhouses.

Besides being intellectually interesting in its own right, drawing such connections between the Americanist tradition and queer theory allows lesbian/gay anthropologists to locate lesbian/gay in[**queer**]y within anthropology's grand tradition. This task is worth pursuing, given that lesbian/gay studies is not yet a widely accepted subfield, or career path, within anthropology, and its acceptance will benefit our profession in multiple ways.[3] Pursuing this task will also encourage lesbian/gay anthropologists to recognize that queer theory is not entirely without precedent within our discipline, and that *we* have much to gain, as lesbian/gay scholars, by consulting the perspectives on culture and marginality developed by Americanist colleagues in earlier times.[4]

Case in Point: Queer Reflections on a Gay English Conversation

To show how Americanist perspectives can benefit anthropological interests in lesbian/gay studies, let me turn to some of the issue that I am exploring in my current study of Gay Men's English – specifically, questions concerning the distinctive properties of a Gay English text, and the meaning implied by the term 'gay text' itself.

At issue here, in part, are formal properties of text structure, features of text content, as well as pragmatic choices that enable speakers to make linguistic claims to a public gay identity. But listening is as important as speaking in such cases, since the distinctiveness of Gay English text also depends on the reaction it elicits from its audience (what I have termed elsewhere the *performative effect* of Gay English text) and the gay-related inferencing that such text inspires.

Consider the example below in this regard, an exchange between the maitre d' and a would-be customer at a bookstore/coffeehouse in the Dupont Circle area of Washington, DC. The bookstore/coffeehouse is a 'heterosexual' space by DC standards; that is, the majority of customers are heterosexual persons; management does not attempt to cater to a lesbian/gay clientele. I was with a group of friends on Saturday evening, waiting for a table. I was standing near the maitre d's podium when speaker A began the conversation, and I was able to follow the exchange and take notes for later analysis.

Example I: *But you people are more fun*

Source: Leap, 1996: 2
Setting: The waiting area of a bookstore/cafe in Dupont Circle, Washington, DC
Speakers: A – customer [42-year-old, Euro-American male, spokesperson for a mixed-gendered party of five]
B – maitre d' [mid-twenties, Euro-American male]

A: Table for 5 – how long do we wait ?
B: Table for 5 [pause, consults list] about one hour.
A: 1 hour. [consults with group] Nope, can't do it. That is too long.
B: Try the Mocha House. They might not be too crowded tonight.
A: Yeah, OK, we can go there. But you people are more fun.
B: Well, I don't know about that. [while he says this, moves head to side, drops voice level, gives trace of smile]
A: Yeah, you're right. [establishes direct eye contact with maitre d'] Maybe the Mocha House is more fun, but I still like your dessert drinks here.
B: [not breaking eye contact] Well, you'll just have to come back and try us again sometime.

I was first attracted to this conversation because my carefully honed ethnographic intuition (what my students term a use of *gaydar*) led me to believe that one (and probably both) of the speakers were gay men. However, queer theory cautions against using such prediscursive assumptions about identity as the basis for exploring textual distinctiveness, since identity is a product of text construction and has no independent status of its own.

But when I focused my attention on the details of text construction, I found very few occurrences of the sentence forms and conversational structures that were prominently displayed in the other Gay English conversations I had previously observed and recorded. I was able, however, to locate indications of 'gay presence' in at least two different places within this seemingly gender-neutral text: the maitre d's recommendation of the Mocha House (lines 5–6), and the maitre d's curiously personal concluding comment (lines 14–15).

Let me comment briefly on the content, and the gay-related significance, conveyed through each of these statements.

The reference to Mocha House caught my attention for several reasons. The Mocha house, a smaller and much more intimate facility, is a fifteen-minute walk from the café. If this café was full, the Mocha House (a smaller, more intimate locale) was certainly going to be crowded. So why send a party of five so far out of their way, when they were still likely to end up waiting in line?

Answer: the Mocha House is just around the corner from two of DC's most popular gay restaurants, and is adjacent to a three-block area filled with other gay-oriented businesses. Mocha House itself is often a site for informal gay social exchange. Distance and congestion aside, the indirect reference to DC gay life signalled by the maitre d's recommendation was likely to be noticed by another gay man, especially if he was equally interested in using the exchange as an site for self-disclosure. Speaker A's reply to this recommendation, 'OK, we can go there. But you people are more fun' (lines 7–8) becomes an interesting form of acknowledgment of that message; certainly, it extends the spirit of the maitre d's comment in an equally playful fashion.

I found a different sense of gay message in the closing refrain. The focus here is not gay locale, but gay icon – specifically, the classic refrain (*why doncha' come up sometime and see me*) delivered by the fabulous Mae West in the film *I'm No Angel.* I cannot claim that the maitre d' was deliberately imitating Ms. West in this closing statement. But the parallel that caught my attention does not depend on proof of intentionality. The statement prompts recollection of a previous text strongly connected to gay meaning. It converges with the multiple meanings of Mocha House, as just described, and – for me – it further confirms the likelihood that this text was a site for Gay English performance.

An Americanist Perspective on (Gay) Authenticity

By referring to Example I as a Gay English text, I acknowledge that there are properties associated with this text that yield to a Gay English interpretation. The absence of explicit gay references and of syntactic constructions unique to Gay English conversations is not important here. At issue is the speakers' inclusion of textual materials that can convey gay associations to those who wish to construct them, material included specifically for that purpose for other reasons; and the willingness of the listener to acknowledge that presence and interpret the text accordingly.

In this sense, 'Gay English text' – and perhaps, 'Gay English' itself – becomes a performative by-product of textual reading, one of several interpretations that can be given to such an exchange by persons associated in some fashion with the events in the textual moment, for instance, the speakers themselves, the immediate audience, and (thanks to the publication of this paper) a more detached group of observers.

The performative nature of a Gay English text is not dependent on principles of 'majority rule,' however. If one person (speaker, listener, or observer) identifies 'gay presence' within the text, that identification makes it a **gay** text, as far as that individual is concerned. The interpretation is valid – or, authentic, in the sense I use the term, below – even if other persons do not find anything 'specifically gay' within textual form or content, or others decide to ignore or erase gay presence once they discover it.

Americanist researchers also encountered instances where differences in point of view at the cultural site led to multiple interpretations of textual meaning; for instance, Boas's (1902) encounters with esoteric and exoteric doctrine on the Northwest Coast, Paul Radin's description of 'the thinker' and 'the man of action' in 'the world of primitive man,' Esther Goldfrank's (1926) reflections on variable narrative in Isleta pueblo folktale performance, or James Owen Dorsey's (1884) representations of Omaha ethnographic facts even if 'Two Crows denies it.'

Such discoveries came at a time when colleagues in sociology and other sciences were using 'social norm' and 'deviation' to organize their studies of social variability. Americanist scholars (as a group) theorized variability somewhat differently, by shifting the focus of research from the social norm, and reluctant compliance with totalizing social rule, to the individual and his/her creative movements within social space.

Hence, while Paul Radin writes about the limiting conditions that physical environment, population size, and economic and social practices impose on 'the world of primitive man,' he notes that an acceptance of such determinism does not prevent individuals from reflecting on local experience with (using Radin's terms) a 'ruthless realism and objectivity' (1953: 325). In fact, it is the very '... sense of the proportion of things which the realities of life impose on us' (346) that prompts primitive peoples to work within the context of material limitations, while actively pursuing metaphorical and symbolic practices – folktales, narratives, proverbs, songs, ritual – which ensure that they are not disadvantaged unduly by those limitations.

In a similar sense, Edward Sapir (1924) used the distinction between 'culture, genuine and spurious' to separate cultural experiences that affirm and nourish the human spirit from cultural experiences that degrade and impede self-development and self-expression. Elsewhere (as reported in Irvine 1994: 145), he made the same distinction by contrasting two different forms of individuality: '*culture carrier*,' a passive compliance with culturally imposed directives and roles, and, '*real persona*,' a conscious affirmation of 'integrated entity' (to use Sapir's own words), regardless of the pressures and demands from the larger social whole.

The tension between Sapir's 'spurious' and 'genuine,' between 'culture carrier' and 'real persona,' defines a broad social terrain, and gives individual social actors room to negotiate the terms of daily experience in diverse ways. But if the psychological locus of culture is the individual or a specifically enumerated list of individuals, as Sapir claimed (Irvine 1994: 141), then it is not so important to debate whether such negotiations uphold or violate social norms; what matters is whether such negotiations allow individuals to maintain (or, in Sapir's words, to 'hold on to') their individuality.

Much as was the case for other Americanists, Sapir did not write directly about homosexuality, or attempt to theorize co-sexual experiences, so we can only speculate about how he might have interpreted same-sex identification and co-sexual desire within the genuine/spurious framework.[5] Even so, Sapir's foregrounding of the individual in his discussion of genuineness and authenticity directly addresses notions of queer textual performativity in at least two ways: First, foregrounding the individual restores a sense of *person* to the starting point for performative social action; it re-personalizes an otherwise de-personalized 'body' (in the sense of Butler 1990: 139, 142). Second, foregrounding the individual insists (and, thereby, recasts Butler's claim [1990: 25, 142]) that the doer – while certainly a product of performative action – is still present, somehow, within the deed.

Viewed in these terms, an authentic gay text becomes a text that affirms gay individuality – a site in which speakers and/or listeners are able to express and embellish 'real [gay] persona' in unencumbered, self-affirming ways.[6] By my reading, this is exactly what was going on in the linguistic negotiations between customer and maitre d' in Example I. The presuppositions underlying this exchange did not obligate either party toward self-disclosure; in fact, several features (for instance, the at-work setting for the maitre d', the public location of the exchange, the possibility of eliciting negative reactions from a stranger) cautioned the speakers against such an action. Yet neither speaker was willing to be silent in the face of such constraints. Both speakers considered Gay identity to be something worth sharing, the conditions of risk notwithstanding.[7] And, judging by the length and the tone of the exchange, both speakers certainly enjoyed using the conversation as a site for carefully negotiated, mutual disclosure.[8]

The politics of expression and disclosure that are at issue in this example resemble the politics underlying other forms of gendered text, and other texts 'from the margin,' in American English.[9] I do not claim that there is anything 'uniquely gay' in the linguistic negotiations that I have discussed here; indeed, an activity does not need to be 'unique' in order to be authentic, in the affirmative, self-fulfilling sense of Sapir's usage. The presence of the activity within the text and the contextual significance of the presence are what matters, under this formulation. Queer theory makes the same claim, by insisting that studies of lesbian, gay, and other marginal experiences be oriented 'at the site' and 'in the moment,' since only in these terms can the constructed nature of such experiences be fully explored within the textual moment. Sapir and other Americanists may not have used that terminology, but they certainly advanced similar arguments when they theorized human behaviour, and – much as I have suggested through my analysis of Example I here – proponents of queer theory can benefit greatly from their insights.

NOTES

1 Thanks for Elizabeth Sheehan, Alan Hersker, Steve Murray, Lisa Valentine, and Regna Darnell for their help and encouragement as I developed the arguments presented in this chapter. I dedicate this chapter to the memory of William S. Willis, Jr, distinguished anthropologist and Americanist historian, who taught all of his graduate students at Southern Methodist University unforgettable lessons about theory, marginality, and resistance.

2 I make these comments, mindful that there is no single 'canon' or central set of claims within 'queer theory.' De Lauretis (1991), Doty (1993), Champagne (1995), and the papers in Beemyn and Eliason (1996) and in Warner (1993) offer additional perspectives on these issues.

3 I am assuming here that queer theory, like other trends in present-day lesbian/gay studies, has a legitimate place in the 'house of anthropology' (borrowing Kath Weston's [1993] creative phrasing), and that the methods and theories guiding and emerging from such inquiry have much to offer the discipline as a whole. However, as long as anthropology remains indifferent to queer theory (or only barely tolerant of its claims), then anthropologists with such interests have no choice but to turn to literary criticism, textual philosophy, popular culture studies, and other external disciplines in order to find support for their work. Under such an arrangement, theory-building in queer anthropology is more likely to support the claims being developed within those outside disciplines than to propose anthropological insights into queer experience. Ellen Lewin and I discuss this problem in greater detail in Lewin and Leap 1996.

4 This observation acknowledges the biases and shortcomings in some areas of Americanist ethnographic description, but assumes that these weaknesses do not restrict the usefulness of such research for queer theory or other, more contemporary ethnographic projects.

5 Herdt and Boxer (1992) use Sapir's distinction between genuine and spurious culture to make additional arguments about authenticity in gay culture.

6 The site, not the setting, is the critical element in the textual moment, according to this argument.

If 'Gay text' is the consequence of a displayed (or performed) gay persona, then gay text can emerge in *any* setting where such performance can unfold.

7 I discuss other ways in which 'language of risk' is a factor shaping Gay English conversations in Leap 1996.

8 Other gay men foreground similar characteristics of Gay English text-making when they tell me (in formal interviews and informal discussions) that 'talking gay' is a lot of fun.

9 For example, Gay men's linguistic negotiations when 'coming out' to friends and family are strikingly similar to the uses of language that women are forced to employ when disclosing their status as rape survivors, and to the cautious declarations through which persons who are HIV-positive confirm that status in public domains.

REFERENCES

Bammer, Angelika, ed. 1995. *Displacements: Cultural Identities in Question*. Bloomington: Indiana University Press.

Beemyn, Brett, and Mickey Eliason, eds. 1996. *Queer Studies: A Lesbian, Gay, Bisexual and Transgender Anthology*. New York: New York University Press.

Benedict, Ruth. 1934. *Patterns of Culture*. New York: Houghton-Mifflin.

Boas, Franz. 1902. 'The Ethnological Significance of Esoteric Doctrines.' *Science* 16(n.s.): 872–4.

– 1920. 'The Classification of American Languages.' *American Anthropologist* 22: 367–76.

– 1929. 'Classification of American Indian Languages.' *Language* 5(1).

Bolton, Ralph. 1995. 'Coming Home: The Journey of a Gay Ethnographer in the Years of the Plague.' In Ellen Lewin and William Leap, eds, *Out in the Field*. Urbana: University of Illinois Press.

Butler, Judith. 1990. *Gender Trouble*. New York: Routledge.

– 1993. *Bodies That Matter*. New York: Routledge.

Champagne, John. 1995 *The Ethics of Marginality: A New Approach to Gay Studies*. Minneapolis: University of Minnesota Press.

de Lauretis, Teresa. 1991. 'Queer Theory: Lesbian and Gay Sexualities – An Introduction.' *differences* 3: iii–xviii.

Devereux, George. 1937. 'Institutionalized Homosexuality of the Mo[j]ave Indians.' *Human Biology* 9: 498–527.

Dorsey, James Owen. 1884. *Omaha Sociology*. 3rd annual report of the Bureau of American Ethnology (1880–2). Washington: Government Printing Office.

Doty, Alexander. 1993 *Making Things Perfectly Queer: Interpreting Mass Culture*. Minneapolis: University of Minnesota Press.

Fuss, Diana, ed. 1991. *Inside/Out: Lesbian Theories, Gay Theories*. New York: Routledge.

Goldfrank, Esther. 1926. 'Isleta Variants: A Study in Flexibility.' *Journal of American Folklore*. 39: 70–8.

Herdt, Gilbert, and Andrew Boxer. 1992. 'Introduction: Culture, History and the Life Course of Gay Men.' In Gilbert Herdt, ed., *Gay Culture in America*, 1–27. Boston: Beacon Press.

Irvine, Judith, ed. 1994. *Edward Sapir: The Psychology of Culture – A Course of Lectures*. Berlin: Mouton de Gruyter.

Leap, William. 1996. *Word's Out: Gay Men's English*. Minneapolis: University of Minnesota Press.

Lewin, Ellen, and William L. Leap. 1996. Introduction to Ellen Lewin and William L. Leap, eds, *Toward a Lesbian/Gay Anthropology*. Urbana: University of Illinois Press.

Manalansan, Martin. 1994. 'Searching for Community: Filipino Gay Men in New York City.' In *Dimensions of Desire. Amerasia Journal* 20: 59–73.

– 1995. 'Performing Filipino Gay Experiences in America: Linguistic Strategies in a Transnational Context.' In William Leap, ed., *Beyond the Lavender Lexicon*, 249–66. Newark, NJ: Gordon & Breach Publishers.

Murray, Stephen O. 1995. 'Stigma Transformation and Relexification in the International Diffusion of *gay*.' In William Leap, ed., *Beyond the Lavender Lexicon*, 297–317. Newark, NJ: Gordon & Breach Publishers.

Murray, Stephen O., and Manuel Arboleda. 1987. 'Stigma Transformation and Relexification: "Gay" in Latin America.' In Stephen O. Murray, ed., *Male Homosexuality in Central and South America*, 129–38. New York: Gai Saber Press.

Newton, Esther. 1993. *Cherry Grove, Fire Island: 50 Years in America's First Gay and Lesbian Town*. Boston: Beacon Press.

Parker, Andrew, Mary Russo, Doris Sommer, and Patricia Yaeger, eds. 1992. *Nationalisms and Sexualities*. New York: Routledge.

Radin, Paul. 1953. *The World of Primitive Man*. New York: E.P. Dutton.

Rubin, Gayle. 1991. 'The Catacombs: A Temple of the Butthole.' In Mark Thompson, ed., *Leatherfolk*, 119–41. Boston: Alyson Press.

Sapir, Edward. 1924. 'Culture, Genuine and Spurious.' *American Journal of Sociology* 29: 401–29.

Sedgwick, Eve Kosofsky. 1993. 'Queer Performativity: Henry James' *The Art of the Novel*.' *GLQ* 1: 1–16.

Warner, Michael, ed. 1993. *Fear of a Queer Planet: Queer Politics and Social Theory*. Minneapolis: University of Minnesota Press.

Weston, Kath. 1993. 'Lesbian/Gay Studies in the House of Anthropology.' *Annual Review of Anthropology* 22: 339–67.

Williams, Walter. 1986. *Spirit and the Flesh*. Boston: Beacon Press.

Contributors

Karen L. Adams is an associate professor of linguistics in the English department of Arizona State University. She received her BA in political science and her PhD in linguistics from the University of Michigan. Her current research interests include the construction of opposition as well as gendered identity in televised political debates, political commentary shows, and gang graffiti. She has also published on classificatory systems in Austroasiatic languages. Among her teaching specialties are pragmatics and discourse analysis, sociolinguistics, and language and gender, in addition to occasional co-taught courses in anthropological linguistics.

Margaret Seguin Anderson is a member of the Hartley Bay Tsimshian community through marriage (to Clarence Anderson in 1984) and custom adoption. Her PhD in Linguistics is from the University of Michigan, and she taught for almost twenty years in the Department of Anthropology at the University of Western Ontario. In 1992, she joined the University of Northern British Columbia, where she has served in three administrative positions. She is currently the Regional Chair for UNBC's Northwest Region, and continues to work with First Nations in that region, including the Nisg̱a'a.

Ellen Basso is Professor of Anthropology at the University of Arizona at Tucson. Trained in social anthropology at the University of Chicago, her research has focused upon the people of the Alto Xingu region in central Brazil. Over the years she has become interested in the study of discourse as an opportunity for synthesizing her concerns with ritual performance; psychology and language; the connections between historical consciousness and explanatory functions of narrative in non-literate societies; and biography as a historical genre.

Charles L. Briggs is Professor of Ethnic Studies at the University of California, San Diego. Having conducted research in New Mexico and Venezuela, he is interested in the discursive construction of social inequality based on concepts of race, ethnicity, gender, and class, particularly in law and medicine. His publications include *Learning How to Ask: A Sociolinguistic Appraisal of the Role in Social Science Research* (1986), *Competence in Performance: The Creativity of Tradition in Mexicano Verbal Art* (1988), and an edited volume, *Disorderly Discourse: Narrative, Conflict and Social Inequality* (1996).

Barbara Burnaby is a Professor in the Modern Language Centre and the Department of Curriculum, Teaching and Learning of the Ontario Institute for Studies in Education of the University of Toronto. Her research includes English as a second language for adult immigrants, adult literacy, and language in education for Aboriginal peoples in Canada. Her more recent publications focus on Canadian language policy.

John J. Cove is Professor of Sociology and Anthropology at Carleton University in Ottawa. His North American research has focused on the Northwest Coast and has included commercial fishing activity, oral traditions, and land claims. More recently, he been exploring aboriginal relations to the criminal-justice systems of Canada, Australia, and New Zealand.

Danielle E. Cyr is Associate Professor in the Department of French Studies at York University in Toronto. Her research includes Micmac grammatical and lexical description, and ethical perspectives in fieldwork research on minority/endangered languages.

Regna Darnell is Professor of Anthropology and Director of the Centre for Research and Teaching of Canadian Native Languages at the University of Western Ontario. Previously, she taught for twenty-one years at the University of Alberta, teaching Cree language and culture in collaboration with native speakers and doing fieldwork with the Plains Cree of northern Alberta. Her current research, in collaboration with Lisa Valentine, is on performing First Nations identity in English in southwestern Ontario (Ojibwe and Iroquoian). She also works in the history of anthropology and is the biographer of Edward Sapir. She is a fellow of the Royal Society of Canada.

Raymond J. DeMallie is Professor of Anthropology and Director of the American Indian Studies Research Institute, Indiana University. A specialist in Plains Indian ethnohistory, DeMallie has worked most extensively with the

Sioux (Lakota and Dakota) and the Assiniboine. His interests centre on social systems and religion, and in particular on the use of native-language texts to understand culture through time. He is the editor of *The Sixth Grandfather: Black Elk's Teachings Given to John G. Neihardt* (1984) and of the Plains volume of the Smithsonian Institution's *Handbook of North American Indians* (forthcoming).

J. Peter Denny teaches cross-cultural cognitive psychology at the University of Western Ontario. In addition, he studies cultural differences in thinking by means of lexical semantics and by symmetry analysis of decorative designs. He also tries to work out the culture history that is associated with societal preferences in cognition. He is a consulting editor of the journal *Cognitive Linguistics*.

Raymond D. Fogelson, Professor of Anthropology, of Human Development, and of Social Sciences at the University of Chicago, conducts research on the ethnology and ethnohistory of Indians of the southeastern United States. He is also concerned with issues involving Indian identity, especially with problems of tribal recognition and the repatriation/rematriation of physical remains and material culture. The conjunction of anthropology, the presentation and representation of native peoples, and popular culture, particularly as manifested in world's fairs and resorts, constitute a third focus of research.

Jane H. Hill is Regents' Professor of Anthropology and Linguistics at the University of Arizona. She has worked on a wide range of issues in linguistic anthropology, with a special focus on the sociolinguistics of Native American languages. She has done fieldwork on three Uto-Aztecan languages: Cupeño, Mexicano (Nahuatl), and Tohono O'odham (Papago). She is currently president of the American Anthropological Association.

Dell Hymes is Commonwealth Professor of Anthropology, and Commonwealth Professor of English (Emeritus), at the University of Virginia. Franz Boas and anthropology entered his life as an undergraduate at Reed College, linguistics through graduate work at Indiana University. He has taught at Harvard, Berkeley, and the University of Pennsylvania, where for twelve years he was Dean of the Graduate School of Education. That involvement is reflected in his most recent book, *Ethnography, Linguistics, Narrative Voice*. He founded the journal *Language in Society*, and was its editor for twenty-one years. With retirement he hopes to finish a number of books having to do with Native American ethnopoetics.

William L. Leap is Professor of Anthropology and a member of the core faculty in Women's / Gender Studies at American University in Washington, DC. His publications include studies of American Indian languages, American Indian English, gay men's English, language and AIDS, and public/private sexualities. He is currently studying intersections of race, ethnicity, and class in Washington, DC, Cape Town, South Africa, and Havana, Cuba.

Bea Medicine, true to her nomadic ancestors, was an 'academic nomad' – teaching at Dartmouth, Stanford, and several state universities, which she preferred. She retired from California State University–Northridge and lives on Standing Rock Reservation in South Dakota. She also taught at the Universities of British Columbia, Calgary, Toronto, and Alberta, where she is an Adjunct Professor, and at the Saskatchewan Indian Federated College. She received the first Martin Luther King / Rosa Parks Outstanding Minority Professor award at the University of Michigan and at Wayne State University; the Outstanding Minority Researcher award from the American Educational Research Association; the Distinguished Service Award from the American Anthropological Association; and the Malinowski Award from the Society for Applied Anthropology. An Outstanding Alumna at South Dakota State University, she was Research Coordinator of Women's Issues for the Royal Commission on Aboriginal Peoples, Ottawa, Canada. At present, she serves as a School Board member in Wakpala, South Dakota. Besides anthropological articles, she has published poetry and prose, and has produced a film made in Russia.

Stephen O. Murray earned a PhD in sociology from the University of Toronto with a dissertation that was a social history of American anthropological linguistics (a revised version was published in 1994 as *Theory Groups in the Study of Language in North America: A Social History*). After postdoctoral work in anthropological linguistics at the University of California, Berkeley, he has worked in public health and authored or coauthored a dozen books, including *Taiwanese Culture, Taiwanese Society: A Critical Review of Social Science Research Done on Taiwan.*

Deanna Nyce is Tsimshian by birth and Nisg̱a'a by marriage (1967) and through custom adoption (1970). She moved to the Nass Valley at the behest of husband Harry's grandparents, Eli and Mary Gosnell and Peter and Angus Nyce. Deanna graduated from the NITEP program at the University of British Columbia in 1984, and completed her MEd at UBC's Ts'kel Program in 1990. She is an employee of School District 92, and was seconded to the Ministry of

Education from 1990 to 1992 and to the Wilp Wilxo'oskwh! Nisga'a from 1993 to the present.

Douglas R. Parks is Professor of Anthropology and Associate Director of the American Indian Studies Research Institute, Indiana University. His primary interests are language documentation and ethnohistory, as well as language pedagogy. His work focuses on northern Caddoan languages (Arikara, Pawnee, and Kitsai) and Sioux dialects, especially Assiniboine and Yanktonai. Publications include *A Grammar of Pawnee* (1976), *Ceremonies of the Pawnee* by James R. Murie (edited by Parks, 1981), and *Traditional Narratives of the Arikara Indians* (1991).

Dick Preston is happily married, with a large family, is nominally retired, and hopes to keep going for many years. He is continuing his sojourning and work with the people of the James Bay region, focusing on TEK (Traditional Ecological Knowledge), establishment of a community-based cultural centre that includes seasonal bush activity loci, and completion of a book, *The Cree Frontier*, tracing the emergence of the Cree concept of community. Other intellectual interests include the cultural dimensions of globalization, the relation of cultural meanings to truth, and the optimistic implications that Edward Sapir offers social science.

Robin Ridington received his BA in history from Swarthmore College and his PhD in anthropology from Harvard University. He is Professor Emeritus of Anthropology at the University of British Columbia. His publications include *Trail to Heaven: Knowledge and Narrative in a Northern Native Community*, *Little Bit Know Something: Stories in a Language of Anthropology*, and *Blessing for a Long Time: The Sacred Pole of the Omaha Tribe*. He is currently an independent writer and researcher living on Retreat Island, British Columbia, and is interested in the theory and practice of anthropological poetics.

Blair A. Rudes's work with the Tuscaroras began in 1973, with research on the history of the Tuscarora language that led to a doctorate in linguistics from the State University of New York at Buffalo in 1976. His continuing research on the Tuscarora language and culture resulted in the publication of a two-volume collection of Tuscarora texts in English and Tuscarora in 1987 by the Canadian Museum of Civilization that was co-authored with the Tuscarora historian Dorothy Crouse. He recently completed work on a Tuscarora-English/English-Tuscarora dictionary with sponsorship by the Ontario Ministry of Education, which has been published by the University of Toronto Press (1999).

Barbara Tedlock is Professor of Anthropology and chair of her department at the State University of New York at Buffalo. Her honours and awards include appointment to the National Humanities Faculty, a Weatherhead Fellowship at the School of American Research (Santa Fe), NEH and ACLS fellowships, and a visiting appointment at the Institute for Advanced Study in Princeton. Her books are *Time and the Highland Maya*; *Teachings from the American Earth: Indian Religion and Philosophy* (with Dennis Tedlock); *Dreaming: Anthropological and Psychological Interpretations*; and *The Beautiful and the Dangerous: Dialogues with the Zuni Indians*. She recently completed a term as co-editor-in-chief of the *American Anthropologist*.

Dennis Tedlock is McNulty Professor of English and Research Professor of Anthropology at the State University of New York at Buffalo. His books are *Finding the Center: Narrative Poetry of the Zuni Indians*; *Teachings from the American Earth: Indian Religion and Philosophy* (with Barbara Tedlock); *The Spoken Word and the Work of Interpretation*; *Popol Vuh: The Mayan Book of the Dawn of Life*; *Days from a Dream Almanac*; *Breath on the Mirror: Mythic Voices and Visions of the Living Maya*; and *The Dialogic Emergence of Culture* (with Bruce Mannheim). He recently completed a term as co-editor-in-chief of the *American Anthropologist*.

Lisa Philips Valentine is an Associate Professor in the Department of Anthropology at the University of Western Ontario. A linguistic anthropologist, her ethnography of communication, *Making It Their Own*, was the culmination of years of research with the Severn Ojibwe of Northern Ontario. More recently, she has received grants from the Social Sciences and Humanities Research Council with Regna Darnell and Allan McDougall to study the use of contemporary English discourse in various First Nations communities, examining issues of identity and cross-cultural (mis)communication. The relationship between discourse and power at the governmental and community levels has become increasingly central in her work and publications in recent years.

H.C. Wolfart accords primacy to the evidence of the text; this may well reflect his early background in the classical tradition and subsequent study at Freiburg im Breisgau of Sanskrit and Classical Arabic. Introduced to the Algonquian languages at Cornell, and to Mayan inscriptions at Yale, he began his intensive study of Cree texts under the guidance of Charles F. Hockett and Floyd G. Lounsbury. In grammatical works and literary essays alike, Wolfart draws on a very rich and diverse body of texts, consisting initially of Leonard Bloomfield's collection of 1925 and the historical and mythological narratives he recorded in Alberta between 1967 and 1977. The altogether exceptional texts which Freda Ahenakew, herself a Cree speaker, has since 1981 been collecting in Saskatchewan are the first to be prepared for publication by Ahenakew and Wolfart, with several volumes already in print.

ANTHROPOLOGICAL HORIZONS

Editor: Michael Lambek, University of Toronto

This series, begun in 1991, focuses on theoretically informed ethnographic works addressing issues of mind and body, knowledge and power, equality and inequality, the individual and the collective. Interdisciplinary in its perspective, the series makes a unique contribution in several other academic disciplines: women's studies, history, philosophy, psychology, political science, and sociology.

Published to date:

1 *The Varieties of Sensory Experience: A Sourcebook in the Anthropology of the Senses*
Edited by David Howes

2 *Arctic Homeland: Kinship, Community, and Development in Northwest Greenland*
Mark Nuttall

3 *Knowledge and Practice in Mayotte: Local Discourses of Islam, Sorcery, and Spirit Possession*
Michael Lambek

4 *Deathly Waters and Hungry Mountains: Agrarian Ritual and Class Formation in an Andean Town*
Peter Gose

5 *Paradise: Class, Commuters, and Ethnicity in Rural Ontario*
Stanley R. Barrett

6 *The Cultural World in Beowulf*
John M. Hill

7 *Making It Their Own: Severn Ojibwe Communicative Practices*
Lisa Philips Valentine

8 *Merchants and Shopkeepers: A Historical Anthropology of an Irish Market Town, 1200–1991*
Philip Gulliver and Marilyn Silverman

9 *Tournaments of Value: Sociability and Hierarchy in a Yemeni Town*
Ann Meneley

10 *Mal'uocchiu: Ambiguity, Evil Eye, and the Language of Distress*
Sam Migliore

11 *Between History and Histories: The Making of Silences and Commemorations*
Edited by Gerald Sider and Gavin Smith

12 *Eh, Paesan! Being Italian in Toronto*
Nicolas DeMaria Harney

13 *Theorizing the Americanist Tradition*
Edited by Lisa Philips Valentine and Regna Darnell

www.ingramcontent.com/pod-product-compliance
Lightning Source LLC
Chambersburg PA
CBHW060817120726
47909CB00006B/1965

* 9 7 8 0 8 0 2 0 8 0 7 7 6 *